P9-CEP-022

*FOREIGN ECONOMIC POLICY FOR THE UNITED STATES*

# FOREIGN ECONOMIC POLICY FOR THE UNITED STATES

EDITED BY

Seymour E. Harris

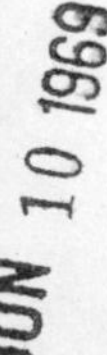


GREENWOOD PRESS, PUBLISHERS
NEW YORK 1968

Reprinted with the permission of the
Harvard University Press

First Greenwood reprinting, 1968

Library of Congress catalogue card number: 68-8335

PRINTED IN THE UNITED STATES OF AMERICA

## CONTRIBUTORS

Sidney S. Alexander, Consultant on European Recovery Program, Department of State; Assistant Professor of Economics, Harvard University

Thomas Balogh, Fellow, Balliol College, Oxford

Paul A. Baran, Economist, Federal Reserve Bank of New York

Robert W. Barnett, Adviser, Division of Japanese and Korean Economic Affairs, Department of State

Thomas C. Blaisdell, Jr., Director of the Office of International Trade, Department of Commerce

Eugene M. Braderman, Assistant to the Associate Director, Office of International Trade, Department of Commerce

Winthrop G. Brown, Director, Office of International Trade Policy, Department of State

Robert B. Bryce, Assistant Deputy Finance Minister, Canada

John M. Cassels, Chief, British Commonwealth Branch, Department of Commerce

Allan G. B. Fisher, Research Department, International Monetary Fund

J. K. Galbraith, formerly Chief, Division of Occupied Areas, Department of State; now on the Editorial Board, *Fortune*

Lincoln Gordon, Professor of Business Administration, Harvard University; Special Adviser on European Recovery Program, Department of State

Camille Gutt, Chairman of Executive Board and Managing Director, International Monetary Fund

Gottfried Haberler, Paul M. Warburg Professor of Economics, Harvard University

Alvin H. Hansen, Lucius N. Littauer Professor of Political Economy, Harvard University

Seymour E. Harris, Professor of Economics, Harvard University

Harry C. Hawkins, formerly Counselor for Economic Affairs, American Embassy, London; now Professor of International Economics, Fletcher School of Law and Diplomacy

Randall Hinshaw, Economist, Federal Reserve Board

Calvin B. Hoover, member, President's Committee on Foreign Aid; Professor of Economics, Duke University

Edward S. Mason, member, President's Committee on Foreign Aid; Dean of the Graduate School of Public Administration, Harvard University

Kirtley F. Mather, Professor of Geology, Harvard University

Paul A. Samuelson, Professor of Economics, Massachusetts Institute of Technology

John D. Sumner, formerly Adviser on Economic Affairs, U. S. Embassy, Chungking, and Adviser, Office of Financial Development Policy, Department of State; Professor of Economics, University of Buffalo

Robert Triffin, Chief, Division of Exchange Control, International Monetary Fund

Henry C. Wallich, Chief, Foreign Research Division, Federal Reserve Bank of New York

## ABOUT THIS BOOK

United States international economic policy should be of great concern to 140 million Americans, and perhaps of even greater importance to 2 billions living abroad. The latter are dependent upon the foreign economic policy of this country to yield the goods and services which will pull them out of the morass into which many have fallen; to provide economic leadership to a world seeking economic stability and prosperity; and with improved economic conditions, to relieve powerful political tensions.

This book of twenty-five chapters is the work of twenty-four experts, most of them practicing economists. Even the ten academic economists who have contributed to this volume are, or have been, engaged in government work and most of them in the subject matter covered in this volume. No one can fairly claim that this is a product of the ivory tower.

In the opening chapter the editor comments on many relevant problems, agreeing (and even disagreeing occasionally) with the contributors. This chapter will give the reader an over-all view of the ground covered and of many of the issues treated. On the basis of a rich experience in international economic relations, Mr. Thomas Blaisdell, Assistant to the Secretary of Commerce, then deals with the administrative complexities of United States international economic policy.

We then turn to studies of individual countries and areas (Part II), concentrating on those of especial concern to the United States. Each chapter is the work of one who has had special opportunity to study the country or area; and each author emphasizes the international economic problems of the country under consideration, and particularly the aspects of concern to this country. Dr. John Cassels (Chief of the British Division of the Department of Commerce) and Randall Hinshaw, Economist of the Federal Reserve Bank, study the British experience; Dr. J. K. Galbraith (formerly Chief Economist with the Strategic Bombing Survery of Germany, and formerly Chief,

Division of Occupied Areas, State Department), Germany; Robert W. Barnett (Advisor, Division of Japanese and Korean Affairs, State Department, and with the Far Eastern Commission), Japan; Mr. Robert B. Bryce (Assistant Deputy Minister of Finance, Canada), Canada; Dr. Henry Wallich (Chief, Foreign Research Division, Federal Reserve Bank of New York), Latin America; Dr. Paul Baran (expert on Russia, with the New York Federal Reserve Bank), Russia; and Professor John Sumner (formerly Advisor on Economic Affairs, U. S. Embassy, Chungking), China.

This country has fought for international economic coöperation, and although the fruits so far have been disappointing, the creation of the International Monetary Fund, the International Bank for Reconstruction and Development and the International Trade Organization (ITO), the most important products of this facet of United States foreign economic policy, are a major achievement. In the opening essay in Part III, The Honorable Camille Gutt, Managing Director of the International Monetary Fund, gives the reader an insight into the problems confronting the Fund and its potential contributions. Mr. Alan G. B. Fisher, head of one of the research divisions of the Fund, examines the Fund, the Bank and the ITO, emphasizing their strength as well as their weaknesses and their interrelations. It remains for Mr. Winthrop Brown, the Chief United States negotiator responsible for the General Agreements on Tariffs and Trade at Geneva, and Mr. Harry Hawkins, of the American delegation of the various conferences on the ITO, to discuss the trade agreements and the ITO. The charter of the ITO is a unique document; and the world has never witnessed so great a disposition to coöperate in the economic field as is revealed in the proportions of the reduction of trade obstacles at the Geneva Agreements on Trade.

Part IV, devoted to the European Recovery Program (ERP), is the work of four economists and one outstanding geologist. Dean Edward Mason and Professor Calvin Hoover served with the President's Committee on Foreign Aid; Professor Lincoln Gordon was special advisor to the State Department on the ERP, and Professor Sidney Alexander, consultant with the State

Department on the ERP. Our geologist is Professor Kirtley Mather.

Our hope is that the first four parts will be readily comprehensible to undergraduates and informed laymen. We even anticipate that these parts of the book may be helpful in clarifying our foreign economic policy and contributing to its improvement. We have reserved for Part V the difficult theoretical issues; thus it offers some nourishment to advanced students and professional economists, although large parts might well be digestible by the nonprofessional.

No problem is more important than that of international equilibrium; for the current disequilibrium is the source of many of our economic and political difficulties. We have, therefore, asked five experts in the field of international economic relations to consider the relevant problems: Mr. Thomas Balogh, fellow of Balliol College; Professors Gottfried Haberler and Alvin Hansen, of Harvard University; Professor Paul Samuelson, of Massachusetts Institute of Technology; and Dr. Robert Triffin, Chief of the Division of Exchange Control of the International Monetary Fund. Unfortunately, there is still substantial disagreement on the problems of international equilibrium; but few will deny that advances are being made in this difficult field. Professor Haberler presents what may now be called an approach to the dollar shortage problem which is highly unorthodox in its orthodoxy; but Dr. Balogh will have none of it. His essay is of special interest because it reflects a viewpoint held by many in England: a distrust of United States economic leadership, an anticipation of continued disequilibrium, and a plea for strengthening the position of the smaller countries vis-à-vis the United States. Need the reader be reminded that the theoretical issues discussed here are of great importance for the practitioner? For example, there is the issue of the extent to which disequilibrium originates in mistaken policies which might be reversed, and the extent to which the explanation is structural maladjustment resulting from war. Those who emphasize the former would put much of the responsibility for recovery upon those responsible for policy and would not rely primarily on American aid.

My thanks are due to my efficient secretary, Miss Lillian Buller, to Mrs. Anna Thorpe for typing part of the book, and to Mrs. Margarita Willfort for research help, and to the Academy of Political Science for permission to publish Dean Mason's essay. The Graduate School of Public Administration made available funds which helped greatly.

SEYMOUR E. HARRIS

Cambridge, Mass.
June 12, 1948

# CONTENTS

## PART I
## *POLICY AND ADMINISTRATION*



## PART II
## *INDIVIDUAL COUNTRY AND AREA STUDIES*

## PART III

## INTERNATIONAL ECONOMIC COOPERATION



## PART IV

## THE EUROPEAN RECOVERY PROGRAM

PART V

## *PROBLEMS OF INTERNATIONAL EQUILIBRIUM*

# PART I

# *POLICY AND ADMINISTRATION*

# 1

## *ISSUES OF POLICY*

Seymour E. Harris

### *Complications of American International Economic Policy*

Two devastating wars and the threat of a third, promising to be more destructive than the last, ideological warfare, the breakdown of isolationism, and a world-wide depression in the interwar period explain the growing importance of foreign economic policy. Conditions have changed greatly since 1914 when tariffs, immigration laws, protection of American investments, copyright conventions, *et hoc genus omne* were the significant problems of foreign economic policy. Even in the thirties, the appointment of an economic advisor in the State Department was a matter for comment. In 1947, the world produced 10 per cent less than just before World War II and yet had 200 million more people. This fact and the increased maldistribution explain in part the rising international economic tensions. A rough estimate reveals that whereas the average per capita income of a large part of Europe was one-half that of the United States just before the war, it was but one-quarter in 1946.

Without major wars, there was no reparation problem to vex governments before 1918. With a tolerably functioning gold standard, the problem of varying exchange rates did not greatly trouble pre-World War I governments. Modern government has recourse to exchange depreciation and similar beggar-my-neighbor measures as a means of exporting unemployment, and arrogating an excessive part of world trade to its citizens. Exchange control, clearing agreements, other quantitative restrictions, and numerous other devilish weapons of economic warfare proliferated in the interwar period; and under the chaotic conditions of recent years it has not been possible to get rid of the vexatious forms of restrictionism and discrimination. Besides having to face the problems raised by measures of this type, this country has to take a stand on cartels and commodity agreements, often introduced with the connivance or at least blessing of government and aimed at exploiting consumers; on state trading agreements which put the private trader in a poor bargaining position; on increasing tendencies to expropriate American investors abroad; on the problems of accessibility to raw materials in a world facing renewed pressure on resources; and on development in backward areas. Perhaps more important than any of these, though related to some of them, are the problems raised by the dollar shortage and international disequilibrium, and above all the use of economic measures to support political objectives, for example, the maintenance of our system of society.

## *A Unified Foreign Economic Policy*

### OBJECTIVES

Because of United States leadership in world affairs, its foreign policy is of great concern to all, and especially to this country. Above all, our foreign policy seeks the security and well-being of the American people. Basing itself on authoritative statements of official spokesmen of the government, the Brookings Institution includes among the fundamental principles of American foreign policy the following:[1]

1. The security and well-being of the United States can best be achieved in a peaceful world order based upon mutual respect, equal treatment, and adherence to the pledged word among nations.
2. The creation of a peaceful world order requires the establishment and maintenance of a system of organized international relations based on a developing code of international law, suitable procedures for the peaceful settlement of disputes, and collective action for the removal of threats to the peace and for

[1] The Brookings Institution, *Major Problems of United States Foreign Policy*, 1947, pp. 23-24.

the restraint or suppression of aggression. *It also requires economic cooperation among nations and the removal of economic causes of international friction, which can best be achieved in an expanding and relatively stable world economy that provides for all nations nondiscriminatory access to supplies and markets, to transportation facilities, and to investment opportunities.* [My italics.]

3. The sovereign equality of all nations should be recognized, and the territorial integrity and political independence of nations that respect the rights of others should be assured. Territorial changes should generally be made only in accordance with the freely expressed wishes of the peoples concerned.

### WORLD DEPENDENCE ON UNITED STATES ECONOMIC CONDITIONS

In the economic field, it is necessary above all that each country achieve stability, an expanding economy, equal access to raw materials and investment opportunities; and that the causes of economic friction be removed.

This country will not make its maximum contribution to the attainment of world-wide stability and economic growth unless it succeeds in stabilizing its economy. It is largely true that as goes the American economy so goes the world. With about two-fifths of the world's income, and an even larger proportion of industrial output and savings, with about one-third the world's export trade, with virtually a monopoly of the convertible currencies required to equilibrate the balance of payments, and of free capital, with about two-thirds the world's consumption of oil and pulp and as much or more of many other vital items, the United States not only is the number one economic power, but in no small part determines conditions elsewhere.[2]

It is, therefore, imperative that the United States stabilize its economy at high levels of employment and income; for unless it does, the reduction of income here will result (1) in curtailed purchases from foreign sources, induced in part by the fall of United States income, and in part by the rise of trade restrictions which accompanies depression, and (2) in a large decline of capital and merchandise exports from this

[2] Cf. Dr. Balogh's essay. He is fearful of the great economic strength of the United States, and particularly of the likelihood of its pulling down the rest of the world.

country, with disastrous results upon the economies of the rest of the world.

A correct foreign program, therefore, is conditioned upon appropriate domestic policies by the United States. This country must not only achieve stability at high income levels; but it must also convince the rest of the world that these are our goals, and that we are sufficiently literate and skillful in modern economics and politics to reach our target. By now it is clear that the U.S.S.R. is convinced that a crash is inevitable in the United States and, therefore, the time for a *rapprochement* is postponed until capitalism flounders, at which time the Russians' bargaining position will be at its peak. Nor are doubts concerning future economic conditions in the United States limited to the Eastern countries. Even in Great Britain, many are disposed to adopt trade and investment policies which will shield her from the effects of an American depression. Again, the widespread enthusiasm for industrialization and development programs in backward areas springs in part from the impression made by the decade of the thirties, when the depression here contributed greatly to the instability and decline in agricultural countries, and notably in Latin America.[3]

An impartial appraisal of American history and American prospects will find much support for the doubts, expressed or implied, concerning the future of the American economy. The United States experienced an unprecedented depression in the thirties which aggravated the decline abroad; and depressions have occurred periodically in American history. And despite the unprecedented prosperity since 1940, history is not reassuring. After years of discussion, the United States is not prepared with a substantial public investment or (and) consumer spending program to offset later declines in spending. Even the Employment Act of 1946 reflects the unwillingness of the Congress to take bold measures to deal with deficient demand and unemployment. The government is equally inept in treating exuberant economic conditions. In its farm policies, in its wage policies, in its premature removal of controls, in

[3] Cf. essays by Dr. Balogh and Dr. Wallich, and my *Economic Problems of Latin America*, 1944, Chap. 1.

its tax reduction policy, in its unwillingness generally to deal with bottlenecks and to make the most effective use of scarce resources, in its almost fanatical aversion to planning of any kind, the government has greatly contributed to the inflation which must inevitably end in collapse. Only continued large military budgets and the ERP can save the country from a collapse. Oddly enough, the U.S.S.R., basing itself on Marxian theory, is convinced of an impending collapse in the United States; but by adopting aggressive tactics and thus stimulating United States military expenditures and assuring the ERP, the U.S.S.R. puts off the day of the inevitable crisis. Once the source of excess demand associated with war or preparation for war dries up, the alternatives seem to be either a major depression, or continued prosperity made possible by spending for military purposes inclusive of ERP.

### *A Consistent Trade and Currency Policy?*

Before discussing the inconsistencies of United States trade and related policies, we should first discuss our objectives in trade policy. The United States for many years has supported multilateralism, inclusive of the most-favored nation treatment and, along with these, convertibility of currencies. This policy finds expression in the Hull program of Reciprocal Trade Agreements and the Geneva Trade Agreements.[4] In some respects, it is rather surprising that the United States, which is not nearly so dependent on trade as many other countries, should have taken the lead in the program to liberalize trade practices. In part, the explanation undoubtedly lies in the return to power of the Democrats, with a long free-trade tradition; in part, in Secretary Hull's keen interest in trade expansion; and in part in the country's strong international economic position which makes possible a reduction of tariff barriers without disastrous international effects on its reserve position.

Other countries are not so enthusiastic as the United States about reducing trade barriers and establishing convertibility of currencies. Their reserves are not adequate to undertake the

[4] Winthrop G. Brown discusses the Geneva agreements in this volume.

risks of multilateral trade and convertibility. In order to induce the outside world to embark on a program proposed by the United States, which includes not only reduction of tariff barriers and convertibility of currencies, but also international control of exchange rates, it was essential to offer insurance against a breakdown. Obviously France, for example, could not afford to give up its bilateral trade agreements and introduce convertibility of the franc so long as the practice did not become general, and a large cushion of reserves was not provided. She could not allow conversion of francs into other currencies while the British would not permit conversion of £ sterling and the Italians that of the lira. Any country which embarks on a program of convertibility prematurely will become a favored market for the world's exports and a source of dollars; and her reserves will quickly vanish. The British learned that lesson in the summer of 1947. The Bretton Woods program had proposed to achieve convertibility and relative stability of exchange in part through making available a large pool of currencies and gold for the use of members. As an incentive for following the lead of the United States, this country was prepared to provide a substantial volume of dollars. As we shall see, the amounts made available were inadequate; and bilateralism became almost the exclusive means of assuring trade for many countries. Few countries could afford to open their markets to all on equal terms and to make their currencies convertible. Reserves were too small; and for most countries the volume of exports relative to imports inadequate.

United States policy has not consistently supported the principles of Bretton Woods and the International Trade Organization (ITO). In recent years, this country has imposed quotas on watch imports and on sugar, and in 1947, the wool interests almost succeeded in imposing serious obstacles to trade in wool. Particularly in its farm policy the United States government supports programs which are inconsistent with its avowed objectives. One objective of American farm policy has been to raise prices through restrictions on output and limited control over demand, with the result that prices of farm products in the United States rose above world levels. The American government, then, dumps cotton on foreign markets and under the ITO asks for special exceptions which would promote the subsidization of farm products. High national prices for farm products result not only in demands for subsidies for exports in order to maintain foreign markets, but also bring about restrictions on imports of farm products. Surely the country needs a farm policy integrated with the professed liberal trade policies of the government.

### *Relation of Reserves to Trade Policy*

No genuine advances towards economic liberalism will be achieved until the shortage of reserves in gold, dollars, and other convertible currencies is treated adequately. The Bretton Woods program was the first step in this direction; but it is far from sufficient. Even total advances and credits by the United States of close to twenty billion dollars in the first two and one-half years after the war were not adequate to correct the dollar deficiency. The ERP, with an anticipated cost of fifteen to twenty billion dollars, is the next important move; and before equilibrium is once more established, others may follow.

Pumping dollars into the foreign exchange market will not, however, be enough. What is required above all is an improvement in the competitive position of the rest of the world vis à vis the United States. These countries must sell more and buy less relatively. This does not mean that export trade for the United States will have to be reduced; but it does mean that our proportion of export trade must decline.

We should consider certain United States policies in the light of this objective of reducing our competitive position, for unless the competitive position of the United States deteriorates, and the ratio of its imports relative to exports increases, the prospect is either a growth of economic nationalism abroad, or a permanent ERP.

First, it is necessary that the ERP strengthen the economies of European and other countries, making it possible for them to produce more goods for export and at reduced cost and to produce for themselves goods formerly imported. Second, the

United States should support the development and industrialization programs of the backward nations insofar as they promise increased stability, less dependence on imports, and industries that will ultimately be able to survive without crutches. In this manner, these countries will become less dependent on their relatively unstable agricultural income, and on handouts from the United States. Third, the United States should practice a more responsible lending policy than she did in the interwar period. This may well mean less enthusiasm and support for private lending than seems consistent with the objectives of present United States policy. Unless private lending is controlled, to prevent excess lending, as in the twenties, or a complete turning off of the capital spigot, as in the thirties, the only alternative seems to be public lending. Fourth, if the source of disequilibrium is a shortage of dollars, even the Reciprocal Trade Agreements are not the proper policy. What is then required is not a reduction of tariffs in this country and similar concessions abroad, but rather a rise of tariffs abroad and a reduction here, or at least a relative rise of obstacles abroad. Actually, despite the Reciprocal Trade Agreements, obstacles to trade abroad have probably increased relative to those in the United States. Obviously, the ideal solution would be growth of net export potentials abroad and an increased willingness on the part of the United States to increase purchases abroad in response to lowered tariffs and higher incomes here.

Finally, the relative export position of the United States will not deteriorate as long as our superiority tends to increase. In the last decade this country has become the world's largest shipper, the greatest air power for commercial use, and the world's largest producer of synthetic rubber. We resent the exclusion of American films abroad and we are making every effort to wrest from France her leadership in the fashion industry. No country can continue to export, and only export, unless it is prepared to give goods away. The theory of comparative costs suggests that leadership in every industry is still compatible with an export and an import trade. But unfortunately, the analysis is not so simple as that. For long periods of time, the country losing export markets may not be able to adjust its economy by an expansion of new export industries and by a reduction of imports. Disequilibrium follows. It is easy to rely too much on the theory of comparative costs, and dismiss the transitional difficulties.[5] Unfortunately the need of self-sufficiency in shipping, rubber, and similar items for defense strengthens the position of the protectionists; but it also makes it less likely that the dollar shortage problem will be solved. We not only develop industries which can survive only through subsidies (for example, rubber and shipping), but in doing so, we establish conditions which will make necessary the continued provision of dollars, not likely to be repaid.

## *Individual Country Studies*

### THE UNITED KINGDOM

In order to understand our foreign economic policy, we must study problems of countries closely related to the United States. Part II presents a survey of seven countries and areas, and through a discussion of the European Recovery Program (ERP) in Part III, we deal with the over-all problem of much of Europe.

Of particular interest to Americans is the economic status of the United Kingdom, for in the struggle to maintain democratic institutions, she is our most likely co-fighter and one of our strongest allies. The miracle of modern Britain is not the large losses suffered in recent years, but rather the remarkable position attained and held even in the thirties, when per capita income was roughly equal to that of the United States. With a population per square mile twelve times that of our country and with scanty natural resources, the British have made the most of their genius, of their industrial leadership, and of their limited resources. As Dr. Cassels well argues in this book, their recent losses are not to be attributed primarily to nationalization or mistakes of the Socialist Government. Robert Young, a great railroad man, should have known better when writing in the *Atlantic Monthly* than to blame the Socialist Government for the lack of oranges and automobiles in Great Britain

[5] Cf. discussion pp. 35-36 and Professor Haberler's essay on dollar scarcity.

in the early postwar period. Is it necessary to remind him that there had been a war which cost the British in capital resources the equivalent of around two years' income? In 1947 it became fashionable among distinguished British economists to blame the government for the loss of reserves, and for international disequilibrium generally. Undoubtedly, like all socialist governments, the British Government, aware of damage done by the war and pressed by the voters, embarked on an ambitious program of capital investment, inclusive of housing; and this expansion reduced exports and tended to raise imports. But it should be pointed out that the United States, with its system of free private enterprise, experienced a sixty-billion dollar investment program in two years, also excessive relative to the requirements of a stable economy and according to past standards. Nor is there any evidence that the Churchill Government was less anxious to rebuild the country quickly, nor that distinguished British economists had protested the ambitious investment programs before 1947.

It is important for the United States to aid the British until they can restore equilibrium. In many respects, the British difficulties are of a temporary nature. Thus, their large deficit on domestic investment account has to be made up, and this will take time. From 1940 to 1945, net disinvestment at home amounted to £1408 million, that is, the country lived on its capital to this extent. The actual deficit might roughly be estimated at £1400 million (disinvestment) plus £1800 million (normal rate of net investment for six years) plus 50 per cent of £3200 million to cover the increased cost of investment or, in all, £4800 million. In 1946, however, net investment was £714 million, or about 2 1/3 times the average of 1938 and 1939, and in 1947, the country actually made up about one-twelfth of its deficit in domestic investment, not an excessive rate on this account.[6] (I leave out of account the disinvestment abroad of £4,747 million from 1939 to 1945—Lend-Lease is included in this total only for £161 million.) Disturbed by the yawning deficit in the country's international accounts, the government

[6] The excess over normal was £400 million at current prices, in comparison with a deficit of £4800 million in current prices.

in late 1947 announced its plans for reducing *gross* investment: The mid-1947 rate had been £1550 million, the original forecast for the calendar year 1948, £1600 million, while the revised figure for annual rate by the end of 1948 was £1320 million.[7]

Excessive capital investment undoubtedly contributed to the British adverse trade balance and rapid depletion of reserves. It was not, however, the most important factor by any means. As Dr. Cassels and Dr. Hinshaw indicate, the most important factors contributing to the sizeable losses of reserves in 1946 and 1947 were the large rise in the price of imports, the heavy burden of foreign expenditures abroad, and the payment of dollar debts on account of foreign interests. It does not follow, as Dr. Hinshaw so well makes clear, that a depression and a decline in the prices of foods and raw materials will extricate the British from their current difficulties. Offsetting the resulting fall in prices of British imports by the estimated reduction in exports and export prices in response to falling incomes abroad, Hinshaw concludes that a major depression may do the British more harm than good. For this reason among others it would facilitate American foreign economic policy if this country continued to lead the way to world-wide prosperity.

One of the most difficult problems to assess is the long-run position of the British. It is well not to put on blinders: their economy seems to have suffered a number of serious economic hemorrhages, and there may well be some involvement. Inability to keep up with the advances in technology abroad; the increased competition of newly industrialized areas; growing economic nationalism, with unfortunate effects on the British export position; the high prices of imports relative to exports; the preponderant weight of luxury and semi-luxury products in the British export trade, commodities shunned by planned economies in a disordered world; the increased costs of mining coal; the loss of a large part of invisible income on investments, shipping, and the like, the source of payments for one-third of their prewar imports; the burden on a country with a heavily

[7] H. M. Stationery Office: *National Income and Expenditure of the United Kingdom, 1938 to 1946* (April 1947), Cmd. 7099, pp. 19, 26; and *Capital Investment in 1948* (December 1947), Cmd. 7268, pp. 4-5.

concentrated population and industry in an unstable world;—all of these suggest a deterioration of the British position, and unless large improvements in productivity (inclusive of reduced loses through unemployment) are made, a deterioration in the standard of living for the present population, or a declining population at prewar standards will inevitably result. United States policy should, therefore, envisage the possibility of a British economy stabilized at a lower per capita real income than in 1939. Much progress may indeed be made in raising man-hour output, also by better distributing manpower between essential and parasitic industries, and between domestic and export industries. But though aware of stodginess on the part of many British business leaders, I do not share the view of my compatriots who, comparing British and American methods, blame British business leadership for competitive losses. The problems are much more complicated. Assembly-line methods are not open to a country with one-seventh the national income of the United States and correspondingly smaller markets, with a concentration on industries emphasizing the highest skills, and with deficiencies of capital, in part the result of a generation of relatively unsatisfactory business. In short, the British are confronted with perplexing short-run problems which may well be solved with our aid and which, if not solved, will have serious long-run repercussions, and with, alas, long-run problems associated with a weakening of Britain's political position and with economic factors adumbrated above.

### CONQUERED COUNTRIES

Germany and Japan made little recovery in the first three postwar years, with unfortunate effects upon the American taxpayer. In the first three quarters of 1947 industrial production in Germany averaged only 44 per cent of 1937 output in the American Zone and 33 per cent in the British Zone; and in 1947 total production in Japan was about 24 per cent of that of 1937.[8]

In the last year or two, there has been a disposition to blame the Morgenthau Plan for the slowness of Germany's convales-

[8] United Nations, *Economic Report, 1945-47,* pp. 76, 131-32. Cf. Essays by J. K. Galbraith and Robert W. Barnett.

cence. Surely few would defend that plan today as a realistic approach to the German problem, though in 1944 it reflected a widespread fear of German rearmament. Distrustful of German militarism, the American people may well have been disposed then to pay a high price for the pastoralization of Germany, though the cost of the program had not yet been dimly revealed. In 1947-48, the American public, aware of the costs of deindustrializing Germany and more fearful of current Russian aggression than of potential German militarism, seems determined to scrap the Morgenthau Plan *in toto*. A revision of the Level of Industry Plan in August 1947, which increased the base of production for Western Germany from the low level given by 1932 output to the higher level of 1936, reflects the abandonment of the principles approved in Quebec in 1944.

Saying that deindustrialization of Germany is out of the question is not tantamount to asserting that Germany's failure to recover was the result of the Morgenthau Plan or of the Directive JCS 1067 and the Level of Industry Plan of early 1946. Even the Yalta and Potsdam Agreements, aside from losses of territory involved, were not so bad as is now frequently contended.[9] It is well to retain perspective. Germany had fought a war, costly in men, capital, and morale. The loss of Eastern Germany and reparation payments out of capital, both likely outcomes of a lost war, were also bound to have unfortunate effects. At least in part the decisions at Yalta and Potsdam were the inevitable effects of war; and it would be as fair to blame Yalta and Potsdam for all the decisions taken as to hold the judge responsible for the criminal who is sent to jail.

More dependent upon outside sources of supplies as a result of dismemberment, Germany obviously could not survive a thorough deindustrialization. Somehow, the increased imports of necessities would have to be paid for out of exports of manufactured products, unless the United States was prepared to cover the deficits or allow Germany to adjust to her depleted resources through a reduced standard of living and even through starvation.

Given the objective of making Germany self-supporting, it

[9] Cf. J. K. Galbraith's essay.

became proper United States policy to stop the drain of reparations to Russia and in particular to discourage reparations out of current output, to introduce a more generous level-of-industry plan and make a concerted effort to stop the Balkanization of Germany. Provision of a working currency (and ultimately a unified currency), a customs union for the Western Zones, temporary aid under the ERP to refurbish industry with equipment and raw materials—these are the roads to recovery. Germany's slow recuperation has been costly to the United States, not only because of the resulting large appropriations to provide her with minimum needs for food, clothing, medicine, and the like, but also because the unavailability of Germany as a market for Europe's exports and as a source for Europe's chemicals, machine tools, and coal greatly contributed to the current European crisis. Unless Germany can once more occupy an important place in Europe's economy—though not so vital as in the prewar period—the United States will carry a severe and long continued burden. In its threat to Europe's recovery, the Morgenthau Plan was unwise, but substantial damage was not done by it. Unable to obtain required raw materials, food, and capital, Germany is producing far below the Level of Industry Plan of 1946. American policy, however, has already raised the targets above those anticipated in 1944 and 1945. The problem, as in 1946 and 1947, remains that of approaching the targets.

In a well rounded study of Germany's economic problems, Dr. Galbraith eschews the "one cause" approach and also minimizes the significance of the Morgenthau Plan, the Potsdam Agreement, and the Level of Industry Plan. With partition and economic prostration of the country, the Level of Industry Plan and reparations are largely academic questions. Shortages of raw materials and food and the excess of money relative to supplies available at controlled prices account for the absence of incentives to produce. A worker can obtain rations with a few hours of work, and many with liquid assets will not work at all. Galbraith holds the United States policy of "calculated inadequacy" partly responsible for Germany's failure to produce at levels more nearly equal to her potentials; and our government's refusal to support the German Social Democratic Party, which has a positive program of nationalization suited to Germany's needs, is another mistake.

Japan faces problems similar to those confronting Germany, although concentration of control largely in the United States has facilitated the management of Japan's economy. Like Germany, Japan is dependent upon foreign sources of supply of raw materials and food, and upon exports of manufactured goods to pay for them. As Mr. Barnett shows, reparations have not so far been a serious factor in the Japanese recovery, other than to contribute an element of uncertainty, for the victors have been unable to agree on the division of the spoils. De-cartelization and Level of Industry Plans plague Military Government in Japan as in Germany.

An examination of Barnett's essay will convince the reader that Japan's problems seem almost insoluble today, and, therefore, the Japanese deficit is likely to weigh on the American economy for many years. Dependent upon the United States for virtually all their imports now, the Japanese have been able neither to produce exports on an adequate level, nor to recover prewar markets. Japan's neighbors are determined to keep her weak, irrespective of the unfavorable effects upon themselves. Her foreign trade position is aggravated by her large losses of shipping, and is related to many weak spots at home. With unbalanced budgets, 'with large accumulations of purchasing power, with money incomes much above the amount that can be used on rationed markets, incentives to produce are lacking. Farmers hoard and city workers malinger. Unless the problem of inflation can be licked, a revival of domestic output and production for export will not be achieved; and as a condition of improvement, substantial imports of food and raw materials financed by the United States will be required.

Another problem confronting American authorities is the alternative between generous subsidies now to bring the Japanese economy back swiftly, or more costly, though smaller, constant outlays until Japan recovers. The greatest obstacle is the disappearance of Japan's markets. In summary, one of the most costly legacies of the war is the support of the economies of conquered nations.

## SPECIAL STUDIES OF OTHER COUNTRIES

Latin American countries, Canada, and China are also areas in which the United States has a special interest. The international economic problems of these countries are in some respects similar; and in others, dissimilar. All are short of dollars and are embarrassed by the rising prices of United States exports; and despite the dollar famine, they are frequently hampered by export controls in this country. Latin America and China share an interest in economic development which they hope will be supported by United States loans to finance exports of equipment, raw materials, and technical services. As Dr. Wallich explains in his essay on Latin America and Dr. Hawkins in his study of the ITO, differences prevail between the United States on the one hand and the countries intent on industrialization programs on the other. These countries are not content with the exceptions allowed under the ITO in order to further development programs, nor are they satisfied with the amount of capital being made available by the United States. Impressed by the prior claims of European recovery and fearful of the protectionist advances to be achieved with the support of the infant industry argument, the American Government lends a hesitant support to foreign industrialization programs.

With European and Asiatic markets partly destroyed and with normal sources of supply closed in part, Latin America and Canada are more dependent upon the United States than before the war, both as a source of supplies and as a market. United States quarterly exports to North America averaged $183 million in 1936-1938 and $946 million in the first three quarters of 1947; to South America, $69 and $600 million respectively. Of all United States exports, the percentage gain for exports to North America was not large; but for our exports to South America the rise was from 9.3 per cent in 1936-1938 to 16.4 per cent in the first three quarters of 1947. United States imports from North and South America rose from 24.1 and 13.0 per cent in 1936-38 to 38.6 and 20.9 per cent, respectively. In dollar value, quarterly imports of the United States from the other Americas had risen from an average of $231 million in the years 1936-

1938 to an average of $814 million in the first three quarters of the year 1947.[10]

United States prosperity in the years 1945-1948 has served to maintain boom conditions in the other Americas, as an examination of the contributions of Mr. Wallich and Mr. Bryce will readily show. Prosperity in the United States is imperative for the other Americas; for, without it, they will suffer a deterioration of their economic conditions, recourse to economic warfare, and unfavorable political effects.

Prosperity in the other Americas has contributed to their unfavorable balance of payments, for with higher incomes, there is a tendency to import more and export less. Mr. Bryce shows, for example, that while Canada's income in 1947 rose by 12 per cent, her imports increased by no less than 25 per cent. But the difficult balance of payments problems confronting the other Americas are not merely a reflection of favorable economic conditions. In fact, the economic rise in the Americas over prewar conditions has generally been less than in the United States. For example, gross national product in the United States had risen 10 per cent more in 1946 over 1938 than in Canada;[11] and industrial output was as follows in 1947 (*1937=100*):

| | |
|---|---|
| Canada, September | 162 |
| Chile, September | 154 |
| Mexico, 2nd quarter | 135 |
| United States, September | 168 |

Source: UN, *Monthly Bulletin of Statistics* (December 1937), pp. 22-26.

Since countries that expand relatively rapidly are the ones that tend to have an adverse balance of payments, improved conditions in the Americas are not sufficient to explain their loss of reserves and the restrictive trade practices imposed in the last year or two.[12]

Several others factors are relevant. The first is the large meas-

[10] A Report to the President by the Council of Economic Advisers: *The Impact of Foreign Aid upon the Domestic Economy* (October 1947), pp. 84-85.

[11] United Nations, *Economic Report, 1945-47*, pp. 47-48; *Economic Report of the President*, January 1948, p. 109.

[12] Cf. Bryce's discussion of Canadian restrictions imposed in 1947; also see H. Chalmers, *Current Trends in Foreign Trade Policies: Review of 1947*, 1948, pp. 1-5, 10-12.

ure of inflation in Latin America, a factor tending to raise imports and reduce exports. By 1947 five Latin American countries had suffered an average rise in the cost of living over prewar conditions of almost 200 per cent, or about three times the rise in the United States.[13] Second, these countries had been denied exports from the United States in the war years as a result of our fairly strict export controls; in 1946, and later years, Latin Americans crowded United States markets in an attempt to purchase the commodities denied them during the war. Unfortunately, the reduced purchasing power of the dollars they had accumulated in the years 1942-1945 became a source of grievance. A third factor was the large sales on credit or for inconvertible currencies by the other Americas, with the result that a substantial part of exports did not yield dollars or their equivalent. Canada's generous financing of British needs is a case in point: exhaustion of her reserves is explained in no small part by her grants and advances to the United Kingdom and repurchase of Canadian assets held by the British. In 1946 Canada had an adverse balance on current account with the United States of $603 million, and a favorable balance (that is, an excess of credits with other countries) of $954 million, the favorable balance with the United Kingdom being $495 million and with other sterling areas, $162 million.[14] Unfortunately, the excess of receipts from countries other than the United States could not be used to pay for the excess of imports from the United States. As Bryce shows, *all* Canadian *debits* on capital account were $2606 million in the years 1946-47; and though her reserves rose by $667 million in 1945, they declined by $994 million in 1946 and 1947. Her postwar *credits* of $1850 million at the low income of Canada corresponded to advances of $33 billion at the high income of the United States.

Mr. Bryce well summarizes Canada's economic problems. In particular, the breakdown of multilateral trade is bound to injure greatly an economy that buys much more from the United States than she sells there, and sells more to Europe than she buys from the latter. Financing export trade by sales for soft

[13] UN, *Economic Report 1945-47*, p. 56.
[14] UN, *Economic Report*, p. 49.

currencies or credits does not provide the dollars required to purchase the vast supplies of imports bought by a full-employment economy. Canada's close economic ties with the United States, not bolstered by a common currency, are perhaps the source of her most serious problem—the shortage of dollars. Bereft of the usual support of her important European markets and facing depletion of important natural resources, Canada must find new outlets for exports, especially of manufactured goods. And she faces severe United States competition, aggravated by the fact that a large part of Canadian industrial output is under the control of United States parent companies.

American foreign economic policy will have to steer a middle course between encouraging an all-out development program in Latin America on the one hand, which will surely bring economic nationalism, reduced trade, and an even lower standard of living for its proponents, and a *status quo* on the other, which will deprive the other Americas of the increased stability and higher productivity, likely accompaniments of a well balanced industrialization program. There is no guarantee that higher incomes in Latin America will result in more sales in their markets by United States exporters; for the relation between industrialization and higher incomes on the one hand, and an expansion of trade on the other, is not so direct and simple as the great British economist Marshall argued a generation ago. Unfavorable effects of industrialization on the volume of United States exports may, however, be welcome over the next decade or so. Since *the* international economic problem over a generation or more has been excessive United States exports relative to imports, any measures which reduce our exports or increase our imports should be helpful. Obviously it would be better to raise our imports than depress our exports; but unless we show a greater disposition to increase imports than we have indicated in the last generation, the way out is continued excesses of exports, financed and paid for by American lenders or taxpayers, or a collapse of our export trade.

Another facet of our international economic policy relates to temporary aid to the other Americas. Here the question of priorities troubles our policy makers. Obviously, the ERP is higher on the priority list than aid to accelerate Latin American development or even to help the other Americas pay for their controlled excess of imports from this country. Besides, these countries will be aided greatly by the off-shore purchases under the ERP insofar as payments are made in United States dollars and insofar as export restrictions do not hamper the free use of the dollars in this country.

As Professor Sumner demonstrates, China suffers from the same economic diseases as Latin America, and in particular from inflation and excessive enthusiasm for industrialization. Unfortunately, her inflation is much more advanced, and the case for industrialization weaker. War and civil war have prostrated the Chinese economy; and her inability to achieve political stability, a condition for substantial United States aid, prevents her from receiving as much help from abroad as she might otherwise have obtained.

### *International Agencies*

In recent years the United States has taken the lead in setting up international agencies for dealing with economic problems. In this volume we limit our detailed discussion to the Fund (International Monetary Fund), the Bank (International Bank for Reconstruction and Development), and the ITO (the International Trade Organization). If space were available, we might have discussed many other organizations, and especially the FAO (Food and Agricultural Organization).[15]

In general, the objective of the agencies is economic coöperation on the international front. Thus the Fund is to provide resources to tide countries over temporary disequilibrium in their balance of payments; and to use the resources made available to force upon members exchange rate policies compatible with the interests of all nations, and an early termination of exchange control and similar restrictions on trade. The task of the Bank is to provide funds for reconstruction and development out of a pool and with the aid of guarantees provided by

[15] Cf. Dept. of State, *Participation of the United States Government in International Conferences, July 1, 1945-June 30, 1946* for an insight into the numerous agencies and international economic conferences.

the participating members. ITO is intended as an agency for reducing obstacles to trade, inclusive of control over cartels; for exorcising quantitative agreements except under stipulated conditions; for excluding discriminatory trade practices except under circumstances specifically described; for underwriting development programs through allowing special favors to backward countries; for sponsoring full employment policies, with attendant favorable effects upon trade.

Messrs. Gutt, Fisher, Brown and Hawkins describe the functions of these agencies and their interrelationships as well as the political difficulties confronting them and their disappointments to date. As, for example, Mr. Gutt points out, it was not possible to determine or achieve equilibrium exchange rates late in 1946; and if rates low enough (vis à vis the dollar) to keep imports down to a desired level had been agreed upon with Europe and Latin America, then the inflationary effects would have been serious, and the exchange rates would have been depressed below the optimum level, yielding the maximum supply of dollars. Despite the proposals in the ITO Charter and the Fund, it was frequently necessary to rely upon quantitative restrictions and even multiple rates (for example, a low valued currency for exports, and a high rate for purchase of essential imports) to conserve the scarce reserves of many countries.

Again, loans by the Bank so far have been at a disappointingly low level. Indeed, as Mr. Fisher suggests, many countries are unable to absorb large loans without strengthening inflationary forces; but for the most part, restricted activities of both the Fund and the Bank are to be associated with a shortage of dollars which had not been clearly foreseen in 1944 and 1945.

Finally, Professors Fisher and Hawkins reveal that many concessions had to be granted in the ITO charter if it were to be an acceptable document. Yet the charter is a step in the right direction; and substantial reductions in trade obstacles were made as a result of the tariff negotiations at Geneva—the details will be found in the essay by the United States negotiator, Winthrop G. Brown.

That the international agencies so far have played a limited role is not unrelated to the economic policies of this country.

Early enthusiasm for UNRRA, the Fund, and the Bank has been dimmed by the large shortage of *dollars;* and by the reluctance of Congress to appropriate additional funds to international agencies when the major voting strength resides elsewhere. UNRRA had taught American authorities that dollars might be used by an international agency to support economies at political loggerheads with the United States. It is, therefore, American policy to tag and trace the dollars made available by the American taxpayer under American directives. From June 30, 1945, to June 30, 1947, the United States, through loans and gratuities, made $15.6 billion available to foreign interests. Of this total only $3 billion were private loans and gifts, while total *dollar* disbursements of the Bank and Fund amounted to but $148 million.[16] Obviously the waning enthusiasm of the American government towards international agencies rests in part upon the determination to make the most effective political use of funds provided. This is not, however, the only explanation of the submergence of the Fund and the Bank: unfortunately the time schedule of recovery anticipated by the Bretton Woods architects has not been realized. *Inter alia,* an intensification of the dollar shortage, political instability, delayed recovery in Europe and Asia, the persistence of inflationary forces—all of these interrelated factors account for the much greater demands upon the American economy for relief and recovery, the inadequacy of the resources available to the international agencies, and the need of delaying stabilization measures as well as development programs. So long as chaos continues and prices skyrocket, the province of agencies with responsibilities to stabilize and expand economies will continue to be a limited one.

It is clear, then, that the international economic agencies are to play a less important part than had been hoped or even anticipated in the late war years. One reason for the disappointing contribution of the Fund is Russia's failure to join. Quotas late in 1947 of $7961 million are, therefore, substantially less than had been estimated at Bretton Woods. Unfortunately, even this overstates the deflation of the contribution of the Fund. Of all

[16] Report to the Senate Finance Committee by the National Advisory Council on International Monetary and Financial Problems, *Foreign Assets and Liabilities of the United States and its Balance of International Transactions,* 1947, p. 168.

the important currencies, the dollar alone is sought; and so far, in dollars, quotas are but $3050 million (United States and Canada) and the assets held by the Fund late in 1947 were but $2286 million. As might be expected, the currency sold by the Fund was almost exclusively in dollars: $473 million in dollars and $6 million in pounds sterling. The more important currencies purchased for these dollars were (in millions of dollars): United Kingdom pounds sterling, 240; French francs, 125; Netherlands guilders, 52. At the end of December 1947 the *Bank* held but $51 million in dollars, $411 million in United States Government obligations, and $216 million in non-interest bearing notes payable in dollars. Loan commitments, primarily to France and Netherlands, were $497 million, and unused balance of commitments, $197 million. It is clear that approximately one billion dollars made available by the Fund and Bank over the period of operation (one year for the Fund and one and one-half years for the Bank) is not a large amount compared with dollar deficits of the world vis-à-vis the United States of five to ten billion dollars yearly. The Fund, indeed, has more than two billion dollars in dollars that might be made available over several years; but the Bank early in 1948 had but about one-half billion dollars in dollars uncommitted. The fact that prices of United States exports early in 1948 were at least 50 per cent higher than they were in 1944 also contributes to the reduced significance of the Fund and Bank. Quotas and subscriptions in dollars are now worth but two-thirds as much in goods as in dollars of 1944 purchasing power.[17]

In summary, disappointment in the achievements of the Fund and Bank and other international agencies are then to be associated with the intensity of the economic crisis, the inadequacy of resources made available, in turn the result of concentration of demands on the dollar market and the rise of prices, and the unwillingness of the United States to entrust additional funds to international agencies which it did not control. The European Recovery Program in part reflects the determination to tie appropriations to control of use by the United States.

[17] Figures mainly from International Monetary Fund, *International Financial Statistics* (February 1948), pp. 3-9.

A final comment in this section relates to the French devaluation of early 1948. Above all, the participating countries at Bretton Woods had agreed to renounce their sovereign rights to pursue exchange policies without due consideration of the rights of others. Hence the French devaluation was a disappointment to all those who viewed the international agencies as symbols of the coming of age of sovereign nations in their economic relations. France, in early 1948, paid little or no attention to the agreements signed by her Government or to the pleas of the managers of the Fund. Despite earlier advances from the Fund and in violation of her obligations, France embarked on a multiple currency program and a discriminatory policy, unhappily reminiscent of the thirties. Not content with a depreciation of the franc in dollars by more than 40 per cent, she established a "quasi" free market in the franc, with resulting disordered cross rates, and gave her exporters large advantages in the American market which were denied them in soft currency markets. One of the anticipated results was purchase of British goods for francs, with profitable sales in the United States, France receiving dollars and the British, unwanted francs. The price of stopping this misuse of British resources would be the imposition of minute controls on the British exporters which France was unwilling to put upon her exporters.

### *The European Recovery Program (ERP)*

This volume contains five essays dealing with the ERP, the authors of four of these having been intimately associated with the evolution of ERP, two as members of the President's Committee on Foreign Aid and two as Advisors to the State Department on the ERP. Dean Mason deals primarily with the ERP as a political weapon to be used to strengthen the economies of the sixteen coöperating nations and Western Germany in their struggle to maintain their independence and economic institutions. An examination of the targets set up by the participating countries and their likelihood of reaching them is the theme of Professor Calvin B. Hoover's chapter. Since the program may cost this country fifteen to twenty billion dollars, it is important to examine the reserves and current production of vital resources, both of the United States and other countries, and to draw some conclusions concerning what can be spared. One of the country's leading geologists, Professor Kirtley Mather, undertakes this task in Chapter 17 of this volume. Operating problems and policies under the ERP are the subject matter of Professor Lincoln Gordon's chapter. Among the questions he discusses are the controls required in the American economy, the management of foreign currencies received for goods to be shipped under the ERP and not transferred into dollars, the relation of stock-piling programs to the ERP, administrative problems relative to the distribution of aid. Finally, Professor Sidney S. Alexander examines numerous important issues: the choice between distress or standard of living as criterion of aid; Europe's problem of diverting adequate resources to exports; the relatively large gains of income anticipated for Western Europe in relation to the aid under ERP.

With five essays dealing with the problems raised by the ERP and with a volume devoted exclusively to this problem, my comments can be very brief.[18] In Part II, we shall deal with the economic problems of individual countries which are of special concern to this country, with emphasis upon the issues of special interest to the United States. The ERP is an attempt to treat the economies of sixteen countries plus Western Germany as a unit; and, therefore, Part IV may be considered as a supplement to the preceding part of this book, and since the ERP is a frontal attack on international disequilibrium and dollar shortage, Part IV is a bridge between Parts III (International Economic Coöperation) and V (International Disequilibrium).

In dealing as a unit with the sixteen European countries requiring aid and in making self-help a condition of American aid, the United States Government proposes to solve the problem of Europe's production and dollar crisis once and for all. Professor John D. Sumner, in his essay on China, shows that there has been a precedent to making aid conditional upon corrective measures undertaken by the recipient.

It is not necessary to discuss in detail here the causes of Eu-

[18] Seymour E. Harris, *The European Recovery Program,* Harvard University Press, 1948.

rope's crisis in 1947. As we show later, dollar shortage is an old phenomenon, the crisis of 1947 reflecting also a famine engendered by crop failures, excessive investment, the breakdown of Western European trade relations with Eastern Europe and Asia, and slow political and economic recovery. Undoubtedly mistaken policies, evident in unrealistic investment programs, high exchange rates, weak fiscal policies, in turn related to political instability, all contributed to the crisis.

Whether the ERP proves successful will depend largely on the recipient countries. They will have to show an increased disposition to trade, make the most effective use of aid as incentives to increased production, and improve their monetary and fiscal policies in order to raise output as rapidly as underlying conditions allow. Above all, they will have to strike a balance among exports, domestic consumption, and domestic investment, which will reconcile the need for equilibrium in the balance of payments, the maintenance of consumption at a level consistent with maximum production, and which will provide an amount of investment, not so large as to endanger the attainment of the required consumption and export goods, and yet not so small as to keep productivity from rising adequately.

Much also will depend upon American administration, and the political situation in Europe. This country should provide aid with a minimum of interference in the internal affairs of the countries receiving it. It will be necessary to lay down broad lines of policy in the agreements signed with each country, and to use the threat of nonrenewal of aid should agreements be flagrantly violated. All that this country can ask is the most effective use of the resources made available in terms of repercussions upon output and trade balance; and to achieve this, proper financial and monetary policies will have to be adopted.

Ultimate success of the program will also depend upon the manner in which our government deals with the *real* and monetary effects here. The fact that fifteen to twenty billion dollars may be made available under the ERP on top of large additional military expenditures makes all the more necessary a vigorous anti-inflationary program. At full employment the *additional* expenditure of five to ten billion dollars yearly for ERP and defense will greatly strengthen the inflationary pressures, unless the United States makes the most effective use of fiscal and monetary policy by keeping taxes up and restraining the amount and speculative use of bank credit, and mobilizes other anti-inflationary weapons—for example, allocations, inclusive of export control, conservation measures and, in very special cases, price control and rationing. Should the government succeed in keeping investment down to the minimum amount required and in reducing private spending by a courageous tax policy and savings campaign, and should it eliminate public spending on nonessentials, then the adverse effects of the ERP will be greatly reduced. In particular markets where serious shortages prevail, the government has pruned European demands and diverted them to other markets; but it may be necessary to take additional measures in mal-provisioned markets.

### *Equilibrium in the Dollar Market*

For over a generation, exchange markets have been short of dollars. In order to understand the dollar problem, we should consider that of international equilibrium and exchange rates. In ordinary markets, an excess of demand over supply is soon reflected in a rise of prices, and higher prices restore the equilibrium of supply and demand. But the dollar market is no ordinary market. First, the price of dollars in gold does not move significantly except in the most unusual circumstances—the rise in the dollar price of gold in 1933-34 was a most unusual move. Hence the pressure for adjustment is on the other currencies. Second, other currencies do not respond to excess supplies vis-à-vis the dollar by the required fall in their price and rise in the dollar, for their dollar value is under control. Third, equilibrium is not necessarily established even should exchange rates respond freely to market pressures. A decline in the price of the franc, for example, may be accompanied not by a reduction of supplies of francs offered but rather by a rise of supplies as an initial fall stimulates the offer of additional francs for dollars. Moreover, should the authorities allow the franc to find its "equilibrium" level, and should a price be found at which supply and demand once more are in equilibrium, then the cost may be a serious fall of imports and a lowering of production and living standards, induced by the reduction of imports and the offer of more exports at reduced prices. Equilibrium in the dollar-franc market might then bring political disequilibrium, and the latter in turn would disequilibrate the exchange market.

So far we have assumed that the path to equilibrium is through movements in exchange rates; but in classical economics, the orthodox approach to equilibrium is price movements induced by gold outflows from France, for example, and inflows into the United States, which would make French exports on world markets cheaper and French imports more expensive, and United States exports more expensive and imports cheaper. (Classical economics also discussed as a special case the required price movements under fluctuating exchanges.) The persistence of a balance of payments disequilibrium raises some doubts concerning the adequacy of the classical analysis.[19]

In the interwar period, Keynes and others had shown that the required adjustments in costs and prices had not taken place; that even to the extent that they had, they were inadequate, at current elasticities of demand, to stop the one-way flow of gold. Classical economics had not allowed sufficiently for institutional obstacles to adjustment, the result being the maintenance of exchange rates and gold reserves at the expense of unemployment at home following a rise in interest rates, a reduction of money, and a curtailment of investment. Professor Alvin Hansen in this volume further develops the thesis, first clearly presented by Keynes, that the test of disequilibrium is in the effects of exchange policy upon the domestic economy. In Hansen's view, disequilibrium is evident also in unemployment brought on by a high level of costs in relation to prices; and it is possible to distinguish the external from the internal causes of disequilibrium. In a companion essay, Professor Gottfried Haberler clearly presents the classical position which relates equilibrium to the absence of substantial movements of gold and exchange rates. Although he is prepared to use purchasing power parity as a guide, the main symptom is to be substantial movements in exchange or gold.

[19] Cf. my essay on "Dollar Shortage," *Economic Journal*, June 1947.

Equilibrium exchange rates, however defined, are not easily revealed. Even if the measure is the relative purchasing power of two currencies as compared with prices and exchange rates in a base (normal) period, many difficulties emerge. Was the base period normal? What of the influence of nonmerchandise items on exchange rates? Are the appropriate price indexes those of international or domestic commodities? Has the *normal* price relationship moved since the base period because of fundamental changes in economic structure? If the answer to the last question is yes, then to what extent is the *normal* rate of exchange affected? Dissatisfaction with the usefulness of the purchasing power parity as a guide explains the approaches of Professors Hansen and Haberler.

In 1948, the problem is even more complicated than in the interwar period when the purchasing power parity theory might still have been adequate. In attempting to set equilibrium rates in the present disorderly exchange markets, the economic practitioner will have to take into account the effects of present and anticipated controls, the uncertain flows of capital, the recourse to trade restrictions, probable large price movements, and many other factors. Whereas, for example, an exchange rate of $4 = 1£ may be appropriate on the assumptions that the British control export prices, favor exporters through allocations of materials and man-power, scrutinize imports, and obtain ten billion dollars of foreign aid over the next five years, this rate may be far from the equilibrium rate should any or all of these conditions not be fulfilled. Professor Hansen's guide of unemployment brought on by disequilibrium exchange rates, of course, would not be very useful in a period of overemployment; and the absence of gold and exchange movements, the barometer for Professor Haberler, is not helpful in the current controlled situation.

In part the difficulties in the exchange markets originate in political factors, which are not treated at all in the classical analysis, and not adequately even in the reservations made by Keynes. Undoubtedly, part of Europe's shortage of dollars is to be associated with an unwillingness to cut consumption standards adequately and trim investment programs to enable Europe to export more and import less. Were the controlled economies of Europe prepared to cut their imports and raise their exports, each by a few per cent, then a substantial part of the deficit in their international accounts might well be wiped out. At first it may seem that this overall treatment neglects the problem of specific shortages, for example, iron and steel, grains. But if the effect of a reduction of imports and a rise of exports is a corresponding increase of dollars or other convertible currencies, then the required supplies should be made available. This analysis is subject to the reservations noted below. First, resources made available by curtailed consumption and investment programs may not yield the export products required, and certainly not without a substantial lag. (We assume that markets will be found.) Second, pruning of investments is a double-edged measure: beyond a certain point, it will reduce net income; and similarly a reduction in consumption will have unfavorable effects on income. Despite the theoretical possibilities outlined above, we conclude that in the light of the instability of many of the European governments and their consequent unwillingness to impose unpleasant sacrifices on their citizens, the suggested program for raising exports and reducing imports by the amount required to remove the need of foreign aid, will not be forthcoming.

In his very interesting paper on dollar shortage, Professor Haberler marshals as strong a case for the adequacy of classical theory in explaining it, international disequilibrium, and the like, as could possibly be made; and his essay is a reminder that the classical analysis may be scrapped too readily. Yet I am not *entirely* convinced by the growing number of economists who, like Haberler and Harrod, just to mention two, seem inclined to rule out dollar shortage as a fraud or at least as a phenomenon easily fitted into classical theory.

First, the classical theory is only a shell and not a fully developed theory which can adequately explain recent developments in international economic relations or point the way out of current difficulties. In an essay in this book which reminds Americans that there is not universal contentment with United States leadership in world economic policy, Dr. Thomas Balogh points out some of the gaps in classical theory—for example, the inadequate treatment of transitional periods and the assumptions of full employment, of high elasticities of demand, of equal bargaining strength among countries.

Second, attempts to prove that dollar shortage is a mirage are not successful. Consider Professor Haberler's paper, which is likely to exercise considerable influence. His evidence is the manageable proportions of the current balance of the United States over most of the twenties and the thirties. Yet the balance on current account was $14.5 billion in the years 1919-1939, when our gold stock rose from $1.5 to $17.6 billion. In every year but three there were favorable balances on current account. Surely the mobilization of two-thirds of the world's gold supply by the United States is both an indication of dollar scarcity, and an embarrassment to those who would explain international relations merely in terms of classical theory. Professor Haberler is prepared to exclude capital movements in the twenties as an indication of dollar shortage, on the grounds that they were exports from capital-rich to capital-poor countries. (These outward movements explain the relatively small inflow of gold in the twenties.) In view of subsequent history which showed an inability on the part of foreign countries to finance the credits of the twenties, one might contend that they reflect dollar shortage, and, therefore, that the appropriate barometer of dollar shortage for the twenties might well be gold imports *and* long-term capital movements. Furthermore, Professor Haberler minimizes the inflow of gold in the thirties by suggesting that the short-term inflow of capital should be deducted from the inflow of gold; and that the large current balances in 1938 and 1939 reflect war preparations. It is convenient not to include capital exports in the twenties but to exclude capital imports in the thirties. I am not prepared to deal with capital movements in the manner suggested, however, nor to write off an excess of exports because they are explained by political developments. The dollar problem is the result of a concatenation of forces—inflation in Europe, indeed, but also rigidities and inflexibilities, *continued* relative advances by the United States, political and military events. Relative price movements are not an adequate explanation.[20] We should emphasize especially the strong economic position of the United States, with vast supplies of goods for sale at relatively favorable prices, while the rest of the world is short of resources and (or) is impoverished as a result of two world wars.

Third, although Professor Haberler makes an important contribution in stressing the inflationary aspects of the current situation and the corrective influences to be exercised by direct attacks on inflation, inclusive of higher taxes, restraints on investment and consumption, nevertheless he goes too far. He knows only too well that in the interwar period the *orthodox monetary* approach to international equilibrium failed dismally, and even the *unorthodox* approach through exchange depreciation was only a partial success. Exchange adjustments may help indeed; but that they will be a cure-all is far from true. Professor Haberler would readily admit the last point. In a brilliant essay in this volume, Professor Paul A. Samuelson suggests (as does Dr. Balogh) the inadequacies and uncertainties of the approach through revision of exchange rates. Incidentally, Dr. Triffin's essay also deals with the relative appropriateness and effectiveness of changes in exchange rates as against control of exchanges and deflation; and he finds that exchange control is frequently to be preferred. Does Professor Haberler, an economist of the liberal school, suggest that *planned* economies of the forties and fifties can and should succeed in bringing about equilibrium through use of orthodox weapons, when the *unplanned* economies of the twenties and thirties, under much more favorable conditions, failed? In short, Professor Haberler rightly distinguishes the plight of the impoverished countries from that of the others which, after a transitional period, are expected to become self-supporting, and he correctly separates the political from the economic aspects of the dollar shortage. Granting all that, I nevertheless contend that an inflation theory of international disequilibrium which fails to take account of the political obstacles, of the rigidities, of the low elasticities of supply of, and demand for, exports, and of the failure to achieve equilibrium over thirty years of successive transitional periods,

[20] Cf. my "Dollar Scarcity," *Economic Journal.*

and which puts too much faith in the long-run theory of comparative costs, cannot be safely used to guide economic practitioners interested in the dollar problem. On the other hand, I am prepared to admit that Professor Haberler has made an important contribution in reminding us that inflation is a relevant consideration and in distinguishing the economic and political aspects of the dollar shortage.

Since 1914 this country has poured eighty billion dollars into the dollar market, primarily through grants and secondarily through loans; and now promises to provide about twenty billion additional dollars. These movements will continue until the chaos caused by war and impending war is removed, and recovery abroad is well on its way; and until, as a result of this improvement, the competitive position of the rest of the world vis-à-vis the United States improves, and the latter shows a willingness to raise its purchases relative to its sales. Correct tariff policies and responsible lending policies by the United States will help greatly.

A country will not excel in every industry, and certainly not by an equal proportionate degree. Each country will presumably concentrate on the industries in which it has the largest advantage and rely on foreign countries to supply commodities in which it has the smaller advantage or is at a disadvantage. There should then be no problem of disequilibrium. Actually, the United States may excel in too many industries; and the British, for example, suffer losses in many. In response to losses of reserves or exchange depreciation, the British should ultimately establish their position through price, cost, and factor movements which would induce the exports required to pay for imports. But in practice, price and cost movements do not necessarily take place or they may require too much time, the relatively favorable industries in Britain's declining economy do not cut their costs and prices adequately, or the factors do not move adequately or quickly enough from the depressed industries, no longer in a position to export. Sales abroad then do not recover sufficiently, and reserves disappear, or the economy is stifled through restrictive monetary policies; and the adjustments assumed under the theory of comparative costs do not take place.

For many years, the British, for example, have exported too little and imported too much. Yet the adjustments assumed in theory failed to take place.[21]

[21] Cf. Professor Haberler's essay, Chapter 24.

# 2

# ECONOMIC ORGANIZATION OF THE UNITED STATES FOR INTERNATIONAL ECONOMIC POLICY[1]

Thomas C. Blaisdell, Jr., and Eugene M. Braderman

### *Breadth of U. S. Economic Interests*

Most people are well aware that the world has grown smaller in terms of our relations with other nations. It is doubtful, however, that the awareness extends much beyond a superficial understanding of the complexity of our foreign relations. This is particularly true in the economic field.

The fact is that today much of our foreign policy centers around economic matters, and economic and commercial policies are of prime importance in all of our international negotiations. The United States is now the greatest single economic force on earth and the kind of foreign economic policy we follow now and in the next few years will inevitably determine in large measure the policies to be followed by the rest of the world. The United States has taken the lead in world-wide efforts to promote industrial and agricultural reconstruction and a renewal of world commerce, for we know that enduring peace must be based upon increased production and an expanding flow of goods and materials among all nations for their mutual benefit.

In meeting our international responsibilities today, the character of the activities of our government has changed tremendously. To fully understand the extent of this change consider-

[1] The authors' views do not necessarily reflect those of the Department of Commerce.

able time and study are required. In this short chapter it will be impossible to do more than touch upon some of the highlights in this story.

Most people have recognized that tremendous problems confronted the world as an aftermath of the war. They realize the need for relief and for aid in rebuilding towns and cities, fields and factories that had been destroyed by war. Our people came to know the United Nations (UN) in a general way, the United Nations Relief and Rehabilitation Administration (UNRRA), and perhaps one or two other international organizations in which the United States was actively participating. But how many of our citizens know that there are dozens and dozens of regional and international organizations in the economic field in which the United States participates? And how many people realize that within our own government foreign economic policy is not determined in any one place, but is the responsibility of many agencies and cabinet departments?

In describing the organization utilized by our government in fulfilling our expanded responsibilities in the international economic field, it is necessary to give attention to several kinds of relationships. In the first instance I shall describe how the work is carried on by government here at home. Then I shall describe the character of our representation abroad. Finally I shall relate both our work here and abroad to our participation in various international economic organizations.

### *Activities of U. S. Government Agencies in Formulating Foreign Economic Policy*

In the field of foreign relations the Department of State is at the hub of the governmental wheel. However, many agencies and departments are active in various aspects of our foreign economic relations and these are coördinated by the Department of State.

Historically, the State Department was organized largely along geographic lines. The preoccupation of the department was with political relationships and little attention was given to the economic forces which affected them.

The organization of the Department of State and its lack of

attention to international economic affairs reflected the general attitude of the government as a whole. While the Department of Commerce for many years had been active in fostering, promoting, and developing our foreign commerce, economic and commercial relationships in the field of foreign policy were largely outside the realm of government activity. The concern of government in the international field was largely with trade promotion and trade protection and with the informational services that were necessary to the American business community in carrying on their normal private commercial transactions with citizens of other countries.

The first appreciable projection by government into the field of foreign economic policy after World War I came about as a result of the great depression. In an effort to restore life to international trade movements the London Economic Conference was called in 1933. Unfortunately the participants in this meeting were unwilling to give sufficient concrete recognition to the necessity for stimulating a wider interchange of goods and services among nations by a mutually advantageous lowering of barriers in all national markets. The U. S. made a further effort to break down these artificial walls in 1934 with the enactment of the Reciprocal Trade Agreements Act. With the passage of this act tariff policy was transferred by the Congress in part to the executive branch of government.

The extent of activity of the executive branch in this field has been considerable. It was clearly recognized tnat coöperation with other nations of the earth in seeking a soundly expanded, sustained, mutually advantageous interchange of goods and services was essential. The alternative was to withdraw behind artificial barriers into economic isolationism and narrow self-sufficiency, a certain deterrent to economic peace and, therefore, to political peace as well.

Under the reciprocal trade agreements program the Department of State was made responsible for acting as the central agency in coördinating the work related to these agreements. The full resources of all the executive departments were brought to bear on this activity through two interdepartmental committees, the Trade Agreements Committee and the Committee for

Reciprocity Information, both of which are still operating today. The Committee on Trade Agreements, which makes recommendations relative to the conclusion of all trade agreements, is composed of representatives of the departments of State, Agriculture, Commerce, Labor, Treasury, Navy, Army, and the U. S. Tariff Commission. The Committee for Reciprocity Information, with approximately the same representation, is responsible for according reasonable opportunity to interested persons to present their views on any proposed or existing trade agreement.

With the outbreak of World War II the Government found that it was subjected to greater and greater demands in the economic, commercial, and financial fields. Our foreign economic activities were expanded into new and broad areas, including wartime commercial policy, allocation of supplies, foreign funds control, lend-lease, the regulation of exports, procurement of strategic materials, and related matters.

Many agencies were created to look after these new responsibilities. The State Department was expanded; the activities of the departments of Commerce and Agriculture were subject to far-reaching changes during this period; and many new agencies were added to the roster. Some of these were the Board of Economic Warfare, the Lend-Lease Administration, the Office of Foreign Relief and Rehabilitation Operations, the U. S. Commercial Company, and the Office of the Coördinator of Inter-American Affairs, and a host of others with greater or lesser responsibilities in the foreign economic field.

The story of our wartime economic activities is, of course, much too large and complex to be treated here, even from an organizational standpoint. It is sufficient to point out that the problems with which we dealt during the war did not, by and large, cease with the end of that struggle. In one form or another they have been carried over into the postwar period.

Upon the United States, with its tremendous productive facilities intact, was thrust the major responsibility for economic reconstruction. There was the immediate problem of relief and rehabilitation of devastated areas. There was the need to get the productive machinery of Germany and Japan and other occupied areas operating once more. And there were many long-run obligations. Measures had to be taken to promote stability in international economic relations. Coöperation with other nations was required to promote higher standards of living, full employment, and economic progress and development.

In order to carry out these responsibilities the nature of the work done by the several agencies of government underwent a profound change as compared with the prewar period. The involvement of diplomacy with questions of trade, finance, transportation, agriculture, and the like moved foreign policy out of the orbit of a single department and made it the proper concern of many federal departments and agencies. Changes in agency organization were required to make this participation effective. The Department of State added many new divisions until its officers were working in such diverse fields as commercial policy, petroleum, international labor affairs, international finance and investment, foreign economic development, and in the foreign policy aspects of many commodities such as various foodstuffs and industrial raw materials. Furthermore, the department continued its wartime activity in the fields of international aviation, telecommunications and shipping. The Department of Commerce also actively participated in most of these fields and to a lesser extent so did the departments of Agriculture, Treasury, Interior, Labor, and others.

Two general methods were developed to relate federal agency participation to the making of our foreign policy. The first is close consultation on a staff to staff basis between the State Department and individual agencies on international matters that lie within the special competence of a particular agency. For example, the State Department consults with officers of the Department of Labor on labor problems, with the Civil Aeronautics Administration of the Department of Commerce and the Civil Aeronautics Board on aviation matters, with the Department of Agriculture on agricultural problems, with the Department of the Interior on petroleum matters, with the Office of International Trade of the Department of Commerce on a great variety of economic and commercial policy questions, and so on. Such consultation has enabled the State Department to inform itself of activities of other federal departments and has permitted these departments to provide guidance and advice in the development of the international aspects of their programs.

The second method by which federal agencies participate in the making of foreign economic policy is through the interdepartmental committee mechanism. A great many of these committees have been created in the last few years. One of the most important is the Executive Committee on Economic Foreign Policy, which examines problems and developments affecting the economic foreign policy of the United States and formulates recommendations in regard thereto for the consideration of the Secretary of State. Along with the Department of State on this committee sit representatives of Treasury, Agriculture, Commerce, Labor, Interior, U. S. Tariff Commission, and the Department of Defense. The work of this committee has become so complex because of the nature of our international economic activities that a great many subcommittees have been created to handle continuing problems. An idea of the vast scope of this work can be gained from an examination of the subjects with which this committee and its subcommittees have been concerned. The following are just a few examples—economic policy toward China, customs procedure, foreign patent protection, foreign travel, inter-American economic affairs, international commodity problems, private monopolies and cartels, and state trading.

Another of the very important interdepartmental committees is the National Advisory Council on International Monetary and Financial Problems (NAC), which was established by act of Congress to coördinate the policies and operations of representatives of the United States on the International Monetary Fund and the International Bank and of all agencies of the government which make or participate in making foreign loans or which engage in foreign financial exchange or monetary transactions. The secretaries of Treasury, State, and Commerce, the Chairman of the Board of Governors of the Federal Reserve System, and the Chairman of the Board of Directors of the Export-Import Bank make up the membership of this council.

Another of the important interdepartmental committees is

the Advisory Committee on the Second Decontrol Act of 1947. This committee is composed of representatives of the departments of Commerce, Agriculture, State, Interior, and the Office of Defense Transportation. It advises the Secretary of Commerce regarding various aspects of export and import control, export priorities, and allocations.

There are many other interdepartmental committees operating in other parts of the foreign economic sphere. In transportation and communications, for example, there are the Air Coördinating Committee, the Radio Advisory Committee, the Telecommunications Coördinating Committee, and the Shipping Coördinating Committee. The existence of these committees is mute evidence of the fact that our foreign economic relations are highly complicated and require that the resources of many government agencies be brought to bear upon them. Through these interdepartmental committees, and others too numerous to mention, nearly every department or agency has been drawn into the deliberations that shape our foreign policy.

## *U. S. Representation Abroad*

### THE FOREIGN SERVICE

The principal instrument through which the United States is represented in other countries is the Foreign Service of the United States. The Foreign Service is the eyes, ears, and representative of our interests abroad; it is also the means for carrying out American foreign policy in every part of the globe. Most persons think of the Foreign Service primarily in terms of the role it plays in the diplomatic field. They may thus be startled to learn the extent of its activities in the economic field. Foreign Service officers negotiate treaties, conventions, and protocols affecting international trade, tariffs, shipping, aviation, communications, and a multitude of related problems. They observe, analyze, and report on economic conditions and trends of significance in the country to which they are assigned. Some of the major fields covered include agriculture, commercial intelligence, commodity and industry reporting, finance, labor, minerals and petroleum, trade promotion and protection, transportation and communications, and a host of other matters that are of concern to the federal agencies in Washington in developing our foreign economic policy and in serving American business and the public as a whole.

Missions headed by ambassadors or ministers are to be found in all countries with which we maintain diplomatic relations. The ambassadors and ministers are stationed in the capitals of the respective countries and their offices, residences, and staffs are known as embassies or legations. In addition, the United States maintains consular offices in important cities or towns throughout the world to care for the commercial interests of its citizens and to protect its seamen. Consular offices normally are under the jurisdiction of our diplomatic missions except in the case of distant colonies where no diplomatic establishment exists.

Each overseas mission is headed by a Chief of Mission who may be either an ambassador or minister. The ambassador or minister is the personal representative of the President of the United States accredited to another government. He is responsible for seeing that the entire embassy staff works to serve the American people and to carry out American policy in the country of assignment. As the personal representative of the President, he appears at important state functions and maintains relations with top government officials, constantly discussing with them problems affecting relations between their two countries. Under the Chief is the Deputy Chief of Mission who is responsible to him for the execution of policy and the efficient operation of the mission. It may be said that he combines the duties of Chief of Staff and Executive Officer. He also acts as Chargé d'Affaires in the absence of the Chief of Mission.

Under the Chief and Deputy Chief of Mission, there are five coequal sections. These are the political, economic and commercial, information and exchange, consular, and administrative sections. In a large embassy such as London or Paris, each section is headed by a separate officer with an appropriate staff. At a smaller post, with only a few officers, one man may supervise several operations.

The Economic and Commercial Section is headed by a chief who may be either the Counselor of Embassy for Economic

Affairs or, if no counselor is assigned to the post, the Commercial Attaché. The chief economic and commerical officer coördinates and directs, as instructed by the Chief of Mission, all the economic activities of the U. S. Government in the area concerned. He provides the Chief of Mission with the economic information needed in the formulation and implementation of policy and is responsible for all economic and commercial reporting. The Economic and Commercial Section is broken down into subordinate units which correspond, by and large, to its basic responsibilities. An Agricultural Attaché handles matters relating to agricultural products; the Labor Attaché is concerned with matters of employment, social security, wages, and so on; the Commercial Attaché and his staff handle a wide variety of matters relating to foreign commodities and industries, commercial laws, finance, tariffs, trade agreements, and the like. Just as the various units of this section must not be separate watertight compartments, so the Economic and Commercial Section in turn must be closely integrated into the general organization of the mission. The exact boundaries of the political and economic functions cannot be charted. Only by closest teamwork can the over-all work of the mission be accomplished.

The economic organization necessary in American consulates naturally varies greatly depending on the importance of this function at each particular post. Thus in many of the smaller consulates, economic and commercial work is merely a part-time function of a general consular officer and includes promotion and protection of American shipping generally and the certification of invoices of goods shipped to the United States. At other posts, however, the work is much broader and warrants the assignment of a special officer or special staffs. At a few of the latter consulates, an organization approaching that described for the Economic and Commercial Section of a mission is necessary. Generally speaking, all economic and commercial reporting is centralized in the mission and the consular posts receive their instructions from the mission and send their information to Washington through the mission. This method of routing applies to all areas of the world except where no mission is maintained.

Back home the Foreign Service is administered within the Department of State. Under the Secretary of State and the Assistant Secretary of State for Administration the principal officer responsible for foreign service operations is the Director General of the Foreign Service. He is assisted by a deputy who supervises the operations of the Office of Foreign Service. Under this office there are six divisions, namely: Foreign Service Personnel, Foreign Service Administration, Foreign Service Planning, Foreign Reporting Services, Foreign Building Operations, and the Foreign Service Institute.

The Division of Foreign Service Personnel handles all recruitment, assignment, and transfer of foreign service officers and employees; the Division of Foreign Service Administration administers the service in its various operations; the Division of Foreign Service Planning handles the programs and plans for current and future operations; the Division of Foreign Reporting Services coördinates the actual dissemination of the reports from the field to all government agencies which require them; the Division of Foreign Building Operations is charged with the construction and maintenance of government-owned offices and residences utilized by the Foreign Service; and the Foreign Service Institute conducts training programs for foreign service personnel.

In accordance with the intent of the Foreign Service Act of 1946 to make our Foreign Service an organization fully representative of the views and needs of all government departments, there was created by that act a Board of the Foreign Service. This board is made up of three Assistant Secretaries of State, the Director General of the Foreign Service, and representatives from the departments of Agriculture, Commerce, and Labor having comparable responsibilities in their respective departments. The Board of the Foreign Service is charged with making recommendations to the Secretary of State concerning all the functions of the service. Policies and procedures governing the selection, assignment, rating, and promotion of foreign service officers fall within its province as well as those governing the administration and personnel management of the service.

In order to effectively carry out its responsibilities, the Board of the Foreign Service has created various sub-boards which assist it in its work. The most important of these are the Staff Board, which is responsible for reviewing over-all programs and policies for the Foreign Service; the Appointments and Assignments Board, which concerns itself with appointments, assignments, and transfers of foreign service officers; and the Committee on Foreign Reporting Services, which is concerned with the reporting needs of all government agencies. There is, in addition, a Board of Examiners which operates under the general supervision of the Board of the Foreign Service and which is responsible for the conduct of the written, oral, and physical examinations leading to appointment in the Foreign Service.

The ramifications of foreign service operations are much too broad to cover in any detail in this chapter. The Foreign Service Act of 1946 is the first major change that has occurred in foreign service administration since the passage of the Rogers Act in 1924. The basic concept underlying its operations is that of a single unified service which can represent the needs of all the American people and of all government agencies in our work abroad. There have been created under the act new branches of the service such as the Foreign Service Reserve Corps and the Foreign Service Staff Corps to meet special problems. The merit system has been more firmly established and many other changes have been made to assure our government the best possible representation throughout the world.

### OVERSEAS REPRESENTATION OUTSIDE OF THE FOREIGN SERVICE

Despite the overriding predominance of the Foreign Service in our representation abroad, this government does maintain other personnel in various parts of the world. These other services are largely specialized in nature.

The Treasury Department maintains its own representatives in key cities abroad where financial problems are of sufficient importance, from the standpoint of the United States, to warrant full-time representation. The Treasury representatives are members of the staff of that department but are attached to the embassies as financial advisers to the ambassadors and as representatives of the Secretary of the Treasury. Their general function is that of reporting on financial developments in the respective countries where they are stationed, and on all international financial matters which are of importance to the United States Government. Their reports are made available not only to the Treasury Department but also to other United States agencies interested in the subject matter.

The departments of the Army, Navy, and Air Force likewise maintain representation abroad. Army, Navy, and Air Force officers are customarily attached to our foreign missions to advise the Chief of Mission on military problems and to perform other functions for the U. S. Department of Defense. Although these officers are subject to the authority of the Chief of Mission they are not a part of the regular Foreign Service.

The Department of Commerce relies principally on the Foreign Service for its representation abroad. However, certain offices of that department maintain their own representatives in various parts of the world or send them abroad for temporary duty. The Coast and Geodetic Survey, for example, during the past few years has been sending consultants to the twenty other American Republics to act in an advisory capacity in the fields of coastal hydrography, tides and currents, geodesy, geomagnetism, seismology, and map and chart production. In many cases, these consultants have assisted in establishing services similar to those performed by the Coast and Geodetic Survey in the United States, and have rendered valuable technical aid in carrying out national programs in these subjects.

The Civil Aeronautics Administration also has representatives abroad. Civil aviation missions have been sent to a number of foreign countries, or foreign field offices have been maintained to facilitate the safe and efficient operation of United States flag air carriers and to permit other countries to draw on the Civil Aeronautics Administration's technical knowledge and that of the United States aviation industry as a whole for civil aviation programs best adapted to their needs. In addition, the Weather Bureau has established a few weather stations abroad and has maintained limited representation in the Philippines and in other countries.

These technical representatives of the Department of Commerce as well as specialists in a multitude of other fields are being sent abroad from time to time to handle special tasks. The work which they perform may often seem to be highly technical yet they all fit into the pattern of expanded activity in the international economic field. As our work becomes more and more diversified, albeit highly specialized, changes constantly occur in both the form and the substance of our representation abroad. More and more there is a need for centralizing our activity in a single body, logically the Foreign Service. How this may be accomplished is exemplified by the handling of a scientific mission, recently sent abroad on a special assignment, which is not unlike others that have operated independently. In order to assure consistency with other programs this mission on science and technology has been attached to the U. S. Embassy in London. It has been operating as a regular unit of the foreign service establishment and its work complements that of the five sections described earlier. The principal difference, however, is that this group has been staffed by temporary personnel who have been given appointments in the Foreign Service Reserve.

Another major projection of our economic work abroad was a direct outgrowth of the war. It is part and parcel of our occupation responsibilities in Germany, Austria, Japan, and Korea. Surrender and occupation have meant that the United States, along with other Allied Governments, has had to undertake the tremendous task of transforming the economic life of the occupied areas into going concerns. Responsibility for this work in Japan was turned over to the Supreme Commander for the Allied Powers (generally known as SCAP). To the economic agencies under SCAP has devolved the task of revitalizing Japan's economy. In Germany the responsibility has been assigned to the Office of Military Government (OMGUS), which has its headquarters in Berlin with related sub-divisions in the U. S. Zone. This work has been modified somewhat by the creation of Bizonia in Western Germany though the basic problems confronting the United States have been the same.

Responsibility at home for our activities in occupied areas

has been in the hands of the Department of Defense. Coördination with our foreign policy and with the work of the several agencies interested in foreign economic activities abroad has been achieved through the operation of several interdepartmental committees similar to those which have been described earlier.

In relating briefly the activities now being performed for the United States Government in other countries, it has been impossible to go into detail or in fact to mention all the instances where such representation exists. What I have tried to do is to outline briefly the work of the Foreign Service as our major organ in foreign representation and to cite sufficient examples of other foreign economic activities to give some idea of the vast extent and scope of our foreign economic operations today.

### *U. S. Participation in International Organizations*

The needs of the war and the desire for continued peace after the war produced a concept of international coöperation which far exceeded anything that had gone before. The foreign economic policy of the United States today is guided by this larger concept of international interdependence. Our government has tried, in concert with other nations, to hammer out the structure for world-wide international coöperation in the economic field. At the top of this structure, under the United Nations, is the Economic and Social Council with its several commissions and sub-commissions. Working in coördination with and under the general guidance of the Economic and Social Council are several specialized agencies which are concerned with definitely delimited areas and with specific tasks of international readjustments and development.

Among the most important of these specialized agencies operating in the international economic field are the Food and Agriculture Organization, the International Civil Aviation Organization, the International Labor Organization, the International Bank for Reconstruction and Development, the International Monetary Fund, and the International Trade Organization. The work of some of these organizations will be discussed in later chapters. Of importance here is the fact that the new role of the United States Government in international organizations has demanded some modification in our existing administrative structure. Consistency of policy in dealing with the UN and its affiliates depends in great measure on the degree to which the staffs of federal departments and agencies accept and act upon common government programs. This has meant once again a broadening of the field of diplomacy. It has become imperative that the international policies of our government be clearly known throughout the federal establishment and far down the administrative line in each of the agencies involved.

Once again the Department of State is chiefly responsible for coördinating the efforts of our government in making our international organization activities effective. However, the major support for particular programs of specialized international organizations must of necessity rest with the federal agencies most able to insure fulfillment by our government of its obligations. Thus the bulwark here at home for our work in the International Labor Organization is the Department of Labor, for the Food and Agriculture Organization it is the Department of Agriculture, for the International Bank and Monetary Fund it is the Treasury Department (and the NAC), and a similar situation must obtain with respect to the International Trade Organization, the International Civil Aviation Organization, and so on. The responsibility of the Department of State in such cases is to assure that the actions taken are consistent with our foreign policy. Here again inter-departmental committees such as those which have been mentioned above are useful instruments in effecting that coördination.

In addition to the organizations attached to the UN, the United States actively participates in other international or regional bodies. The International Telecommunications Union, the Inter-American Coffee Board, the Caribbean Commission, the South Pacific Commission, and the Inter-American Economic and Social Council are but a few. They all serve to illustrate in a small way the breadth of our international economic interests and the effect these activities have on our daily lives.

## PART II

# *INDIVIDUAL COUNTRY AND AREA STUDIES*

# *INTRODUCTION*

Seymour E. Harris

Eight papers on economic problems of six countries and one area constitute Part II of this volume. The emphasis is on the international aspects, and particularly upon those which concern the United States. In Great Britain, the central theme is the adverse balance of payments. The contributors weigh the extent to which mistaken socialist policy, the aftermath of war, inclusive of higher import prices and Government expenditures abroad, and the assumption of dollar obligations for others account for the adverse balance of payments. They also want to know whether relief may be expected from a world-wide depression, internal measures, and the ERP. German deterioration is not to be explained by any single cause: partition, niggardly economic support policies by the United States, political difficulties, lack of incentives, mismanagement of currency (related to the others and a cause of further deterioration), an ineffective administrative setup—these and other causes explain the present impasse. Somewhat similar explanations are relevant to the Japanese economy, though Japan has not suffered from partition. Here again a disturbing monetary situation, imbalance of exports and imports, the absence of incentives stand out. In both countries, vigorous programs of help and economic reform are indispensable if these economies are not to cost the American taxpayer several billion dollars yearly for many years.

Problems of other countries under consideration range from the relatively minor ones of Canada to the almost hopeless ones of China. Canada's economy is sound, even though suffering from boom conditions and a shortage of dollars. The short-run aid and correctives required, and the development of export markets for manufactures are within the realms of probabilities. Nor are Latin American countries so prostrated as most of the rest of the world. The burden of financing exports to countries short of dollars has in turn contributed to an imbalance in foreign exchange markets. A growing imbalance in international accounts and the related inflationary situation are the short-run problems; the extent of industrialization the long-run problem. Russia's problem is primarily that of how much economic isolation she can afford; the extent to which she will milk the satellite countries and make their economies complementary to hers; and that of financing the large imports to Eastern Europe required for their industrialization programs. China faces a production, exchange, and inflation crisis, and a political situation so deteriorated that in the absence of the communist threat, the United States would not be prepared to offer substantial aid. Both the short-run and long-run problems seem almost insoluble. Even industrialization does not offer cheerful prospects.

# 3

## *ANGLO-AMERICAN ECONOMIC RELATIONS*[1]

John M. Cassels

From the earliest period of our colonial history to the present time our economic relations with Britain have been uniquely important to us. To Britain, on her side, relations with the United States have become increasingly important as this country developed. These relations have involved, and always will involve, more than just the exchange of goods between the two countries. They include also the performance of services, the provision of capital, the transfer of experience, and the participation of both countries in world affairs. Our economic relations with Britain have undergone marked changes in the course of time, and they have been by no means free from conflicts of interest, but on the whole they have been mutually helpful, and the gains from the continuing of our close relations are likely to be great, not only for us and for the British, but also for the world at large.

American trade with Britain was orginally based on our ability to supply her with raw materials which she needed, and her ability to provide the manufactured goods that were needed here. The War of Independence was fought, in part, for freedom to develop our own industry and trade. Today we are able to provide most types of manufactured goods economically for ourselves. We meet the British in foreign markets as competitors both in the sale of finished products and in the purchase of many types of crude materials. There still remains, however, a substantial basis for direct trade with the United Kingdom,

[1] The views expressed are not necessarily those of the U. S. Department of Commerce.

an even greater scope for advantageous triangular exchanges, and a common interest in the promotion of sound international trade relations generally. Prior to the first World War there was a net inflow of capital into the United States and much of it came from Britain. Now we are exporters of capital and the United Kingdom is temporarily in need of financial assistance. Over the longer run we are likely to be more concerned about capital investments in British dominions and colonies than in Britain itself, but this also will represent a type of Anglo-American relations which can give rise both to economic ties and to economic friction.

During past centuries we have learned a great deal in technology, in business management, in public finance, in industrial relations, and in socio-economic organization, from the experience of the United Kingdom—in a very real sense our "mother country." More recently our own progress, particularly on the technological side, has been so rapid that it has given us much to contribute in return. In the broad field of world affairs, the fact that two great nations like the United States and Britain have fundamentally similar objectives and have good understanding with one another is of tremendous importance. The differences in our background of experience and our present situation are, perhaps, no less important, since they help to broaden the basis from which we approach world problems and bring a better balance into the policies we are likely to adopt.

*Our Loan to Britain and the 1947 Dollar Crisis*

Victory in World War II depended on the "total" mobilization of economic resources. Our alliance with Britain, therefore, involved the closest kind of economic coöperation through Lend-Lease, Combined Boards, and so on. We contributed greater material wealth to the winning of the war than the British did, but our contribution was made with much less economic strain than theirs.

The population of the United States is nearly three times that of Britain, and in terms of resources the disparity is even greater. Britain was in the war for two years before we entered it, and throughout the whole period of the struggle her people were literally on the fighting front. Her war effort cost her the equivalent of four years of her national income and it meant a tremendous distortion of her internal economy and of her external trade. Her industrial plants were devoted to the maximum production of munitions and military supplies. Her agriculture was expanded and reoriented to meet wartime needs. Unessential imports were cut out entirely and her exports were reduced to about 30 per cent of their prewar volume. She was also forced to liquidate about one-fourth of her foreign investments—mostly to pay for supplies from us before Lend-Lease arrangements came into effect. For a nation normally concentrating on the manufacture of civilian goods and dependent for her prosperity on foreign trade, this obviously meant an extraordinarily difficult period of readjustment when the war was over.

In recognition of this situation, although we terminated Lend-Lease immediately after V-J Day, we entered into negotiations with Britain for the extension to her of a special line of post-war credit with long-term repayment provisions. This was intended to meet her balance of payments deficits during the period necessary for her to regain a position of approximate equilibrium in her international transactions. It was assumed, without disagreement, that the transition period should be over about the end of 1948, but on the amount of credit likely to be required there was a substantial difference of opinion between the British and American experts participating in the negotiations. Finally, the figure of three and three-quarter billion dollars was accepted as the amount to be submitted to Congress, and by July 1946 the British were able to start drawing on this credit. Then followed the period of unexpectedly heavy dollar expenditures. Within thirteen months the total amount of the United States loan had been practically used up, and the gap between Britain's international payments and receipts in 1947 promised to be 50 per cent larger than it had been in 1946.

This situation was naturally referred to as the "British crisis." There is no question that the position was a critical one for the

United Kingdom, but the events actually have much broader significance. Britain's difficulties were accentuated symptoms of the over-all problem of world recovery. Looking back now it is clear that in 1945 (and in 1946), prevailing views about the speed and ease with which the world could recover from the effects of the war erred on the side of overoptimism. Judgments with respect to Britain's prospects were not greatly at fault in regard to the rate of her internal recovery, but the assumptions made in 1945 about price movements were wrong, and there was a general failure to foresee the difficulties which would be created for Britain by the abnormal conditions which have continued throughout the world as a whole.

The volume of Britain's industrial production in 1947 was above the prewar level by something like 10 per cent. Her agricultural production is also at a higher level. Her exports, ever since the middle of 1946, have been above prewar in volume terms, while her imports have been held down to less than 70 per cent of prewar in 1946 and approximately 75 per cent in 1947. By her production efforts, her export drive, and her acceptance of "austerity" living standards, the United Kingdom has made considerable progress towards recovery.

Had her problems been limited to the meeting of her *general* balance of payments deficits during the period from 1946 to 1948, she could almost certainly have made ends meet with the aid provided for through the combined credits from this country and from Canada. Her deficits for the three half-year periods from January 1, 1946, to June 30, 1947, were successively: $965 million, $695 million, and $1,300 million. The total for the period was $2,960 million. Before the successive adjustments made in her export and import programs during the second half of 1947, it had been anticipated that the deficits for the second half of 1947 would be of about the same magnitude as in the first half, but it was confidently expected that a reduction of perhaps 50 per cent could be made in the figure for the first half of 1948, and that in the second half of 1948 Britain would come close to balancing her accounts completely. On this basis her total deficits for the three postwar transition years would have been in the neighborhood of $5 billion and could have been covered by the United States credit of $3.75 billion plus the Canadian credit of $1.25 billion. The fact is that Britain's individual progress towards recovery, as reflected in the figures given above, has been both creditable and encouraging. The so-called "British crisis" must, therefore, be explained in large measure by other factors.

In the first half of 1947, the drain on Britain's United States dollar resources because of the payments she felt she had to make in that currency to countries other than the United States was greater by almost $100 million dollars than the net amount she owed this country for goods and services received directly. During that period she paid us $705 million on her own current account and she paid to third countries $800 million. In addition to this she paid $115 million for food that had been sent to Germany. The payments to third countries included: $220 million to Canada; $225 million to Central and South American countries; $270 million to Sterling Area countries; and $55 million to European countries.

Britain's expenditures of United States dollars, resulting from the claims of non-United States areas, was *six times as great* as it had been in the last half of 1946 (see Figure 1). This may reasonably be regarded as the fundamental cause of the financial problem with which Britain is presently confronted. Britain has, in fact, been suffering a disproportionate share of the impact of the general shortage of United States dollars in the world at large.

Underlying this general "dollar shortage," of course, is the desperate shortage of goods which exists in many countries in Europe and elsewhere. Because their needs for goods have been so urgent, they have had difficulty in sending out exports in sufficient quantity to offset more than a limited proportion of the imports required. During the past two years, the rest of the world has been paying the United States through the immediate delivery of goods for no more than about 40 per cent of the supplies which we have been exporting. For many months after the end of the war, the United Kingdom was shipping a large part of her outgoing supplies to countries which did not fully repay her either in goods or in dollars and could not have done so in the existing circumstances without the greatest difficulty. As noted above, she has also been compelled to pay United States dollars for an increasing proportion of her imports from other countries, because they in their turn had an urgent need of goods from the United States which could only be paid for in American currency.

Two more technical matters connected with the Anglo-Ameri-

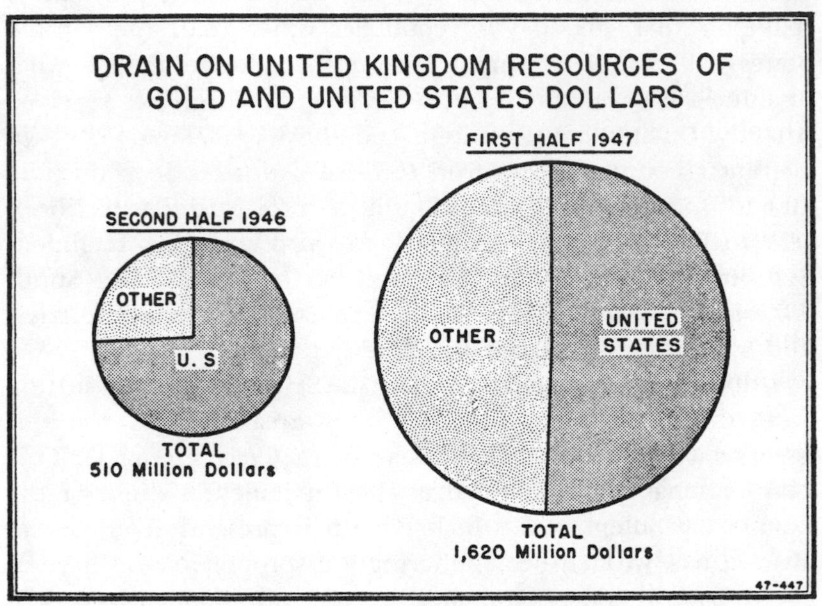


FIGURE 1

can Financial Agreement deserve brief consideration: (a) the provision in Article 7 requiring Britain to make currently earned sterling convertible into dollars after July 15, 1947; and (b) the provision in Article 9 requiring that there should be no discrimination against the United States in the purchasing of imports for Britain. Although lengthy arguments have taken place over these provisions, it may be readily shown on logical grounds that in the present circumstances the first is impossible of complete fulfillment, and the second would make sense economically only if interpreted in a sense very different from that which is ordinarily given to it.

CONVERTIBILITY

Our "export surplus" has been increasing. Before the war it was little more than half a billion dollars per year. In 1946 it was 8 billions and in the first half of 1947 it was running at an annual rate of 12 billions. Since the export surplus is not offset by imports, international settlements for amounts equal to the value of the surplus must be effected in other ways. Countries obtaining these exports from us may pay for them by transferring assets to us (securities, gold, and so on), or by securing from us financial assistance in the form of loans or grants. In 1946, when our export surplus was 8 billions, receiving countries transferred to us assets amounting in value to 2 billion dollars and we extended credit to the amount of 3 billion and made grants (including civilian supplies for occupied areas) of 3 billion dollars. The corresponding figures for the first half of 1947 (on an annual rate basis) were: 4.8 billion; 4.8 billion; and 2.4 billion. Thus, during the first six months of 1947, we were extending financial assistance at the rate of 7.2 billion per year.

Since each country is presumably buying no more goods and services from the United States than represent its effective demand for the items concerned at present prices (and present rates of exchange), and since each is selling as much to us as it finds advantageous at the prices it can obtain with existing tariff barriers, all those whose balances of payments with us are unfavorable have a strong incentive individually to acquire United States dollars and thereby avoid the necessity of making unwanted changes in their trade with this country. The total of the quantities of United States dollars that other countries wish to secure at the present rates of exchange is greater than the total supply available.

In these circumstances, the pressure on the United Kingdom to supply United States dollars to countries having claims on her was bound to be tremendous even without any formal obligation to make sterling convertible. The situation was parallel to that which would exist in the case of any commodity, say steel, for which a price ceiling was established below the market value. If one of the users of steel were put under the obligation of reselling whatever steel it obtained (at the ceiling price) to any creditor who wished to have his account settled in this way, it is obvious that this firm would be left with insufficient steel for its own use. This was confirmed by experience. Britain had to suspend the convertibility of pounds into dollars on August 20. In the five-week period during which she was attempting to operate under the conditions prescribed in Article 7 of the Agreement, the drain on her gold and dollar reserves amounted to nearly one billion dollars.

### NONDISCRIMINATION

As long as prevailing exchange rates are widely at variance with the ratios which would tend to bring international payments into equilibrium, any attempt to enforce nondiscrimination, as the term is interpreted commercially, is likely to lead to some absurd economic results. The commercial definition of nondiscrimination is based (among other things) on the relative prices of goods from different sources, measured against one another on the basis of the established rates of exchange. An economic interpretation of the meaning of the term would take account of the fact that, if exchange rates are not such as to result in market equilibrium, the price comparisons on which the commercial definition is based become completely misleading.

Britain has a limited number of dollars with which to buy things in the United States and has to make them go as far as she can in the purchase of essentials. This means that she probably cannot afford to buy less essential products here (e.g., apples, oranges, walnuts, and so on). On the other hand, when she plans the expenditure of the resources she has available in other currencies (which we will not accept) she finds that, after buying all she can get of essentials, she has some purchasing power left over which she could spend with advantage on limited quantities of fruits and other semiessentials. On the basis of the commercial definition of nondiscrimination, Britain would be prevented from buying these semiessentials from any other source, so long as our prices for them were nominally at a competitive level when compared at established exchange rates. This would mean that Britain had to go without certain imports which she could use to advantage, and that international trade would be unnecessarily and unnaturally curtailed.

The dilemma is, of course, an artificial one. The Financial Agreement is more than a simple business contract. It was intended to deal with fundamental economic problems and should be interpreted with that in mind. If exchange rates do not reflect the market values of currencies in relation to one another, any price comparisons made by using them will involve corresponding distortions. If, for example, the dollar under free exchange conditions were to cost 25 per cent more than it does today in terms of British pounds, there would be no discrimination in an economic sense in Britain's paying prices in other markets which, when computed at the established exchange rate, appear to be 25 per cent higher than what would be charged by American suppliers. The magnitude of the differential which would be justified on economic grounds might be difficult to estimate precisely, but some realistic correction of this sort is clearly needed. Even an approximation to the proper figure would afford a helpful basis for distinguishing practically between those cases in which there is "real" discrimination and those in which it is only "apparent."

Returning to the more basic problems of our export surplus and the dollar shortage, it might appear that a simple solution could be found through the adjustment of exchange rates—a lowering of the value of the pound and of other currencies in terms of American dollars. Eventually some fundamental alterations in exchange rates will be necessary, but this does not provide us with a panacea for our present problems. Depreciation must be rejected as *the* remedy for current difficulties because the blind operation of purely economic forces could not be depended on to bring about, in all respects, the results to be desired in the present abnormal state of world affairs. For example, a general depreciation would have the effect of making countries which can ill afford to pay the present United States prices pay even more for what they bought from the United States. It should also be remembered that free exchange rates would prove to be highly speculative, therefore unsettling, in the current period, and would lead to further adjustments and speculative movements after the current abnormal shortages have been overcome.

Some exchange rate adjustments may be helpful in the very near future, and further steps towards equilibrium rates will be appropriate and necessary during the next three or four years as more stable trade patterns develop, but they should be designed to correspond with the longer-run relations between the countries concerned rather than regarded as a means of dealing with current emergency problems. One of the important benefits from the Marshall Plan will be the time which can be gained in this way for the gradual working out of the more stable relations under which more dependence can be placed on exchange rates for the automatic guidance of trade. In the meantime it is important that we should be consistent in recognizing that, while these rates are not performing the functions traditionally expected of them, many direct controls on international dealings of all sorts will be indispensable.

### *The Marshall Plan and Britain's Recovery Prospects*

Britain will be one of the countries principally affected by the Marshall Plan. She will benefit from it directly, she will benefit from the recovery of other countries, and her own recovery will have an important relation to world recovery. Less than justice is done to the Marshall Plan when it is referred to as a European Recovery Program. It is a general recovery program in which the treatment is applied in the areas where the underlying ailment of our global economic organism centers at the present time. The significance of this may be seen from the analysis of Britain's problems outlined above. If Britain cannot pay Canada and other suppliers with American dollars, they must cut down on their imports from the United States or sell more goods in this market. This would mean a drastic distortion of trade and would cause serious financial difficulties. On the other hand, if Britain gets aid from us, some of the dollars will be paid for Canadian food and Canada will have the means of paying for more of the essential imports that she customarily buys from us. The same will be true of other countries receiving assistance and of other countries supplying them with imports. This is the purpose of providing, under the Marshall Plan, for what is referred to as "off-shore procurement"—that is, the use of aid funds for the procurement of supplies from sources other than the United States. With this in mind, estimates of the financial assistance needed to accomplish the objectives of the program have been related not only to the deficits of the seventeen receiving countries with the United States, but also to their total balance of payments deficits with all Western Hemisphere countries. This does not quite equal the total deficits of *all* countries with the United States, but since the seventeen countries concerned have a very large proportion of the world's trade, the figure arrived at in this way represents the greater part of the total world deficit with us under conditions assumed to exist during the period of the program.

One other point should be noted here to avoid misunderstanding. The fact that U.S. dollars would flow back through Canada and other supplying countries does not mean that we would be contributing "financial" aid to them. The benefit to them would come through our facilitating the continuance of trade with a minimum of distortion. Actually, other supplying countries will share with us the responsibility of providing the financial assistance required. In some cases they will probably be contributing a greater amount in proportion to their national incomes than we ourselves contribute. This has been true of postwar aid to date and may well continue to be true of some of the British Dominions during the next four years. Canada, for example, in the two-year period from July 1, 1945 to June 30, 1947, assisted through grants and credits at a rate equal to nearly 7 per cent of her national income. When a further allowance is made for the submarket prices charged to the U.K. for wheat and other foodstuffs, Canada's contribution amounted to at least 8 per cent of her national income. The corresponding rate for the United States was 3 per cent. In 1948, in spite of the fact that the financial strain on Canada has been causing increasing difficulty, it is almost certain that her contribution will continue to be on a parity with ours in relation to her national income.

In the case of Britain—a direct recipient of financial assistance—we are naturally interested to know what her prospects for recovery are, and how we may expect them to be affected by the Marshall Plan. As has been already pointed out, the volume of Britain's production and exports, by the end of 1946, was above its prewar level. In 1947 it was higher than in 1946, but not as much higher as it had been hoped. Stocks of certain basic materials had been run down in 1946 to levels that made efficient operations more difficult and, in the case of coal, meant that nearly 6 million additional tons of the 1947 output had to be used to bring winter reserves back up to a safe minimum level. The railways of the country also proved to be in worse condition than had been realized at the end of the war, and transportation difficulties interfered with the maximization of production. On the agricultural side Britain suffered from the worst winter she had had in forty years, followed by a summer so dry that her potato crop was reduced to a level which necessitated rationing. At the same time her production of milk in particular had to be curtailed for lack of feed. International responsibilities led her to keep more men in the armed services and in civilian services abroad than was consistent with her need for manpower on productive jobs at home. Finally, some of the reductions made in working hours, together with incentive problems, resulted in a smaller output of the things most needed for recovery progress than was theoretically possible.

Her general balance of payments position was adversely affected by the upward movement of all prices (lessening the real value of her income from foreign investments), and by the more rapid increase in the prices of things she had to import than in the prices of the things she had for export (making the terms of trade continually more unfavorable to her). With respect to her American dollar deficit she suffered from the difficulty of obtaining essential supplies from areas where other currencies were acceptable in payment.

The year 1947 was a disappointing one for Britain, but in its later months foundations were being laid for a fresh attack on her problems in 1948. As a nation she is now realistically accepting inescapable consequences of the war and is adapting her economic programs with characteristic resilience to the circumstances with which she is confronted. Miscalculations which resulted in the past two years from deficient coordination in the development of her programs should henceforth be minimized by the centralization of management authority in the hands of Sir Stafford Cripps. The British people are accepting continuing austerity in their standard of living, and cutting construction projects back to levels that meet only the most urgent needs. Exports are being pushed at the expense of domestic consumption. Imports are limited to commodities of the most essential character. Working hours have been lengthened, and efforts are being made to guide labor and other resources into employments that can contribute most significantly to the nation's recovery. Special emphasis is being placed on coal production, and the output of railway equipment has already been sharply increased. Vigorous steps are being taken to deal with inflation.

By the end of 1947, Britain had come three and one-half million tons of attaining the 200 million ton goal for coal production which at midyear had seemed to be far beyond her reach. The mechanization of her mines is proceeding steadily. Each month 200 mechanical cutters and 200 loaders are being installed. The output per man-shift is almost back to its prewar level and the labor force in the mines is gradually increasing. The output target for 1948 is 211 million tons—still 7 per cent below prewar, but 7 per cent higher than 1947 and 16 per cent above the wartime low in 1945. In all export industries production is on the upgrade and, with a few exceptions, the levels in all important lines are higher than 1938.

The all-out export drive begun after the crisis of mid-1947 has brought good results (see Figure 2). By the end of the year, iron and steel exports were already ahead of the target levels set for the middle of 1948; nonferrous metals were at the target level for a date still six months away; exports of vehicles (including ships) were at 88 per cent of their midyear target levels, while pottery and glass were within 17 per cent of theirs. Coal exports in 1948 should amount to 15 or 16 million tons.

Britain plans to have her exports expanded by the end of June, 1948 to a volume 35 per cent greater than they were before the war; by the end of the year the level planned for is 150 per

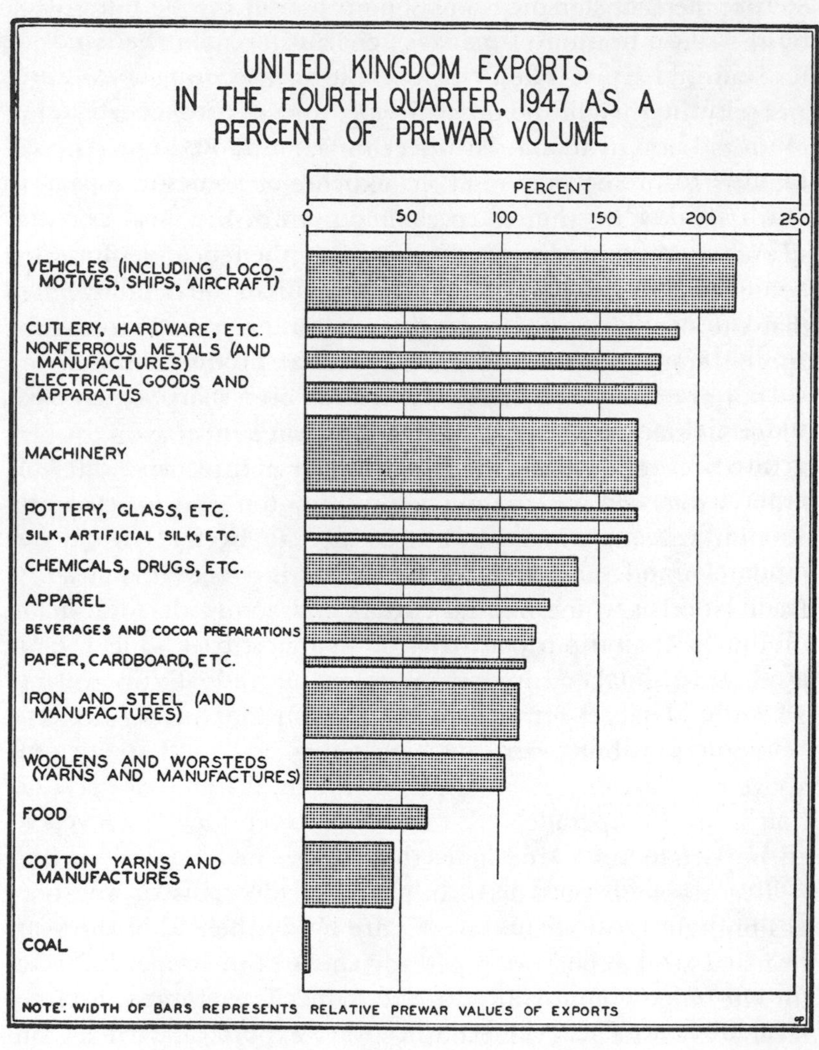
UNITED KINGDOM EXPORTS
IN THE FOURTH QUARTER, 1947 AS A
PERCENT OF PREWAR VOLUME
PERCENT
0
50
100
150
200
250
VEHICLES (INCLUDING LOCO-
MOTIVES, SHIPS, AIRCRAFT)
CUTLERY, HARDWARE, ETC.
NONFERROUS METALS (AND
MANUFACTURES)
ELECTRICAL GOODS AND
APPARATUS
MACHINERY
POTTERY, GLASS, ETC.
SILK, ARTIFICIAL SILK, ETC.
CHEMICALS, DRUGS, ETC.
APPAREL
BEVERAGES AND COCOA PREPARATIONS
PAPER, CARDBOARD, ETC.
IRON AND STEEL (AND
MANUFACTURES)
WOOLENS AND WORSTEDS
(YARNS AND MANUFACTURES)
FOOD
COTTON YARNS AND
MANUFACTURES
COAL
NOTE: WIDTH OF BARS REPRESENTS RELATIVE PREWAR VALUES OF EXPORTS

FIGURE 2

cent. It is hoped to increase receipts from international transactions over those of 1947, while continuing to limit expenditures so that the British deficit on current account for the first half of 1948 will be no more than £135 million, compared with £335 million in 1947. The estimated Western Hemisphere deficit of £185 million would be offset in part by a sterling area surplus. With aid now available through the Marshall Plan, Britain will be able to protect her reserves and have a little more time to reach a balance in her international payments.

Without financial assistance, Britain's food consumption would be reduced to a critically low level; her general standard of living would be unsatisfactory; the rate of capital formation would be below prewar, in spite of the need to make up for wartime arrears and losses; the restoration and renovation of her industrial facilities would be delayed; and her progress towards greater industrial efficiency retarded. Her difficulties would have repercussions on other countries, some trade adjustments which should be brought about gradually would have to be made precipitately, and other features would be introduced into world trade patterns which would be inconsistent with the attainment of the best results for all nations in the period which comes after these abnormal transitional years. From Britain's point of view the Marshall Plan should mean a quicker, less painful, and more successful recovery.

### *Britain's Internal Economic Organization*

There has been a natural tendency for many people in this country, and for some in the United Kingdom also, to attribute Britain's current difficulties, in considerable part at least, to the fact that she has had since July, 1945 a Labor Government committed to economic planning and to a limited program of nationalization. The evidence does not support this conclusion. Regardless of the views which anyone may hold about the longer-run advantages or disadvantages of giving more conscious recognition to the public interest in the planning and direction of economic affairs, the postwar program of the British Government deserves a thoroughly objective appraisal.

Some responsible leaders of the Conservative Party have themselves stated that, had they been in power, they would have found it necessary to do many of the things which the Labor Government has done; and that, if they were to win the next election, few of the fundamental steps taken in the past two and a half years would be reversed. They take pride in the fact that some of the measures put into effect by the Labor Government (for instance, their extended national insurance scheme), were designed by the Coalition Government while Mr. Churchill was still Prime Minister. Many other characteristics of Britain's present program, such as coal allocation, food rationing, and price control, are emergency measures continued since the war because of her recognition that conditions still are far from normal. Certain other controls, as we know, were abandoned for a time and have had to be reinstituted because of the 1947 crisis.

The nationalization of the Bank of England made practically no change in its organization or its functions. The central banks in most countries are public or quasi-public institutions. In the case of coal, because of the importance of this resource as a basis for the whole economy of the nation, and because of the highly unsatisfactory conditions that have existed in the industry for decades past, nationalization was to be foreseen long before the war. Power and transportation, falling in the class of natural monopolies, were recognized as requiring either public control or public operation. Britain has a background of successful experience in the municipal operation of public utilities and, being a small country, the choice of this method on a national scale represented no departure from principles that had been put to the test and proved widely acceptable. When we turn to the land of the country, we are concerned again with a national resource of the greatest importance to a people as crowded for space as the British are. Land has not been nationalized, but the uses to which it may be put have been brought under supervision by public authorities, and the increases in land values which do not arise from direct improvements by the owners themselves are in the future to be absorbed by taxation. In a country where the natural interest of the people in their land has for long been gaining increased recognition, these recent measures are in no sense revolutionary. It would be impossible to demonstrate conclusively whether efficiency has been impaired or improved in those segments of the British economy where socialization has taken place, but it is clear that the steps so far taken could have had very little to do directly with the creation or aggravation of her economic difficulties.

Conceding this, the critics of the Labor Government still may argue that, if it had given less attention to its socialization program, it could have dealt more effectively with current emergency problems and could have had better working relations with industry. There is undoubtedly some truth in this line of reasoning, but other considerations must be added before a balanced judgment can be made. Working relations with labor have probably been of greater importance during the past two years than the relations of government to management. Had the Conservative Party been in power, serious losses of output through strikes would have been almost certain to occur. Under a government representing the workers themselves, the time lost through industrial disputes has been negligible—no more than one hour per worker per year.[2] Industrial peace was of inestimable value to the country, and it could hardly have been expected to continue if the government had abandoned the principles it had undertaken at the time of its election to put into effect. Therefore, whatever diversion of government attention from emergency problems may have resulted, it must be weighed against the very great gains that were obtained through the coöperation and support of the trade unions and the working population as a whole.

Members of the Government would not deny that there have been some grave miscalculations and errors both in the planning and in administration of their program. The United Kingdom has its troubles with inflation—"suppressed inflation." Since the prices of most commodities have been controlled and essentials have been rationed, people have had more money coming into their hands than they needed for their ordinary living expenses. This meant a weakening of the money-wage incentive, a tendency for labor to be employed in "inessential" services, and a failure

[2] The corresponding figure for the U. S. was one day per worker per year.

to reflect in the budgets of individual citizens the stringency of the nation's economic situation. The degree of inflation, however, and its consequences, have undoubtedly been less serious in Britain than in most other countries. Another error Britain made (along with the United States and practically all other countries) was in underestimating the duration and the stringency of the postwar transition period. Through the overoptimism of the nation and through lack of centralized authority for economic planning in the government, Britain was led, immediately after the war, to set herself a series of objectives on the various economic fronts which could not all be attained simultaneously. Her original over-all plans for capital expansion, colonial development, improvement of living standards, shortening of hours, raising of the school-leaving age, increase of exports, assistance to war-devastated areas, and for discharging the heavy international responsibilities of a Great Power have had to be scaled down as a result of experience.

In the interpretation of these developments we may easily be misled if we fail to see them in their proper perspective. It was natural that a people long under the strain of war should assume that victory would bring them material benefits instead of increased hardship. It was only to be expected that the new postwar government would require time to integrate its machinery for planning. It would have required clairvoyant gifts to foresee all the adverse circumstances here and there throughout the world which have had an impact during the past two years on Britain's economic conditions. The encouraging thing to note is the adaptability which the British have shown in adjusting themselves to the realities of the situation—their capacity to learn quickly from experience and to face their problems squarely. Their sense of national unity is strong. Moderation and reasonableness predominate in the political life of the country. Industrial relations are good. Management is coöperating with the government in the all-out production and export programs. Trade unions, in spite of their traditions and their very recent advocacy of a shorter working week, have agreed to the lengthening of hours in essential industries. Consumers are accepting present and prospective deprivations stoically. One of the nation's greatest assets is its will to win the "Economic Battle of Britain."

Over the longer run Britain's experiments in economic management will deserve our close attention. In the modern world, with all its complexities, with its giant enterprises and its giant unions, with its dynamic forces and its tendencies to instability, the problem of insuring that each nation's institutions work effectively for the common welfare has become to all a matter of paramount importance. However well we may think our type of economic system works in the United States, we must face the fact that it is not proving entirely acceptable in many countries of the world. At the opposite extreme are the dictatorial systems in which we see an intolerable sacrifice of the liberties of individuals. Between the two extremes is the British system. In Britain essential liberties are highly prized, the respect for law is exceptionally strong, and the government is democratic. The British approach to the problem of social well-being is pragmatic and they are less likely than almost any other people to allow doctrinaire principles to lead them to impractical conclusions. It will be well for the world to have the benefit of their pioneering in this troublesome field and it should not be surprising if we ourselves discover lessons of real value to be learned from their experience.

### *Anglo-American Participation in International Economic Affairs*

The objectives of the United States and Britain in international economic affairs, while they do not correspond completely, have many elements in common. On many issues the two countries naturally lend support to one another, at the same time broadening each other's policies by approaching the problems from somewhat different points of view. On questions where the countries differ, there is commonly a tendency for the British position to parallel more closely the positions of other nations and to lead in the direction of more widely acceptable solutions. The fact that these two important countries, each maintaining its independence of action, have demonstrated considerable capacity for working together is certainly one of the notable features in the international picture and is one which should prove helpful in dealing with world problems.

Anglo-American economic coöperation during the war was, of course, extraordinarily close and successful. In the period immediately following the liberation of the western European countries, the continuation of the allocation authority in the hands of Anglo-American Combined Boards created ill-feeling on the part of other countries which was allowed to fester too long before the arrangements changed. In UNRRA, although objectives were less clear than in the wartime programs, the joint work of the United States and the United Kingdom along with others brought good results. In the setting up of the existing international financial institutions (the Bank and the Fund) and in their operation to date, British and American views diverged. The wishes of the United States have had a dominant influence on what has happened; the long-run results for the world still remain to be seen.

More recently, the interaction of the policies of the two countries has been exercising an important influence on international plans for the expansion of world trade and employment. From the start there has been substantial agreement on the objectives, but considerable disagreement about the means that can best be employed in attaining them. The two countries readily joined forces in supporting the establishment of an International Trade Organization. They differed, however, not only in the relative importance they attached to the various functions it might have, but also on the rigidity with which certain principles were to be applied. A comparison of the original "Proposals" taken over to London in December, 1946 with the revised document which resulted from the preliminary international discussions at that time shows clearly the benefits which follow from the merging of complementary points of view. In the revised proposals, more stress was laid on: measures to maintain high levels of employment; the promotion of development in backward areas; and the flexibility to be provided in carrying out charter provisions, particularly during the period of postwar difficulties. Modifications which the British pressed for reflected their concern about economic stability and their characteristic willingness to qualify the application of doctrines which fit imperfectly with the realities of any given situation. It is generally conceded that the changes made at London were important and necessary improvements in the draft with which the conference started.

With respect to tariff reductions—to be effected through the Geneva Trade Agreements Conference—there was a common recognition by the United States and Britain of the advantages to be expected from the development of freer trade, but some reluctance on the British side to give this a top priority among the international problems of 1947. When the conference was held, the actual bargaining involved in working out reciprocal concessions was conducted in a friendly fashion and significant tariff adjustments were effected. On the question of imperial preferences, however, opposing positions were so stubbornly maintained that the success of the whole conference was, for a time, endangered and proceedings were seriously delayed. This issue is one on which the feelings have been strong for many years and on which there is need for better understanding. Commercial self-interest is involved on both sides, but there are also more fundamental questions. Our approach has tended to stress consistency in the adherence to general principles and the fulfillment of commitments (obtained from Britain under the Lend-Lease and Loan Agreements) on which we put a rather different interpretation than do the British. We have regarded imperial preference as a form of discrimination which should be eliminated from international dealings. Rightly or wrongly, the British, on their side, have viewed imperial preference as one of the important means of maintaining close economic relations between the areas that make up the Commonwealth and Empire. Although their territories do not happen to be contiguous, they consider that the extent of their political unity justifies them in giving one another lower tariff rates, without violating the general principle that nondiscrimination should prevail in the trade between independent nations.

Furthermore, on the basic question of economic relations among British areas, Americans generally have tended to underrate the importance that is now attached to intra-empire cooperation as a means of minimizing, for the countries concerned, some of the risks arising from business fluctuations. Very popular during the past few years in the United States has been the belief that an expansion of international trade would in itself lessen the danger of depression and unemployment. We have been tempted to look on this method as an alternative to less popular measures affecting the operations of our internal economy. It must be admitted, however, that the reasoning with which the thesis has been supported has not been convincing. The fact that an increasing export surplus tends to stimulate business does not logically lead to the conclusion that a general expansion of trade will contribute to economic stability in all countries of the world simultaneously. British economists lay greater stress on the governmental measures that must be employed to combat depression. Many have doubts about the promptness and vigor with which such steps would be taken, when necessary, in the United States. If these doubts proved correct, other countries economically interdependent with us would suffer adverse effects. On the other hand, a group of countries with political machinery to facilitate concerted action, and with corresponding views about the types of internal measures called for, would presumably have an advantage in working together for the attainment of greater stability in their economies.

# 4

## *PROSPERITY, DEPRESSION, AND THE BRITISH EXTERNAL PROBLEM*

Randall Hinshaw[1]

During the war the view was widely expressed that the principal contribution the United States could make toward a long-range solution of the British balance-of-payments problem would be to maintain a high level of domestic prosperity. It was argued that, under prosperous conditions, American imports of goods and services would be at a high level, and that this would provide Britain with adequate markets for its exports, not only in the United States, but throughout the world. In an article written just before the end of the war, Lloyd A. Metzler and the present writer attempted to estimate the postwar British balance of payments under conditions of world prosperity.[2] The conclusions of this article, which was concerned only with the post-transitional period, were moderately optimistic. Subject to certain qualifications, it was concluded that in a prosperous world British exports of goods and services would be at a level approximately sufficient to balance external accounts, including payment for the volume of imports demanded under prosperous conditions in Britain.

In recent months a widely different view of the British problem has been given expression. According to the latter view, prosperity in the United States and elsewhere, instead of helping Britain to meet its foreign expenses, actually makes the problem more difficult by increasing the cost of British imports.

[1] The conclusions presented in this chapter represent the personal opinions of the author and do not necessarily reflect the views of the Board of Governors of the Federal Reserve System.

[2] "World Prosperity and the British Balance of Payments," *Review of Economic Statistics* (November 1945).

In fact, it has been suggested, more or less seriously, that a moderate—though probably not a major—depression abroad would ease Britain's external plight by improving British terms of trade. While this would seem to be an exaggerated view of the situation, the British balance of payments in recent months has taken such an unfavorable turn that it is well to reëxamine the problem in the light of developments since the end of the war.

TABLE 1

BRITISH BALANCE OF PAYMENTS ON CURRENT ACCOUNT[a]

(*Millions of pounds sterling*)

| | 1938 | 1947 |
|---|---|---|
| Payments | | |
| Imports, c.i.f. | 921 | 1783 |
| Less freight, etc. | 86 | 209 |
| Imports, f.o.b. | 835 | 1574 |
| Government payments abroad | 16 | 211 |
| Total payments | 851 | 1785 |
| Receipts | | |
| Exports, f.o.b. | 533 | 1125 |
| Net invisible receipts | 248 | −15 |
| Total receipts | 781 | 1110 |
| Balance on current account | −70 | −675 |

[a]Source: *White Paper on United Kingdom Balance of Payments*, Cmd. 7324 (February 10, 1948).

## *Elements of the British External Problem*

In Table 1, the British balance of payments on current account for 1938 is compared with the balance for 1947. It can be seen from this table that there have been three major adverse developments in the British current position since 1938: (1) a huge increase in the merchandise trade deficit; (2) a marked increase in government expenditures abroad; and (3) a sharp contraction in income from overseas investments and other invisible sources, with the result that a substantial surplus has been converted into a deficit.[3] Those who hold that a depression in

[3]An additional unfavorable factor in the British balance of payments is the

the United States would benefit the British position would appear to be thinking almost solely in terms of the balance of trade. With respect to (2), it is clear that the high level of government payments abroad is a direct consequence of the war and is only secondarily related to boom conditions abroad, while with respect to (3) it would appear that an external depression would only make matters much worse than at present. Accordingly, we shall first center our attention on the trade balance in an effort to determine whether the adverse effect of world prosperity on the cost of British imports is likely to outweigh the favorable effect on net receipts from all sources.

British imports and exports, together with the balance of trade, are shown for selected periods in Table 2. The quarterly figures are expressed at annual rates.

After rising at an alarming rate for four successive quarters, the British trade deficit reached an annual rate of nearly £800 million in the third quarter of 1947. The major factor accounting for the mounting deficit has been the rapid rise in world prices. In a situation such as this, where imports are initially larger than exports, a given percentage increase in both import and export prices adds a larger absolute amount to the value of imports than to the value of exports. In these circumstances, a doubling of prices on both sides is a serious matter: it not only doubles the value of imports and exports; it also doubles the trade deficit. Actually, both import and export prices in Britain are well over twice the 1938 level and, of the two series, import prices have registered the greater increase. British import prices in the third quarter of 1947 were two-and-a-half times as high as in 1938, while British export prices were two-and-a-third times as high. To show how unfavorable these price developments have been, it may be pointed out that, at 1938 prices, the trade deficit for the third quarter of 1947 would have amounted

---

large external short-term sterling debt. This debt, which arose as a consequence of British participation in the war, amounted in 1948 to between £3 and £4 billion. The debt is largely in the form of foreign-owned British Treasury bills and bank balances, and thus the interest burden is small—probably less than £20 million a year. Reduction of the debt, which has been proceeding on a modest scale, increases the net requirements for foreign exchange beyond the amount indicated by the deficit on current account.

to an annual rate of only £271 million instead of the actual figure of £794 million.

### *Depression and the British Balance of Payments*

Nevertheless, the thesis that an external depression would help Britain must be viewed with marked skepticism. A plausible case for this proposition can be made only by soft-pedaling

TABLE 2

BRITISH IMPORTS, EXPORTS, AND TRADE BALANCE, ANNUAL RATE[a]

(*Millions of pounds sterling*)

| | Imports c.i.f. | Exports f.o.b.[b] | Balance |
|---|---|---|---|
| 1937 | 1028 | 596 | −432 |
| 1938 | 919 | 532 | −387 |
| 1942 | 996 | 276 | −720 |
| 1943 | 1232 | 239 | −993 |
| 1944 | 1307 | 282 | −1025 |
| 1945—III | 1099 | 454 | −645 |
| IV | 939 | 533 | −406 |
| 1946—I | 1118 | 790 | −328 |
| II | 1270 | 934 | −336 |
| III | 1315 | 1010 | −305 |
| IV | 1476 | 1120 | −356 |
| 1947—I | 1455 | 1072 | −383 |
| II | 1814 | 1134 | −680 |
| III | 2051 | 1257 | −794 |
| IV | 1812 | 1331 | −481 |

[a]Source: British Central Statistical Office, *Monthly Digest of Statistics*.
[b]Includes re-exports.

some of the more important repercussions of a decline in foreign incomes. Of course, a depression which *spread* to Britain might solve the British external problem (by its impact on the volume of British imports), but this is clearly not the line of reasoning entertained by those who believe that a foreign depression would be a blessing to Britain. Such a cure would be worse than the disease. Those who adhere to the thesis under discussion assume that, by appropriate domestic policies, Britain is able to isolate itself from the depression, and they do not favor a solution which involves a reduction in the volume of British imports, since imports are already at austerity levels.

It is of course true that a depression abroad would result in a fall in the cost of British imports. Moreover, the fall in the price level of imports, which consist mainly of foodstuffs and raw materials, would probably be greater than the fall in the price level of exports, which consist chiefly of manufactures. These favorable price developments, however, must be weighed against the virtually certain accompaniment of a serious decline in the volume of British exports.

Consider for a moment the British trade deficit, which in the second half of 1947 was running at an annual rate of £637 million. If a depression abroad were to result in a 20 per cent reduction in import prices—and if export prices as well as the volume of exports and imports were to remain unchanged—this deficit would be reduced to an annual rate of only £251 million. But the matter cannot be left here, since a foreign depression would result in a fall in the volume of British exports. If, in the above case, the fall in import prices were accompanied by a 30 per cent drop in the volume of exports, the trade deficit would be virtually the same as in the second half of 1947 (£639 million as against £637 million). And if, along with the drop in export volume, British export prices were to fall by, say, 10 per cent, the trade deficit would be 15 per cent larger than before the assumed depression. At the same time, income from invisible sources would be sharply reduced, and the whole problem of achieving balance might be much greater than at present.

That this unfavorable train of events is not of merely hypothetical significance is indicated by evidence that the volume of British exports is highly sensitive to income changes abroad. That is to say, the foreign income elasticity of demand for British products appears to be unusually high. This is hardly a matter for surprise, since a large segment of British exports is in the luxury or semiluxury category. The demand for expensive motor cars, fine woolens, and other quality products is notoriously affected by changes in the level of consumer income, for when income falls such items either can be dispensed with entirely or can be replaced by cheaper substitutes.

Comprehensive estimates of the foreign income elasticity of demand for British products are not available, but in the case of one important British customer—the United States—it is possible to make such a computation for the interwar period. In Figure 3, the volume of American imports from the United Kingdom for the period 1923-37 is correlated with American national income (at constant prices).[4] Both series are expressed as indexes on a 1937 base. It is readily apparent from this chart that in the interwar years the volume of British exports to the United States was sensitive to changes in the level of American real income. The American income elasticity of demand for British products, as computed from the data in the chart, is 1.6, indicating that, for the period covered, a 10 per cent change in American real income was accompanied, on the average, by a 16 per cent change in the volume of goods purchased from the United Kingdom. It is interesting to note that the American income elasticity of demand for British goods appears to be much higher than for foreign products as a whole; the over-all American income elasticity of demand for products purchased from overseas, as calculated from interwar data, is about unity.

It is not clear whether British exports are as sensitive to income changes in other countries as to income changes in the United States, but there are reasons to believe that this is the case. In the two years from 1929 to 1931, the total volume of British exports declined by 37 per cent. This decline appears to have been of much greater proportions than the decline in real income abroad during the same period. While the latter decline can be only approximately estimated, it appears to have been of

[4] The volume of American imports from the United Kingdom was computed by dividing the import value figures by a price index of American imports from Britain. The price index, which was constructed at the Federal Reserve Board by Miss Lucy Axelbank, is based on about sixty commodities and was derived by means of the "ideal" formula. It is reproduced in a previous article by the author ("American Prosperity and the British Balance-of-Payments Problem," *Review of Economic Statistics* (February 1945), p. 7). The income figures here used are the annual estimates prepared by the Department of Commerce, and are divided by the consumer price index of the Bureau of Labor Statistics. Since the recently revised (and conceptually somewhat different) Department of Commerce income figures are not available for years prior to 1929, the former income estimates have been used throughout.

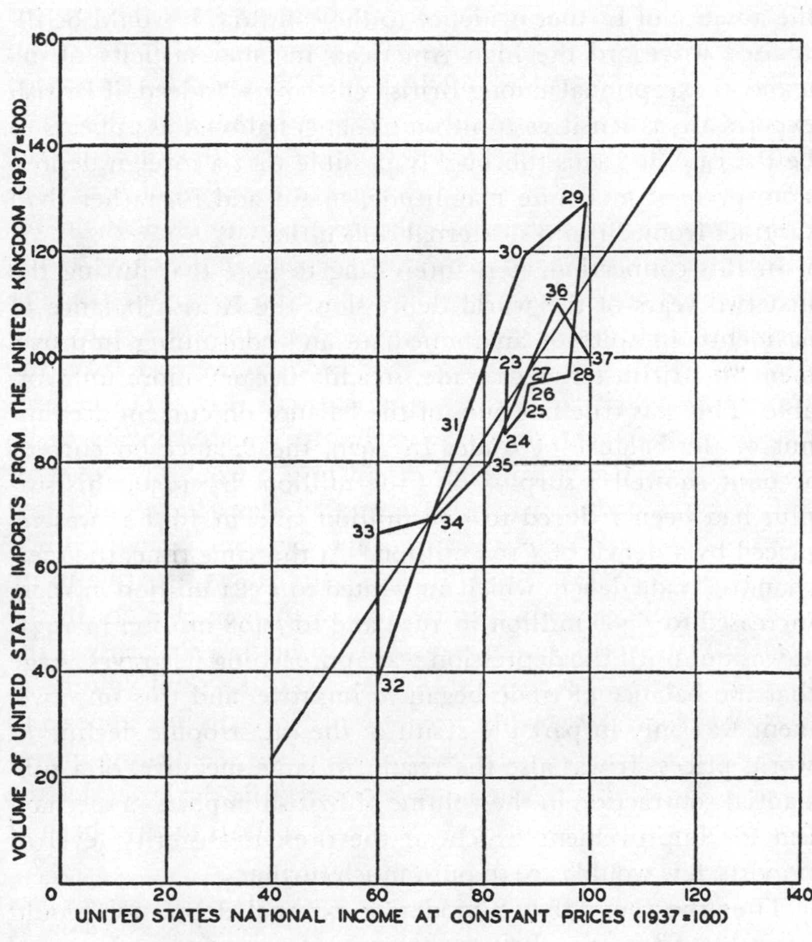
VOLUME OF UNITED STATES IMPORTS FROM THE UNITED KINGDOM (1937=100)
UNITED STATES NATIONAL INCOME AT CONSTANT PRICES (1937=100)
160
140
120
100
80
60
40
20
0
20
40
60
80
100
120
140
29
30
36
37
23
28
27
26
25
31
24
35
33
34
32

FIGURE 3

the order of not more than 20 per cent.[5] This would suggest an exceptionally high world income elasticity of demand for British exports. Unfortunately, the picture after 1931 is obscured by the rapid growth of trade restrictions, but it is clear that, in the absence of further evidence to the contrary, it would be ill-advised to regard the high American income elasticity of demand as exceptional among British customers. Indeed, if British exports are as sensitive to income changes abroad as appears to be the case, it seems thoroughly possible that a foreign depression, even of moderate magnitude, might add to, rather than subtract from, Britain's external difficulties.

In this connection, it is interesting to note that during the first two years of the world depression, the British balance of payments, in spite of an immediate and continuing improvement in British terms of trade, steadily became more unfavorable. This was true not only of the balance on current account but of the balance of trade. In 1929, the balance on current account showed a surplus of £103 million. By 1930, this surplus had been reduced to £28 million, and in 1931 it was replaced by a deficit of £104 million.[6] At the same time, the merchandise trade deficit, which amounted to £381 million in 1929, increased to £386 million in 1930 and to £408 million in 1931. It was not until the depression was approaching its gravest stage that the balance of trade began to improve, and this improvement was only in part the result of the catastrophic decline in world prices. It was also the result, in large measure, of a substantial contraction in the volume of British imports—a mechanism for improvement which, at the present austerity level of imports, few would care to push much further.

Thus the thesis that a moderate external depression would favorably affect the British balance of payments, whereas a major depression probably would not, receives little support

[5] According to a composite index of real income prepared by the author in another connection, the combined real income of twenty countries (excluding the United Kingdom but including the United States) fell by 18.7 per cent in the two-year period 1929-31. This index is described in Hinshaw and Metzler, *op. cit.*, p. 169.

[6] *Statistical Abstract for the United Kingdom* (1937), p. 438. Since 1931, the British balance on current account has shown a deficit for every year except 1933, when the balance was neutral, and 1935, when there was a small surplus.

from the experience of the early thirties. At that time, the reverse was the case; in the early months of the depression, the British external position steadily grew worse, and it was only when the depression had achieved major proportions that improvement came.

## *British Prospects in a Prosperous World*

In the light of recent developments, it is easy to be unduly pessimistic concerning long-range British prospects. In the article cited earlier, the authors made an estimate of the post-transitional British balance of payments under conditions of world prosperity. In this estimate, which appears in Table 3, it was assumed that the volume of British imports would be somewhat greater than before the war.

TABLE 3

ESTIMATED POST-TRANSITIONAL BRITISH BALANCE OF PAYMENTS UNDER CONDITIONS OF WORLD PROSPERITY

(*Millions of pounds sterling*)

| | |
|---|---|
| Payments | |
| Imports, c.i.f. | 1288 |
| Less freight, etc. | 188[a] |
| Imports, f.o.b. | 1100 |
| Government payments abroad | 64 |
| Total payments | 1164 |
| Receipts | |
| Exports, f.o.b. | 795 |
| Net invisible receipts | 272 |
| Total receipts | 1067 |
| Balance on current account | −97 |

[a]Current estimate.

In some respects, the figures in Table 3 now appear overoptimistic. A much lower level of import and export prices than in 1947-48 was assumed, as well as a much lower level of government expenditures abroad. However, despite the very poor showing in 1947, it would be too early to conclude that the post-transitional level of net invisible income has been seriously overestimated. With the restoration of the British merchant fleet, with prospects of increased receipts from tourist expenditures in Britain, and with some measure of recovery in income from overseas investments, it would appear probable that net invisible receipts will gradually climb to a much higher level.

Also assumed in Table 3 is a volume of exports about 20 per cent above the annual rate attained in the third quarter of 1947. With the less favorable price relationships now prevailing, an increase in exports of this magnitude would not be sufficient to restore balance in British external accounts. Under conditions of adequate foreign demand, however, there is no reason to assume that exports could not be expanded to the required level. Indeed, official export targets announced in September, 1947 go far beyond the increase in exports assumed in Table 3; the target set for the end of 1948 calls for a volume of exports about 40 per cent higher than in the third quarter of 1947.

TABLE 4

REVISED ESTIMATE OF POST-TRANSITIONAL BRITISH BALANCE UNDER CONDITIONS OF WORLD PROSPERITY

(*Millions of pounds sterling*)

| | |
|---|---|
| Payments | |
| Imports, c.i.f. | 1993 |
| Less freight, etc. | 276 |
| Imports, f.o.b. | 1717 |
| Government payments abroad | 100 |
| Total payments | 1817 |
| Receipts | |
| Exports, f.o.b. | 1681 |
| Net invisible receipts | 136 |
| Total receipts | 1817 |
| Balance on current account | 0 |

The revised balance in Table 4, which takes into account unfavorable developments since the end of the war, is based on the following assumptions: (1) the level of import and export prices prevailing in the fourth quarter of 1947; (2) a volume of imports 10 per cent higher than in the fourth quarter of 1947 (equivalent to about 85 per cent of the 1938 volume); (3) a volume of exports 30 per cent higher than in the third quarter of 1947; (4) a reduction in external government payments to £100 million (the official target for 1948); and (5) *half* the level of net invisible income estimated in the previously cited article. Under these rather conservative assumptions, the deficit on current account entirely disappears. Under assumptions not much more favorable, the prewar volume of imports could be restored and a modest program of external debt reduction could be undertaken.

### *Conclusion*

In the last analysis, the effect on a country of changes in external economic conditions must be measured in terms of real income. The question with which we have been concerned is not whether Britain, in a depressed world, could maintain full employment; it may be assumed that, with appropriate policies, full employment can always be maintained. But, as recent experience amply demonstrates, full employment in itself is not a sufficient condition for British prosperity. Nor are British terms of trade the sole additional consideration. To determine the impact of external depression on British real income, we must ask the following question: What measures would be required, under depressed external conditions, to maintain full employment in Britain? Broadly speaking, it would appear that the British would have two alternatives: (1) they could attempt to maintain employment in the export industries, either by sterling depreciation or by export subsidies, or (2) they could permit exports to decline, and proceed to move in the direction of greater self-sufficiency. Full employment could be maintained in either way. If they were to choose the first course, it is not at all clear that British terms of trade would become more favorable than under conditions of external prosperity; indeed the terms might become much less favorable. If, in these circumstances, the terms of trade should deteriorate, both the British balance of payments and British real income would be unfavorably affected by an external slump. If, on the other hand, the

British were to choose the second course, and were to attempt to become more self-sufficient, the terms of trade no longer would be the crucial issue. Indeed the terms, as conventionally derived, would be almost bound to improve but, paradoxically, British real income would be almost bound to decline. Moreover, an improvement in terms of trade under these conditions would not necessarily lead to an improvement in the British balance of payments. Indeed, as has already been shown, if British export prices were more or less rigid, and if the volume of exports were to fall by a greater proportion than import prices, balance-of-payments difficulties would actually increase.

Present British external difficulties are mainly the direct and indirect result of the war; and if the foregoing analysis is correct, these difficulties would be augmented, rather than diminished, by the emergence of deflationary tendencies abroad.[7] With imports at austerity levels, the solution of the British balance-of-payments problem largely depends upon whether Britain can achieve a sufficient expansion of exports. In the first postwar years, the major obstacles to such an expansion were on the supply side, and the disappointing results achieved were traceable, not to marketing difficulties, which were virtually nonexistent, but to the difficulty of allocating sufficient resources to export production. In the long run, however, Britain's ability to attain the required level of exports will depend primarily on the level of foreign demand, which in turn will depend chiefly on the level of foreign income and employment.

[7] The latter statement does not apply to a fall in British import prices resulting from an improvement in supply conditions abroad, particularly if the improvement in supply is due to an increase in productivity. In these circumstances, a price decline, if unaccompanied by a significant decline in foreign demand, would be a distinct boon for Britain. But everything hinges on the *cause* of the improvement in the terms of trade.

# 5

## *THE GERMAN ECONOMY*

J. K. Galbraith

The distinctive feature of the popular discussion of the German economy since the end of the war has been its almost unrelieved incompetence. It has been the wonderland of the one-cause dialectic. During the past three years production in western Germany has been very low—far lower than, under any formulation of American policy, would have been desirable. There have also been unmistakable signs of stagnation. Depending on the observer this malperformance has been attributed more or less exclusively to too many people on too little land, to shortages of food and raw materials, and to a plethora of currency. It has also been blamed on wartime destruction, the shortage of coal, the Potsdam Agreement and former Secretary of the Treasury Morgenthau. One peculiarly fashionable line of argument has placed the entire responsibility on bureaucratic controls and the absence of free enterprise. A few extremists have traced the difficulty to de-Nazification and the dismantling of industry.

A writer who begins on a subject by decrying what others have written is usually suspect and no doubt properly so. In the case of Germany, nonetheless, it is proper to warn the reader that most of what he has been encountering is one-sided, naive and, not infrequently, irresponsible. There could be no more serious ground for questioning the ability of the United States to conduct a responsible foreign policy than the quality of its information on the country that, next to Russia, is the chief subject of its policy.

### *First Considerations*

The problems of the German economy, while not simple,

yield to orderly economic analysis and few novelties are required in the solution. There is, first, the question of goals or objectives which, for the short run, present no serious issue. The immediate object of economic policy in western Germany is to achieve a greater measure of recovery and the ancient question of which of the ends are to be served by the scarce means is largely answered by the extreme scarcity of the means. The latter gives a stark simplicity to the choice that largely grows out of biological requirements.

Elementary considerations of human welfare and decency, the needs of non-German countries and, as a tertiary consideration, the progress of Germany toward self-support all dictate a maximization of output. There would be no escape from this even were it in conflict with long-run policy. There is rarely an alternative to pragmatism in dealing with the situation in hand, and it is normally far better to respect this fact than to allow policy to be made in accordance with more distant or doctrinnaire aims. Nevertheless, it is important to define more distant aims or strategies. It is only by doing so that the circumstances that shape short-run action can themselves be shaped. The long-run policy for German economy, or more specifically for that of the western zones, is not so easily set down as the short-run aims. To this I shall return later in the essay.

## *The Factors of Production*

The diagnosis of the present disorders of the economy of western Germany begins with an extraordinarily bad assortment of the factors of production. It consists, in the largest sense, in a shortage of effective manpower, a shortage of materials, including food, and a substantial excess (in relation to the first two) of capital plant. A distinction needs to be made between population and manpower. The former, numbering about 50 million in the part of Germany outside the Soviet zone, far exceeds the prewar population of the area. For a variety of reasons, including the substantial disproportion of old people and women to males of working age, this population makes a heavy demand on the food supply without making a compensating contribution to the supply of effective manpower. The shortage of food, in turn, acts to limit the supply of effective manpower. The shortage of materials, with very few exceptions, is coextensive with the requirements of an industrial economy, although the critical deficiency, in addition to food, is coal.

Capital plant, though generally plentiful in relation to manpower and materials, is unbalanced within itself. To a limited extent, most seriously in the case of transportation, this takes the form of bottlenecks resulting from wartime destruction. The main weight of the wartime destruction, however—a simple though often overlooked point—was borne by armament plant, much of which is unimportant for civilian production or by industries, such as for oil synthesis, which were of peculiar importance for war. A more serious unbalance in Germany's capital plant has resulted from partition of the country which, for example, has divorced the electrical and other light industry of the Berlin area from the heavy industry of the Rhenish-Westphalian region. In some cases the line of partition runs between different stages in integrated industrial processes. Finally, there is some unbalance as the result of the heavy expansion of the metal and metal working industry at the expense of civilian industry during the war years and the preceding years of preparation. But even German's most purely civilian, and accordingly its relatively neglected industries (always excluding agriculture, of course), have a capacity well in excess of postwar rates of production.

### *The Problem of Organization*

Badly assorted or not, factors must be organized. Lack of a system of incentives or drives to their employment and organization is the second problem of the German economy. Here one needs to have recourse to something that might be called "the economics of the shattered economy." Certain problems arise in Germany that are more or less peculiar to an advanced stage of deterioration. Their analysis calls for a balanced distribution of emphasis between the role of incentives to individual effort and the need for a central organizing authority which makes it possible for these incentives to have effect.

Postwar discussion of the problem of organization in Germany has turned almost entirely on the absence of an effective system of money and concomitant incentives and this lack has not been without importance. But it is quite possible, as the German experience has shown, for an economy to be so badly wrecked that the forces making for further disintegration operate with a cumulative effect that frustrates any possible catalysis from individual effort. Since the end of the war, to cite a widely known case, insufficient coal production in Germany has acted to keep down fertilizer and food production and, until recently, an inadequate food supply has been an important cause of low coal production. In a broad sense such deteriorative tendencies have characterized the whole relationship between materials, manpower, and capital plant since the end of the war. Although raw materials imports, on which Germany is heavily dependent, have been organized externally by the United States and United Kingdom, they have remained critically scarce. This, and especially the food shortage, has kept down production and limited the supply of effective manpower. It has also limited the production of domestic materials, most importantly coal, and the combined result has been low exports and limited means for commanding further imports. To check or reverse cumulative deterioration requires measures above and apart from incentives to factor employment.

The only way in which this deterioration can be reversed is by organized action—that is, by planning. In the last few months the Ruhr has provided an important demonstration of what is required. Daily coal production is now (March 1948) about 75 per cent of prewar. This has been accomplished by according the recovery of coal mining a unique priority. Special rations have been granted to miners and their families; an incentive system has been established permitting them to buy consumer's goods; the mines have been given an overriding claim on steel and other mine supplies. It is fairly clear that coal production could not have been restored except by singling it out for this kind of organized action. And this restoration of coal production was a strategic step in the larger design for restoring the economy of western Germany.

During the past two years it has been asserted with increasing frequency and vehemence that if, somehow, the German economy could be freed from materials and manpower regulations, price controls and other bureaucratic paraphernalia then recovery would be expedited. I would not want to defend either the design or administration of present economic controls in Germany. Yet there never has been the slightest possibility of getting German recovery by this wholesale repeal, and it is quite possible that its reiteration has delayed German recovery. The question is not whether there must be planning—the assignment of priorities to industries for reconstitution and rehabilitation, the allocation of materials and manpower, the supplying of incentives goods and all the rest—but whether that planning has been forthright and effective. The currency that has been given to the notion that there is something unhealthy or evil about such action has, very possibly, helped make measures more tentative and self-conscious and less forthright than they would otherwise have been.

In this connection one of the serious handicaps to recovery in western Germany is the character of the bizonal government now being established at Frankfurt. There are grounds for doubt whether this government is strong enough for the tasks of pulling the economy together. Not only is it a government of delegates from the provincial *(Land)* governments but it also must depend, at least for the time being, on the executive establishments of the several Land governments to carry out its measures. The American prototype would be a legislative body in Washington composed of state governors or designees of the state legislatures which would depend on the executive departments of the states to carry out its measures. Such a constitution has undoubted charm for a believer in state's rights. But no one would expect such a government to be very effective in getting enforcement of, for instance, an antidiscrimination law in the state of Mississippi. He should not expect a similar government in Frankfurt to be very effective in getting Bavaria, which has none too much food, to surrender part of its stock to the Ruhr, which has far less. The German economy will require strong administration for several years to come—and sooner or later it will get the administration it requires. The wisdom of giving the Germans a preliminary lesson in ineffective parliamentary government is, to say the least, doubtful.

*Incentives for Germany*

Given an organizing authority, a generalized system of incentives to the employment of factors may then be properly emphasized. In Germany now there is no such system. German prices have been substantially frozen since 1936. Both price controls and the rationing system survived the war. A black market exists, but it is relatively small and its prices are so far above prevailing price and income levels as to make it generally inaccessible to the masses of the people.

The distribution of goods in Germany consists, in the simplest terms, of a grant of food to each member of the population, the amount being graded more or less to the character of the work being performed. For workers the marginal utility of money, beyond what is necessary to buy the ration and pay rent and a few other charges, is effectively zero. Accordingly there is little encouragement to work more than the number of hours necessary to earn the ration and pay the rent. There is a positive incentive to spend the remaining time cultivating home gardens, searching for unrationed food or conserving energy. In addition many Germans, including a considerable proportion of the erstwhile middle classes, have a stock of money that is adequate for all current or foreseeable purposes. By common estimate there has been a sevenfold increase in the means of payment in Germany as a whole since the beginning of the war. The volume of transactions has fallen by at least half. Some millions of Germans, therefore, are able to avoid gainful employment. The incentive to live on liquid capital is strengthened by the knowledge that someday something will happen to the present stock of money which will almost certainly have the effect of making it even less valuable. (This was written before the monetary purge of June 1948.)

Almost since the surrender there has been discussion of monetary reform in Germany. Action was delayed first by the need to work out a plan that would be applicable to the peculiar circumstances of the German economy and when this hurdle had been surmounted,[1] by the difficulty in getting quadripartite (especially Russian and French) agreement. More recently the need for proceeding with monetary reform in the western zones has been recognized, although with reluctance. The step would establish two German currencies and would confirm, even more definitely than the establishment of a government for the British and American zones, the partition of Germany. It is possible, however, that the delay has not been without its advantages. The conversion of the currency would not, of itself, have solved the basic problems of the German economy. But once deteriorative forces had been checked or reversed and, in particular, some small supplies of consumer goods were making their appearance, the conversion could have greatly strengthened incentives and so accelerated recovery. It would, however, seem reasonably certain that the time is now ripe for such action.

### *The Potsdam Agreement*

Perhaps the most frequently cited obstacle to German economic recovery in the last three years has been the Potsdam agreement providing for the economic disarmament of Germany and for reparations, and the subsequent Level-of-Industry agreement of March 1946. (The latter was amended for the British and American zones by the subsequent bilateral agreement of August 1947). These have been the subject of general and often frenzied attack as restraints on the German economy and as indirect imposts on the American taxpayer.

The fact is that neither the Potsdam economic provisions (as distinct, for example, from the territorial provisions) or the Level-of-Industry agreement, have had any important bearing on the German economy. These declarations have not been implemented by actual dismantling of plant except for limited categories mainly of armament factories. Had it been possible to exceed the stated levels of output during the past three years,

[1] The so-called Colm-Dodge-Goldsmith Plan (after its authors Gerhard Colm, Joseph M. Dodge, and Raymond Goldsmith) which became official American policy in 1946, provided for a new currency in exchange for the old with a ten for one write-down, a simultaneous writing down of claims, a provision for equalizing loss between holders of real property and other assets, a provision for handling war losses, and a fairly stiff capital levy.

it does not seem likely there would have been any great hesitation in doing so. In general these levels have, however, been far above achievable production. The first level-of-industry plan allowed an annual production of 5.8 million metric tons of steel from a capacity of 7 million tons of which perhaps two-thirds would have been in the British and American zones. Last year steel production in the bizonal area was 2.95 million metric tons. The revised level-of-industry agreement allows a maximum production in this area of 10.7 million metric tons, a figure that so far from being a limitation on output, must be regarded as a highly optimistic target.

This is not to imply that the economic policy implicit in Potsdam and the Level-of-Industry agreement was above reproach. On the contrary, it is doubtful if prohibitions on certain classes of civilian industry and the placing of ceilings on other types was ever a satisfactory insurance against future German military strength. It is also uncertain whether the excess plant and machinery that this policy made available was a serviceable type of reparation.

Now the question of security from Germany has been made academic by the breakdown of four-power collaboration. It is doubtful if the restraints imposed by the first Level-of-Industry agreement would have been as severe in their effects as the removal of the Berlin industrial area from the German economy. As matters now stand, not only Berlin but the entire Soviet zone have been effectively removed from the German economy—or, if Germany is viewed from the east, all of the industry west of the Elbe, including the Ruhr, have been removed. As long as this condition persists, Germany as an independent instrument of military power does not exist.

This *de facto* partition, coupled with economic prostration, has also made the question of reparations largely academic. There is no chance for reparations from current production which, from both an economic and an engineering point of view, are almost certainly to be preferred to reparations from capital assets. Germany does have a considerable surplus of machine tools which, with some other classes of equipment, could be put to use in other countries. Limited dismantling of this kind is now going on but it is a matter of no critical consequence either to Germany or to the countries receiving the equipment.

*Aid to Germany*

The final requirement for recovery of western Germany is a supply of external resources. In respect to this requirement the position of Germany is different in urgency but not in kind from that of other western European countries. Since the end of the war, it has been necessary for the United States to supplement the resources of all of the former belligerents in western Europe and the Marshall Plan represents only a new designation for an established policy. In the case of western Germany the ratio of contributed to internally available resources has been especially large and it may safely be assumed that the need will be considerable for some time to come.

How long and in what volume western Germany (and also western Europe as a whole) will have to be supplied, cannot be predicted. It depends, among other things, on the extent to which western Europe is divorced in its trade relations from eastern Europe. The terms of trade between western and eastern Europe are, it can be guessed, capable of being much more favorable to western Europe than trade between western Europe and the western hemisphere.

The amount and duration of aid also depends on the standard of living that is deemed to be tolerable—it may be observed that for Germany this is far lower than would have been thought conceivable ten years ago—and it also depends on the consistency with which what may be termed "the principle of calculated inadequacy" continues to dominate the foreign economic policy of the United States. This latter principle consists in recognizing an aim or goal and in appropriating somewhat less than the amount of money and employing something less than the amount of administrative vigor that would insure achieving the goal. In the case of Germany, which in many ways has been an admirable example of the principle in operation, the need for supplying food and materials to the German economy, not only for welfare but for recovery, has been recognized. This has been done in a sufficient quantity to keep most Germans alive, but in an insufficient amount to enable them to contribute with any effectiveness to this end. A not greatly larger supply might well have meant the difference between subsistence and a considerable measure of recovery.

A distinctive feature of the principle of calculated inadequacy, also well-exemplified by Germany, is that, as a result of the annual economy in cost and energy, the total expenditure of both over a period of years is considerably magnified. This, however, does not prevent devotees of the principle from being known as "budget-balancers," "watchdogs of the Treasury," "men of sound business judgment," or by the other honorofic titles that are reserved for the unintelligently parsimonious.

### *Some Remaining Problems*

It could hardly be claimed that the foregoing discussion exhausts the problems of German economic policy for the near future. There are the questions of how German output is to be allocated between Germany and the remainder of western Europe and between current consumption and investment within Germany. These have been subjects for heated controversy since the end of the war and, by and large, have been resolved in favor of the German economy and, to an increasing degree, in favor of current consumption in Germany. The latter has, in part, been a reflection of the fact that in an economy like that of Germany, conventional differences between consumption and investment *vis à vis* future production largely disappear. Coal allocated to the production of consumer's goods—or rather to certain critical categories of consumer's goods—may as frequently result in larger future production as coal allocated to the production or maintenance of capital equipment.

Mention should also be made of the problem of internal economic organization—and particularly of nationalization. Here, as in the case of state's rights, there has been a strong tendency to make an export package out of policies that are deemed appropriate for the United States. While nominally American policy in Germany has been one of neutrality on the nationalization of industrial properties, there is no doubt that the latter has been tacitly discouraged. One formula has been to urge the postponement of decision until it could be decided by a competently elected government for the Reich as a whole, a formula for a distant decision indeed. The German Social Democratic party (SPD) reformed after the war with its old objective of state ownership of primary industries and with a somewhat more energetic desire to implement it. As a result, American policy has been at variance with that of the SPD—an extremely serious matter, for not only has this party the strongest hold on German workers but it is also, for this sector of the German community, the effective alternative to Communism. The counterpart of opposition to nationalization has been the tendency for Americans in Germany to become aligned with the Christian Democrats, the clerical party of the center, and with the bourgeois Liberal Democrats (LDP) on the right. These parties are both defensive rather than programmatic which means that the United States finds itself supporting, as in Italy and elsewhere after the war, efforts to maintain a political vacuum. This negativism will one day be recognized by all except its advocates as an effective boost for Communism. There might conceivably be some excuse for discouraging public ownership in Germany were this the alternative to vigorous private entrepreneurship. That is not the case. The coal and steel properties of the Ruhr, the principal targets of the Social Democrats, present an extremely confused problem of title and would be almost as difficult to put into private ownership as to put under public management. Some properties were owned by the now nonexistent Reich government; some are owned by war criminals and are in custody of Allied property control officials; many are parts of industrial combines which, in greater or less measure, it has been official military government policy to dissolve.

## *Conclusion*

The shape of long-run economic policy for Germany is wholly subordinate to the question of whether, and how long, the partition of Germany endures. Partition, in the last analysis, is the result of the collapse of confidence between Russia and the western powers and presumably will last as long as tension continues. Although neither Russia nor the United States or United

Kingdom can actively espouse a policy of partition, neither will consent to the reuniting of Germany, except in a context of some mutual confidence.

If a *rapprochement* between Russia and the West at some future date is a possibility, then there is a chance for the reconstitution of Germany. It would still be my view that long-run policy should call for a fairly free development of the economic resources of a reconstituted state—and accordingly there is, in this respect, no serious conflict between long- and short-run aims. I am not persuaded that economic disarmament or economic restraints are either very good economics or offer very good security. My preference would be to concentrate on the outlawing of German military power and on backing this with unequivocal enforcement. The least of all Germany's potential misfortunes is the loss of so much of her sovereignty as is implied by forbidding her a military establishment. So long as she has no military power, she will neither make war nor be reckoned useful in a war. This is not, as has been suggested, a purely mechanical formula for dealing with German security though neither is it a complete solution. It is a complete substitute for economic disarmament without its obvious disadvantages. One of the discouraging features of American foreign policy since the end of the war has been the tendency to by-pass simple and straightforward measures of this sort in favor of more subtle if spurious designs.

If the unification of Germany is not assumed, then the need for a long-run policy of maximizing the use of western Germany's resources is clear. It is the only alternative—and it may not be a complete one—to a continuing subsidy from the outside. There are no problems of security so long as one assumes, as one must, that the area lies within the orbit of the western countries. Indeed actual occupation or garrisoning of some sort is probably implicit in the notion of partition.

However, it is not easy or wise to assume away the idea of an eventual unification of Germany—certainly the Germans themselves have not done so—and this creates serious problems in connection with measures which, while important for recovery in western Germany, may be at variance with eventual unification. Monetary reform in western Germany is a case in point. Far more serious are the problems connected with efforts to integrate the western German economy with that of France and the Low Countries. If permanent partition is assumed, the industry of western Germany—notably but by no means exclusively that of the Ruhr—can and should be considered an integral asset of the western European community. Subject possibly to some gestures in the direction of internationalization—such as that announced for the Ruhr at the London conference of the western powers on Germany in February 1948—it is possible that France would agree. This could mean, for example, that investment in the French steel industry would be made with an eye to the availability of Ruhr steel. Rehabilitation of the Lorraine industry and the concomitant investment would take a correspondingly lower place in the French capital budget.

If, however, Germany is to reappear as a national entity, it is unlikely that France would concur in any such planning and few would say that she should. Here, perhaps, is the most serious dilemma of German policy. As to the best escape I have, at the moment, no suggestion. It may well be that no decision should be made until the lines of permanent relations with Russia, on which the issue ultimately turns, are a good deal more distinct than at present.

# 6

## *OCCUPIED JAPAN: THE ECONOMIC ASPECT*

Robert W. Barnett

On September 2, 1945, Japan surrendered. Reduced to the territory upon which it had lived as a self-sustaining island state in the midnineteenth century, but vastly enlarged in population, with wasted economic resources and institutions and distrusted by its neighbors, Japan awaited Allied determination of the role it could and should play in the postwar Far East.

This essay is a report on events affecting the Japanese economy since that time. The Allies have attempted and failed to deal with Japan's obligations to pay them reparations, revealing in that failure political sensitivities which stand in the way of recovery of Far Eastern countries and recovery in Japan. Japan itself has begun to shake off the postsurrender bewilderment and lassitude which prevented it from effectively applying its own efforts to its own resources. However, even maximum effort would not have sufficed to attain self-support. In order to survive, Japan must trade; that trade has revived slowly, in large part because of instability and the lagging recovery of economic productivity outside Japan. The United States, in consequence, has had to support a mendicant Japan still distrusted in Asia. To remove that distrust, Japan has begun to reform its economic institutions, looking towards withdrawal of the pattern of Allied authority to which it has, since the surrender, submitted.

### UNITED STATES AND ALLIED RESPONSIBILITY

Because of its dominant role in the military offensive of the Allies against Japan, because General MacArthur was the commander who imposed upon Japan Allied authority and control, and because the resources of the United States would be required to cope with Japan's postwar problems, the United States maintained, in September 1945, that it should have the controlling voice in the occupation of Japan and that its Allies should cooperate in this undertaking as advisers. This position was held from the time of the surrender until December 1945, when, in deference to the insistence for responsibility in the occupation of the United Kingdom, the U.S.S.R., China, and several other interested countries, the United States agreed to the establishment of the Far Eastern Commission. By its terms of reference, this agency had authority to formulate the policies, principles, and standards in conformity with which Japan should fulfill its obligations. Such policies would be adopted by a majority of its participating governments, the U.S.S.R., the United Kingdom, the United States, China, France, the Netherlands, Canada, Australia, New Zealand, India, the Philippines, including the concurring votes of the United States, the United Kingdom, the U.S.S.R., and China. It was agreed at the same time that the Commission would respect the "existing control machinery in Japan including the chain of command from the United States Government to the Supreme Commander and the Supreme Commander's command of occupation forces." This meant that in the field of actual implementation of policy, cognizance would be taken of the fact that General MacArthur had already received instructions from the United States Government and had acted on those instructions in setting up an administration and putting in motion occupation programs. The terms of reference went further. The right of the United States Government to issue unilateral interim directives on matters of urgency was recognized. The Commission reserved the right, however, to review the actions of the Supreme Commander and the policies upon which he acted. An Allied Council for Japan comprising Chinese, Soviet, British, and American representatives was established in Japan to consult with General MacArthur. To General MacArthur's armed forces was added a contingent of British Commonwealth troops. This has been the pattern of authority for the occupation of Japan.

### BASIC ECONOMIC POLICIES

General MacArthur's initial directives, dispatched to him by the United States Government alone, included, in addition to their strictly military and broad political provisions, the instruction to destroy Japan's economic ability to create munitions. He was, on the other hand, to encourage development of democratic institutions and processes. He was to direct the Japanese themselves to assume responsibility for avoiding acute economic distress, accomplishing just distribution of available supplies, satisfying the needs of the occupation forces, and fulfilling Japan's reparations obligations. He was to supervise the Japanese and, where necessary, direct them to meet their obligations. He was to be responsible for conduct of all of Japan's foreign economic relations. In a Far Eastern Commission decision adopted in June 1947, the ten other countries of the Far Eastern Commission associated themselves with the United States in substantially approving these same basic principles.[1]

These principles implied occupation economic programs of three sorts. Japan was to pay reparations and the Allies were to determine in what manner. The Japanese economy was to be reformed. Japan was expected to support itself.

## II

### REPARATIONS: CAPITAL REMOVALS CONCEPT

During the war years the Far Eastern countries, suffering from both war devastation and Japanese exploitation of their resources, felt that Japan's resources should play a major role in the rehabilitation of Asia. Thus, even before the Far Eastern Commission began its business, there was an urgent demand for reparations. The Potsdam Declaration assured Japan that it would be permitted to maintain industries for its economy. It also stated that Japan should pay just reparations in kind. The problem of reparations was discussed by the Far Eastern Commission within that framework.

Mr. Edwin Pauley, Personal Ambassador of President Tru-

[1] *Activities of the Far Eastern Commission: Report of the Secretary General*, United States Government Printing Office (1947), p. 49.

man appointed to study the problem of reparations from Germany and Japan, brought to the problem the broad concept that reparations should be accomplished quickly, should contribute to maximum long-term welfare and productivity, and should not conflict with early revival of normal peacetime commercial activity in Asia. Reparations in cash or out of current production did not seem to meet this standard. Reparations in the form of industrial removals did and could contribute, furthermore, towards the end of correcting swiftly the uneconomic distortion of Japan's wartime industrial structure. Industrial removals have been accepted as the proper form for reparations without serious challenge either from within the United States Government or internationally.

### INDUSTRY: FOR REMOVAL AND RETENTION

In the spring of 1946 the Far Eastern Commission placed the problem of reparations high on its agenda and acted with comparative rapidity in approving proposals which the United States Government, after careful screening of Mr. Pauley's recommendations, put before the Commission. These proposals were intended to make immediately available for removal a pool of Japanese industrial facilities. This prompt international action was possible because the so-called "interim" United States proposals merely dealt with what was obviously surplus to Japan's peace needs in industries universally acknowledged to have war use alone or to have been overexpanded during the war. They were not intended to define ultimate levels of retained industry for Japan.

To match the above "interim" removal decisions, which were intended to serve the interests of claimant countries, with "interim" retention decisions specifically designed to meet a need in Japan, the Far Eastern Commission authorized the Supreme Commander to designate particular industrial plants and facilities within permitted capacity levels which would be permanently immune from future removal as reparations. This was intended to be an answer to Japanese plant managers and owners who maintained that they could not reasonably be expected to invest capital in the reöperation or in the repair of damaged or deteriorated plant so long as reparations questions remained undecided. Table 1 indicates, in broad terms, those capacities of industry within which the Supreme Commander was authorized to make his determinations of what specific plants should be removed and what remain.

TABLE 1

| Industry | Unit | Peak Production (a) or Estimated Capacity (b) | FEC Interim Decisions for Determining Obvious Industrial Surplus | Assured for Retention |
|---|---|---|---|---|
| Pig Iron | m.t./yr. | 4,306,000 (a) | 2,000,000 | 800,000 |
| Steel Ingot | m.t./yr. | 7,821,000 (a) | 3,500,000 | 2,000,000 |
| Steel Rolling | m.t./yr. | 4,876,000 (a) | 2,775,000 | . . . |
| Machine-Tool Production | pieces/yr. | 54,000 (b) | 27,000 | 7,500 |
| Shipbuilding | gross tons/yr. | 1,900,000 (b) | 150,000 | . . . |
| Thermal Electric Power | kilowatts | 3,750,000 (b) | 2,100,000 | 1,000,000 |
| Primary Aluminum | m.t./yr. | 130,000 (b) | -0- | -0- |
| Sulphuric Acid | m.t./yr. of 62% acid | 4,850,000 (b) | 3,500,000 | 3,000,000 |
| Caustic Soda | m.t./yr. | 144,000 (a) | 82,500 | . . . |
| Chlorine | m.t./yr. | 240,000 (b) | 75,000 | 28,000 |
| Soda Ash | m.t./yr. | 672,000 (a) | 500,000 | 207,000 |
| Aircraft | . . . | . . . . | -0- | -0- |
| Arsenals | . . . | . . . . | -0- | -0- |
| Ball and Roller Bearing | ¥ = yen | ¥300 million (1943–44 prices) (b) | ¥32.5 million | |
| Synthetic Oil | bbls./yr. | 1,500,000 (a) | -0- | -0- |
| Synthetic Rubber | m.t./yr. | 900 | -0- | -0- |

### LEVEL OF INDUSTRY: FINAL DECISIONS ON AVAILABILITY

Delay in making final decisions on the availability of industrial facilities prevents reparations claimant countries from having a clear idea of what may be the character and value of reparations to their postwar recovery programs. It produces adverse practical and psychological effects upon both the Government and business of the defeated country. The making of final decisions in the case of Japan has been approached in a systematic but laborious fashion.

Demands for reparations, security considerations, and Japan's own peaceful needs have been related elements in the Commission's consideration of the Japanese level of industry problem. The Commission ruled, as a first step, that only industrial capacity surplus to Japan's peace needs would be considered available for removal as reparations. It then agreed that the average per capita consumption during the years 1930-34 would be used in determining what should be considered the legitimate needs of a Japanese peace economy. This statistical base would, it was agreed, be adjusted to take into account factors in Japan's situation which have changed since 1930-34; these factors might include population increases, technological developments, employment, and balance of payments problems. The Commission agreed, further, that use of the 1930-34 data would not necessarily imply the required levels of capacity in any particular industry, but rather would be used to determine the over-all pattern of Japanese industry sufficient to meet Japan's recognized general consumption needs.

In a subsequent action the Commission decided that when specific levels for various industries could be determined, in accordance with the above standards, those levels would not constitute a continuing strait jacket upon Japan's future industrial structure. So far as Japan is concerned, therefore, "level of industry" has a limited meaning. It merely determines reparations availabilities. To this general principle, however, there is an exception. The iron and steel, light metals, metal working machinery, shipbuilding, oil refining and storage, synthetic oil, and synthetic rubber industries will not be permitted to expand beyond agreed levels prior to October 1, 1949. After that date, expansion would not be prevented if, for economic reasons, expansion seemed necessary or desirable to the Japanese. The above decisions established a conceptual framework within which negotiations regarding reparations availabilities in particular industries should have developed on a purely technical basis. Unfortunately, political considerations have so influenced and distorted discussion that final technical agreements have not been concluded.

Meanwhile the Commission did agree that the Japanese Government should bear all the costs within Japan of handling reparations, but that the claimant country would pay the costs of transportation and reinstallation of reparations goods outside Japan. This decision should operate to restrict actual removals, when they occur, to facilities clearly of use and value to recipient countries. The Supreme Commander has been issued other instructions by the Commission and the United States Government similarly administrative in character, with regard to standards for selecting, valuing, and allocating reparations. These instructions outline how, but not to whom, reparations should be distributed.

### REPARATIONS SHARES

No removals occurred, however, because the Far Eastern Commission countries could not decide how to share reparations. Desiring to expedite agreement on the shares question and to help General MacArthur set up an administrative machinery for handling reparations, the United States Government issued a unilateral directive to General MacArthur in April 1947, instructing him to start limited deliveries to China, the Philippines, the Netherlands, and the United Kingdom. These four were named because their needs were urgent, because their territories were occupied by and they fought against Japanese armed forces, and because the percentages assigned them were considered beyond cavil. China could draw up to 15 per cent, and the United Kingdom, the Philippines and the Netherlands up to 5 per cent each of industrial facilities available for removal as reparations, providing they presented evidence that facilities requested would alleviate relief needs in an immediate and practical way. Late in 1947 some machine tools were claimed and were removed early in 1948.

Negotiations on reparations shares, however, remained stalled. Considerations of prestige seem to have outweighed what should have been the economic advantage of promptly receiving the available reparations. Had there been a clear, practical, and immediate use for Japanese surplus plant facilities in neighboring Far Eastern countries and a sufficiently stable economic environment to justify the costs of installation, it is hard to believe that some compromise on the shares controversy could not have been found.

### REPARATIONS FROM CURRENT PRODUCTION

It might be asked why claimant countries continued to desire industrial reparations when they knew that plants in Japan steadily deteriorated in value, that removal and reinstallation presented in many cases gigantic engineering difficulties, and that to realize the potential productive value of capacity would require outlay of capital needed in the exigencies of the postwar situation for more immediate consumption purposes. It might also be asked why alternative forms of reparations were not insisted upon. Intellectual inertia may explain, in part, failure to find a substitute for Mr. Pauley's interpretation of the intent of Potsdam. A better answer, however, may be that gradually it was recognized that certain prerequisities were necessary for a program of reparations out of current output—the logical alternative to a capital removals program—an enormous movement of raw materials from which Japanese exports on reparations account could be produced which in turn required an economically productive and politically stable Far East. The Far East could not meet these prerequisites. The Far Eastern countries realized, moreover, that the United States Government would desire to assert a strong claim against whatever trade surplus the Japanese could develop for repayment of its occupation costs. Dependent in many ways upon the United States, most of them would be loath to challenge that claim; in fact, in principle they recognized it. Finally, Asia does need industry; "industrialization" through reparations has a political appeal. Hence, it seemed to be accepted, with some resignation, that reparations would be in industrial facilities, or there might not be any at all.

## III

### ECONOMIC SELF-SUPPORT: DELAYED EFFORTS

Despite the lack of a reparations settlement, it began to be seen that Japan could not shirk indefinitely its immediate economic responsibilities without bringing about either a disastrous collapse of all aspects of its economic activity or an intolerable increase in the relief burdens borne, on its behalf, by the United States. Prevention of collapse was a precondition for successful accomplishment of the broad and progressive objectives of the occupation: development of a democratic and peacefully inclined people. Rehabilitation was a precondition for survival. Surrender found Japan in a state of shocked fatigue and bewildered by the prospect of putting in order its economic affairs in ways acceptable to the Allied authority. Yet for more than a year the headquarters of the Supreme Commander pursued a general policy of nonintervention in economic recovery aspects of Japan's domestic economic life, concentrating rather on the reform objectives and giving impetus to Japanese Government programs having as their objectives stabilization and rehabilitation of Japan's economic life, mainly by hints, suggestions, and exhortations which emanated from all levels of the Supreme Commander's headquarters.

After several directives were issued in the initial stage of the occupation looking towards the reduction of government expenditures, financial reform, and the control of credit, the Supreme Commander decided to allow the Japanese Government a freer hand in domestic economic recovery. Successive conservative governments, however, seemed to oppose genuine financial reform and failed to exercise effectively the free hand they were given. Although an Economic Stabilization Board to give over-all supervision to the internal economy was established during the first year of the occupation, it was not until March, 1947 that its activities began to respond to an urgent need for effective governmental controls. General MacArthur at that time sharply notified Premier Yoshida that unless the Japanese Government undertook determined measures in the economic sphere, the unstable and inflationary condition of the Japanese economy, together with its attendant maldistribution of food and other necessities, would become increasingly serious and Japan's achievement of social and political objectives would be endangered. The Japanese Government, which was in the meantime passing from the leadership of conservative Premier Yoshida to that of Socialist Premier Katayama, responded to this warning with measures designed to arrest inflation, stimulate production in key sectors of Japanese industry and mining, to increase food collections, and to improve food distribution.

### ALLIED ATTITUDE TOWARD REHABILITATION

The Far Eastern Commission ruled, in both 1946 and 1947, that Japanese food imports should, in light of the world food shortage, be the minimum required to prevent such starvation and widespread disease and civil unrest as would endanger the safety of the occupation forces, and that no imports exceeding that level should be permitted which would have the effect of giving preferential treatment to the Japanese over peoples of any Allied or liberated area. But with that possible exception, the Supreme Commander and the Japanese Government were not materially hampered in their efforts to stabilize Japan's economic situation by harsh or repressive international decisions at the policy level. On the contrary, a genuine willingness to lay the policy foundation for expansion of Japanese industry and trade along mutually beneficial lines seemed to have been shown.

The Commission's policy granting portions of Japanese industry immunity from reparations removal has been mentioned above. The Commission authorized the Supreme Commander to take the steps to stimulate Japan's production of commercially exportable goods, insuring that goods produced were those desired by countries requiring Japanese exports. It directed him to develop an overall import and export program. Despite the strongly possessive interest of the Far Eastern Commission countries in ultimate disposition of stocks of Japanese gold and silver, they authorized their use in a revolving fund designed to aid in generally reviving Japanese trade and industry. They agreed to advise the United States Government in recommending ways in which Japanese imports and exports could be facilitated. They sent representatives to Japan to conduct trade on a strictly intergovernmental basis, and when the Supreme Commander permitted private merchants to enter under quotas established by an Inter-Allied Trade Board for Japan sitting in Washington, a movement into Japan began of private businessmen with legitimate business interests there. Yet there was a line beyond which the Far Eastern countries refused to give their blessing to the process of Japan's trade expansion. When first presented with the possibility, few of the Far Eastern countries desired any movement of Japanese merchants abroad.

### INTERNAL PROBLEMS: INFLATION

Japanese inflation gives clear indication of the weakness of the Japanese Government and the difficulties the Japanese people have had in putting their economy on a stable footing. At the time of surrender when Japan's wartime rationing and price controls, though weakened, were still in effect, the note issue of the Bank of Japan stood at 41 billion yen. Five months later prices had risen by 50 per cent and the currency issue stood at 62 billion. Japanese financial authorities, conscious at that time of the perils of this inflationary trend, evolved a drastic currency conversion scheme which was put into effect in March, 1946. The entire outstanding note issue was temporarily called into the banks and a new issue of 15 billion yen put in circulation. These monetary controls proved inadequate to cope with the underlying causes of price inflation, particularly since complementary tax measures to "mop up" excess funds were long delayed and since regulations governing outflow from the banks were lax. Concomitant measures necessary for stimulation of production and control of distribution of goods were not applied and government expenditures substantially increased so that by December, 1947, yen in circulation amounted to over 200 billion. An analysis of the underlying causes of this inflationary trend was presented to the Allied Council for Japan by General MacArthur's staff in April, 1947:

> Japan's economy today is characterized by a great scarcity of practically every type of goods, aggravated by unequal distribution of monetary purchasing power and deficit financing of both governmental and industrial operations. In an economy of scarcity, a stable and proper relationship between wages and prices depends upon the successful operation of other economic controls such as allocation of critical materials to the most essential uses, effective rationing of consumer goods, strong enforcement machinery and sound finan-

cial policies. Without such controls, consumers bid against each other for the limited supply of goods and services and obtain a considerable part of their wants at exorbitant prices through black market channels. Producers, similarly, are driven to the black market for part of their supplies of raw materials. Prices are forced up and, in turn, increase the pressure for wage increases to meet the rising cost of living. These wage increases cause further demands for price increases, and the cycle goes on. Without an effective program of economic stabilization, this spiraling may result in an uncontrollable inflationary situation.

### FOOD SUPPLY

The weakening, in fact the virtual collapse, of governmental controls over food collection and distribution immediately following the surrender aggravated the vicious influence of the black market in food on general price and wage trends which had been progressively perceptible even during the war. The application of satisfactorily effective distribution controls could not, however, have removed the need for food imports. A Japan confined to its islands is a food deficit area. The following data illustrate the point.

In 1939, Japan's population per square kilometer was 169, compared with 16 for the United States. Moreover, only 15 per cent of its mountainous islands was cultivated, thus making Japan's density of population, in proportion to cultivated areas, 11 per hectare as compared with 0.8 in the United States (5 in China). Prior to the war, Japan had to import, despite "gardening" methods of cultivation, 20 per cent of the food it consumed and even with those imports the standard of nutrition in Japan was unsatisfactory. To meet that prewar standard today, Japan requires 6 million tons of imported grains and other foods to supplement its normal indigenous crops.

Since the surrender, Japanese food production has been comparatively good and the Japanese farmer has suffered no shortage of cereals in his diet. However, as against the 6 million tons general requirement needed to maintain prewar urban standards, only 1.5 million tons has been procured from abroad in a short world market and made available to supplement Japan's own supplies.

During 1947, direct intervention of military government in

the Japanese Government's food collection and distribution program has reduced farmer hoarding and brought about more equitable distribution of supplies. The gap between minimum and satisfactory levels of food consumption which still remains, however, produces direct and indirect effects upon the stability and productivity of the Japanese economy as a whole.

### INDUSTRIAL PRODUCTIVITY

Inadequate food for workers in Japan's factories and mines has impeded labor recruitment, reduced working efficiency, and contributed to absenteeism. Industrial productivity has been hampered also by shortage of raw materials (both indigenous and imported), by postwar psychological slackness and perplexities, by lack of effective government planning and administration, and to some extent by the disturbing effect upon normal private incentive of the variety of economic programs instituted by the Allied occupation authority. The index for industrial activity stood at only 40.8 for November, 1947 (100 = 1930-34).

### COAL

Of these factors, none has been more important than raw material shortages. Coal is the life blood of the Japanese transportation system and an essential prerequisite for industrial recovery as a whole. Historically, Japan has been self-sufficient in coal, except for high-grade coking coal. During the war indigenous coal production rose to over 50 million tons annually. Prewar levels of production were much lower. Yet in January, 1946, the monthly index of Japanese coal production stood at only 46, with 1930-34 at 100. A year later it stood at 78, but even then only 2 million tons monthly were mined. Recognizing the seriousness of the situation, the Supreme Commander directed the Japanese Government to take measures designed to encourage owners and to induce workers to increase production. These measures bore fruit in September, 1947. In January, 1948, 2.8 million tons were mined. The index stood at 95.6, closely approximating prewar normal production. Even this improvement, however, left Japan short of minimum requirements, nor was Japan's maximum capacity to produce yet realized.

### TRANSPORTATION: RAIL AND WATER

Japanese rail transportation has had a first claim upon coal. Because of this claim and despite wear and tear and general deterioration of equipment, government railway operations have remained at levels comparing favorably with railway activity prior to the war. This activity, however, is to some extent an index of weakness, since it reflects the impact of the crushing war losses Japan suffered in merchant shipping, both that used for overseas and coastal hauls. Japan began the war with some 6 million tons, which were sunk by Allied air and naval attack with such effectiveness that less than 1 million remained operable at the time of Japan's surrender. With new construction, repair and salvage, Japan's operable merchant shipping fleet at the end of 1947 was approximately 1.5 million tons. Some of this tonnage has been involved in repatriation operations; it is not, as was the case with Japan's prewar fleet, an important source of foreign exchange earnings and a vital element in Japan's balance of payments.

### OTHER INDUSTRIES

Higher productivity in certain priority industries proceeded from the improvement in the output of Japan's coal mines. This was true particularly of fertilizer producing capacity such as the sulphuric acid industry, whose index of monthly production rose from 31 in January 1946 to 110 in November 1947; and the ammonium sulphate industry, which rose from 60 to 156. At the same time, however, the ceramics industry, which uses indigenous clays, and could find foreign markets for its output, has not recovered commensurately, almost entirely because of its inability to secure coal allocations. Likewise Japan's machinery industries, which depended on coal allotted to the iron, steel, and thermal power industries, was able to rise in this period from 15 to only 45 of the 1930-34 level, or at about the same rate as industry generally.

A critical lack of imported industrial raw materials provides another explanation for Japan's sluggish industrial recovery towards 1930-34 levels. Coking coal for steel, pulp for rayon, petroleum products for its shipping, and so on, practically every line of Japanese production suffered from shortage of imports. The prewar Japanese cotton industry developed on a base of Chinese, American, and Indian raw cotton imports. Severed from its sources of fibre supply, cannibalized to meet urgent war needs, severely damaged by Allied air attacks, Japan's operable spindleage, in 1945, had fallen from a prewar 8.5 million to some 2.5 to 3 million. In January, 1946 the monthly index of cotton textile production stood at 4.5 of 1930-34 levels. This index had risen to 14.8 by November, 1947, but the remarkable fact is that it was not higher. The Commodity Credit Corporation has made available ample raw cotton supplies to the industry. An acute need for textiles exists throughout Asia. Yet, because the Japanese must pay for American cotton in dollars and because other dollar income is not available and therefore sales must be for dollars which are scarce throughout the world, buyers cannot be found for a substantial part of Japan's present 50 to 60 million yards monthly output. In early 1948 the Japanese textile industry, though still active, faced the prospect of having to curtail operations. The problem of disposal for dollars of Japanese cotton textiles in foreign markets presented wide and alarming implications.

### SELF-SUPPORT: DEPENDENCE ON TRADE

Japan cannot find within itself a complete solution to self-support. It must export to survive. This fact is not a new discovery; nor is it a fact influenced, fundamentally, by the nature of Japan's political system and economic institutions. In 1930, before Japan had distorted its industry for war, had begun its China campaign, or had begun to create economic satellites elsewhere in Asia, John E. Orchard, in discussing Japan's population problem, stated, "Industrialization is more than a solution of the population problem. It is the key to the future of the country. . . The progress of Japan's industrialization depends very largely upon the country's ability to expand foreign trade."[2]

In 1938, G. C. Allen still could state, "In view of her growing population and her shortage of industrial raw materials, a fail-

[2] John E. Orchard, *Japan's Economic Position* (1930), pp. 48, 418.

ure to expand the export trade must inevitably lead to a fall in the standard of living."[3] Japan's population in 1937 stood at 72 million. Now it is between 78 and 79 million. Students of demography believe that by 1960 Japan's population may have risen to 90 million. What was true of prewar Japan carries, if for no other reason than its enlarged population, compounded significance in the Japan of today.

### PATTERN OF TRADE

Even though levels of Japanese foreign trade are above those of a year ago, its pattern and nature have begun to carry disturbing suggestions of the difficulties Japan will encounter in attaining self-support and occupying a sound economic position in the world. In the autumn of 1947, the Supreme Commander reported on Japan's trade position. His report showed that during the period September 1945-1947, 95.7 per cent of Japan's imports came from the United States; 38.2 per cent of its exports went to the American market. Japan's imports from Asia amounted to 3.2 per cent of total imports, its exports to Asia 41.7 per cent (see Tables 2 and 3).

Imports from the U.S. were primarily cereals, fertilizer, petroleum products, and medicinal supplies. Exports to the United States were primarily silk, which encountered a soft and shrinking demand, and strategic metals from Japanese wartime stock piles which are now largely exhausted. Cotton textiles figured dominantly in Japan's exports to Asiatic markets but, as mentioned above, sale of textiles has been complicated by the terms of the Commodity Credit Corporation loan of over $200 million which required that repayment should be in dollars. Even so, demand has been sufficiently strong that some 60 per cent of this self-liquidating loan has been repaid out of dollar sales, but the balance will be increasingly difficult to repay.

As shown above, in the two-year period from September 1945 to September 1947, the total value of Japan's imports amounted to $691 million, while the value of its exports amounted to $255.8 million. Imports from the United States alone amounted to $661.2 million, exports to the United States amounted to

[3] G. C. Allen, *Japan: The Hungry Guest* (1938), p. 253.

$97.8 million. It is not shown above that Japan no longer can rely upon favorable invisible factors, foreign exchange earnings in dividends and from shipping and other services which in 1936 amounted to some $38 million. The trade deficit on U.S. dollar account represents a United States Government "advance" of

TABLE 2
IMPORTS INTO JAPAN, BY CONTINENTS AND PRINCIPAL COUNTRIES OF ORIGIN
(Subject to Revision)
(*in millions of U. S. dollars; figures rounded to nearest tenth*)

| Imported from | Value | Sept. 1945 through Sept. 1947 Per cent of Total Import |
|---|---|---|
| Total Imports | 691.0 | 100.0 |
| Asia: Total (U.S.S.R. excluded) | 22.2 | 3.2 |
| Korea | 2.7 | .4 |
| China—total (including Manchuria, Kwantung, Formosa) | 8.6 | 1.2 |
| India, Burma, Ceylon | .0 | .0 |
| Netherlands East Indies | .9 | .1 |
| Philippines | 2.0 | .3 |
| Hong Kong | 4.0 | .6 |
| Singapore | 4.0 | .6 |
| Other Asia | .0 | .0 |
| North America: Total | 661.2 | 95.7 |
| United States | 661.2 | 95.7 |
| Other North America | .0 | .0 |
| Europe: Total (including U.S.S.R.) | 6.9 | 1.0 |
| United Kingdom | 6.9 | 1.0 |
| Other Europe | .0 | .0 |
| Africa: Total | .0 | .0 |
| Oceania: Total | .7 | .1 |
| South and Central America: Total | .0 | .0 |

$563 million, financed, in part, by the Commodity Credit Corporation, but largely by United States Congressional appropriations.

Although Japan had, in the autumn of 1947, favorable balances with all countries with which it did business except the United States, the Philippines, and Singapore, repayment of its dollar obligation is not soon in sight. The United States advances to Japan have had the effect of making Japan a hard currency area, with resulting contraction of exports. The present situation is not one which need remain permanently unchanged, however. Already an agreement for carrying on Japanese trade in sterling, exclusive of cotton textiles, has been made with the

TABLE 3

Exports from Japan, By Continents and Principal Countries of Destination

(Subject to Revision)

*(in millions of U. S. dollars; figures rounded to nearest tenth)*

| Exported to | Value | Sept. 1945 through Sept. 1947 Per cent of Total Exports |
|---|---|---|
| Total Exports | 255.7 | 100.0 |
| Asia: Total (excluding U.S.S.R., Turkey) | 106.7 | 41.7 |
| Korea | 34.4 | 13.4 |
| China—total (including Manchuria, Kwantung, Formosa) | 13.8 | 5.4 |
| India, Burma, Ceylon | 12.6 | 4.9 |
| Netherlands East Indies | 18.8 | 7.3 |
| Philippines | 1.2 | .5 |
| Hongkong | 13.9 | 5.5 |
| Singapore | 2.0 | .8 |
| Other Asia | 10.0 | 3.9 |
| North America: Total | 97.8 | 38.2 |
| United States | 97.7 | 38.2 |
| Other North America | .1 | .0 |
| Europe: Total (including U.S.S.R., Turkey) | 38.8 | 15.2 |
| United Kingdom | 20.6 | 8.1 |
| Other Europe | 18.2 | 7.1 |
| Africa: Total | 7.9 | 3.1 |
| Oceania: Total | 4.5 | 1.8 |
| South and Central America: Total | .1 | .1 |

sterling area. Terms of trade, which now are not in Japan's favor, ultimately may improve as the world price structure reverts to a pattern in which the prices of manufactured goods rise in relation to prices of raw materials.

### PREWAR PATTERN

The table below indicates the scope and pattern of Japan's trade relationships (excluding Korea and Formosa) in 1936, the last year prior to the outbreak of war in China. What does it imply for the future? (See Table 4.)

Even in 1936 Japan's exports to the United States and its possessions amounted to 24.5 per cent of the total and its imports to 31.9 per cent; but it should not, now, be overlooked that Japan was at that time building up urgently needed stock piles for military use or for Japan's war-distorted industry; nor should it now be disregarded that the use of silk, which constituted more than half of Japan's sales in the United States market, has largely been supplanted by nylon.

### TRADE WITH CHINA

What is known of it invites speculation upon what may have been the long-term economic, as distinct from the obvious military, motivation underlying the prewar expansion of Japan's trade with North China and Manchuria. From 1936 through 1939, Japan's exports to the yen bloc areas of China (primarily Manchuria, Kwantung, and North China) mounted to one-third of total Japanese (nonmilitary) exports and one-sixteenth of total Japanese imports. Though the excess of even the nonmilitary exports was doubtless caused, to some extent, by Japan's military purposes, Japan's exports of industrial plant, mining equipment, and transportation facilities served, concurrently, to lay the foundation for an integrated and progressively productive raw material-fabricating relationship between the Continent and Japan. That trade and those hopes are ended today by the civil strife which is sweeping across large parts of China. Japanese business, however, learned to rely upon the coking coal, iron ore, salt, cereals, and soy beans of that area; to learn to do without them imposes a strain upon Japan's ingenuity in meeting these requirements elsewhere.

### TRADE: OTHER AREAS

Looking elsewhere, Japan sees a divided Korea with production reduced from prewar levels, and in any case reluctant, for political reasons, to restore the economic relations which Japan imposed upon it in the period from 1910 until Korea's liberation. Formosa is now tied to a much distressed Chinese economy.

TABLE 4

JAPAN: TRADE WITH PRINCIPAL COUNTRIES IN 1936[a]

*(in million yen)*

| | Exports | Imports | Balance of Trade | Percentage of Total Japanese Exports | Percentage of Total Japanese Imports |
|---|---|---|---|---|---|
| TOTAL . . . . . . . | 2693.0 | 2764.0 | − 71.0 | 100.0 | 100.0 |
| Great Britain . . . . | 147.3 | 72.9 | + 74.4 | 5.4 | 2.6 |
| British Dominions[b] . | 144.2 | 299.8 | −155.6 | 5.3 | 10.8 |
| British Colonies[c] . . | 463.7 | 507.7 | − 44.0 | 17.2 | 18.4 |
| United States . . . . | 594.3 | 847.5 | −253.2 | 22.1 | 30.7 |
| U. S. Colonies[d] . . . | 64.1 | 36.7 | + 27.4 | 2.4 | 1.3 |
| Netherlands . . . . | 15.4 | 4.6 | + 10.8 | .6 | .2 |
| Netherlands Colonies[e] | 135.9 | 113.5 | + 22.4 | 5.0 | 4.1 |
| France . . . . . . . | 43.5 | 19.9 | + 23.6 | 1.6 | .7 |
| French Colonies[f] . . | 45.3 | 22.5 | + 22.8 | 1.7 | .8 |
| Belgium Luxembourg | 16.2 | 16.0 | + .2 | .6 | .6 |
| Italy . . . . . . . . | 4.5 | 3.8 | + .7 | .2 | .1 |
| Other Colonial Areas . | 38.4 | 6.8 | + 31.6 | 1.4 | .2 |
| Manchuria . . . . . . | 498.1 | 239.4 | +258.7 | 18.5 | 8.6 |
| China . . . . . . . | 159.7 | 154.8 | + 4.9 | 5.9 | 5.6 |
| Siam . . . . . . . . | 43.0 | 8.8 | + 34.2 | 1.6 | .3 |
| U.S.S.R. . . . . . . | 31.4 | 21.3 | + 10.1 | 1.2 | .8 |
| Iraq . . . . . . . . | 19.0 | 2.9 | + 16.1 | .7 | .1 |
| Iran . . . . . . . . | 4.7 | 1.6 | + 3.1 | .2 | .1 |
| Turkey . . . . . . . | 4.3 | 4.5 | − .2 | .2 | .2 |
| Germany . . . . . . | 35.1 | 115.5 | − 80.4 | 1.3 | 4.2 |
| Sweden . . . . . . | 8.8 | 23.1 | − 14.3 | .3 | .8 |
| Norway . . . . . . | 6.2 | 17.9 | − 11.7 | .2 | .6 |
| Finland . . . . . . | 3.2 | 6.6 | − 3.4 | .1 | .2 |
| Switzerland . . . . . | .8 | 14.0 | − 13.2 | . . . | .1 |
| Latin America[g] . . . | 77.5 | 128.7 | − 51.2 | 2.8 | 4.7 |
| Egypt . . . . . . . | 40.9 | 45.7 | − 4.8 | 1.5 | 1.7 |
| Other . . . . . . . | 50.5 | 27.5 | + 23.0 | 2.0 | 1.5 |

[a]Based on statistics compiled by Miriam S. Farley, in the publication, *The Problem of Japanese Trade Expansion in the Post-War Situation* (New York, 1939).

[b]Includes Australia, South Africa, New Zealand, Canada, and so on.

[c]The word "colonies" is used here to denote all possessions which are not fully self-governing. Group totals are, in fact, slightly larger than shown, as Japanese statistics do not list separately all of the smaller colonial possessions. "British colonies" include India, Strait Settlements, Hong Kong, and so on.

[d]Includes Philippines, Hawaii, Puerto Rico, Canal Zone.

[e]Includes Netherlands East Indies, Curaçao, Dutch Guiana.

[f]Includes French Morocco, Syria, Indo-China, French Somali, Senegal, Algeria, and so on.

[g]Includes Argentina, Panama, Brazil, Uruguay, Venezuela, Chile, Mexico, Peru.

The Philippines, Netherlands East Indies, Indochina, Malaya, Burma, and Siam need Japanese exports, but general political instability or postwar readjustment of their economies has hampered production of the oil, minerals, and other industrial and agricultural raw materials with which they might pay for Japan's output. Moreover, as exports from that area expand, there may continue to be, as is now the case, a tendency for exporters, particularly in the colonial areas of European powers, to seek dollar payment which would mean sales in the United States market or, if in the Japanese market, for dollars covered by U.S. appropriations. Prospects of developing trade with India, probably on some kind of barter basis, appear more bright, and Japan may be able to obtain Australian wool on similar terms. Europe, with which Japan had an unfavorable balance of trade before the war, is unlikely to be willing to part with goods except for payment in hard currency; nor is it likely to pay dollars to buy imports from Japan in the near future. The varied prewar trade with South American countries, never bulking large in amounts or values, is unlikely to revive unless there is a resumption of personal contacts between South American and Japanese traders able to appraise each others' tastes and demands.[4] Japanese trade, as it expands, is unlikely to conform soon or exactly to the prewar pattern.

## OBSTACLES TO TRADE: SPECIFIC AND GENERAL

Both specific and general obstacles obstruct recovery of Japanese trade with all parts of the world. Specifically, for example, Japanese traders have not been permitted by Japan's neighbors to go abroad and will trade inefficiently until they are permitted to do so. Foreign traders in Japan, who were until September 1947 representatives of governments exclusively, have found lack of an exchange rate, with what that implies, a nuisance and an obstruction to concluding deals. One immediate and fundamental difficulty is the fact that nearby markets and sources of raw materials in Asia, upon which Japan depended prior to and during the war, have been disturbed by political instability and

[4] Roswell H. Whitman, "Economic Recovery in Japan," *Military Government Journal* (January, 1948).

have suffered profound postwar economic dislocations. As stable conditions are restored, Far Eastern countries may desire to protect their own industries through tariffs or other devices. Restoration of any approximation of Japan's prewar patterns of trade must be a two-way operation in which the mere fact of Japan's desires, needs, and efforts may not be a decisive consideration. But until it occurs, in reliance upon United States assistance lies Japan's only hope for preventing economic chaos.

Nothing is more clear than the fact that Japan does not now support itself. It leans upon a United States loath to bear the burden of financing Japan's trade deficits. Yet the United States has justified appropriations for that purpose both on the grounds that a victor undertakes certain obligations to its former enemy and because a stable economic environment is prerequisite for achieving the long-term objectives for which the war was fought and the military occupation established. That assistance cannot be provided indefinitely. Hence, except in the unlikely event that Japan can pay in exports to the United States for imports it now procures in the United States, Japan must, despite the discouraging immediate outlook, find in the Far East or elsewhere in the world a way to trade and the key to its self-support. An amelioration of world conditions would not necessarily benefit Japan, however, if rehabilitated governments in Asia chose to throw up obstacles, for political, emotional, or short-run economic reasons, in the way of revival of what in purely economic terms might be mutually beneficial trade with Japan.

## IV

## REFORM: THE ANSWER TO ASIA'S DISTRUST

An ugly remembrance of war lingers in the mind of Asia, particularly in those countries which were occupied by Japanese armed forces. Time has not healed the wounds inflicted by Japan's wartime brutality and exploitation nor eased the social strains and conflicts which the withdrawal of the Japanese brought to the surface in many of the war-weakened Far Eastern societies. Reparations will not compensate for losses suffered. In many of the Far Eastern countries there persists a deep, resentful, and in some ways irrational fear that Japan's recovery will place Asia once more in the disadvantageous competitive position which was intolerable before the war.

The immediate interests of private merchants and the foresight of wise government planners may help to suppress this fear. It will not be removed unless the peoples of Asia understand Japan's essential weakness. Sir George Sansom has pointed out:

> It is difficult to see how she can by her own unaided efforts build up her resources even to a moderate standard while an industrial output which would permit her to make war must be out of the question for as long as can be reasonably foreseen. It may be objected that Germany, on her knees in 1918, became a formidable industrial and military power within 20 years. That is so, but the cases of Japan and Germany are not comparable. Germany had land frontiers across which she could draw strength from contiguous states. The economy of Europe was dependent even after 1918 upon the existence of a prosperous Germany, or at least it was so regarded by the victorious powers who therefore handsomely subsidized German recovery and condoned breaches of the so-called Versailles *diktat*. But the economy of Eastern Asia is not dependent upon a prosperous Japan, though a rehabilitated Japan could probably make important contributions to the economic progress of Asiatic countries. . . . The immediate problem is not how Japan can be prevented from developing a high war potential but how she can support her population.[5]

Recovery of the Far Eastern countries themselves is an essential prerequisite for Japan's self-support; not contrariwise. Nevertheless, the peoples of the Far East may resist Japan's recovery and damage their own interests in doing so, unless there is clear evidence that Japan is cleansed of the militaristic and exploitive elements, economic, psychological, and political, in its society. Even allowing for skepticism regarding the permanent effect of reforms, Japan's attempts in this direction may be regarded by the peoples of the Far East as the assurance that a self-supporting Japan would advance and not menace their own welfare and development.

[5] Sir George Sansom, "Conflicting Purposes in Japan," *Foreign Affairs* (January 1948).

### OBJECTIVES OF ECONOMIC REFORM

The broad outlines of the Supreme Commander's economic reform program were laid down in the United States Basic Directive of September 1945. The Far Eastern Commission gave that program international benediction. The occupation authority was to encourage labor unions, dissolve excessive concentrations of wealth, purge undesirable personnel, reform Japan's system of land tenure, and reform Japan's financial system.

### FINANCE

Towards the end of destroying those aspects of the Japanese financial structure that were used to promote war, while strengthening those aspects which could contribute to an early and healthy recovery of Japan, the Supreme Commander established a system of control, supervision, and approval over governmental budgets, instituted supervision over the tax structure, controlled the finances of the Imperial Household, and took measures to free private finance from excessive bureaucratic or monopolistic control. Institutions principally concerned in Japan's prewar and wartime programs of financial colonization and economic penetration of conquered areas were closed. A capital levy law and a war indemnity tax brought about redistribution of private fortunes, provided funds for the Government, and cancelled war damage claims. The Government's accounting procedures were reformed, the ordinary tax structure was reorganized, and procedures were established for disposition of state-owned property. Most important, in the long term, Japan's new constitution provided for control by the Diet over public finance.

### MONOPOLY: THE ZAIBATSU

The Zaibatsu, a small number of families and monopolistic enterprise closely associated with the Japanese Government, exerted a dominant control over the prewar economy of Japan. Ten major Zaibatsu families, through 67 holding companies and affected enterprises, asserted effective control over 75 per cent of Japan's financial, industrial, and commercial activities both at home and abroad. The Supreme Commander has supervised the Japanese Government in taking steps towards breaking up the Zaibatsu and dispersing its properties among a larger number of independent and competitive enterprises in Japan. A Holding Company Liquidation Commission was created with power to liquidate and to disperse concentrated economic power. In due course the Holding Company Liquidation Commission designated 83 holding companies for dissolution and named 56 persons who were considered to have controlled the 10 major Zaibatsu families, taking over their securities for liquidation purposes, establishing control over their other properties, and preventing them from reassuming positions of economic importance. Meanwhile, the Japanese Government was directed to dissolve all control associations and to repeal all laws and legislation which had fostered their growth and to prepare legislation prohibiting international cartels and execution by Japanese firms of restrictive international contracts. It passed an Anti-Trust Law, established a Fair Trade Commission for its enforcement, and in December 1947, passed a Deconcentration Law under which it would be determined whether and how some 325 operating enterprises, through which Zaibatsu power was exercised, should be reorganized into smaller, independent businesses. These were important steps, but the permanent and full success of the program will not and cannot be determined until it is seen how quickly and how effectively the ownership of liquidated properties passes into the hands of new economic leadership able and desiring to participate positively in the operation of the Japanese economy.

### LABOR UNIONS

Japan has had labor unions since the earliest days of its industrialization. Fairly active in the nineteen-twenties and early thirties, this movement became, shortly after the outbreak of war with China, captive of the wartime Governments and the military who stripped it of its freedom. After 1940 it had become almost completely impotent. The first step taken by the Supreme Commander in the labor field, after establishing his authority, was to dissolve the wartime labor front organizations, divorce the police from labor administration, and secure elimination of repressive labor laws. The framework of basic labor rights was created in a Trade Union Law and the Supreme Commander helped to institute sound collective bargaining procedures. Encouraged to adopt democratic labor legislation, the Japanese Government has, further, adopted an elaborate pattern of labor laws which compares favorably with those of progressive democratic countries. These include a Labor Relations Adjustment Law (September 1946), a Labor Standards Law (April 1947), a Workman's Accident Insurance Law (April 1947), a Seamen's Law (April 1947), and an Employment Security Law (August 1947). Legislation providing for unemployment insurance was introduced in the Japanese Diet in August, 1947.

Japanese workers responded in a startling way to the opportunities thus provided them to organize. By August 1946, three million Japanese workers belonged to labor unions. By November 1947, this number exceeded 4.5 million. The Supreme Commander has given considerable freedom to the Japanese labor union movement, abridging that freedom only by prohibition of strikes considered inimical to the objectives of the occupation. In no instance have occupation troops intervened in strikes, but a strike of all government workers planned for the spring of 1947 was called off as a result of the Supreme Commander's pressure on labor leaders.

## LAND REFORM

Japan's prewar system of land tenure was one in which land owners actually operated only half the farm lands of Japan. The remainder was cultivated by tenants and part tenants who constituted about 70 per cent of the 5,700,000 Japanese farm families. Traditionally, they were compelled to deliver half or more of the yields from their rented plots to landlords who wielded enormous power, dominated local politics, provided officers for the army and navy, and gave their support to Japan's most reactionary political parties.[6]

Undertaking to remove economic obstacles to the strengthen-

[6] W. N. Gilmartin and W. I. Ladejinsky, "Promise of Agrarian Reform in Japan," *Foreign Affairs* (January, 1948).

ing of democratic tendencies in the Japanese agrarian system, the Supreme Commander as early as December 1945 directed the Japanese Government to start a program of agrarian reform which would redistribute the land equally among Japan's 5½ odd million farm families. The Land Reform Law of October 21, 1946, represented the legislated result of this instruction. This law provides for purchase by the Japanese Government of approximately 5 million acres, or 70 to 80 per cent of the tenant-cultivated land of Japan, for resale to tenant farmers within a two-year period ending December 31, 1948. Approximately one-third of all Japan's farm land will be involved in the transfer. Compensation of the land owners is to be at price levels established by law. Resale of the land to tenant cultivators after consolidation into economic farm units will be at the same prices. Tenant payments will be made over a 30-year period and will not exceed one-third of the gross income of the land, but can be reduced, delayed or cancelled by the Government in the event that farm prices drop or crops fail.

In the Supreme Commander's Report on the First Two Years of the Occupation, issued in August 1947, the difficulty of accomplishing the economic and political objectives of the agrarian reform program was clearly stated. "The task of altering the basic structure of Japanese agrarian economy requires more than the creation of administrative machinery of reform. It entails also the re-education of the great mass of Japanese farmers to their newly acquired democratic rights and privileges." On this subject, W. N. Gilmartin and W. I. Ladejinsky state that "The most formidable part of the task is to put them [the land reforms] into effect. It is understandable that the immediate prospect of so basic a change in a tradition-ridden agrarian society should stir up great passions."[7] Even though execution of the program as a whole has been slow, some encouragement can be found in the fact that by the end of 1947, the Government had bought more than 3.4 million acres of land from the landlords, or over 70 per cent of the total which the plan envisages. Tenants, however, bought up only a negligible portion of the government purchases and in many cases tenant purchasers

[7] *Foreign Affairs* (January, 1948).

merely assumed ownership of land they were already cultivating. The limited and slow assertion of tenant interest in these properties can be explained in part, but unfortunately in small part, by technical difficulties. Education will be essential to overcome obstacles inherent in the traditional feudal mentality of the farmer and to assure successful execution of the program as a whole.

### THE "PURGE"

In accordance with the Potsdam Declaration, the Joint Chiefs of Staff directive, and subsequent controlling policies, the Supreme Commander has taken steps to purge from Japanese political and economic life persons who shared the responsibility for Japan's program of aggression. Applied first in the fields of education and police and later applied to the political, social, and economic fields, the purge has affected directly or indirectly some 800,000 to 900,000 Japanese. There has been a tendency, moreover, on the part of individuals, fearful of the purge, to withdraw themselves completely from political or economic activity. This was the case even though the economic phase of the purge was not begun before April, 1947. At that time, some 3,200 persons holding policy positions in some 300 companies were screened. By December 1947, 416 of these persons had been removed or excluded from public service. This, of course, is not a large number in terms of Japan's resources of leadership in economic spheres, but fear of purging may have kept some economic talent from stepping forward into positions of responsibility where screening would take place.

### DEPTH AND PURPOSE OF REFORMS

The reform programs which the Supreme Commander has required the Japanese to undertake may be considered to have removed blocks to Japan's democratization. Whether the Allied concept of economic democracy will endure depends, of course, upon the will and character of the Japanese people themselves. The reform programs had to be undertaken if Japan was to fulfill the obligations laid upon it at the time of its surrender. That, however, is a legal consideration far outweighed by more fundamental considerations. Reform, by giving the Japanese people themselves a stake in their society, is an antidote for totalitarianism. Only a reformed Japan is likely to be an acceptable neighbor in the eyes of Far Eastern countries. The weak Japan of today cannot thrust or shoulder itself into the good graces of the countries of the Far East. Through its reforms, Japan can make it easier for its neighbors to offer that coöperation, in supplying raw materials, in opening up markets, and in exchanging economic services upon which Japan's survival will depend.

## CONCLUSION

The purpose of occupying Japan has been to make possible Japan's early readmission into the family of nations. Its overseas territories have been stripped away, its military establishment dissolved, and the reform of its political, religious, and educational institutions has been got under way. Similarly clear and rapid progress towards Allied objectives in the economic sphere has not been made. For this the Allies themselves have not been without fault. They have not made final decisions on how much industry is necessary for a peaceful Japan nor on how the Allies should share, as reparations, what is surplus. Their failure, in this respect, may have been induced, to some extent, by the unstable conditions throughout Asia which complicate planning, at best difficult, for the removal and reinstallation of industrial plant. Unstable general conditions have also stood in the way of any genuine revival of that trade upon which Japan's self-support depends. For the time being, the United States has undertaken to cover, on a relief basis, Japan's deficits in food and other minimum requirements. These deficits have been larger than they need to have been because a weakened Japan, so long as it is condemned to live at a level no better than that sufficient to prevent disease and unrest, could not apply a maximum effort in exploiting even those resources, such as coal and skilled labor, already at hand. The United States, in early 1948, was in process of expanding its concept of relief to cover the procurement of raw materials and industrial spare parts necessary to resuscitate Japan's economic system as a whole.

An act of faith underlies the efforts being made towards the reform and recovery of the Japanese economy. Neither Japan nor the Allies can see clearly the kind of world into which an independent Japan will be, in due course, admitted, nor what kind of a Japanese economy can survive in that world. What is clear is that presurrender hopes may not soon materialize—hopes that economic Japan eventually would enter a world free of fear where trade could expand unhampered by restrictive practices and where production and commerce would be stimulated by the credit resources of private, national, and United Nations institutions concerned in increasing productivity and welfare the world over. Upon realization of these hopes depends the stability, if not in fact the survival, of the democratically inclined Japan now being shaped for independence by Allied authorities.

# 7

## *SOME ASPECTS OF CANADIAN ECONOMIC RELATIONS WITH THE UNITED STATES*

Robert B. Bryce

Canada's economic relations with the United States are dominated by the effects of the general scarcity of American dollars in the world outside the United States. Consideration of the problems brought about by this situation and the action taken to deal with them will bring out and illustrate most of the currently important aspects of the economic relations between the two countries. This approach would appear to be of more use and interest than an historical review or analytical catalogue.

By way of background, it is worth while to recall that Canada consists of about twelve and a half million people, scattered for the most part along the area just north of the United States boundary, concentrated here and there in fair-sized urban centres, and spreading out on the prairies to a wide extent. Its economy has been built largely upon East-West lines to create a nation, despite the natural tendency in many portions toward a North-South orientation with adjacent American territory. Its large area—slightly greater than that of the United States—has many fertile and productive patches, considerable mineral and water power resources, and extensive soft wood forests, the exploitation of which by relatively modern methods enables it to support a small population at an average standard of living closer to that of the United States than any other country manages to attain, even in normal times. A great part of the area, however, is cold and unproductive, able to support only a handful of people under frontier conditions of life. During recent decades the main primary industries of agriculture, forestry and mining have been highly developed and have been matched by the growth of a large manufacturing industry, partially based upon them, as well as those service trades and industries which occupy such a large proportion of a modern industrial state. This Canadian economy by 1947 managed to achieve a gross national product of about thirteen billion dollars—roughly one-eighteenth that of the United States, at a price level roughly comparable.

In speaking of the present "scarcity" of American dollars faced by Canada, in common with most other countries, it is desirable to make clear that the use of that term implies something abnormal and not corrected by the usual workings of the price system. Normally, the economist would regard all things having a price as being scarce to the degree measured by the price, and would not speak of shortages except in relative terms based upon price. This would apply to currencies as well as to goods. Now, however, the price system is not working over large areas of economic life—being restricted or suspended by action of one kind or another. So scarce are many essential goods and currencies which will buy them, that societies and their governments in many cases will not tolerate the social consequences of the unfettered price system. Under such circumstances we may legitimately speak in terms of a shortage of U. S. dollars throughout most of the world, without having to stop to discuss whether there would be any absolute scarcity if prices and exchange rates were something other than they are.

The origins and nature of this world dollar shortage are described elsewhere in this volume.[1] At this point, it is important to observe, first, that its present extent and intensity (March, 1948) were not foreseeable in 1945 and 1946, when some of those affected might have taken steps to anticipate it and protect themselves, at least in part; and, secondly, that it is now so widespread that not only Europe and the sterling area but almost all other major economic units outside the United States are forced to restrict and curtail their use of dollars, thereby limiting greatly the freedom of action of any one country such as Canada in ad-

[1] *See* Introduction and Professor Haberler's essay, Chapter 24.

justing to the situation. Those countries which by nature or emergency needs must depend upon trade, and particularly upon multilateral trade, are bound to be in difficulties, unless neutrality or particular good fortune has safeguarded their exchange position.

The nature of Canada's economy and balance of payments has been such that she was highly vulnerable in these circumstances. Originally organized to supply overseas demands for exports of primary products, yet located and developed in such a way as to depend heavily upon imports from the United States, Canada has multilateral trade and convertibility of exchanges built into her economic structure. Prosperity for Canada has only been possible in the past on the basis of large-scale exports of foods and raw materials to Britain and the continent of Europe, as well as large exports in recent decades of forest mineral, and farm products to the United States.

During the thirties, when exports to Europe languished, they were supplemented by a less natural trade with other Dominions of the British Commonwealth, fostered by imperial preferences in their markets and fed by the establishment and growth of Canada subsidiaries or branches of American manufacturing businesses. Imports from overseas, on the other hand, were before the war much less in total than imports from the United States. Not only was the United States the natural source for such items as coal and oil, steel and cotton, but both the consumer and the business man in Canada have had large and natural demands for American finished goods. The Canadian consumer reads the advertisements in American magazines, hopes and attempts to achieve the American standard of life, which, of course, implies buying a wide range of goods, from oranges to motor cars, from the U.S.A. Machinery and equipment in Canadian business are normally of American design and standards, even if wholly or partially made in Canada, and even apart from price and lower costs of shipment, the American producer of capital equipment enjoys a great advantage in the Canadian market over all overseas competitors.

As a consequence, Canada depended before the war upon a surplus of exports to Europe and elsewhere overseas, to get dollar exchange to pay for a surplus of imports from the United

States. In the one period of prosperity between the wars—the period 1926-1928—Canada had a favorable balance on current account of roughly $200 million with the continent of Europe, a rough balance with the United Kingdom, an unfavorable balance with the United States of $275 million, and a small favorable balance with the rest of the world.[2] At the culmination of the boom in 1929 and 1930, Canada's current balance with the United States (and also, it may be noted, with the United Kingdom) was so heavily adverse that it could not be offset by the favorable balances with Europe and elsewhere—already dwindling as a result of plunging wheat prices—and the balance of payments was only maintained by heavy investments of United States capital in Canada in those years—investments not unconnected, of course, with the construction boom in Canada at the time, and the heavy imports of machinery and equipment from the U.S.A.[3] When by the later thirties Canada had recovered in some measure from the depression, her unfavorable balance with the United States was much smaller because she had no domestic boom to draw in heavy imports; by this time continental Europe was buying much less and Canada was depending upon a favorable balance with the United Kingdom and other parts of the sterling area to secure dollars required in the United States for current purposes and for some beginning at reduction in external debt.

This trans-Atlantic triangular trade has been of more than financial importance. It has enabled Canada to build up a specialized export economy, yet with a domestic economy patterned upon and supplied by the United States. Without it, Canada must have had a lower standard of life—having either to export at greater disadvantage to other markets or to import goods from overseas at higher costs and less suited to North American demands. More even than that, however, Canadians saw in this trade triangle a means of preserving some measure of independence from the United States on the one hand, and of maintaining a North American character on the other.

With this background, with a vivid consciousness of their

[2] See the *Report of the Foreign Exchange Control Board* (Ottawa, March, 1946), page 6.

[3] See *The Canadian Balance of International Payments Preliminary Statement, 1947*, by the Dominion Bureau of Statistics (Ottawa, 1948).

usual dependence on trade for income and employment, and with a realization that nations that have been friends and allies in two world wars are worth restoring and strengthening, Canadians naturally were concerned with the recovery and reconstruction of Britain and continental Europe after the war. The Canadian Government was widely and strongly supported in Parliament and by the public in measures for relief grants and reconstruction credits. Indeed, these attitudes and policies had had effect earlier on a much larger scale with the financing of war requirements of allied countries on a basis similar to Lend-Lease but larger in relative magnitude.[4] Canada, of course, participated in UNRRA, and by that action exported substantial amounts on relief without payment during 1945 and 1946. Also she participated on quite a substantial scale with the United States and Britain in the less widely known military relief operations during 1944 and 1945. Finally, she provided in 1947—with the outlines of her own foreign exchange problem already evident—an appropriation of twenty million dollars for post-UNRRA relief.

From the balance of payments viewpoint, however, much the most important action that Canada took in the initial postwar period was the provision of credits to Britain and various other countries—mainly to Western Europe—for purchases in Canada. Under general enabling legislation passed in 1944 and expanded in 1945, Canada granted credits of $242 million to France, $125 million to Holland, $100 million to Belgium, $30 million to Norway, $19 million to Czechoslovakia, $3 million to Russia, $15 million to the Netherlands Indies, and $60 million to China. These credits were granted normally for long periods, with interest rates slightly above those for which the Canadian Government borrowed at home for comparable periods. In granting these credits and later in extending the period of their use, it was usually stipulated that the borrowing countries would fi-

[4] See the *Final Report of the Canadian Mutual Aid Board* (Ottawa, 1946). The total aid supplied by Canada of this nature during the war amounted to approximately three and one-half billion Canadian dollars, which was on a net basis—i.e. Canada paid allied countries for war supplies and services received and did not secure the equivalent of "reverse Lend-Lease." Canada, it may be recalled, did not receive Lend-Lease aid from the United States, but paid for her war requirements from the United States.

nance a portion of their purchases from Canada by payment in United States dollars or the equivalent. The reason, of course, was the need—and the possibility—of getting some current return from exports to these countries, which could be used by Canada in paying cash for imports required from the United States.

The credit to the United Kingdom overshadowed in magnitude those noted above, for it was a total amount of $1250 million on terms practically identical with the terms of United States credit to the United Kingdom, that is, more favorable financially than others, but linked with conditions concerning import and exchange control measures. In form, the credit to the U.K. could be used anywhere for any purpose over the five-year period. In fact, the magnitude of British requirements in Canada made it certain that all the credit, and more, would be needed for buying in Canada. There was in the agreement provision for consultation in regard to its working out, and Canada and the United Kingdom have in the past twelve months agreed from time to time upon the rate at which this large credit will be drawn upon, or the ratio between the drawings on it and purchases for United States dollars. In granting this, the Canadian Government made clear that its intention was to help make possible the restoration of multilateral trade, the removal of discrimination in import controls, and the convertibility of currencies. In the two years that have since elapsed, these goals have, of course, proven far more difficult of achievement than they then appeared.

Two aspects of these credits should be noted. First, the total—about $1850 million (apart from relief grants, and so on)—is large by comparison with those of the United States and other countries, taking into account the relative income and wealth of the countries. If the United States had granted credits on a similar scale in relation to national income, they would have totalled roughly thirty-three billion dollars—enough to include the proposed ERP total in addition to all postwar credits already granted. Canada was willing to act on this scale because of the importance which Canadians attached to the revival of trade and the economic reconstruction abroad, which was necessary as a basis for it. The program was not regarded as one of generosity but of long-range self-interest, which required some temporary cost and risk. The magnitude of this program should be borne in mind in assessing what Canada should be expected to do under the ERP program.

The second aspect worth noting here is, of course, that these credits meant that Canada would be foregoing foreign exchange receipts from exports at a time when she was increasing her own imports from the United States and paying cash for them. It was anticipated that this would lead to some loss of exchange reserves, but a loss that could and should be taken as part of the price of restoring trade. In the event, of course, the loss of reserves has been much larger than anticipated, in part because the use of the credit to Britain has been more rapid than was expected, but mainly because the value of Canadian imports from the United States increased so rapidly that Canada's total surplus on current international account dwindled away to almost nothing in 1947.[5] In addition, considerable exports of

[5] The following figures for Canada's total balance of payments with all countries may be of interest in this connection:

| | *1945* | *1946* | *1947* (Preliminary) |
|---|---|---|---|
| *Current Account* | | ($ Millions) | |
| Total Exports | 3,474 | 2,393 | 2,723 |
| All Other Current Credits | 978 | 966 | 1,010 |
| Total Current Credits | 4,452 | 3,359 | 3,733 |
| Total Imports | 1,442 | 1,822 | 2,535 |
| All Other Current Debits | 1,468 | 1,083 | 1,113 |
| | 2,910 | 2,905 | 3,648 |
| Current Balance | +1,542 | + 454 | + 85 |
| *Capital Account* | | | |
| Relief and Other Grants | − 858 | − 97 | − 38 |
| Official Credits Utilized | − 105 | − 750 | − 563 |
| Other Capital Movement (net) | + 88 | + 142 | − 227 |
| Total, Ex Reserves | − 875 | − 705 | − 828 |
| Change in Reserves of Gold and U.S. Dollars Increase (−), Decrease (+) | − 667 | + 251 | + 743 |

capital to the United States took place and were permitted by the exchange control authorities.

Canada's shortage of United States dollars has arisen not only from the difficulties in selling exports for cash or getting imports from Europe, which are understandable, but also from the consequences of the boom within Canada which has given rise to a large volume of imports, and the rise in American price levels which has greatly increased their cost. The boom in Canada—no lesser term does it justice—is based upon a conjunction of three circumstances: the very high level of export sales (sustained in part by credits), a surprising and record-shattering level of private investment, and a high level of consumption supported not only by high disposable incomes, but also by a high propensity to consume. Under these stimuli gross national expenditures have climbed at rates and to levels that brought about increasing prices and increasing imports.

In some cases the higher imports are linked directly to these stimulating forces—for example, a large part of private investment expenditure is on steel, machinery, and equipment from the United States, and certain types of exports themselves have a considerable content of steel or other imported materials or parts. In some measure imports are linked to general productive activity—for example, coal and petroleum, which bulk very large in the totals at present. In other cases, the imports represent simply the spilling over of demand, either consumers' or business', when domestic supplies are not sufficient to meet the abnormal requirements. It is tempting to the economist to try to sum up these tendencies and developments in a "marginal propensity to import" which might be applied to national income or expenditure, but under present Canadian circumstances any such over-all figure would be a gross oversimplification, and in any event there are not sufficient statistical observations to determine a curve of any use in analysis.

For those who wish to know the aggregate figures anyway, it might be noted that between 1946 and 1947 Canada's gross national expenditure increased by roughly $1.4 billion dollars, or about 12 per cent, while total imports of goods and services increased by roughly $730 million, or about 25 per cent. Some of the high level of imports in 1947 was due to temporary, abnormal factors—for example, the filling up of pipe lines and other additions to inventories (estimated at 6 per cent of gross national product); the abnormal postwar demands for plant, machinery, and equipment, much of which is imported from the United States; the abnormal deferred demands for consumers' durables, in which United States imports are also prominent; and the anticipation of import restrictions. Some of these, however, are not much more temporary than the similar factors accounting for the high level of gross national expenditure, and any conception of normal import requirements must be related to the form and nature, as well as the magnitude of expenditures required to sustain income and employment.

Canada's import experience in 1947 tempts one to use it as an illustration—not perfect but useful—of the consequences of overabundant employment in such an open economy. If imports are available, and the capital exchange resources with which to pay for them, excessive national expenditure in relation to productive capacity may be expected to lead to an adverse balance of payments, instead of inflation of prices and costs. Other circumstances, of course, will affect the situation; inflation and other influences from abroad may counteract and complicate this rather simple and obvious generalization, which, however, is one that those concerned with vulnerable, open economies must bear in mind.

Canada had emerged from the war with gold and exchange reserves that were quite substantial by comparison with any prewar standard, even allowing for differences in price levels—a total of $1508 million in December, 1945 compared with $393 million in 1939. This did not represent an improvement in Canada's balance of indebtedness in United States dollars during the war, but in effect was the result of United States investment in Canada during the war, and the sales by Canadians of U. S. assets. Total current account receipts and payments in dollars or their equivalent—which early in the war were very seriously out of balance—eventually turned out to be almost equal, as a result of efforts by Canada to conserve dollar resources and American war purchases in Canada under the Hyde

Park Agreement and otherwise.[6] Canada remained, at the end of the war, a huge debtor to the United States, in 1945 owing nearly $5 billion in all, including equities in Canadian property, and holding as offsets, in addition to her reserves, only about $1 billion.[7] Of course, Canada's balance of indebtedness to the United Kingdom was greatly reduced during the war because of the sale of United Kingdom holdings of Canadian securities to finance war purchases, and the noninterest-bearing loan made by Canada in 1942. When all of the postwar Canadian credit has been advanced to the United Kingdom, the indebtedness of each country to the other should about balance.

Although Canada removed her restrictions on imports in mid-1945 and was selling substantial amounts on credit, her exchange reserves continued to increase until mid-1946, partly because imports were not yet available in volume from the United States, partly because American capital continued to flow into Canada. In 1946, however, exports declined from the high levels at the end of the war, sales on credit increased, and imports from the United States began to rise rapidly. During the second half of the year, therefore, Canada's exchange reserves fell off sharply and the decline continued into and through 1947, as the rise in the value of imports far outstripped the modest increase in exports, and as the inward capital movement was reversed to a substantial net outflow.

It is natural to wonder how far this reversal of the movement in the Canadian exchange position vis-à-vis the United States was due to the return in July 1946 of the Canadian dollar to parity with the United States dollar, from the ninety-cent level at which it had been held since the war began. This change was made by the Canadian Government for the explicit purpose of dampening the inflationary effects upon Canada of rapid price increases in the United States and elsewhere.[8] A careful

[6] See F. A. Knox "Canada's Balance of International Payments, 1940-45," *Canadian Journal of Economics and Political Science* (August 1947), pp. 352 and 361, and also the *Report of the Foreign Exchange Control Board,* (Ottawa, March, 1946), pp. 20-29.

[7] See *The Canadian Balance of International Payments Preliminary Statement, 1947.*

[8] See statement by Minister of Finance in *House of Commons Debates* (July 5, 1946), pp. 3180-85.

consideration of the elasticities of demand and supply of the main Canadian imports and exports from July 1946 to the present leads one inevitably to the conclusion that this change in rate could have had very little effect on the current account balance, because price was clearly having little influence on the volume of trade. On the capital account there may have been some nonrecurrent effects, as the lower rate probably offered some inducement to Americans to acquire or hold Canadian dollar assets in anticipation of a possible appreciation, a motive which no longer applied after the change, while some Canadian debtors with outstanding U. S. obligations had probably been waiting for the return to parity to take advantage of favorable market conditions to refinance in Canada and redeem their U. S. obligations. On the whole, it would appear that the return to parity played a relatively small part in the development of the exchange shortage, and mainly in the form of reducing Canada's indebtedness at an inconvenient time.

By early 1947 it was evident that unless the increase in the volume of imports or their prices was reversed, or unless Canada had bumper crops to swell her cash exports, some action would be necessary to restrict imports. The full seriousness of the British and general European difficulties and outlook were not yet evident, however. The negotiations at Geneva for tariff reductions and the drafting of the ITO Charter were just beginning, and Canada was most vitally concerned in their success. The Canadian authorities felt that action by Canada to introduce restrictions on imports, added to all the other difficulties being faced at Geneva, might well prove "the last straw" to those engaged in the negotiations and might help cause the conference to fail. This would have meant failure in the key point of American and Canadian plans for long-term international economic policy. The Canadian Government, therefore, withheld action until the Geneva negotiations were completed, when it was able to act in accordance with both the letter and the spirit of the agreements reached, and when it was possible to secure the modifications in the Canada-U.S. trade agreement that were necessary to permit the control of imports without abrogating that agreement and losing the valuable tariff treatment it provided for Canadian exports. This period of waiting, of course, during which the necessity for eventual restriction of imports became clearer week by week, resulted in the reduction of Canada's exchange reserves to uncomfortably low levels, although it did enable a large volume of useful imports to be acquired, many of them for capital purposes, and it also served to moderate in considerable measure the inflationary pressure in Canada that would have been more acute had imports not been available.

Following announcement of the Geneva agreements, the Canadian Government announced and put immediately into effect a program to meet and overcome the shortage of U.S. dollars with which Canada was faced.[9] The emergency portions of that program consisted of quantitative restrictions on imports, heavy excise taxes on certain nonessential goods, restrictions on travel expenditure, and a short-term line of credit from the Export-Import Bank to supplement Canada's dwindling exchange reserves. The longer-term and more positive side of the policy, which was emphasized in the announcement, was to increase exports to the United States, partly by expansion of total exports and partly by diversion of exports from other areas. Subsidies on gold production, which was seriously depressed, were also announced. The Government stated that its long-term objective was to develop Canadian resources and industry in a way that would permanently reduce the lack of balance in Canadian-United States trade. The Government later revealed that informal proposals had been made to the proper American authorities for a further trade agreement between the two countries, more far-reaching in its effects than that negotiated at Geneva. In regard to immediate issues, the Canadian Government indicated that Canada's ability to supply and finance exports to Europe would depend upon implementation of the Marshall Plan and the use of some United States funds for purchases in Canada.

The most spectacular and unusual part of this program was

[9] The program was announced by the Minister of Finance, The Honorable D. C. Abbott in a broadcast November 17, 1947, which was published in leading Canadian newspapers of the following day. A more detailed explanation appears in the *House of Commons Debates* (December 16), pp. 323-339.

the restriction of imports. It was calculated to reduce imports by about three hundred million dollars or 12 per cent of the 1947 levels—plus whatever can be accomplished in the restriction of capital equipment and materials, which is hard to forecast. This reducation from the high levels of 1947 does not look large to an outsider, but it must be noted that the great bulk of Canadian imports consists of coal and oil, cotton and other raw materials, steel and machinery, fruits and vegetables, and other items which it is hard to regard as luxuries or even nonessentials. Many items could not be substantially restricted without the institution of consumer rationing—a step which a Government could hardly be expected to undertake readily under North American conditions of today. Restrictions on imports of capital equipment must be imposed with some regard to existing commitments and to local, regional, and industrial development. Given these conditions, the restrictions actually imposed constitute a fairly severe curtailment of the imports of nonessential items.

The major point of principle involved in the restrictions was the issue of discrimination versus nondiscrimination. There was much immediate logic in discrimination because most of the world outside the United States is short of Canadian dollars as well as U.S. dollars, and needs to increase exports to Canada as well as elsewhere. It appears antisocial internationally at the present time to restrict British, French, or Italian exports, however nonessential their use may be. Moreover, Canada's balances of trade and payments with nearly all countries other than the United States are favorable, and if there is to be a general movement to bilateral balancing, Canada might be inviting trouble and retaliation in cutting imports from a long list of countries to which she is exporting. On the other hand, Canada has at Geneva and elsewhere taken the same view as the United States in opposing the principle of discrimination in the application of exchange restrictions. If such discrimination is widely practiced abroad, Canadian exports are more likely to be placed at a disadvantage than they are to be favored. Finally, Canada's marginal imports from nearly all sources at present are paid for, from a short term viewpoint, in United

States dollars, because credits are limited, balances are settled in United States dollars, no clearing arrangements are in force, and few countries seem likely to increase or decrease their purchases in Canada as a direct result of increased or decreased Canadian purchases from them.

After weighing the conflicting considerations, the Canadian authorities came down strongly on the side of the principle of nondiscrimination in regard to the source of imports, but they applied the choice of items to be restricted and the bases of quotas in such a way as to do as little harm as possible to the export trade of countries that are in balance of payments difficulties. As a consequence, items that are prohibited are prohibited from all countries. Items that are restricted to a quota are divided into five or six major groups and quotas allotted to individual importers for each group as a whole, within which the importer may select items and sources of supply, subject to the area division which I will describe. In applying quotas to areas, the world outside Canada has been divided into two groups—one containing all those countries having balance-of-payments difficulties, and the other group including the United States, Switzerland, the U.S.S.R., and a handful of other small countries not known to be in balance-of-payments difficulties. Imports from each group of countries are restricted to total values for each group of restricted items that are some multiple of the value in a standard prewar period. This has the effect of seriously restricting the imports from the few countries not in dollar difficulties whose exports are now high compared to prewar levels, while permitting considerable expansion in the recent level of imports from all those countries that are short of dollars.

Notwithstanding the care it exercised in applying these restrictions in the way I have described, the Canadian Government has been strongly attacked in Parliament for adopting the principle of nondiscrimination, and it has been charged with doing so because it was forced into it by the United States. This the Canadian Government has denied, and it has defended the principle of nondiscrimination as well as the selective application of it. It has also emphasized that the restrictions on imports are to be temporary, and that anyone taking advantage of their protective effect to build up domestic production of excluded items cannot expect to have his vested interest recognized.[10]

The restrictions on imports of capital goods and structural materials (and moving picture films) are to be exercised administratively rather than by quotas, in order that due regard may be had for the end use and all the relevant circumstances. It is still too early, at the time of writing, to form any judgment as to how this control will operate and what savings in exchange it can effect. It is hoped in its application to secure the coöperation of industry in converting and expanding industrial capacity in those directions which will assist in securing a better balance in trade with the United States and the "dollar area"; for example, branch plants and subsidiaries of United States concerns are being persuaded to develop a more balanced trade with their parents and to obtain a share of export markets in the dollar area.

A word should be said about the curious spectacle of Canada borrowing from the Export-Import Bank—curious because Canada normally borrows from private American banks or sells securities in United States markets, and because the Export-Import Bank is not expected to lend to those who can borrow privately. The answer lies in the time factor. A relatively modest loan was required as an assurance against adverse contingencies and in order to give time for the other measures to take effect. The lender would need to know in advance the whole program in order to understand the purpose of the credit. In the case of a program of this kind, it was not considered possible to divulge in advance the nature and details of the program to private groups. Moreover, the amount required immediately as a standby was more than could be expected from a private loan, while a public market issue could hardly be considered under the circumstances, as the whole program was sure to be a subject of considerable public controversy in Canada as soon as it was announced and for some months thereafter. Consequently ar-

10 See for example the statement of the Minister of Finance on p. 1081 of *House of Commons Debates* (February 10, 1948), explaining that no assurance could be given even regarding the duration of the restriction, to enable Canadian producers to meet demands arising from the restrictions on imports.

rangements were made for a relatively short-term credit from the United States' own lending institution, with the expectation that Canada would subsequently investigate the possibilities of loans from banks or other institutional or private investors. Canada did investigate shortly afterwards the possibilities of a loan from New York banks, but found that the time was not favorable for such an operation, particularly as the banks were in considerable uncertainty and under some pressure to curtail loans, as a result of developments in monetary policy in the United States.

On the export side, the immediate problem is the recreation of an export surplus and the sale of a large portion of it for United States dollars. The important restrictions will, of course, help to make an export surplus, but an increase in exports would be a more constructive method, both to Canada and to others. There are, however, serious obstacles to any large, immediate increase. Canada is already fully employed, and the possibilities of increased production are limited, although there may be a few manufacturing lines that could expand and a few localities where primary production could be increased if markets were particularly favorable. The acute shortage of steel and electric power and the fairly general shortage of labor make it difficult to expand to meet opportunities that may arise. Moreover, the Government has relatively little control of production, distribution, and use of goods except in the case of steel, wheat, and a few minor products, and consequently has very limited power to direct resources into exports. Indeed, there would appear to be some danger that when domestic demand cannot expend itself on imports because of restrictions, it may ultimately result in diverting resources away from exports. Canada realizes the need for additional exports, and although the present level is very high, efforts are being made, both privately and by Government authorities, to expand them.

The amount of her exports which Canada can now afford to finance by credits or grants under present circumstances is limited, and in the case of the United Kingdom these limits are quite serious. In part, this arises from the fact that Canada is selling certain of her products, notably wheat, at prices determined by long term contracts, substantially below current world price levels, trading some of the present high returns for greater stability in the future. Some exports can be diverted from countries that cannot pay in cash to those which can, but the numbers of the latter are limited, and in any event it is highly desirable that such countries as Britain, France, and Holland should get the foodstuffs, raw materials, and industrial products they require from Canada. Yet they have great difficulty in paying in any currency that Canada can use to purchase her own requirements in the United States.

It is this situation which leads Canadians to hope that the ERP will permit substantial offshore purchases in Canada from United States funds, by or for Britain, France, Holland, and other European countries. It was this "offshore purchase" principle that helped so greatly to overcome Canada's acute dollar shortage in 1941 and 1942, for the financial aspects of the wartime Hyde Park Agreement consisted almost entirely, in the last analysis, of "offshore purchases" in Canada for the United States Services and for Lend-Lease requirements. Such purchases will not in themselves solve the dollar problem for Canada, for she must herself contrive to create a sufficient exportable surplus to cover that portion of her exports financed by herself, and as much more as is necessary to restore her exchange reserves to tolerable levels. Substantial ERP purchases will be required even to make possible the volume of exports to participating countries that are necessary for Canada to balance her accounts and purchase the restricted volume of imports from the United States, let alone any increase. Nor must it be thought that ERP will meet all such problems. A considerable part of Britain's problem and some part of Canada's arise from the requirements of the sterling area, apart from the United Kingdom and her colonies; India, Pakistan, and Australia, in particular, have serious dollar problems that apparently fall quite outside ERP.

Before closing it would seem desirable to say a little about future problems. Mention has already been made of the emphasis given by the Canadian Government to the positive side of its program in balancing its accounts, its intention to develop

Canadian resources and industry in order to bring about a better balance in trade with the United States, and the hope of a more far-reaching agreement for the reduction of tariffs between the two countries. This desire to turn more to trade with the United States reflects, I think, a consciousness of the importance of not having to rely so heavily upon trans-Atlantic trade as in the past. Canadians have a very keen realization of the importance to them of Britain and Western Europe, both economically and politically, and they have shown a readiness to act on that conviction both in war and afterwards. Nevertheless they also realize, I believe, that Britain and Europe have been forced by circumstances to a situation where they must, even over the long run, export more, or import less, or do some of each. Even with the aid contemplated under the Marshall Plan, Europe will remain poorer than it used to be, and very likely faced with less favorable terms of trade. She will have debts to repay not only to the United States, but to Canada too. Canada must, therefore, as part of North America, expect to import more from Europe over the long run. Whether she must also expect to export less to Europe than before is still uncertain. Nevertheless, Canada needs to export more than she did before the war, if she is to pay for anything like her current level of imports and to sustain something approaching full employment. For the reasons mentioned, Britain and Europe are not the best places to look for expanded markets. Consequently it is natural that she look to the United States. Later there should be opportunities elsewhere overseas—in the Far East, Africa, South America, India, and the Middle East—but none of these looks particularly promising in the near future.

Canada may be helped in achieving more balanced trade with the United States by the general shortage of food and raw materials that seems likely now to last for some years, and by the better relative prices for foodstuffs and raw materials, in comparison with industrial products, to which this shortage has led. The improved terms of trade of the primary producers appear likely now to persist for some time, despite the reluctance of industrial workers, both in North America and abroad, to accept the lower real incomes that this implies. Moreover, as long as the United States remains prosperous, she herself seems likely to offer to Canada and others a considerable market for foodstuffs and/or raw materials. Canada should be able to take advantage of this substantial nearby market at favorable prices to help correct some of the lack of balance in her trade. Like the rest of the world, she is uncertain how long American prosperity will last, on which this market is based, but at present there is sufficient confidence in the outlook in the United States to afford a basis for developing additional exports.

Despite these opportunities for primary production, I doubt whether Canada can achieve a balanced trade with the United States, or a satisfactory general level of trade and employment, without substantial industrial exports, either to the United States or to markets able to pay in American dollars. Now, perhaps for the first time, it is possible to contemplate such exports. Canada's industrial capacity has been increased greatly as a result of the war. Labor has learned new skills, and it has been found that Canadian labor can be fairly quickly trained to industrial processes. Management has gained in knowledge, efficiency, and confidence. It has been found that with market opportunities, Canadian business can produce at costs that frequently compare well with those in the United States—not in all lines, of course, but in some. Consequently there is a new willingness among Canadians to contemplate reduction or removal of tariffs on industrial products and competition with the United States, provided American markets are as open as Canadian. Moreover, there is a deliberate effort under way to develop and utilize natural resources with the correction of our trade balance in mind.

It must be recognized that there are important institutional difficulties in the face of industrial exports. Canada does not have a sufficiently large home market in many items to afford a secure base for low cost production that can be used for export promotion, and she needs to rely on some assurance of export markets to achieve competitive costs. Secondly, many important Canadian industrial concerns are subsidiaries or branches of American firms, and quite apart from any cartel complications, it is difficult for the child to compete with the parent in the latter's home market or in third markets. This is an aspect of our problems being explored at the present time, and there appears to be a better chance of overcoming it than was earlier believed. Another aspect of Canada's peculiarly close relationship with the United States that affects our ability to compete is the tie-in between our labor unions. With Canadian unions frequently forming part of large American unions, and subject to some considerable degree of influence as well as stimulus from the American side, Canadian industry cannot rely upon large wage differentials as a secure basis for competing with American producers.

Another problem in the competition with American industrial products is the great technological lead of American industry. In the cheap and standard products, one must expect overseas countries to make a very determined drive to enter the North American market and to compete with North American products abroad. Therefore, Canadian industry must expect to seek markets for more complicated, more expensive, and more specialized products, appropriate to the highly developed industrial economy of North America. In this field technological development is so rapid and so important that there is a great advantage to those whose size and wealth permit the experience and expense that lead to new developments. It will be difficult for all relatively small industrial powers, I believe, to overcome the large lead that the United States now has, in new processes, new materials, new designs, and new methods of cheaper production. This is one of those dynamic factors which seem to defy any quantitative or precise analysis or appraisal, but perhaps it merits more attention by students of international trade.

One aspect of the problem of industrial exports which provides grounds for hope is the trend in U.S. tariff and commercial policy. Viewed from north of the border, there appears to be a consciousness of the need for a more liberal import policy and substantially lower tariffs, not only in administration circles but in important sections of public opinion. Real reductions have been made in American tariffs in the past fifteen years, especially in their real burden when allowance is made for higher prices. Tariffs are still high in many items, of course, and they are reinforced by customs procedures and laws that are strongly protective in conception and execution. Canadians hope and even expect that means will be found to get U.S. tariffs down considerably more, not only on Canadian goods, but on those from overseas countries as well. It is not possible in this paper to go into the problems and prospects of tariff relations between the two countries, but it does seem worth noting that Canadian authorities feel it is desirable and feasible to work toward agreement on further substantial reductions.

As yet, only the negative and emergency measures in the Canadian program to meet the dollar problem have been implemented to any considerable degree. Over the long run, the positive measures to increase exports to the United States would seem the ones most deserving of emphasis. In the present world situation, however, it seems to be good sense to emphasize the negative aspects—the restriction of imports to Canada, and of the Canadian use of her own resources for domestic purposes. Canada is already producing at near maximum capacity. Only by reducing imports and consumption or domestic investment can she hope now to build up an export surplus. Only by creating an export surplus can she provide the rest of the world with the real resources it needs from Canada for reconstruction and recovery. Only if that export surplus is directed to overseas countries rather than the United States will it be going where it is most needed in the general interest. Negative measures in the present Canadian program, together with the positive measures of the Marshall Plan, will be needed to secure these results.

# 8

## *SOME ASPECTS OF LATIN AMERICAN ECONOMIC RELATIONS WITH THE UNITED STATES*[1]

Henry C. Wallich

Our relations with Latin America, after reaching a height of friendliness during the war, appear to have entered upon a temporary lull. The change in atmosphere, which is apparent from a variety of public and private utterances on both sides[2] and which recent official emphasis on the Pan American System cannot altogether conceal, is to some extent a natural reaction from the war years. The wartime pitch of emotional intensity, particularly on the side of the United States, could hardly have been sustained permanently. A letdown is quite understandable and will no doubt yield in time to a more considered attitude.

There also are, however, a number of concrete difficulties. Latin America not unreasonably is disappointed with the looks of postwar reality, after the glowing expectations aroused during the war. Latin Americans hoped, and they were encouraged in this by the United States, that a variety of measures would be taken which would rapidly raise their standards of living.

[1] Although the author is chief of the Foreign Research Division of the Federal Reserve Bank of New York, the views expressed here are his own.

[2] Cf. "Recommendations," *Revista del Banco de la Republica,* Bogota (Dec., 1947), pp. 981-985. Editorial. *Revista Bancaria Brasileira* (Dec. 20, 1947), p. 2; Statement of Diego Molinari, Argentine delegate to the ITO Conference, *New York Times* (Dec. 4, 1947); Olive Holmes, "Latin America and the United States—Problems of Economic Readjustment," *Foreign Policy Reports,* Vol. XXIII, No. 21 (Jan. 15, 1948), pp. 262-271; "Economic Aspects of the Bogota Conference," Department of State *Bulletin* (Dec. 21, 1947), p. 1216; Acierto, *Inter-American Economic Affairs* (Sept. 1947), pp. 3-20; Arthur P. Whitaker, "Rio and Bogota: Pan-American Perspective," *Inter-American Economic Affairs* (Dec. 1947), pp. 23-44.

Among these were exchange stabilization, industrialization programs, the freeing of international trade, and commodity price stabilization. These and other good things were expected to be obtained through United States initiative and money, and with the aid also of the exchange balances that Latin American countries had accumulated in varying degrees.

The reality that Latin Americans now face is very different, and they are understandably disturbed about it. Their reaction almost inevitably takes the form of complaints about the United States. Chief among their complaints are these: (1) wartime exchange accumulations, derived from exports to the United States at OPA ceiling prices, have melted under the heat of American inflation; (2) development loans, which at Bretton Woods were intended to have equal priority with reconstruction loans, have not been forthcoming in any volume; (3) international monetary conditions, which were to be straightened out by the Monetary Fund, continue in disorder; (4) attempts to free international trade, through the ITO Charter, appear to be aimed primarily at depriving growing countries of their protective devices instead of securing broader markets for them; (5) nothing at all has been done for long-run commodity price stabilization; and (6) the recent development of the European Recovery Program threatens to perpetuate the shortage of investment goods as well as of investment funds available to Latin America.

In some United States quarters, on the other hand, there is a tendency to argue that Latin American countries are in large part to blame for their own predicament. A more determined effort on their part to put their houses in order and to draw on their own resources, it is said, would take care of a good many of the problems that are now being dumped at the door of the United States. This country, it is argued, should apply to Latin America criteria similar to the standards of self-help that are now being made a prerequisite for aid to European countries.

There is some truth to the allegations on both sides, but a rational approach should be able to bridge these differences. From the United States viewpoint, it should be recognized that

Latin America is being asked to make substantial sacrifices in terms of hopes and programs. Whatever can be done to satisfy legitimate Latin American needs, within the limits set by the more urgent European program, should be undertaken. Those who are critical of Latin American performance on exchange control, for instance, should consider that in many other fields Latin American countries have managed their postwar transition with a good deal of success.

On the other hand, Latin Americans who are disappointed by current United States attitudes should not overlook the great benefits that will accrue to them from the reconstruction of Europe, both in an immediate financial sense and in terms of more balanced international relations. Finally, they should remember that the United States has fulfilled what two years ago was universally regarded as the main condition of worldwide prosperity: maintenance of a high American income. Full employment here has been mainly responsible for preventing a collapse anywhere in Latin America. Granting that it has been full employment with a vengeance, and has brought a number of disagreeable surprises, there is no doubt that a depression would have been a great deal worse for Latin America.

For the United States, however, this lull in relations with Latin America, temporary though it may be, poses a rather serious question of principle. If the attitudes of our own public and the policies of our government are subject to considerable short-run fluctuations, how will it be possible to find international acceptance of American world leadership which circumstances seem to impose upon this nation? Clearly, there can be no confidence in any country's leadership unless its policies, whatever they may be, are clearly defined and reasonably stable.

National policies and attitudes inevitably are the reflection of national interests. Recent vacillations seem to indicate that as a nation the United States has not yet succeeded in defining clearly and realistically what its interests in the Latin American sphere are. If the United States knew—a matter of instinct and old habit—what it primarily wanted from Latin America, whether it be help in the maintenance of democratic ideals, or markets and sources of raw materials, or military and political support, it would not so easily find itself blowing hot and cold in quick succession. This lack of instinctive certainty in such matters may in part be the result of relative inexperience in international politics. In part, however, it is undoubtedly attributable to the fact that United States interests in Latin America, economically at least, are not really critical. If tomorrow's dinner depended on the nature of our dealings with Argentina, as it does for Britain, the United States would soon be forced to find a basic line of policy and stick to it. But since all that seems to be at stake are export markets of only moderate importance, political friendships most of which the country feels reasonably sure of anyhow, and raw material supplies for which the United States is the only solvent market, United States policy has been able to drift without courting immediate disaster.

This lack of deeply rooted interests in Latin America is reflected also in the practices of American private enterprise. There are few industries that regard their international connections as so vital that they would be willing to make major sacrifices to preserve them, let alone put them ahead of domestic interests. With some exceptions, there has been a tendency on the part of manufacturing exporters to disregard Latin American needs whenever the going became difficult or when the home pastures looked greener. Everybody is familiar with the complaint that we are fair weather sailors in the matter of credit and supplies, while the British are said to be willing to stick by their customers during bad times. Part of the explanation, no doubt, is the older experience and longer view of the British. Another part of it, however, is that very few of our businessmen have to regard Latin American business as their bread and butter. Even for those who have important international connections, the latter are usually the cake and candy of the business which they can forego in difficult times.

I do not want to dwell exclusively on negative aspects, however. In the zigzag line of United States relations with Latin America there is a distinctly upward trend. In the economic sphere the last decade has intensified our trade relations, although the share of the United States in Latin America's trade will fall again as European supplies reappear. United States direct investors have increased their participation in Latin America, while European capitalists have been forced to retreat. Politically, fairly impressive cohesion has been maintained despite recent stresses and strains. The Rio pact for hemisphere defense has been signed, and work toward more intensive co-operation continues in other fields.

There can be no doubt, on the whole, that the efforts made before and during the war to come to an ever closer understanding have borne some permanent fruit. One need not be too concerned, therefore, about short-term fluctuations in United States-Latin American relations and about the alleged present loss of "goodwill," which one often hears about in statements emanating from Latin America. In the long run what will count is, not good will, but the basic nature of our mutual interests. With most of Latin America our interests are complementary and have been made more so by the war. The best way to ensure continued progress in United States-Latin American relations is to disregard temporary disappointments and to go on exploring and implementing these mutual interests.

### *Postwar Developments*

Two major aspects have characterized Latin American economic conditions since the end of the war: the continuance of inflation, and the onset of the dollar shortage. The two are intimately related.

When the war ended, it was widely expected that high war-time prices would wilt under the impact of reduced strategic-material exports and larger imports. For a short time declining price tendencies actually were in evidence in a number of countries, seemingly corroborating these pessimistic expectations. Very soon, however, it became apparent that aggregate exports were rising instead of falling, while the expected flood of imports failed to materialize. During the early part of 1946, therefore, inflationary tendencies originating in the balance of payments resumed sway with new vigor.

These tendencies were intensified by a number of factors

which for the most part were already present during the war. Among them were: pressure for higher wages, the rising cost of such imports as were available, particularly after the lifting of OPA ceilings, intensive investment activity, and credit expansion through borrowing by governments and business. It was this credit expansion that constitutes the chief connecting link between inflation and the dollar shortage.

One might have thought that so long as exports continued in high gear, no lack of foreign exchange was likely to be experienced. The expansion of the money supply through government deficits and business borrowing, however, created a mass of purchasing power greatly in excess of exchange availabilities, and this purchasing power in large part made itself eventually felt as demand for imports. When these became available, balances of payments almost universally turned passive, and the disproportion between exchange reserves and money supplies became apparent. How large a part of reserves was dissipated in the importation of luxury goods is something that only a detailed statistical investigation could show. There is some preliminary evidence indicating that, despite current impressions to the contrary, the proportion of luxury imports was not high. What seems to be undeniable, however, is that import licenses were being granted with very little regard to exchange availabilities. To the authorities of a number of countries it therefore came as a distinct surprise when suddenly they found themselves faced with a very serious shrinkage in resources. The West Coast countries, whose wartime exchange accumulations had been relatively small, were the first to encounter this predicament. The East Coast countries, notably Argentina, had much larger resources to draw upon. Most of the East Coast countries, however, were seriously affected by the inconvertibility of sterling. Their problem was less a general exchange shortage than a specific dollar shortage.

This experience naturally has been a severe disappointment to Latin Americans, although it should not be allowed to obscure the favorable basic fact that virtually all countries have enjoyed good or even booming business conditions. The experience furnishes an interesting commentary on one of the standbys of wartime "postwar" discussions—the importance, for all the world, of continued full employment in the United States. This panacea appears to have proved itself to the extent that, as already noted, full employment in this country has in fact prevented a collapse in any Latin American country. Its validity must be qualified, however, on two counts. In the first place, our full employment has affected different countries in varying degrees, and there is no assurance that by itself it will assure permanently high exports for each individual country. In the second place, it is quite obvious that United States full employment does not solve all problems. Serious difficulties may still arise if the price of United States exports is driven up unduly, or if Latin American countries pursue excessively expansionary policies at home.

### *"Fomento"*

The policies currently pursued by Latin American countries necessarily are mainly concerned with the solution of these short-run difficulties. The dominant long-run preoccupation, however, and one intimately affecting United States-Latin American relations, is economic development—"fomento." Economic development has been a major aim of Latin American economic policy for a long time, but in recent years it has come to overshadow almost everything else. Latin Americans have presented their developmental problems as a key issue at successive international conferences. Instances of this are Chapultepec, where emphasis was placed on postwar exchange control as a means of conserving dollars for development; Bretton Woods, where intensive efforts were made to give development the same priority as reconstruction; and the ITO conference at Havana, where development became a stumbling block to the elimination of quantitative trade restrictions.

Development involves two major ideas: (1) an increase in production and living standards in general, and (2) diversification of production, chiefly in the direction of industrialization. To some extent these two aspects are antithetical. The largest production increase usually can be obtained by more intensive use of existing basic resources, in the direction of a higher degree of international specialization. Diversification in a raw material country, on the other hand, means industrialization and hence points in the direction of less international specialization. Nevertheless, there obviously is a wide range over which these aims are quite compatible.

Even where some sacrifice of productivity seems to be involved, diversification is worthwhile if the country in question is excessively dependent upon foreign markets and particularly upon the sale of only one or two commodities. Experience has shown that in the present uncertain state of international trade, specialization is a gamble that a responsible government must try to avoid. The least that nations with agricultural opportunities, such as abound in most areas of Latin America, should aim at is to be able to feed themselves from their own produce, so that they can sit out a depression without suffering actual starvation.

The stimulation of manufacturing industry, even when the economic benefits are doubtful in the short run, frequently is justified by the favorable long-run effects that a growing demand for more highly skilled labor exerts upon the general level of the population. Experience in raw material countries shows that specialization in a few crops, involving the use of a large illiterate mass of unskilled labor, rarely redounds to the advantage of that group. In one way or another, the masses' willingness to work for a low wage stands in the way of their own progress. The gains from international division of labor therefore flow largely to the owners, or are diverted, through deterioration of the terms of trade, to the consuming population of the industrial countries. One of the best ways of raising living standards in raw material countries is to channel the laboring masses into employment where higher qualifications are required. The general human and educational improvement that comes from such work, at the same time that it increases productivity and living standards, also helps to justify the existence of industries that originally may have been uneconomic.

The effects of Latin American industrialization on United States trade have been much discussed. The easy generalization frequently put forward that our trade is more intensive with industrial than with raw material countries certainly is far from satisfying. Nevertheless, it does appear that the United States, as a seller of heavy equipment, is much more likely to find this generalization true than countries selling chiefly consumer goods. At the same time, Latin American development gives us an opportunity to even up the balance of payments through productive foreign lending. It also offers the prospect that foreign countries eventually will partly free themselves of dependence upon our consumer goods and thus restrain the active tendency in our balance of payments. Perhaps that will be one way toward an organic solution of this balance of payments problem. From the political point of view, the greater stability and responsibility that growing economic maturity is likely to bring to Latin American countries will be welcome to the United States.

Despite the many favorable things that can be said about Latin American development policies, however, one can not avoid certain doubts about several of their aspects. In the first place there is the question of timing. Most Latin American countries still continue in an inflationary phase. The limits, therefore, to which development programs can be pushed without engendering further inflation probably are a good deal narrower than many Latin Americans would like to admit. The experience of Argentina under the five-year plan is a warning example. I very much doubt whether forced saving through inflation can be made a really effective means of financing development, or that anything more than a very mild degree of inflation is a worthwhile price to pay for it.

A second doubt involves the motivation of many small industrial projects. Where the market is so narrow that only small-scale plants are feasible, employing a negligible amount of labor and perhaps relying on imported raw materials, demands for heavy tariff or other protection in the name of development have scant merit. Such "development" may involve little more than the creation of a permanent monopoly for a small group of entrepreneurs. In such cases, labor fails to benefit and the consumer may be permanently worse off.

A third question is the degree to which the drive for development comes from an excess of nationalistic feeling rather than from a desire for higher living standards. It is entirely understandable that rather pronounced antiforeign tendencies should exist in Latin America. But the attempt to become "independent" of foreign countries, in the sense not only of eliminating foreign influence but of becoming self-sufficient, is entirely hopeless for countries with Latin America's economic structure, and its pursuit likely to be ruinous.

Fourthly, Latin Americans may find it advisable to be on guard, in their own interest, against some of the political aspects of development. Ambitious schemes of this type usually have a strong attraction for a growing bureaucracy and for governments eager to consolidate their position by handing out contracts and by purchasing strategically owned land sites, and generally glad to use economic policies toward political ends. If such motives should dictate development policies, much of the money and effort poured into them will be wasted.

In most cases, development involves the importation of foreign capital. It should not be overlooked, therefore, that the attractive new slogan covers an age-old process, the borrowing of money, in one form or another, by a poorer country from a richer one. For the duration of the European Recovery Program at least, most of this inflow of capital is likely to be in the form of private foreign investment, rather than governmental loans.[3] It is interesting, therefore, to survey some of the factors that recently have been influencing the outlook for private investment. Ostensibly, considerable improvements have taken place compared with the discouraging treatment that foreign investors suffered during the thirties. The Monetary Fund and the proposed ITO agreements carry provisions safeguarding the foreign investor as to both the transfer of funds and the investor's competitive position in the country where he operates. Several countries, among them Argentina and Brazil, have specifically provided for limited transfer of profits in their

[3] In his speech at the Bogotá conference, Secretary Marshall stated that for the duration of the European Recovery Program, private investment would have to carry most of the burden of Latin American development.

present exchange control systems. There also has been some liberalization of legislation affecting the rights of foreign investors to develop basic natural resources, and in general the welcome sign has been hung out to American capital.

Nevertheless, the general climate is not yet particularly reassuring. At the end of the war, it is true, there appeared to be a considerable number of United States firms with plans for "going into Latin America." This would have signified a continuation of a trend that had become evident during the war, particularly in the direction of Mexico. It seems, however, that this interest has since cooled off considerably. No doubt the dollar shortage, threatening the nontransfer of profits, has something to do with this. It is also being said, however, that many executives have become discouraged over labor conditions, government regulations, ultranationalistic tendencies, and the general prospects for doing business on a satisfactory basis. If this be true, Latin America would seem to have chased away the goose that was to lay the golden eggs.

If the policy of the United States Government should continue to be that of letting private capital bear most of the burden of financing Latin American development, these countries would have to modify some present practices so as to create genuinely attractive conditions for private enterprise or else give up part of their developmental ambitions. While many of the policies and trends that have tended to scare away American capital could in fact be corrected without undue sacrifice on the part of the recipient countries, many legitimate aspirations are also involved that deserve to be recognized. In most instances, these conflicts of interest should be quite capable of being bridged.

Nevertheless, the active intervention of a foreign element in a national economy, which is the essence of direct foreign investment, is always a possible source of friction. Although this certainly does not imply that direct foreign investment is undesirable, it does seem to suggest that it is perhaps not the final form of international investment. Direct foreign investment is an essential stage, so long as managerial and technical skills are important ingredients of such investment. Eventually, however, it will become desirable to shift the emphasis from direct investment to portfolio investment in foreign equities, that is, stock ownership by individual United States residents in enterprises managed and controlled by Latin Americans. This form of investment would eliminate many of the frictions inherent in direct foreign investment, while preserving most of its flexibility. It is one of the forms in which Europe financed the United States and in which the United States in part financed Canada. It is true that at present the security markets in the United States are almost completely unreceptive to Latin American equities. Eventually, however, this attitude may change. I believe that in facilitating the introduction of Latin American equities in our capital markets, we have an important opportunity for improving the technique of our foreign lending as well as our general economic relations with Latin America.

*Latin America in the European Recovery Program*

The foregoing reflections on development programs refer largely to the longer run. The more immediate outlook for Latin America will be shaped predominantly by the European Recovery Program.

When the Marshall Plan first began to take shape, voices arose in Latin America calling for a similar project for our southern neighbors. The most specific of these suggestions was a Colombian proposal to the Pan American Union for a five billion dollar development loan which was brought up at the Bogotá Conference. Under United States pressure, economic issues were not considered at the Rio conference. There, as well as at Bogotá, it was made clear that this country could not undertake an additional major effort at a time when our resources already were strained by domestic demand. Latin Americans were left to contemplate gloomily the postponement for several years of their development hopes, with the added fear that much of the equipment they had planned to buy would remain unobtainable, even for cash.

While the postponement of development plans is in effect a considerable blow, there is every prospect that Latin America will nevertheless benefit substantially from the ERP in more than one sense. For Latin America, the basic aspect of the program is that if it succeeds in rehabilitating Europe, it will thereby restore Latin America's traditional position in a multilateral network of political and economic relationships. Latin America, being able to lean on Europe as well as on the United States, to that extent will be less dependent on either. Economically at least, the advance of the iron curtain to the shores of the Atlantic would be even more disastrous for most Latin American countries than for the United States.

Apart from this basic structural significance of the ERP, many Latin American countries will benefit immediately in dollars and cents—notably Argentina, Brazil, Cuba, and Uruguay. The report of the Committee on European Economic Coöperation called for Latin American and Canadian supplies to the tune of two billion dollars during 1948 alone. The reworking of the proposals in Washington, where many of the estimates were cut, increased substantially the amount to be spent in the offshore procurement program for the fifteen-month period beginning April 1, 1948.

The golden ring of these figures, however, which are far in excess of Latin American and Canadian sales to Europe in 1947, is marred by a dissonance resulting from the uncertainty over the method of payment. Diametrically opposed to the Latin American suggestion that all shipments be paid by the United States in dollars, is Ex-President Hoover's proposal that no dollars at all be made available for this purpose. Latin America would then be left to finance its shipments by means of credits. The Administration proposal takes an intermediate position, calling for dollar financing to the extent indicated above, but at the same time asking the other American countries to authorize the equivalent of 700 million dollars in grants and credits for the period April 1948-June 1949.

Whatever compromise may be reached on this score should take into account three objectives: (1) it should provide Latin America with an incentive for maximum production, in order to increase over-all supplies available under the program; (2) it should minimize inflationary pressures upon the United States, not only those emanating directly from the recovery program, but also those that would result from the respending by Latin America of dollars received for shipments to Europe; and (3) it should avoid the creation of unmanageable indebtedness on the part of Europe, while at the same time laying a basis for continued healthy exports from Latin America and for conditions favorable to a development program.

Among the means for meeting these objectives might be long-term price maintenance agreements, which Latin America would like to have in any case. They might be combined with stockpiling plans for the United States. Another device might be the use of "delayed availability dollars" which could be given to Latin America in payment of part of its European shipments, and which would remain frozen for a specified period. Finally, a comprehensive development program might be drafted, to be put into execution at a later date, when the abatement of inflationary pressures both here and in Latin America would make its execution less burdensome and more productive.

# 9

## THE U.S.S.R. IN THE WORLD ECONOMY

Paul A. Baran

With the war only recently concluded, and with the contours of the new balance of power still in dim and distant sight, it may be premature to attempt a forecast of the part that the U.S.S.R. will play in the world's future economic developments. It may be useful nonetheless to sketch some of the more conspicuous changes that have occurred in Russia's foreign economic relations as a result of the war and to consider briefly their probable implications.

### I

From the very beginning of its existence the Soviet Government has been determined to conduct Russia's foreign economic relations in strict accordance with the requirements of its domestic economic planning and as an integral part of its foreign policy. Tariffs and exchange regulations were not regarded by Lenin as sufficiently reliable for attaining this end. Nothing short of a state monopoly embracing all of Russia's foreign economic transactions, it was believed, would guarantee the effective management of foreign trade by the central authorities. Established as one of the first institutions of the new republic, the foreign trade monopoly remains today among the most characteristic features of the Soviet economic system. Its organization, to be sure, has undergone in the meantime a number of important changes.[1] Essentially, however, it now operates as it has throughout, in accordance with its basic

[1] The organizational development of the foreign trade monopoly is described in Alexander Baykov, *Soviet Foreign Trade* (Princeton, N. J., 1946), pp. 23-40.

statute promulgated as early as April 22, 1918.[2] As a later official statement succinctly notes:

"the essence [of the monopoly of foreign trade] consists in the provisions that the state itself conducts foreign trade through a specially established agency [Peoples Commissariat for Foreign Trade[3]]; that the state determines the fields and limits within which the specified organizations are to carry on direct foreign trade operations; that the state stipulates, in accordance with the needs of economic progress and socialist construction, by means of an export-import plan, what goods and in what quantities may be shipped out of and into the country; and that the state through a system of licenses and quotas directly regulates imports and exports and the operations of foreign-trade agencies."[4]

The permanency of this institutional framework, underscored by the inclusion of an appropriate provision in the Soviet Constitution,[5] is paralleled by the stability of the basic trend of Soviet foreign trade. As Table 1 shows, not only did it not return at any time to prewar levels either in volume, value, or relation to total world trade, but with the exception of one short interval, it consistently declined throughout the entire interwar period.

This period as a whole may be conveniently subdivided into three distinct phases. The decade from the Revolution to the inauguration of the First Five-Year Plan in 1928 constituted the

[2] Article I of that decree stipulates that "commercial transactions involving purchases and sales of all kinds of products [of the extracting industries, manufacturing industries, agriculture, etc.] from and to foreign states and from and to individual trading enterprises abroad are to be conducted on behalf of the Russian Republic by specially authorized agencies. All commercial import and export transactions with foreign countries outside of these agencies are prohibited." Quoted in I. I. Evtikhiev i V. A. Vlasov, *Administrativnoye Pravo SSSR* (Administrative Law of the U.S.S.R.) (Moscow, 1946), p. 76.

[3] Now called Ministry of Foreign Trade.

[4] Resolution of the Plenary Session of the Central Committee of the Communist Party of the Soviet Union (October 1925) as published in "VKP (B) v Resolutsiakh i Resheniakh S'ezdov, Konferentsii i Plenumov TS.K" (CP of the SU in *Resolutions and Decisions of Congresses, Conferences, and Plenary Sessions of the Central Committee),* part 2 (Moscow, 1941), pp. 34-35.

[5] The Constitution (Fundamental Law) of the Union of Soviet Socialist Republics, Chapter II, Article 14, provides: "The jurisdiction of the Union of Soviet Socialist Republics as represented by its higher organs of state power and organs of state administration embraces . . . (h) foreign trade on the basis of state monopoly." Information bulletin of the Embassy of the U.S.S.R. (Washington, D. C.).

TABLE 1
FOREIGN TRADE OF THE U.S.S.R.[a][b]

| Year | EXPORTS Volume in thousand metric tons | EXPORTS Value In million 1936 rubles | EXPORTS Value As % of total world exports | IMPORTS Volume In thousand metric tons | IMPORTS Value In million 1936 rubles | IMPORTS Value As % of total world imports | Excess of exports (+) or imports (−) (million rubles) |
|---|---|---|---|---|---|---|---|
| | (1) | (2) | (3) | (4) | (5) | (6) | (7) |
| 1909–13 (annual average) | 24,590.8 | 6,513.9 | 4.0[c] | 11,240.7 | 4,994.1 | 2.9[c] | +1,519.8 |
| 1913 | 24,112.8 | 6,596.4 | 3.8 | 15,342.8 | 6,022.5 | 3.2 | + 573.9 |
| 1919 | 0.9 | 0.4 | | 8.5 | 14.0 | | − 13.6 |
| 1920 | 11.1 | 6.1 | | 85.3 | 125.7 | | − 119.6 |
| 1921–22 | 726.7 | 277.9 | | 1,989.1 | 1,187.4 | | − 909.5 |
| 1922–23 | 2,160.8 | 583.4 | | 907.5 | 650.9 | | − 67.5 |
| 1923–24 | 6,736.9 | 1,626.1 | 0.7 | 979.2 | 1,022.7 | 0.4 | + 603.4 |
| 1924–25 | 6,169.0 | 2,447.3 | 0.9 | 1,863.7 | 3,168.5 | 1.1 | − 721.2 |
| 1925–26 | 7,855.8 | 2,963.6 | 1.1 | 1,547.3 | 3,312.6 | 1.1 | − 349.0 |
| 1926–27 | 9,573.0 | 3,417.4 | 1.2 | 1,846.5 | 3,125.6 | 1.1 | + 291.8 |
| 1927–28 | 8,873.7 | 3,424.1 | 1.2 | 2,014.3 | 4,141.3 | 1.3 | − 717.2 |
| 1929 | 14,145.0 | 4,045.8 | 1.4 | 1,936.7 | 3,857.0 | 1.2 | + 188.8 |
| 1930 | 21,486.4 | 4,539.3 | 1.9 | 2,855.9 | 4,637.5 | 1.8 | − 98.2 |
| 1931 | 21,778.9 | 3,553.1 | 2.1 | 3,564.4 | 4,839.9 | 2.6 | −1,286.8 |
| 1932 | 17,967.9 | 2,518.2 | 2.2 | 2,322.1 | 3,083.5 | 2.5 | − 565.3 |
| 1933 | 17,916.3 | 2,167.5 | 2.1 | 1,236.1 | 1,525.1 | 1.4 | + 642.4 |
| 1934 | 17,340.2 | 1,832.4 | 1.8 | 1,025.2 | 1,018.0 | 0.9 | + 814.4 |
| 1935 | 17,190.4 | 1,609.3 | 1.6 | 1,259.1 | 1,057.2 | 1.0 | + 552.1 |
| 1936 | 14,204.0 | 1,359.1 | 1.2 | 1,155.3 | 1,352.5 | 1.1 | + 6.6 |
| 1937 | 12,969.4 | 1,728.6 | 1.2 | 1,285.8 | 1,341.3 | 0.9 | + 387.3 |
| 1938 | 9,682.3 | 1,331.9 | 1.1 | 1,127.2 | 1,422.9 | 1.1 | − 91.0 |

[a]Except for columns 3 and 6, which are calculated on the basis of data published by the League of Nations in *Review of World Trade 1938* (Geneva, 1939), the statistics are from S. N. Bakulin, D. D. Mishustin, *Statistika Vneshney Torcovli*, Statistics of Foreign Trade, (Moscow, 1940).

[b]It should be noted that only the figures from 1927–28 on are completely comparable, since in earlier years both the territory and the methods of computation were different. All ruble amounts are in terms of the 1936 parity; one old gold ruble was the equivalent of 4.38 post-1936 gold rubles. To obtain the dollar value of Russian imports and exports, the ruble values have to be divided by 5.3.

[c]Data on total world trade for the years 1910–13, inclusive, were taken from the *Statistical Abstract of the United States, 1914*, and an average for these years was computed. The total trade was then broken down on the assumption, based on the 1913 League of Nations statistics, that 52 per cent of the total was imports, and 48 per cent exports.

"prehistory" of Soviet economic planning. In spite of the vast economic and political powers held by the state, the reconstruction of the Russian economy, devastated by seven years of war, foreign intervention, and civil strife, was largely left to "automatic" forces. Although economic planning was explored as to theory, prepared for from the point of view of organization, and even actually attempted, it was confined at that time to certain specific sectors of the economy (for example, electrification and the restoration of the Ukraine metallurgical industry) without any attempt being made to modify significantly the direction of the country's economic development. To reach prewar levels of output as fast as possible was the avowed goal of the Soviet Government, and the strengthening of its political base by healing the wounds of the foreign and civil wars and by raising the standard of living of the population was one of the principal objectives of its economic policy.

Russia's foreign trade was conducted accordingly. Its almost complete breakdown in the first four to five years after the Revolution was followed by a partial recovery in the middle twenties. The restoration of agricultural production made possible the resumption of agricultural exports, and the structure of imports expressed on the whole the "consumer-oriented" economic policy of the government. Until 1924-25 the bulk of the imports consisted of consumers' goods or of raw materials needed for their manufacturing in Russia: "......Throughout the period the *total* import of producers' goods remained at a lower level than in 1909-1913; there were fewer imports of machinery, boilers, apparatus and parts, iron and steel goods, rubber in sheets, and roller latex, chemicals and pharmaceutical products. . . . ."[6] Limited only by the amounts of foreign exchange secured through exports, gold sales, and insignificant borrowing abroad, Russian imports in the years of reconstruction contributed somewhat to the alleviation of the worst consumer goods' shortages, and at the same time replenished equipment, repair parts, and raw materials indispensable to the restoration of the Russian economy.

The situation changed sharply towards the end of the re-

[6] Alexander Baykov, *Soviet Foreign Trade*, p. 46.

construction period. At the crossroads between the "drifting" of the N.E.P. years,[7] and an all-out effort to solve Russia's basic economic and political contradictions by a rapid increase and reorientation of its industrial and agricultural output, the Soviet Government, after a lengthy and dramatic period of violent controversy, adopted in 1928 the latter course. The inauguration of the First Five-Year Plan, the specific programs and goals of which were the subject of thorough exploration and the cause of further intense dissent, marked the beginning of actual economic planning in Russia. The aims of this planning are known: industrialization and the socialization of agriculture were to be accomplished in the shortest possible time in order to develop the productive resources of the country, raise the living standard of its population, and assure the economic independence and military impregnability of the Soviet Union.

Foreign trade was to play a major part in this ambitious effort. Russian industry, even after having reached prewar levels of output, was too small and too backward to serve as a sufficient basis for the expansion envisaged in the First Five-Year Plan. Modern machinery, up-to-date equipment, and technical knowledge had to be imported on a large scale from the leading industrial countries of the world. Since the long-term foreign credits or capital imports that usually facilitated the industrialization of other countries were not available to the USSR, the imports needed for its investment program had to be paid for by exports.

Yet the Russian economy had very few exportable surpluses.[8] Without drastic increase in total output, such surpluses could

[7] This is the familiar abbreviation for the New Economic Policy introduced by Lenin in 1921 and continued until 1928 when the First Five-Year Plan was launched.

[8] Exports of grain and other agricultural raw materials that bulked large in Russia's prewar exports had to be curtailed considerably in view of the markedly increasing domestic demand. This increase was due partly to the growth of the urban population and partly to larger consumption on the part of the producing peasants: "In Russia during the five years 1908-1913, the average production of grains [not including grains used for seed] was 378 kg. per capita, only 2 kg. more than in Germany, a grain-importing country. The production of oats in Russia was 400-500 kg. per horse; in Germany 2,000 kg. Russia was able to export so much grain only because consumption by the population was very low." *Report to the Council of Ministers* (1916), as quoted in A. Yugow, *Russia's Economic Front for War and Peace* (New York and London, 1942), p. 101.

not be looked for either in industry or in agriculture. A significant increase of total output was, however, impossible without imported industrial machinery, electrical equipment, agricultural implements, and the like.

To many inside and outside the Soviet Union the circle appeared vicious. The solution adopted by Stalin's Government was the utmost reduction of domestic consumption with the view to "squeezing out" all possible exports of consumers' goods, and the stimulation of the production of those exportable commodities of which the output could be most easily expanded. The most important of these were furs, lumber, and oil products, the exports of which increased very much during the First Five-Year Plan. Of equal if not larger importance were the growing production and exports of gold made possible by the extensive prospecting during the preceding years.

This export drive, conducted at the cost of considerable domestic sacrifice, was calculated to yield sufficient foreign exchange to pay for the imports upon which the realization of the Five-Year Plan was largely predicated. Matters did not develop, however, as anticipated. The great depression which coincided with the First Five-Year Plan period had a disastrous effect on Russia's terms of trade. Prices of Russia's exports—primarily agricultural products and raw materials—dropped much more than the prices of its imports—chiefly industrial commodities. In order to secure the planned quantities of imports, the volume of exports had to be expanded beyond the original estimates. Shortages of food and other consumer goods at home were disastrously aggravated. The disturbing effect of the depression was somewhat offset, to be sure, by the sharp increase in the purchasing power of gold. Exports of the latter commodity assumed large significance, paying for almost 25 per cent of Russia's total imports. At the same time, the competition among foreign exporters, eager to do business with Russia, enabled the country to secure much more favorable credit terms than previously. Although such credits were granted only on a short-term basis, they enabled the U.S.S.R. to raise its imports during the First Five-Year Plan period by about 2 billion 1936 rubles above the value of its exports.

The original directive concerning the First Five-Year Plan, formulated by the Fifteenth Congress of the Communist Party of the Soviet Union, which instructed the Soviet Government to conduct Russia's foreign trade so as to secure favorable balances and accumulate foreign exchange reserves, was far from being fulfilled.[10] Nevertheless, the imports most essential for the execution of the First Five-Year Plan were obtained, and thus the crucial prerequisites for its success secured. In the words of Stalin,

> ...... of the 1½ billion rubles spent in this period on the equipment of our heavy industry, [half could have been allocated] for importation of cotton, leather, wool, rubber, etc. In that case, we would have had more cotton goods, shoes, clothing. But we would not have had either a tractor industry or an automobile industry, nor would we have had anything like a worth-while heavy metallurgy, nor enough metal for the production of machinery, and we would have been disarmed in the face of a capitalist encirclement equipped with modern technique. We would have deprived ourselves of the possibility of supplying agriculture with tractors and agricultural implements, and would therefore have had to go without bread. We would not have had the modern means of defense without which an independent political existence of a country is impossible, without which our country would become an object of the military operations of foreign enemies.[11]

With the completion of the First Five-Year Plan, the Russian industrialization program became technologically almost self-propelling. The Russian economy was so developed that it became able itself to produce the sinews for its further expansion. By 1935, 99 per cent of all industrial machinery used in Russia was of domestic origin. Imports of tractors and agricultural implements were completely dispensed with under the Second Five-Year Plan. Only 2.3 per cent of the cotton consumed in Russia had to come from abroad in 1936. Of such other commodities as ferroalloys, aluminum, rubber, and automobiles,

[10] Resolution of the Plenary Session of the Central Committee of the Communist Party of the Soviet Union (October 1925) as published in "VKP (B) v Resolutsiakh i Resheniakh S'ezdov, Konferentsii i Plenumov TS.K" (CP of the SU in *Resolutions and Decisions of Congresses, Conferences, and Plenary Sessions of the Central Committee),* part 2 (Moscow, 1941), p. 243.

[11] J. Stalin, *Voprosy Leninisma* (Questions of Leninism) 11th edition (Moscow, 1939), p. 375 f.

only small and ever decreasing proportions of the total domestic consumption were met by foreign supplies.[12]

For only a few items had Russia to continue relying on the outside world. Its imports consisted increasingly of special machinery embodying advanced scientific developments in other countries, and certain raw materials and consumer goods that could not be produced or were not to be found in Russia (crude rubber, coffee, tea, and the like).

"High-pressure" exports of goods sorely needed at home, to pay for imports urgently required for investment purposes, could thus be discontinued. Shipments of grains, lumber, hides, leather, flax, and other raw materials drastically declined. Tractors and machine tools appeared for the first time among commodities *supplied* by Russia to foreign countries![13]

In the years of the Second Five-Year Plan, from 1932 to 1937, the total volume of Russian foreign trade dropped by about 75 per cent from the exceptional heights of 1929-31, and during the rest of the interwar period remained almost negligible relative to the world's total trade.[14]

Had it not been for the need to repay the short-term foreign debt incurred during the First Five-Year Plan and the urgency of building up large stockpiles of strategic and critical materials against the worsening international situation, the export decline under the Second and Third Five-Year Plans might have gone even further. By the end of the decade Russia might have fallen behind even little Belgium, Denmark, or Sweden among the countries participating in world trade.

Such a development would have been fully in accord with the general economic policy of the Soviet Government during the Five-Year Plans. It would be erroneous to conclude from it,

[12] Cf. P. Belov, "O Voennoi i Ekonomicheskoi Moshchi Sotsialisticheskogo Gasudarstva" ("On the Military and Economic Might of the Socialist State") in *Bolshevik* (1940), No. 4, p. 47f. Cf. also Alexander Gerschenkron: *Economic Relations with the U.S.S.R.* (New York, 1945), p. 58.

[13] For the composition of Russian imports and exports during the entire period see Tables 2 and 3.

[14] This is not to say, to be sure, that in some commodity markets Russian exports did not continue to play an important role. With respect to high quality lumber, some grains, oil products, ores, furs, and a few other items Russia remained a significant (or even exclusive) source of supply. Cf. *Statistisches Jahrbuch fuer das Deutsche Reich, 1938* (Berlin, 1939).

however, that the economic philosophy of Russia's ruling party regards the attainment of autarky as desirable *per se*. Neither in the writings of the founders of the Soviet state nor in other publications dealing with this subject can one find advocacy of

TABLE 2
RUSSIAN IMPORTS OF THE MOST IMPORTANT COMMODITIES[a]
(*Annual averages in million 1936 rubles*)

| Commodities | 1909–1913 | 1929–1932 | 1933–1937 | 1938 |
|---|---|---|---|---|
| Livestock | 51 | 87 | 50 | 47 |
| Rice | 43 | 54 | 8 | 12 |
| Tea | 262 | 76 | 27 | 27 |
| Coffee | 35 | 3 | 0.5 | 1.0 |
| Lemons and oranges | 35 | 5 | 3 | 15 |
| Dried Fruits | 49 | 19 | 3 | 8 |
| Cocoa | 10 | 5 | 4 | 10.5 |
| Herrings | 98 | 20 | 4 | 22 |
| Rubber | 145 | 51 | 60 | 52 |
| Paper | 93 | 25 | 0.8 | 5 |
| Wool | 225 | 182 | 71 | 72 |
| Cotton | 483 | 228 | 44 | 27 |
| Jute | 38 | 26 | 9 | 7 |
| Iron, steel, and their products | 203 | 621 | 191 | 115 |
| Nonferrous metals | 174 | 219 | 149 | 238 |
| Internal combustion engines | 34 | 34 | 19 | 10 |
| Pumps | 21 | 23 | 5 | 5 |
| Agricultural machinery | 177 | 102 | ..... | ..... |
| Machine tools | 31 | 327 | 133 | 236 |
| Electrical machinery and apparatus | 68 | 223 | 60 | 57 |
| Precision tools | 31 | 63 | 26 | 22 |
| Tractors | ... | 229 | ..... | ..... |
| Automobiles | 52 | 98 | 2 | 11.8 |
| Ships | 16 | 49 | 25 | 25 |

[a]Sources: S. N. Bakulin, D. D. Mishustin, *Statistika Vneshney Torcovli*, and A. Yugow, *Russia's Economic Front for War and Peace*.

autarky as a valid principle of economic organization. Just the opposite is commonly asserted, and the advantages and desirability of the international division of labor and of the world-wide exchange of goods and services, were often stressed by Lenin—Russia's highest authority in theoretical matters—and some more recent writers.[15]

If, nevertheless, the actual policies of the Soviet Government

[15] Often in connection with criticisms of the German exponents of the autarky philosophy.

were consistently directed toward rendering the U.S.S.R. economically independent of the outside world, the reasons were of a purely pragmatic nature, and stemmed from the specific conditions prevailing in Russia. Most important among them were undoubtedly security considerations. Viewing the outside world

TABLE 3
RUSSIAN EXPORTS OF THE MOST IMPORTANT COMMODITIES[a]
(*Annual averages in million 1936 rubles*)

| Commodities | 1903–1913 | 1929–1932 | 1933–1937 | 1938 |
|---|---|---|---|---|
| Grain | 2620 | 453 | 143 | 175 |
| Leguminous vegetables | 113 | 32 | 15 | 18 |
| Lumber mill products | 382 | 305 | 231 | 280 |
| Butter | 272 | 89 | 43 | 0.6 |
| Sugar | 179 | 117 | 35 | 34 |
| Oil-cake | 155 | 75 | 33 | 30 |
| Furs | 31 | 309 | 150 | 130 |
| Hides and leather | 175 | 30 | 10 | 8 |
| Petroleum | 160 | 567 | 219 | 102 |
| Manganese ore | 42 | 51 | 27 | 27 |
| Chemical products (including fertilizers) | 38 | 44 | 44 | 25 |
| Cotton textiles | 142 | 204 | 87 | 52 |
| Flax | 370 | 131 | 79 | 27 |
| Iron, steel, and their products | 43 | 28 | 36 | 21 |
| Machines and equipment | 12 | 15 | 30 | 32 |
| Tobacco | 21 | 32 | 10 | 18.5 |

[a]Sources: same as Table 2.

as fundamentally inimical to their social and political system, and expecting foreign attempts at any time to destroy their state and to restore capitalism in Russia, the Soviet leaders throughout were very conscious of the necessity for raising Russia's military potential high enough to defend the country against any hostile coalition. As early as October, 1927 the resolution of the Central Committee of the Communist Party formulating the principles to be followed in the preparation of the First Five-Year Plan stated explicitly:

Taking into account the possibility of military aggression of capitalist countries against the first proletarian state in history, it is necessary to work out the Five-Year Plan in such a way as to give maximum attention to those branches of the national economy in general, and of industry in particular, that will play the main part in assuring the defense and economic stability of the country in time of war.[16]

Once this directive was accepted and the decision made to attain a strong military potential within a short period of time, the strategy of industrialization followed with inexorable logic. To have concentrated investment in those branches of the economy in which Russia might have enjoyed at the time the highest comparative advantages and to have relied on international trade for essential supplies, would clearly have left Russia exposed to the dangers of economic blockade. Convinced, moreover, that business fluctuations and severe depressions represented an inevitable "law of motion" of capitalism, the Soviet planners were anxious to insulate Russia's economic development from the vicissitudes of international markets. The price that had to be paid for this independence was undoubtedly high. Foregoing the advantages of international trade could not but reduce Russia's national income. The allocation of a large share of available resources to defense purposes at the same time curtailed consumption and expansion of consumer goods industries.

Yet in spite of the sacrifices that the defense-orientation entailed in the short run, such an orientation did not militate against the basic long-run objectives of the industrialization program. Calling for emphasis on basic industries and mining as the essential prerequisites for current and potential expansion of military output, it merely reënforced the reasoning underlying the Soviet over-all plan of economic development. Occupying one-sixth of the globe and endowed with natural riches probably second to those of no other country, the U.S.S.R. has at its disposal the wherewithal for the development of *all* branches of a modern economy. Its resources, once explored and employed, can provide the country with sufficient food, raw materials, and fuel for a rapid and harmonious economic expansion. Although many newly created industries were in the beginning bound to work at higher cost than similar industries abroad or some older

16 "VKP (B) v Resolutsiakh i Resheniakh S'ezdov, Konferentsii i Plenumov TS.K" (CP of the SU in *Resolutions and Decisions of Congresses, Conferences, and Plenary Sessions of the Central Committee)*, part 2 (Moscow, 1941), p. 202.

branches of the Russian economy, it could have been reasonably expected that the cost of "infancy" would be fully rewarded in the longer run. At the same time, many a developmental project motivated by defense considerations and appearing very costly in terms of available alternatives had immeasurable advantages from a more general social and political viewpoint. The strategically inspired desire, for instance, to allocate a large share of total investment to the Urals, Western Siberia, Central Asia, and other remote regions of the country happened to coincide with the design of increasing the standards of welfare and civilization in the backward parts of the U.S.S.R.

Much as the wisdom and the urgency of this industrialization and self-sufficiency drive were doubted at the time of its relentless prosecution, later events have fully vindicated the sacrifices that it entailed. Without a heavy industry able to produce annually 30,000 tanks, 40,000 planes, 120,000 guns, and 3 million rifles,[17] Russia could not possibly have withstood the onslaught of Germany and its allies. Without having developed secure bases of raw materials and fuel in the impenetrable depths of the country, Russia could not possibly have carried out its unprecedented industrial evacuation program. And last but not least, without a pool of technically-trained manpower, Russia could not have operated and serviced the tanks, planes, and vehicles indispensable to modern warfare.

All this became generally recognized during the war. Nevertheless, the view was frequently expressed that the victory over Hitler Germany, having corroborated the correctness of the Soviet Government's prewar industrialization and self-sufficiency drive, would also create the conditions for its relaxation.[18] It was expected that with an industrial base firmly established and with Russia's security adequately guaranteed, the Soviet Government would feel able to reduce the speed of its industrialization effort and to place less emphasis on self-sufficiency. It was hoped that, less fearful of a possible economic blockade, it would consider participating on a larger scale in world trade, and would

[17] J. V. Stalin, Election Speech in Moscow on February 9, 1946.

[18] Cf., for example, Alexander Gerschenkron, *Economic Relations with the U.S.S.R.*

attempt to make more extensive use of the benefits of the international division of labor. Specifically, many students of the Soviet economy believed that after the war Russia would concentrate on the reconstruction of its war-devastated cities and the expansion of industries essential for the further economic development of the country, and would rely for many urgently needed consumer goods on foreign supplies. It was held that large reconstruction loans would be made available to Russia which, symbolizing the goodwill of the Western Allies, would help dispel Russia's anxiety about future foreign aggression and would facilitate its transition to a less defense-oriented economy.

All these optimistic expectations were, however, dashed by the rapid deterioration of international political relations. Now, as before the war, the Russian Government feels compelled to regard the capitalist world as basically hostile to the Soviet Union. With Germany removed as an effective threat to Russian security, the United States is looked upon as an even greater potential danger.

At the same time the changing technology of warfare widens still further the discrepancy of power between the industrially advanced and the industrially underdeveloped countries. The chances of filling this gap with substitutes extemporized in case of emergency are becoming progressively smaller. While men armed with "Molotov cocktails" were able to stop the German "tiger" tanks, such miracles could not be expected if the attack were carried out with atomic weapons. "Military capability," which during the last war was still a combination of manpower, previously accumulated stockpiles, and current output of essential materials and munitions, has come to assume a new economic meaning. The strength of the nation's industrial base, its accomplishments in the field of scientific research, the geographical location of strategic plants, are now more than ever the crucial economic prerequisites of successful defense.

Paradoxically enough, this development is not altogether unfavorable to Russia's economic growth. As the production and stockpiling of conventional weapons recede in importance, the economic requirements of defense coincide even more closely with the general objectives of Soviet industrialization. Although the share of income that has to be devoted to investment, and the resulting drain on consumption, may have to be even larger than before, this investment has to be directed to a lesser extent to industries of exclusively military significance. Its bulk can be used for a further expansion of heavy industry and of the raw material base—an expansion that is equally essential to defense and to Russia's general economic future.

The Fourth Five-Year Plan, promulgated in 1946, appears to have been strongly influenced by these considerations. Representing the blueprint of Russia's postwar economic effort, it indicates clearly that the basic principles of the Soviet economic policy, although adapted to changing conditions, will remain essentially the same as before the war.[19] Although providing for a rate of growth substantially lower than under the preceding Five-Year Plans, it continues to strive for expansion of basic industries and for strengthening of Russia's economic independence from abroad.

II

The foregoing may suggest that so far as foreign economic policy is concerned, the Soviet Union merely took up after the war the thread where it had been broken by the German invasion, and that the country's role in world trade will remain as insignificant as in the thirties. Such a conclusion, however, would hardly do justice to the problem, and would overlook the changes that have occurred in Russia's international position as a result of the war.

Most important among them is the political and economic leadership assumed by the Soviet Union with respect to a number of Eastern and Southeastern European countries. Under Communist control, these countries are in the process of carrying out far-reaching social revolutions and establishing economic systems based on principles similar to those prevailing in Russia.

According to the classical Marxian blueprint of socialist internationalism, it might be expected that these nations would join the multinational Soviet Union, thus becoming members of a

[19] Cf. the very informative essay on the Fourth Five-Year Plan by Abram Bergson, "The Fourth Five Year Plan: Heavy Versus Consumers' Goods Industries," *Political Science Quarterly* (June 1947), pp. 195-227.

Communist Commonwealth. This, however, would clearly be a premature conclusion. Not only would such a step contribute to the worsening of the relations between the U.S.S.R. and the Western countries, but the political and economic structure of the Russian-orbit countries is far from permitting their complete integration with the U.S.S.R. Struggling for the stabilization of their power, the Communist regimes in these countries are socializing their economies only gradually. While large parts of trade and industry have been taken over by the state, significant sectors of the urban economy are still in private hands. In agriculture, at the same time, the agrarian reforms carried out immediately after the war have even increased the number of peasant holdings and in this way have strengthened—at least temporarily—the political power of the rural population. It would present tremendous economic and political difficulties to merge into one economic-planning system the fully socialized Russian economy and the partly nationalized, partly privately operated economies of the countries in the Soviet orbit. Moreover, the inclusion in the Soviet Union of these border nations, with their traditionally strong nationalist feelings, could easily become a storm signal for nationalist movements that would undermine the political stability of the young Communist governments.

The difference between the Soviet-orbit countries on one hand and the Soviet Union on the other is not the only obstacle to complete integration. The six countries with newly established Communist regimes differ no less among themselves. With dissimilar historical backgrounds, with political traditions that are frequently of antagonistic character, and with economic structures by no means supplementary, the countries that have recently come under Communist control have still a long way to go before they will be ready to become members of a closely-knit, centrally-planned political and economic entity. Their industrialization plans now being carried out undoubtedly constitute important steps in that direction. It is, however, impossible as yet to discern any more general scheme on which these plans might be said to be based. While there are many signs of close economic coöperation among these countries, and between them and the Soviet Union, it is by no means clear whether the intention is for an early integration of the entire Communist sphere of Europe or only of its new Eastern and Southeastern European components.

In the meantime, however, the enlargement of the Communist area has already had some impact on Russian foreign economic relations. As Table 4 shows, Russia's trade with the countries in this area has expanded considerably. Although data for the

TABLE 4
SOVIET POSTWAR TRADE[a]
*(in millions of Dollars)*

| | IMPORTS | | | EXPORTS | | | BALANCE | |
|---|---|---|---|---|---|---|---|---|
| | Total | From Eastern Europe | | Total | To Eastern Europe | | Total | Eastern Europe |
| | | Value | Percent of total | | Value | Percent of total | | |
| 1937 | 253.1 | 4.5 | 1.8 | 326.2 | 6.3 | 1.9 | + 73.1 | + 1.8 |
| 1945 July–Dec. | 819 | 102 | 12.5 | 111 | 49 | 44.1 | −708 | −53 |
| 1946 Jan.–June | 461 | 50 | 10.8 | 194 | 60 | 30.9 | −267 | +10 |
| 1946 July–Dec. | 456 | 80 | 17.5 | 245 | 102 | 41.6 | −209 | − 6 |
| 1947 Jan.–June | 392 | 117 | 29.8 | 176 | 62 | 35.2 | −216 | −55 |

[a]Based on statistics of Bulgaria, Czechoslovakia, Hungary, Poland, Rumania, and an estimate for Yugoslavia, but excluding the Soviet Zone of Germany. *Commercial* imports and exports only (i.e., excluding shipments on account of Lend-Lease, UNRRA, reparations, etc.).
*Source:* Bank for International Settlements.

second half of 1947 are not yet available, it appears from scattered information that the total volume in 1947 may have been even larger than in 1946. Equally, if not more important, are the changes that have occurred in the structure of the foreign trade of the orbit countries. While before the war they traded relatively little among themselves, in 1946 and 1947 they were each others' largest customers.

It would be rash to draw any definite conclusions from this brief record. The first postwar years have been abnormal in all respects: the industrial economy of the Eastern and Southeastern European countries, although steadily recovering, did not reach prewar levels until the end of 1947. The countries' food situation was badly shattered by drought in Russia and other parts of Eastern Europe. Relief shipments of various kinds, reparation removals partly planned and partly haphazard, transfers on capital account, and sales of surplus war material make it impossible to regard the trade statistics for this period as a basis for any longer-run forecast.

Nevertheless, it is very likely that the trade between countries in the new Communist area will remain much larger than before the war. Realization of their industrial programs is predicated mainly upon large-scale imports of industrial equipment. Some of it will be supplied by the more industrially-advanced parts of the area—Czechoslovakia and Poland—in exchange for ores, oil products, and other raw materials. The bulk, however, will have to be imported from outside. The area as a whole will thus face a problem quite similar to that which confronted Russia under the First Five-Year Plan. It will have to increase its exports considerably in order to pay for the necessary imports.

Such export increases, however, may prove very difficult. In fact, so far as agricultural products are concerned—and they were the most important single item in those countries' prewar exports—a decline in exports is more probable than an increase. The agrarian reforms carried out since the war have tended to raise consumption on the farm and reduce the marketed share of the total agricultural output. Similarly, the export of timber and other raw materials may be seriously curtailed by increasing domestic requirements. An over-all reduction of home consumption, on the other hand, is hardly feasible. The area's absolute living standards are very low, and forcing them still lower may be too onerous politically.[20] What the Russian Government could only afford eleven years after the Revolution, is most likely beyond the present power of the newly established regimes.

Short of abandoning or considerably slowing down the industrialization programs, the only solution of the dilemma is foreign credits. Yet the country most able to furnish such credits—the United States—is least disposed to aid Communist-controlled economies. Under prevailing political conditions, it thus is

[20] It should be also considered that the growth of the area's population and the area's increasing urbanization tend to raise steadily its food requirements.

highly improbable that any significant sums will be lent by the United States or by organizations under its influence to any of the Soviet-orbit countries. Although it is still not precluded that the International Bank for Reconstruction and Development may grant some loans to Poland and Czechoslovakia, the chances of such assistance are rather small.

Nor are the Soviet area's prospects for obtaining sizable credits in Western Europe particularly bright. Not only are the political hinderances about as large there as in the United States, but most Western European countries will hardly be economically in the position in the next few years to grant any credits except on very short term.

Under such circumstances, Russia becomes the only major country from which the Eastern and Southeastern European area might expect any significant help in its industrialization effort. The magnitude, however, of the support that Russia will actually be able to render is very difficult to estimate. There can be no doubt that any such contribution will be made only at a considerable sacrifice to its own economy. It certainly is not belittling the success of Russia's industrialization to say that it is not as yet in any position to export large quantities of machinery and technical equipment, let alone supply them on a long-term credit basis.

Yet having chosen for political reasons to abstain from participation in the European Recovery Program, and having induced the countries in its orbit to follow its lead, Russia seems to have decided to embark upon a long-range scheme of aiding their industrialization programs. The details of this scheme are not yet known. The agreement recently concluded with Poland indicates, however, its possible nature and scope. Under the terms of this arrangement, Russia and Poland agree to exchange in the next four years goods to the value of over 1 billion dollars. The U.S.S.R. is to supply Poland with iron, chromium, manganese ore, oil products, cotton, aluminum, asbestos, automobiles, tractors, and the like; while Poland is to deliver to Russia cotton textiles, sugar, zinc, steel, railway materials, cement, and other goods. Prices are to be determined from time to time in accordance with world market conditions. At the same time,

Russia has granted Poland a credit equivalent to 450 million dollars, to be used until 1956 for its purchases of Russian machinery and industrial equipment. Similar agreements are reported to have been concluded or to be under negotiation between Russia and other members of the Russian orbit. The total volume of trade for which they will provide, and the amount of credits which Russia will grant, can only be guessed. However, if they are drawn up along the lines of the Polish agreement, Russia's trade with the countries in its orbit in the next few years should greatly surpass the levels attained in 1946 and 1947.

But as indicated above, an increase in the total exports of Russia and the Russian-orbit countries is hardly to be expected for the immediate future. An intensification of the economic relations among the six Eastern and Southeastern European countries, as well as between them and the U.S.S.R., could not but lead, therefore, to a reduction of their aggregate exports to the rest of the world. In the absence of foreign credits, their imports from the Western countries would also decline accordingly.

Such a reorientation of Eastern European trade would be the result not so much of conscious design as of a confluence of economic and political circumstances. There can be no doubt that the Eastern European economies would be better off in respect to many commodities by trading with Western Europe or the United States rather than among themselves or with Russia. For most goods that they will need to import for their industrialization programs, the Western countries are obviously cheaper and better suppliers than they themselves (with the possible exception of Czechoslovakia) or Russia. At the same time, Western Europe, at least in the immediate future, would be a more attractive market for most of their exports than any they could find within their own area. How large a deterioration of their combined terms of trade would result from this shift will depend on the future movements of the relative prices of their imports and exports. It could be quite considerable.

Nor can a partial loss of Eastern European supplies fail to aggravate the present economic difficulties of Western Europe. In the last prewar years 17.8 per cent of Western Europe's total imports from non-ERP countries came from Eastern Europe and were paid for to the extent of almost 70 per cent by Western European exports to Eastern European countries.[21] The shrinkage of this trade would increase Western Europe's dependency on supplies from the American Continent, thus complicating further its dollar position. "The loss of non-American sources of supplies can not be measured precisely but it may be roughly estimated that more than 1/4 of the import requirements from the American Continent at the beginning of the 4-year period [1948] is attributable to this cause."[22] This over-all estimate may even understate somewhat the significance of the Eastern European exports to Western Europe. For certain commodities such as timber, feeding stuffs, and some cereals, Eastern Europe was one of Western Europe's most important suppliers. It is in these commodities, at the same time, that the drop in Eastern European exports is likely to be most pronounced. Not only are these the goods of which Eastern Europe's own requirements are now much larger than before the war, but the costs of their transportation are so high as to render their export from Eastern Europe to Western European markets very unattractive.

The conclusion of the ERP Report cited above that ". . . . it is reasonable to expect that the westward flow of food, agricultural and timber products will gradually be resumed" thus does not appear to be well founded. It is much more likely that Western Europe will have to adjust itself to a permanent curtailment of its Eastern European supplies and to the necessity of filling the resulting gap with extra-European trade.

Needless to say, the foregoing considerations assume the present political relations between West and East. Should the political climate improve, and should the Western countries be willing to render some assistance in the industrialization of Eastern Europe, the economic relations both among the Eastern countries themselves and between them and the Western world would assume an altogether different character.

[21] This refers to the imports of the countries participating in the ERP and Spain, and was computed from League of Nations *Network of World Trade* (Geneva, 1942). The implications of the East-West split of Germany for the economy of Western Germany are much larger.

[22] Committee of European Economic Cooperation, July-September 1947, Volume 1, *General Report* (London: Paris, 1947) p. 23.

Given appropriate credit facilities, the Eastern European countries would enter Western markets as large buyers of machinery, industrial equipment, and the like, and would eventually tend—as their present investments succeeded in raising their total output—to expand their exports. The composition of these exports would undoubtedly change, but the volume of their total trade with the West would probably become larger than before the war. In other words, in the foreign economic relations of the six Eastern and Southeastern European countries, Western Europe and the United States could assume the part which at the present time has to be played after a fashion by the U.S.S.R.

Yet such a turn in American and Western European policy toward Eastern Europe for the time being appears to be quite remote. In the meantime Russia's foreign economic policy remains basically determined by a continuous concern with self-sufficiency and defense, as well as the endeavor to support the countries within its political orbit. These requirements are to some extent conflicting. The export of industrial equipment or agricultural implements on credit to Poland or Yugoslavia, for example, certainly does not help to satisfy the urgent requirements of Russia's own war-devastated economy.

The inability of Russia and the rest of Eastern and Southeastern Europe to secure Western help in form of sufficient reparations or loans thus places a double burden on the Soviet economy. Not only does it deprive it of large-scale imports badly needed for its reconstruction, but it forces it to draw on its scant resources for the rehabilitation and development of the countries in its sphere of influence.

This is not to suggest that at the present time Russia is in fact entirely cut off from the industrially more advanced and economically stronger Western countries. Although Russia's total imports are declining toward their prewar volume, their help in overcoming technical bottlenecks in the reconstruction of Russian industry and transportation is undoubtedly very large. The recently concluded trade agreements with Great Britain and Switzerland should prove very important in this respect. Even the current small cash purchases from the United States (amounting in 1947 to only about 150 million dollars)—if not blocked by the current campaign for an embargo of trade with the U.S.S.R.—will probably be of considerable marginal usefulness.

Moreover, there are some other net additions, even if small, to Russia's current resources. The value of Russia's present reparation receipts from its zones in Germany and Austria is not known. It is very unlikely, however, that they will amount to very much in the future. However, unless some changes are made for political reasons, over 100 million dollars annually should be received during the next seven to eight years on reparation account from Italy, Finland, Rumania, and Hungary. The sizable loan (1 billion Swedish kroners) granted to Russia by Sweden in 1946 should also provide Russia with valuable imports without any immediate drain on its resources.

That Russia attaches considerable value to additional imports, even at the cost of having to pay for them with commodities that could be well utilized at home, was demonstrated strikingly by its latest export operations. From its 1947 crop, Russia contracted to ship to Great Britain, Belgium, Egypt, and other countries over 3 million tons of grains, a large quantity even by Russia's best prewar standards.

Yet while this interest in imports is fully understandable, some other aspects of Russian foreign trade policy are rather puzzling. The current gold output of the U.S.S.R. is estimated at about 150 million dollars' worth a year, and its accumulated stock as possibly approximating 2.5 billion dollars.[23] Russian gold exports since the war did not amount, however, to more than 100 million dollars. One would have thought that following the devastation of the war the Russians, pressed for goods of all kinds, would have made use of at least a part of their gold reserves to finance large-scale purchases in the Western Hemisphere. It would also appear that placing gold at the disposal of Poland, Yugoslavia, and such other countries whom Russia wishes to aid in their industrialization efforts might have been a more economical procedure than supplying them with tractors or automobiles

[23] The most recent estimate was made by the Bank for International Settlements and released in December 1947.

that could be well employed in Russia. Yet except for a 28 million dollar gold loan to Poland, no such Russian gold transfers to countries within its orbit seem to have taken place.

Various explanations for this policy might be offered. Since Russian economists, not unlike many American observers, have anticipated a major postwar depression and price decline in the United States,[24] the Soviet Government may have decided to delay the placement of large orders until the sellers' market is over and the purchasing power of gold is appreciably enhanced. It might also be surmised that Russia hopes to improve its bargaining position in future credit negotiations by being able to offer cash payments for a part of its foreign purchases.

All these explanations, however, are hardly satisfactory, since it is difficult to imagine that such gains as Russia might have expected from the hoarding of its gold reserves after the war would have been deemed sufficient to compensate for the disadvantages of postponing essential purchases. Even in the years 1938 and 1939 when the danger of war called for an urgent strengthening of defense industries and for the increased stockpiling of strategic materials, Russia did not use its gold reserves, which are estimated to have amounted at that time to over 1 billion dollars, to finance essential imports.

Difficult to comprehend is also Russia's decision not to join the International Monetary Fund and the International Bank for Reconstruction and Development. Their Articles of Agreement contain, to be sure, a number of provisions that Russia might have found objectionable; yet flexible as they actually are, they could hardly have curtailed Russia's freedom of action.[25] At the same time, Russia's adherence to the Fund would have opened to her an important source of cheap credit, even had the Bank proven unwilling to grant loans.

Less astounding is Russia's refusal to participate in the International Trade Organization. Not unlike other countries tech-

[24] "The boom still continues but the crisis is approaching fast. The outbreak of this crisis will lead to a sharp drop in output and to mass unemployment." E. Varga, in *Novoye Vremya* (New Times) of May 16, 1947. Similar statements were made earlier by the same and other Russian writers.

[25] As a state-trading nation Russia would in any case not be affected by the Articles of Agreement regulating changes in the par values of the members' currencies or providing for eventual abolition of exchange restrictions.

nically backward compared with the United States, it views all the United States' efforts to liberalize international trade on a nondiscriminatory basis as exclusively favoring American interests in the world markets.[26] To quote Professor Varga again: "Should the policy of the United States prevail, the consequences for countries with weaker industries would be fatal."

While Russia could regard its own position as sufficiently well protected by its foreign trade monopoly, that of the orbit countries would appear to be more vulnerable. Even if they should develop sufficiently strong safeguards for their industrialization efforts, the enforcement of the objectives of the International Trade Organization could not but complicate their positions and reduce their joint bargaining power in bilateral trade and credit negotiations. It is this untrammeled bargaining power upon which the U.S.S.R. and the countries in its sphere of influence are determined to rely, particularly in an event of a worldwide depression.

Barring far-reaching changes in international relations, the U.S.S.R. and the countries in its orbit may thus be expected to remain aloof from most international economic organizations. Adhering to its course of "technical-economic independence" from the capitalist world, the U.S.S.R. will no doubt continue to stress its economic relations with the countries of Eastern and Southeastern Europe. Their contacts with the Western world may exceed in the immediate future those of the Soviet Union. Yet in the longer run these contacts, too, are likely to decline. They will be overshadowed by the centripetal forces of economic integration in the Communist part of Europe.

[26] "The economic policy of America, by forcing other countries to accept the most-favored-nation clause, aims at securing larger sales on the world markets and at solving or at least alleviating the problem of demand." E. Varga, *Novoye Vremya,* May 16, 1947.

# 10

# *ECONOMIC RELATIONS OF THE UNITED STATES WITH CHINA*

John D. Sumner

The purposes of this essay are to indicate: (1) the general lines of economic policy which have governed past relations of the United States and China; (2) wartime developments in the economic relations of the two countries; and (3) circumstances influencing current and prospective economic relations between China and the United States. What can be said within the limits of this brief essay is no more than an introduction to a highly complex situation. It is trite, but nevertheless true, also to emphasize at the outset that the current and prospective entanglement of economic and political questions makes it impossible effectively to consider "economic relations" in a purely economic frame of reference.

## *Economic Relations Prior to World War II*

During the nineteenth century the "China Policy" of the United States was concerned almost entirely with insuring equality of opportunity for American commerce.[1] As early as 1842 an American representative negotiated a most-favored-nation agreement with the Chinese Governor of Canton. As the treaty ports were opened, largely by British force, the United States continued to employ the most-favored-nation approach. Indeed, the essential purpose of the famous "open door" policy, later associated with the name of Secretary of State John Hay,[2]

[1] One of the best accounts of U. S. policy in China with which the writer is familiar may be found in A. W. Griswold, *The Far Eastern Policy of the United States* (New York, 1938).

[2] His enunciation of the Open Door policy was contained in circular notes to the several powers in 1899 and 1900.

was to maintain equality of commercial opportunity. Under the so-called unequal treaties of the eighteen-forties and fifties, China lost control of her tariff rates, granted extraterritorial privileges under which foreigners in the treaty ports were subject to their own rather than to Chinese law, and gave foreign shipping access to Chinese territorial waters and the Yangtse River. The United States and other foreign nations enjoyed the benefits of these concessions to British and French power. The open door policy as expressed by Hay included an insistence upon the administrative and territorial integrity of China. However, this emphasis was regarded largely as a means of insuring the primary objective of equal treatment in commercial matters.[3]

During the period of America's emphasis on equality of commercial opportunity, her objectives were nonpolitical and she refrained from attempting to acquire spheres of influence or territorial concessions and bases in China.[4] During the Taft administration, however, there were repeated attempts to use economic means for ends which, in part, may have been political.[5] Long-term American investments in China, including participation of American banking in railroad loans, had been negligible. The State Department, despite the opposition of Britain, France, Japan, and Russia, and the lukewarm interest of American banking groups, endeavored to inject private capital into China on a long-term basis. These efforts were fruitless in Manchuria and served only to tighten Japanese and Russian controls in that area. Farther south, in the Yangtse Valley, a place was finally made for American banks in the foreign banking consortium financing the Hukuang Railway. The American group also joined in a proposed reorganization loan to the Chinese Government and in a loan for the reform of the currency. President Wilson in 1913, however, refused to request American banks to take part in further loans to China, and this episode in "dollar diplomacy" was closed.

[3] Griswold, *The Far Eastern Policy of the United States,* p. 6.

[4] An exception occurred in 1900 when Secretary Hay attempted without success to negotiate for a naval base and concession in Fukien Province. Griswold, *The Far Eastern Policy of the United States,* p. 83.

[5] This and the two following paragraphs are based on the excellent account in Griswold, *Far Eastern Policy.* See especially his Chapter IV on "dollar diplomacy."

In endeavoring to inject American investment into China the Taft administration attempted, however unsuccessfully, to break the financial hold of other powers in China. The reasons for this policy perhaps cannot be stated precisely; Griswold's analysis suggests a desire for political power in China as a means of enhancing the long-run economic position of the United States and, perhaps also, as a protection to the security of the Philippines. To a degree, the earlier emphasis on equality of commercial opportunity was supplemented by a desire for investment opportunity. It must be recognized, however, that this new emphasis appears not to have reflected the pressure of American banking or industrial interests; the State Department appears to have taken the initiative despite the absence of either a sustained or a widespread interest in American financial circles.

Subsequently, the encroachments on China during and following World War I led President Wilson to challenge the increasingly aggressive attitude of Japan. But he was able to accomplish little by either economic or political means. When independent American loans to China failed because of lack of investor interest and effective foreign opposition, Wilson agreed to sponsor American participation in international loans by a British, French, Japanese, and American consortium. The American purpose was to enable China, by means of the international character of the loans, to free itself from financial dependence on individual foreign powers, especially Japan. In 1922, however, American bankers in the consortium made it clear to the State Department that they were not interested in the risks attendant upon further loans to China.[6] American private investment proved a weak reed in Government attempts to stem the tide of Japanese aggression, or otherwise to maintain the political integrity of China. Nor were the exhortations of Dr. Sun Yat-sen, the moving spirit in the emergence of a "new" China, to be more successful.[7]

In the Washington Conference of 1921-22, however, the United States secured Japan's signature to a nine-power treaty

[6] Griswold, *Far Eastern Policy*, p. 470.

[7] In his *The International Development of China* (1922), Dr. Sun advocated the granting of international loans to aid the development of China's economic potential.

which, *inter alia,* recognized the sovereignty and territorial integrity of China and the principle of equality of commercial and industrial opportunity to all nations in China. The limitations of naval armaments also agreed to at the conference, however, acted to give Japan unquestioned naval supremacy in the western Pacific.[8]

China, with the rise of nationalism within its own borders, made progress towards the elimination of the "unequal treaties" which had abridged her economic and political sovereignty. Tariff autonomy[9] was agreed to by the United States and other Western powers in 1928-39; Japan acquiesced in 1930.[10] Negotiations for the ending of extraterritorial rights were interrupted by the war with Japan, but were concluded by the United States and Britain in 1943.[11]

An interesting paradox appears in the history of American economic and political relations with China and Japan. The absolute significance of trade with China has always been small, and throughout this century it has been much less significant than that with Japan. Nevertheless, American diplomacy has endeavored to support China against Japanese encroachments. In 1936, China received approximately 2 per cent of the exports of the United States, and Japan somewhat more than 8 per cent. China contributed about 3 per cent of American imports, and Japan 7 per cent.[12] In 1896, forty years before, China and Japan each received less than 1 per cent of American exports, but Japan's share was slightly in excess of China's. Over 3 per cent of American imports came from Japan, and somewhat less than 3 per cent from China.[13] In 1867, while American trade with China was relatively much larger than with Japan, exports to China approximated only 2 per cent of the total,—while imports

[8] The Washington Conference is described in, for example, K. S. Latourette, *A Short History of the Far East* (1946), pp. 460-479, 520-526.

[9] China's power independently to establish her tariffs was compromised by the first Anglo-Chinese War in 1839-42, and by a second war in 1858-60. See Latourette, *A Short History of the Far East,* pp. 370-376.

[10] Latourette, *History of the Far East,* p. 476.

[11] Latourette, *History of the Far East,* p. 622.

[12] League of Nations, *International Trade Statistics, 1937* (Geneva, 1938), p. 172.

[13] Treasury Dept., *The Foreign Commerce and Navigation of the United States,* V. I (Washington, 1897), p. iv.

from China amounted to approximately $12,112,000, or about 3 per cent of the United States total, the same proportion as in 1936.[14]

American investments in China have been similarly small. Remer estimated long- and short-term U.S. business investments, including ownership of Chinese Government obligations, as approximately 20, 49, and 197 million dollars in 1900, 1914, and 1930 respectively.[15] By contrast, the long-term international investments of Americans have been estimated at 2500 and 14,700 million dollars in 1914 and 1929.[16] The *Census of American-Owned Assets in Foreign Countries*[17] placed U.S. assets in China in 1943 at 122.2 million as compared with 119.4 million in Japan. In comparing American investments in the two countries, however, available information suggests a larger proportion of direct investments in China and a larger proportion of portfolio investments in Japan.[18]

It is difficult to explain the paradox of political support to a minor importer and exporter against the inroads of a more important American customer solely on the ground of expectations of a great future market in China. Such an interpretation puts the Yankee trader in the position of chasing an economic will-o'-the-wisp for a much longer time than business men, or governments acting for them, are ordinarily willing to do.

It would seem that political rather than direct economic considerations have increasingly been the chief determinants of American policy during the present century. A narrow economic interpretation is confronted with the phenomenal growth of American trade with Japan. Such an interpretation could be based, if at all, only on the continuing hope that American capital investment might ultimately find more scope in a developing China than in Japan.[19] This view, however, is made less persua-

14 Treasury Dept. *Annual Report of the Director of the Bureau of Statistics on the Commerce and Navigation of the United States* (Washington, 1868), Part I, p. 47, and Part II, p. 267.

15 C. F. Remer, *Foreign Investments in China* (New York, 1933), p. 333.

16 Eugene Staley, *War and the Private Investor* (New York, 1935), App. A.

17 Treasury Dept. (Washington, 1947), p. 69.

18 See also Royal Institute of International Affairs, *The Problem of Foreign Investments* (London, 1937), pp. 186, 263-267.

19 From the outset, modern Japan has endeavored to minimize the use of

sive by the continued lack of interest of American bankers and industrialists in the China market. It seems probable that the United States, while perhaps influenced in a general way by the hope that China would "someday" translate physical size into economic importance, has been traditionally hostile to *de facto* infringements of equality of economic opportunity, resentful of the aggressive policies of Japan along both economic and political lines, and, of late years, increasingly concerned with national security and the use of force in international affairs.

### *Economic Relations During World War II*

World War II began in the Far Eastern theatre no later than 1937, at which time Japan embarked upon the so-called "China Incident." Prior to Pearl Harbor the United States, while generally sympathetic to the Chinese position, continued to trade with Japan so that with the closing of Chinese ports America was placed increasingly in the position of seeming to aid Japan at the expense of China. Economic support of China was undertaken on a small scale through the Export-Import Bank in 1938. In the period 1938-40, the Bank entered into several so-called commodity loans, amounting in the aggregate to $120 million, which were used by China to finance imports.[20] The United States also coöperated with China and Great Britain in endeavoring to stabilize China's foreign exchange rates; in this connection the United States Treasury in the spring of 1941 advanced $50 million, which amount was later entirely repaid by the Chinese Government.

After Pearl Harbor economic relations were necessarily dominated by a United States desire to "keep China in the war," and various measures were employed to that end. While China had been declared eligible for lend-lease aid in May, 1941, the amount of assistance under the program was extremely small,

---

foreign loans and direct investments. She also proved adept in creating a modern banking structure, in mobilizing savings and credit, and in developing an extreme concentration of economic control.

[20] One loan of $25 million was authorized in 1938; three in the total sum of $95 million in 1940. China, in turn, agreed to deliver tin, tungsten, and other minerals, and wood oil in repayment. See *Annual Reports* of the Export-Import Bank of Washington.

and with the blocking of the Burma Road in April, 1942, materials were transported entirely by air until the reopening of land transport in January, 1945. By V-J-day the total lend-lease transfers, which were largely of a military character, amounted to some $849 million. Subsequently, lend-lease transfers amounted to more than $777 million, of which $49.6 million were "pipe-line supplies" sold to China on credit terms. Aside from pipe-line supplies the post-V-J-day lend-lease aid has been of a military nature, of which a small part was on a reimbursable basis.[21]

Aside from lend-lease aid, of which nearly half the total was extended after the cessation of hostilities, the United States during and shortly after the war advanced nearly $500 million of financial assistance, as well as some technical aid. The $500 million credit extended China by the Treasury was authorized by the Congress in February, 1942. Its purpose was to strengthen the internal political and financial position of the Chinese Government; no terms of repayment were stipulated by the Congress or the Treasury, and their negotiation has not yet been undertaken. It is significant, however, that the credit was characterized as "the financial counterpart of lend-leasing war materials,"[22] and it seems probable that eventual settlement may be on terms comparable to lend-lease settlements generally.

Technical advice was provided China by the Nelson mission in 1944-46 and by individual specialists sent to China under State Department or Foreign Economic Administration auspices. The advice extended to techniques of industrial production, agriculture, standardization, economic planning, and plans for the development of hydro-electric works on the Yangtse River. Negotiations also led in 1943 to the ending of the extraterritorial rights which Americans had enjoyed in China for nearly a century. Work was then begun in the nego-

[21] Committee on Foreign Affairs, House of Representatives, Eightieth Congress, Second Session, committee print, *Text of Proposed China Aid Bill and Background Information* . . . (Washington, 1948), p. 23. Submitted by the Department of State, Feb. 20, 1948.

[22] This phrasing was used in House Report 1739 and by the Secretary of the Treasury in testimony before the House Committee. See State Dept., *Text of Proposed China Aid Bill—*, cited above, p. 22.

tiation of a commercial treaty, signed in November, 1946.[23]

In general, it may be said that economic relations with China during the war period were *ad hoc* in character and, for the most part, did not reflect a coördinated over-all conception of economic relations from a long-range point of view. In the writer's view, certain of these activities had the unfortunate consequence of creating misleading impressions of the long-run intentions of the United States. For example, Generalissimo Chiang Kai-shek apparently was encouraged to believe that hundreds of millions of dollars might be forthcoming to finance a hydro-electric project at the gorges of the Yangtse. And certain Chinese probably gained the impression that America would in the long run favor and lend support to a highly intricate, blueprint type of detailed plan for the economy of all China.

To the extent that these efforts contained a central focus, they were in the nature of a "holding" action designed to keep China in the war. This objective had both physical and psychological aspects, involving the maintenance of the internal strength and prestige of the National Government of China and, after V-J day, the reëstablishment of its authority in occupied China. (In the latter connection, lend-lease services were used both to transport national troops east and northeast and to continue their training and equipment.)

It must be added that the United States, under the Yalta agreement, supported Russia's ambitions in Manchuria, industrially the most important part of China. The Yalta provisions, which in substance appear to have been confirmed in the Sino-Soviet treaty of 1945, provided for the restoration of a Soviet position in Manchuria substantially similar to that of the Czar prior to the Russo-Japanese War of 1904-05. Under the Sino-Soviet Treaty, the Soviet Union received a lease of Port Arthur as a joint naval base, joint and equal ownership of the principal Manchurian railways, and a free lease of half the port facilities of the important port of Dairen; all these concessions were for a period of thirty years.[24]

23 State Dept. Press Release No. 773, Nov. 2, 1946. The treaty had not been ratified by the U. S. Senate as of March 25, 1948. Certain of its provisions have been objected to by American chambers of commerce in China.

24 *Department of State Bulletin,* XIV (Feb. 10, 1946), 201-208.

Sino-Soviet relations in Manchuria and elsewhere are such as potentially to affect the economic relations of China and the United States. The Soviet position in China affords it a basis for influencing Chinese economic policies, both internally and externally. It would be idle at this time to forecast whether the long-run consequence will be that China leans more or less heavily upon the United States or upon Russia for advice and economic assistance. One can only point out that China is not yet fully the master of her own economic and political house.

### *The Immediate Postwar Period*

V-J-day did not bring an end of war in China. Civil war, largely but not entirely deferred by both the Kuomintang and the Communists in the face of Japanese aggression, has been resumed on a far wider scale than during the nineteen-thirties. During the Japanese conflict, the Chinese Communist Party extended its influence and control through broad areas of north China. With the failure of the truce in 1946, during which negotiations between the Government and the Communists took place under American mediation, full scale civil war was initiated and continue in the spring of 1948.

The United States has endeavored to bring about the unification of China and has employed a variety of tactics toward that end. American objectives, in the writer's view, have not been and are not primarily economic. Rather, American policy has been dictated by the desire to avoid either a power vacuum, or the development in the Far East of another threat to world peace and security. In the writer's view, therefore, current economic policies concerning China should be appraised largely in their political setting. One may roughly divide such economic policies and actions in two groups: those which have been general to American foreign policy in the postwar period, and those which, if not unique to Sino-American relations, have been emphasized especially in relations with China.

In the first category belong encouragement of Chinese membership in the International Bank and the Monetary Fund, and participation in the economic activities of the United Nations. In addition, through UNRRA, the United States has contributed $465.8 million[25] toward Chinese relief and rehabilitation and has encouraged China to take part in the reciprocal trade negotiations and in international discussions preparatory to the establishment of an International Trade Organization. In all these activities China has enjoyed full participation. Mention may also be made of economic assistance to China under the United States Foreign-Relief Program under which $45.7 million have been allocated to China, of the children's aid program of the United Nations in which the United States share of the China allocation is $2.1 million, of a lend-lease credit of $49.6 million for civilian supplies contracted for but not delivered before V-J day, and of some $17.6 million of Naval aid in 1945-46.[26]

In the category of United States economic measures or policies especially related to China, reference should be made to (1) Export-Import Bank loans, (2) certain postwar lend-lease and military assistance measures, (3) surplus property sales, and (4) the negotiation of a commercial treaty.

1. Discussion of Export-Import Bank loans must be preceded by reference to President Truman's policy statement of December, 1945, issued immediately prior to General Marshall's departure to China as the President's representative. In this statement[27], the President called attention to the existence of "one party government" in China and advocated the broadening of the Chinese Government "to include other political elements in the country." He then declared that "As China moves toward peace and unity along the lines described above, the United States . . . would be prepared to give favorable consideration to Chinese requests for credits and loans . . . for projects which would contribute toward the development of a healthy economy throughout China and healthy trade relations with the United States." The President reiterated this position in a public statement a year later.[28]

In what was in *some* respects a forerunner of the Marshall

[25] This amount is the U. S. share of 72 per cent of total UNRRA aid. See State Dept., *Text of Proposed China Aid Bill—*, p. 18.

[26] *Text of Proposed China Aid Bill*, p. 18, *et. seq.*

[27] *Dept. of State Bulletin* (Dec. 16, 1945), p. 946.

[28] *Dept. of State Bulletin,* (Dec. 29, 1946), p. 1181.

Plan, loans were made conditional on internal developments; as China moved toward peace and unity along democratic lines she would receive economic assistance. In April of 1946, the Export-Import Bank (with the approval of the National Advisory Council) agreed to set aside $500 million for loans for specific projects; the funds so set aside were never used, and the earmark was allowed to lapse on June 30, 1947.[29] No formal agreement was arrived at between the United States and China concerning this $500 million of Bank Funds. Attention should be called to the phrasing of the President's second statement of policy concerning China, in December 1946, emphasising the conditional nature of financial assistance: "—the Export-Import Bank earmarked a total of $500,000,000. . . . *Agreement* to extend actual credits for . . . *projects would obviously have to be based upon this Government's policy as announced December 15, 1945. So far, this $500,000,000 remains earmarked, but unexpended*" (italics added). It may be noted, however, that limited credits had been signed by the Bank early in 1946, prior to the earmarking, which in the aggregate amounted to $66.8 million.[30]

Obviously, however, neither the prospect of substantial dollar credits from the Export-Import Bank, nor the moral suasion of the United States, was effective in inducing desired internal developments in China. General Marshall returned to the United States at the end of 1946 and issued a statement[31] which is unusual for the frankness and objectivity with which he discussed the obstacles to the ending of civil war in China. In his view, neither "the dominant reactionary group in the Government," nor "the irreconcilable Communists" are free of grave responsibility. He expressed the belief that "The salvation of the situation . . . would be the assumption of leadership by the Liberals in the Government and in the minority parties. . . . under the leadership of Generalissimo Chiang Kai-shek. . . ."

2. Some have criticized postwar lend-lease and related military assistance as having been an obstacle to peace negotiations.

[29] Export-Import Bank, *Fourth Semiannual Report to Congress* (July 31, 1947), p. 8.

[30] Export-Import Bank, *Second Semiannual Report* (July 29, 1947), p. 58.

[31] Dept. of State, Press Release No. 9 (Jan. 7, 1947).

It has been charged that the continuance of military lend-lease gave unfortunate encouragement to reactionary elements in the Kuomintang. As previously mentioned, lend-lease assistance after V-J day continued until June 30, 1946,[32] and, aside from the pipe-line agreement common to the United States policy toward other lend-lease countries, consisted of military goods and services. This aid, nearly as great as that extended prior to V-J day, was defended as necessary to carry out agreements with China to aid in evacuating approximately 3,000,000 Japanese, and to assist the Chinese Government in reoccupying territory held by the Japanese. The United States had also agreed during the war to train and equip thirty-nine Chinese divisions; the training ended on V-J day and the transfer of equipment had been largely but not entirely completed before the beginning of the Marshall mission.[33]

These advances of military aid necessarily increased the ability of the Chinese Government to reëstablish its position in occupied China. Certainly, also, they reduced somewhat the burden which would otherwise have been borne by the Chinese economy. It is most difficult to estimate their effects on the collapse of peace negotiations. The parties in controversy were already lacking in trust of each other, and the United States program was not a new element introduced subsequent to General Marshall's mission.

3. Through sales of surplus property the United States made available to China goods of an estimated original cost of about $824 million. Combat matériel, vessels, and aircraft were specifically excluded from the contract. The terms of sales were somewhat complicated. The return to the United States amounted to $175 million, and consisted of: (1) an offset of an estimated[34] $150 million owed by the United States to China for Chinese currency advances to United States forces; (2) $35 million for

[32] A military aid agreement, however, authorized a continuance of military lend-lease of no more than $40 million, on a reimbursable basis, until Oct. 31, 1946. Dept. of State, *Text of the Proposed China Aid Bill. . .*, p. 23.

[33] Statement by the President, United States Policy Toward China, *Dept. of State Bulletin* (Dec. 29, 1946), p. 1181.

[34] Chinese yuan were advanced in a period of rapid inflation, without prior agreement as to the determination of a rate of exchange appropriate for settlement of the obligation.

the acquisition by the seller of properties in China and government current expenses; (3) the provision by China of a fund of $20 million for cultural, research, and educational activities in China. The "purchase price" thus arrived at was $205 million, but the United States agreed to establish a fund of $30 million to cover costs incurred by China in shipping and other services relating to the property transfer.[35]

Calculations of United States aid to China sometimes include the original cost of the surplus goods sold to China. It is the writer's conviction, however, that the United States was extremely anxious "to get rid of" surplus war property in the Pacific area, that the ratio of the sales price to original cost of the property was in line with such ratios in the case of war surplus sales to other countries, and that it is grossly misleading to consider the transaction only as "aid to China," as many have done. From China's point of view, however, the hope was expressed that the resultant importation of commodities would tend both to mitigate price inflation and to be of use for reconstruction purposes.

4. In the long view, the most important economic negotiation of the two countries may prove to be the Treaty of Friendship, Commerce and Navigation,[36] signed in Nanking in November, 1946. It is considered to be one of the most comprehensive commercial treaties negotiated by the United States. It is of unusual importance in view of the relinquishment by the United States in 1943 of all rights of extraterritoriality.

The Treaty is both lengthy and complex; it is possible here only to summarize certain of its most important economic provisions. (1) In general, nationals and corporations of each country are accorded most-favored-nation treatment in the territory of the other. (2) Business firms are not necessarily accorded "national" treatment in commerce, manufacturing, processing, or mining. That is to say, China may lawfully give its own companies rights or privileges not accorded American firms.

[35] Dept. of State, *Text of the Proposed China Aid Bill. . .*, pp. 26-28.

[36] Dept. of State, Press Release, No. 773 (Nov. 2, 1946), with a copy of the Treaty and Protocol attached. The Treaty has not yet been ratified by the U. S. Senate; American chambers of commerce in China are said to have objected strongly to certain of its provisions.

(3) Each country does, however, generally accord national treatment to the nationals (natural persons) of the other, with certain exceptions including mining, and organizing, participating in, and controlling or managing companies of its own country. (4) If there is a taking of property of nationals or companies of one country, each assures just compensation, the right of the owner to withdraw such compensation in the foreign exchange of his own country over a period of not more than three years, and the right to the most favorable foreign exchange rate in use at the time of application. (5) As to foreign exchange for the payment of imports, interests, dividends, and transfers for such other purposes as loans, there is an assurance of national and most-favored-nation treatment. Each country reserves the right, however, to restrict such transfers on a nondiscriminatory basis. (6) The Treaty contains an article concerning state trading agencies, and stipulates that such agencies in their purchases and sales will be governed only by considerations, such as price and quality, which would ordinarily by considered by a "private commercial enterprise." (7) Shipping may be barred from the waters and ports of either country; only most-favored-nation treatment is assured.

There is not space for comment or further summarization. Suffice it to remark that the days of extraterritorial privilege are over!

### *The Future*

American economic policy toward China, as indicated in earlier paragraphs, has tended in the recent past to make loans contingent upon China's progress toward national unity along democratic lines. The desired result obviously has not been achieved, and China, at the time of this writing, is in desperate straits both economically and politically. Economically, civil war has brought the widespread destruction of facilities of production and transportation, depleted China's foreign exchange resources, brought her monetary system to the verge of collapse, and induced runaway price inflation with its attendant repercussions on the production and distribution of commodities and the honesty and efficiency of government personnel. Politically, the deterioration of economic conditions has weakened the power of the National Government, and reduced its ability either to command the support of the Chinese people or to implement necessary reforms.[37]

In these circumstances, and in view of the deepening rift in relations with the Soviet Union, the United States faces a most serious dilemma. Were international relations less threatening, she might well occupy a passive role with regard to China, and leave the people of that unhappy land to seek their own solution. Confronted with a world-wide clash of ideologies, however, America is reluctant to accept further accretions of communist power. Chinese communists, as virtually all careful observers agree, unfortunately are in fact communists and not merely agrarian reformers.[38]

It appears to be highly probable that Congress will aid the National Government of China by voting economic and military assistance. Such action may well modify the previously stated policy of the United States. In the President's statements referred to in earlier pages, economic assistance was made contingent upon progress in China toward peace and unity along democratic lines. The current proposal of the State Department is based more narrowly. Secretary Marshall described the proposal as giving China ". . . breathing space in which the Government could initiate important steps toward more stable economic conditions."[39] It appears, however, that Congress in the case of China, as in that of Europe, will require a bilateral agree-

[37]For general descriptions of economic and political conditions in China, see the President's message to the Congress of Feb. 18, 1948, and Secretary Marshall's statement to the Foreign Affairs Committee of the House on Feb. 20, 1948, in support of the recommended China Aid Program. *Dept. of State Bulletin* (Feb. 29, 1948), pp. 268-270, 270-271.

[38]Doubt does exist, however, both as to the ability of the Communists successfully to govern China, and the degree to which they would in fact continue with the policy of "gradualism" pursued in communist areas during the second World War and preached by their leaders. For an exposition of the necessity for a gradual evolution of communism in China see Mao Tse-tung, *The New Democracy* (New Century Publishing Co., 1944), *passim.*

[39]The Secretary's statement before the Foreign Affairs Committee of the House, cited *supra.* The statement of purpose in the China Aid Act of 1948, which is Title E of the Foreign Assistance Act of 1948, approved April 3, is much less limited in scope than the corresponding section of the State Department bill. The Act contains reference, among other things, to "the continuing development of a strong and democratic national government. . ."

ment designed to implement the effective use of funds, and to encourage the adoption of other desirable economic measures.[40] (1) China would be asked to enter into an agreement with the United States to make efficient use of commodities provided, and to initiate, "insofar as practicable," financial and related steps toward a more stable currency and the improvement of her economy. (2) Insofar as aid is extended, China will be required to establish a commensurate fund which can be used only for purposes agreed to by the United States. The President will have power to terminate the aid program whenever ". . . he determines that China is not adhering to the terms of its agreement . . ."

In considering future economic relations between the two countries, it is important that sight is not lost of conditions affecting the long- as well as the short-run well-being of the Chinese people. Even if the United States were to concern itself only with political objectives, it seems obvious that political progress in China along lines that would generally be desired by the United States, rests on the support of the Chinese people and the economic conditions which affect them.

Space does not permit an adequate description and analysis either of the Chinese economy or of the conditions of economic progress in that country. Certain matters, however, are sufficiently clear and fundamental as to justify the brief comments which follow.

*Agriculture:* It is usually estimated that from 80 to 85 per cent of China's population is rural, and it seems highly unfortunate that most discussions of economic development have concentrated so heavily upon industrialization. It appears that the average size of farms in China is approximately three to three and one-half acres, and that perhaps a third or more are not more than one and one-half acres in size. (There is, of course, a considerable regional variation in the size of farms.)

[40] It appears at this time that the China Aid Program will be administered by the Administrator of the entire foreign aid program, and that the legislative basis will be identical or nearly so. This brief description of the program is based on the draft legislation prepared by the Dept. of State. The China Aid Act of 1948, as adopted, authorizes the appropriation of $338 million for economic, and $125 million for military assistance to China.

Before the war, it was estimated that about one half of the peasants owned their farms, and that tenants paid approximately one-half of their cash crops as rent.[41] Tax rates in China are extremely high; Chinese agricultural experts informed the writer in 1945 that they estimated taxes in kind in Szechwan Province to take more than 20 per cent of the summer crop.

Under such circumstances it is clearly important that measures be taken to reduce the rent, tax, and interest burdens on the farmer, and at the same time to increase his productivity. The National Government has paid lip service to these objectives, but action has been lacking. Information during the war period, however, indicated that the communists, after abandoning the land expropriation policy of the nineteen-thirties, were gaining popular support by reducing both taxes and rents. An interesting aspect of the situation was that rent reductions which were enforced in communist China were less severe than those prescribed by the unenforced laws of the National Government. Similarly, the National Government planned to provide financial assistance to farmers, but accomplished comparatively little.

The substantial increase of farm productivity, through measures such as better seeds, insecticides, irrigation projects, rural extension work, and the development of local and handicraft manufactures, is possible and practicable, in the view of competent Chinese and foreign observers.

*Transportation.* Clearly, the improvement of transportation is essential in a country so vast as China. Before the war, railway mileage including that in Manchuria was approximately 12,000. Famines would be minimized and the real standard of living increased, if China were to become increasingly an economic unit rather than a series of comparatively autonomous markets.

*Industrialization.* One cannot deny that the "people's livelihood," to use Sun Yat-sen's phrase, may be benefited by an increasing industrialization. The danger, however, is that industrialization be given a higher priority than it deserves in the

[41] The above statements are based largely on R. H. Tawney, *Land and Labour in China* (London, 1932), but they conform approximately to numerous other materials. It must be emphasized that data concerning economic conditions in China are rarely accurate by Western standards.

allocation of China's "scarce resources," and that it be directed toward economically inferior uses. Loose thinking leads many Chinese and foreigners to believe that a forced industrialization necessarily increases the national income to the people's benefit, without reference to the comparative advantage of alternative allocations of productive resources. In China, also, political difficulties have placed an undue emphasis on the development of heavy industry as necessary to political power and national security.[42]

Aside from raw material deficiencies in petroleum, copper, zinc, lead, and other important metals and minerals, China lacks trained manpower at all levels of industrial production. Many Chinese political leaders are influenced by the economic planning of the Soviet Union as well as by the views of Sun Yat-sen.[43] They are sympathetic to the nationalization of important industries or to government participation therein,[44]—and perhaps to over-all economic planning in a detailed blueprint sense. Moreover, as indicated by the unwillingness of China to assure national treatment to American companies in the recently negotiated commercial treaty,[45] there is a tendency toward restriction of foreign capital in many types of business.

This is not the place to discuss either the economic merits of socialism, or the virtues of increasing the international mobility of capital. It seems to the writer, however, that China is so large, and her economic development so limited, that she is in the greatest need of foreign capital[46] on the one hand, and of the flexibility of private enterprise on the other. Certain industries in China are nationalized and will continue to be. The danger,

[42] An excellent anaysis of China's economic potential in relation to military power is to be found in D. N. Rowe, *China Among the Powers* (New York, 1945). It affords little encouragement to those who may assume that China's industrialization will quickly result in substantial military strength.

[43] Sun Yat-sen, *The International Development of China*. See also his *San Min Chu I* (1924).

[44] Sun Fo, influential son of Sun Yat-sen, has expounded the doctrine of the "mixed" economy in which public and private capital will jointly and severally participate in given industries. See his *China Looks Forward* (New York, 1944).

[45] Described above.

[46] The mobilization of private Chinese capital is much handicapped by the comparatively limited use of the corporation, and by the absence of well organized mechanism for private investment. Few Chinese concerns have more than a handful of stockholders; almost none have as many as several hundred shareholders.

however, is that in an excess of zeal the Chinese Government may nationalize so rapidly, and plan so intricately, that economic progress will be long in coming. Moreover, there is a real prospect that industrialization will be aimed towards objectives of autarchy and military power, rather than toward those industries best adapted to Chinese resources and to the needs of her people.

*Commercial Policy.* The implications of certain of the above comments concerning industrialization apply also to Chinese policies concerning trade barriers, exchange controls, and to the rapid development of state trading.

*Price Inflation.* The inflation of prices in China has reached a point where at the time of writing $2 of American currency are reported to be exchangeable for $1,000,000 of Chinese currency; before the war the ratio was approximately one to three. Inflation is a problem of the moment in China, and therefore is in a different category than the longer-run questions referred to above. While inflation is acute, the Chinese economy is essentially rural, and a money economy is less pervasive than in Western countries; also, the Chinese have developed various procedures, such as the collection of taxes in kind, which tend somewhat to minimize the consequences of inflation. At the same time, price inflation in China has been a major cause of corruption in government and military circles, has led to the hoarding of commodities, has reduced long-term capital investment, and has contributed to a socially undesirable redistribution of wealth.

The shortages of commodities have, of course, contributed to price inflation. More important, however, has been the inability of the Chinese Government to finance government expenditures principally through taxes or borrowing from the people. During the later war years, and since V-J day, the major portion of government expenditures have been financed through the printing press. At present, "The civil war imposes a burden on the national budget of 70 per cent or more, and the financing is now carried on by means of paper money."[47]

[47] From Secretary Marshall's statement before the House Foreign Affairs Committee, *Dept. of State Bulletin* (Feb. 29, 1948), p. 269.

Under these circumstances, the remedy of inflation lies in the end of civil war, a rise of output, and in the general improvement of laws and of government efficiency. The answer certainly cannot be found in foreign loans for financing Chinese imports, or for stabilization purposes, though the increased imports associated with foreign loans would tend to restrain inflationary forces. Monetary aid in the form of increased reserves may of course check further rises in the velocity of circulation, especially if accompanied by a reduction of government expenditures, an increase of tax revenues and an increase in the supply of goods. Inflation is too far advanced for purely monetary measures to be effective.

The above remarks can do no more than provide an introduction to a few aspects of the Chinese economic situation; many topics, including population—which is perhaps the most important of all the long-run problems confronting China—have not been mentioned. It is hoped, however, that if the United States is positively concerned with the future development of China, there will be an increasing tendency in this country to recognize that economic and political progress are one and inseparable.

## PART III

# *INTERNATIONAL ECONOMIC COÖPERATION*

# *INTRODUCTION*

Seymour E. Harris

America's foreign economic policy is intimately associated with numerous international agencies, the most important of which are the International Monetary Fund, the International Bank for Reconstruction and Development, and the International Trade Organization (ITO). This part of the book deals with these three important agencies. Perhaps of less importance today but with fair prospects is the Foreign Agricultural Organization (FAO). The United Nations Economic and Social Council which, among other functions, should help integrate the work of the various organizations is also an important factor in international economic relations.

Among the problems with which the four papers in this part of the book deal are the manner of freeing exchange rates, the relation between the expediency of definitive exchange rates and the current inflation, the effect of variations in rates upon exports, the danger of multiple rates and the manner of eliminating them, the repercussions of political deterioration upon the functioning of the international agencies, the clash between advanced and backward countries relative to the Charter of ITO, the integration of state trading with general programs for reducing obstacles to trade, the manner of achieving tariff reductions through negotiations, the relation of multilateralism and full employment. In general, international agencies strive to improve economic conditions by stimulating trade expansion and by discouraging exchange practices and trade restrictions which not only tend to reduce standards of living but also bring economic warfare and, therefore, are threats to peace.

# 11

## *EXCHANGE RATES AND THE INTERNATIONAL MONETARY FUND**

Camille Gutt

Exchange rates are historical facts. They reflect not only prevailing conditions but conditions that have evolved continuously from the past. From 1930 to 1936 the structure of exchange rates throughout the world underwent violent changes. The great depression and its consequences induced every country to change the parity of its currency with relation to gold. By 1939, before the war broke out, the world had adjusted itself to a new pattern of exchange rates. Of course, it was not ideal; it was supported in many instances by high tariffs, import restrictions, and exchange controls. Despite this, in a number of countries the prevailing parity was in a precarious position. If the war had not intervened, further adjustments in exchange rates would have been necessary in 1940 and 1941.

The war itself created new forces which inevitably weakened the whole structure of exchange rates. Of first importance is the tremendous war destruction and its immediate consequence, the impairment of production. Closely related to this is the monetary inflation, realized or latent, which affects the capacity to trade as well as to produce. The countries of Western Europe were cut off from the normal channels of trade for six years or more. The great shipping countries lost about half of their fleets during the war. The commercial and financial services they had provided to customers in all parts of the world were

*This paper is the substance of an address given at the graduate school of Public Administration, Harvard University, February 1948.

greatly reduced. During and after the war they spent much of their accumulated international reserves and wealth and they incurred large foreign debts.

All these factors act on the international economic position of a country, although some of them will in time be overcome. There has already been a great recovery in production and even in trade. Merchant fleets of European countries have now been restored to between 70 and 80 per cent of their prewar level, so that about one-half of European shipping losses has been restored outside Germany and Italy. The commercial and financial services that Europe provided to the rest of the world will also be resumed in time, though probably not on the prewar scale. Some of the wartime deterioration is inevitably permanent in its nature. The loss of international investments will probably never be made good.

One other element must be emphasized. The political upheavals of the war and the political uncertainties of the postwar period have a direct effect on the international economic position of many countries. Particularly important are the changes in Germany, which are of far-reaching economic significance. In the Far East, equally great changes are taking place, not only in the territories of the Japanese Empire, but even in the territories of allied countries.

We must not overlook the effect of the lack of agreement among the great powers in placing a heavy burden on the economies of a number of countries. Resources must be devoted to continuing a scale of armaments that prevents these countries from putting more resources into investment and consumption. In some cases, large overseas expenditures must be incurred to carry out commitments resulting from the failure to conclude peace. For example, noncommercial overseas expenditure of the government of the United Kingdom amounted to $1.2 billion in 1946 and $1 billion in 1947. Nor should we underestimate the internal effects, political and economic, in some European countries of the tension between the United States and the Soviet Union.

The forces that disturb the world economy are still very powerful. During and after the war, the parities of the currencies of some countries were changed with a view to making them better suited to the radically altered conditions in these countries and in the world. It would be folly to assume that these changes undertaken to meet immediate and urgent needs have taken full account of the new conditions created by the war. It takes no prophetic insight to see that many changes will have to be made before the pattern of exchange rates is suited to the radically altered conditions of the postwar world. The great task of the International Monetary Fund is to see that necessary adjustments in exchange rates are made promptly and in an orderly manner and that they are helpful in establishing a new economic balance in a greatly changed world. This is the purpose that has guided the Fund in dealing with exchange problems.

*Initial Parities*

The Fund Agreement provides that members must agree with the Fund on the initial parities of their currencies. In the summer of 1946 the Fund undertook consideration of this problem. A vast amount of data was collected. Many studies were made. Numerous discussions were held. I would not want to leave the impression that all this was done, so to speak, in the mass. In every case a detailed investigation was made of the present and prospective position of each member.

In this work we had in mind both the immediate and the ultimate problem. On the ultimate problem we wanted to know what would be the international economic position of a country after the transition period, and what real exchange rate—that is, the terms of trade—would then be suitable for it. Specifically, we assumed that the country would have completed reconstruction, that the United States would have good but not booming business conditions, that the United Kingdom would have restored its balance of payments without cutting imports below the 1936-1938 level, and that convertibility of major currencies would have been reëstablished, so that countries would be able to use the proceeds of their exports to every country to pay for their imports from any country. We wanted to know what real exchange rate under these assumptions would enable a country to restore a tolerable balance in its international payments.

The immediate problem was of a different order. It was concerned simply with the question of what effect the parity then prevailing in each country would have on its economy and on its trade within the next year or two. In short, we wanted to know whether the prevailing exchange rate would handicap a country in rebuilding its economy and in securing an orderly adjustment to its new international economic position. We wanted to know whether the prevailing exchange rate would help attain by the end of the transition period that tolerable balance of payments consonant with the real exchange rate.

This involves a Fund point of view on exchange rates. It is a practical point of view looking to the effectiveness of an exchange rate in performing its two functions. The first function is to enable a country to export the goods which it can spare in order to secure the means to acquire the imports which it needs. In short, the first function of an exchange rate is to let the exports flow. The second is to keep the imports of a country within its capacity to pay and to allocate imports according to the needs of the community as measured by broader policy considerations. In brief, the second function of an exchange rate is to limit imports.

Under present conditions it is not possible for the exchange rate to perform this second function in some countries. Exchange rates cannot be counted on to limit imports to the proper level or to apportion them among those various goods which the economy most urgently needs. For example, in a country like the Netherlands, in which the shortage of goods is so great that rationing is necessary to limit the demand for consumer goods and allocation is necessary to limit the demand for investment goods, it is inconceivable that the exchange rate could be expected to bring about an adequate limitation of the demand for imports. To do this a country might have to depreciate the parity of its currency so sharply as to offer exceptional bargains to its customers in the sale of its exports. Such a great depreciation might even affect adversely its foreign exchange receipts if its capacity to produce is still limited.

For these reasons it appeared to the Fund that for the present the one practical test which could be applied to determine the suitability of an exchange rate was whether it enables a country to export. A test of the initial parities communicated to the Fund[1] indicated that the proposed parities would not under prevailing conditions seriously handicap exports. That does not mean that there was any general expectation that the initial parities could be continued indefinitely. Obviously, the officials of the Fund were aware that as conditions of world demand changed, as latent inflationary forces began to manifest themselves, a parity which was not then hampering exports might later do so. This was stated very clearly in the first annual report of the Executive Directors of the Fund.

Whether or not the initial parities actually met the expectations of the Fund can be roughly determined by seeing how export trade has behaved in the year or so since the initial par values were established. In fact, for nearly every country in Western Europe exports have increased more rapidly than production. At least until the last of 1947 the initial parities do not seem to have been a handicap to members of the Fund in expanding their total exports. I shall have something to say regarding the direction of their exports in connection with another problem.

In the last few months, however, it became clear that in some countries the initial parity had begun to burden export trade, more particularly exports toward the dollar area. Whether these developing difficulties are proof that an error in judgment was made in accepting the initial par values is a matter of opinion. My view is that, if the necessary changes are made promptly, the wisdom of our original action will be supported. Unnecessary delays in changes will indicate that the members of the Fund are making a serious mistake in continuing the overvaluation of their currencies. Under such conditions the Fund will not hesitate to urge on a member consideration of the desirability of a revision of the parity of its currency.

[1] Brazil, China, the Dominican Republic, Greece, Poland, Uruguay, and Yugoslavia requested a postponement of agreement on the initial parities of their currencies.

What alternative was there in fact to accepting the initial parities? Some people would have wanted the Fund to make a thorough overhaul of exchange rates, adjusting them to what they regard as the real value of the currency, probably something resembling purchasing power parity. Frankly, such a course would have been in practice impossible. The adjustment of a currency on the basis of purchasing power parity implies that all that is necessary is to restore the prewar balance of payments. In fact, most of our members were faced with the establishment of a new balance of payments suited to their altered international economic position. An adjustment on the basis of purchasing power parity assumes that the whole problem in exchange rates is one of inflation. In fact, for many of our members the inflation problem is secondary to the real deterioration in their international economic position.

What can be the meaning of purchasing power parity in countries with rigid price controls and rationing? Many of our members are suffering from latent rather than realized inflation. Should the new rate have been based on the expected inflation or on the realized inflation? The answer seems to be that any purchasing power parity formula, whether of prices or wage rates, would have been an impossible basis for a general revision of exchange rates. That is not to deny that relative prices and costs are of major importance in considering whether an exchange rate will enable a country to export. Obviously they are, and price and wage data were given careful weight by the Fund.

It may be said in passing that to have compelled a country capable of exporting only 50 per cent of its prewar volume to value its currency at a parity suited to exports of 100 per cent of its prewar volume would have forced on that country further inflation. If we assume relative freedom in bidding for international trade goods, then if Czechoslovakia, for instance, was exporting 50 per cent of its prewar volume, if the exchange rate for the koruna had been set at a level that would have resulted in a world demand equal to 100 per cent of the prewar volume of exports, and if Czechoslovakia was unable to produce and export this volume, the effect would have been to bid up the prices of these goods in Czechoslovak korunas to a level higher than necessary to make their export remunerative. But this would not have brought more exports at that time. In short, such an exchange rate, however suitable for conditions two or three years off, would for the time being only have induced additional inflation.

These are among the considerations that led the Fund to accept the initial parities. The judgment of the Fund was that the accepted parities were then performing reasonably well their function of moving export goods and that they were likely to be effective for a year or two to come. Even in the more extreme cases of doubt, such as France, the prospective inflation rather than the realized inflation would have had to be the basis for a change in parity.[2] In the view of the Fund the proper course was to continue the existing parities until they were shown to be an obstacle to international trade. At such a stage the Fund could consider one by one the necessary changes in parity. This was not alone the opinion of the officials of the Fund; it was wholeheartedly supported by the best informed central bank opinion in London, Ottawa, and New York.

### *Changes in Parity*

The policy of the Fund on initial parities carried with it as a corollary the willingness of the Fund to act promptly and favorably whenever a change in parity should become necessary because it threatened the export position of a country. The first annual report of the Executive Directors of the Fund stated that the Fund expected that changes in parity would be necessary when the export capacity of countries had increased and the buyers' market was superseded by a sellers' market. Even before that stage, in individual cases, continuing inflation was expected in time to undermine the parity of the currency in some countries; and here too the Fund was prepared to act promptly.

This raises a difficult question of timing. Suppose that a

[2] The wholesale price index in France (the retail price index is an index of food prices) was 846 in December 1946 on a 1938 base. It was 847 in April 1947. The rapid rise in French prices occurred in May 1947 and the following months. The volume of French exports, which averaged 54 per cent of 1938 in the last half of 1946, averaged 81 in the first half of 1947, with a peak of 92 in June 1947. The decline in French exports occurred during and after the summer of 1947.

country is suffering from a continuing inflation that affects the exports of that country. What should the policy of the Fund be? If all that a country does is adjust the exchange rate to the inflated level of prices and costs, it may restore exports for three months or six months. But in a relatively short time the adjustment in parity will be absorbed and the continuing inflation will make the new exchange rate unsuitable. A change in parity is not an ultimate solution to the export and balance of payments difficulties faced by such a country.

If the adjustment in the parity is to be fully effective, it must be accompanied by measures to halt the inflation. This means, measures must be taken to see that aggregate demand for consumption, for investment, and for government outlay at stable prices will not be in excess of the capacity of the country to produce plus any import surplus that can be financed by loans or grants from abroad. It means that total government expenditure should be reduced and that what is spent should be covered by taxes. It means that investment should be limited to those productive needs which will act quickly on the output of the community, and that investment funds should not be supplemented by new credit from the banking system. And it means that money incomes cannot be increased without a corresponding increase in output, particularly in that part of output which will be available for consumption. These are the elements of the anti-inflation measures that must be taken in conjunction with the change in parity if the change is to be effective. Otherwise, we shall only have bloated incomes and currency chasing short supply in a new spurt of inflation.

Unfortunately, such measures cannot always be taken promptly. In any democratic state time is needed to put through such comprehensive reforms. We have discussed with our members the need for just these policies to make effective a change in parity that was generally recognized as necessary. If there have been delays in getting an obviously necessary change in the parity of one of the major currencies, the French franc, it is because political disturbances prevented such measures from being taken earlier, and it is only recently that progress has been made in putting such measures into effect. In my opinion, it is better to wait three or four months before adjusting a parity, if this delay is necessary in order to have the change in parity accompanied by corrective measures adequate to deal with the underlying cause of the difficulty—inflation.

But suppose a country is not prepared to deal boldly with the inflation problem; what then should be the attitude of the Fund? While the Fund would deeply regret the failure of a country to proceed with strong measures to halt inflation, and while it would not hesitate to continue to urge on a member the necessity for such measures, I think it should not on that account refuse to agree to a change in parity. It is one thing to say that a country which is not taking steps to put its exchange policy on a sound and stable basis cannot expect help from the Fund. That is reasonable. It is quite another thing to say that the Fund will object to a proposed change in parity because a country is not taking adequate measures to keep its currency stable. If the Fund were to take such an attitude it would inflict on a country the continuation of a disastrous exchange rate which is choking its export trade and preventing the country from getting imports which it desperately needs.

## *Free Rates*

A number of our members have not brought their inflationary difficulties under control and are not able even to attempt to maintain a stable exchange rate. Greece is one such country; Italy is another. The action of the Fund in permitting such countries to continue their system of free rates has been criticized. In my opinion there is no other course than to permit a country in which prices rise at an annual rate of 50 per cent or more to keep a system of steadily depreciating rates.

The system in Italy is not, strictly speaking, a free market; it is a controlled exchange market. Exporters are permitted to sell half of their exchange receipts for whatever rate they can get from authorized importers. The other half is sold to the monetary authorities at the average of the market rates that prevailed during the preceding thirty days. This is not a system in which the exchange authorities can sit back and hopefully say that the market is free to do as it pleases.

It would be a serious mistake to assume that under such a system the sole problem of the monetary authorities is to limit the granting of licenses. Even the licensing policy becomes more complex in a country with continuing inflation. Actually, the monetary authorities must be sure that sufficient licenses are issued to encourage the bidding up of exchange rates to a level that will make exporting remunerative, despite inflated demand at home and rising domestic costs and prices. Exchange policy in Italy, therefore, must see that demand for foreign exchange be kept great enough through authorized and licensed imports to bring about a free exchange rate adequate to assure the proper level of exports.

As far as this feature of the Italian exchange system goes, I can see no objection to its temporary use under present conditions. Needless to say, the Fund would be very happy if conditions in Italy made it possible to declare a definitive par value and to keep the lira at parity without restricting export opportunities for Italy. Under present conditions, with severe unemployment, with a large budgetary deficit, and with political pressure to provide food subsidies and wage bounties, it is far better to continue for a time the free exchange system in Italy than to force a premature parity of the lira. We have studied the Italian situation and we hope that it will improve. The problem of overpopulation must be met through emigration of Italian workers. If part of the burden of unemployment could be lifted in this way, then good harvests, an adequate inflow of raw material imports, and aid from abroad would make it possible, without too long delay, to institute an effective stabilization program, and stop the inflation. At such a time the Fund will not be remiss in urging upon the Italian Government the desirability of agreeing on a parity of the lira.

### *Multiple Currencies*

It was stated above that one of the functions of the exchange rate is to limit imports but that under present conditions the exchange rate cannot perform this function in some countries. There has been some question whether exchange rates can, in the future, perform this function. In a number of Latin American countries, the exchange system even before the war involved the use of multiple currencies with a considerable difference between buying rates and selling rates for foreign exchange. The typical system of this sort has a buying rate for exchange from exports which is presumed to be remunerative to the exporters. This same rate of exchange may be applied to imports of essential goods. The purchasers of nonessential and luxury goods pay penalty rates considerably in excess of the buying rate.

A penalty rate on imports may be only another device to collect taxes from consumers of nonessential and luxury goods, with the tax collected at the time the exchange is sold. But in many cases multiple currency rates are not used simply as a means of collecting revenue. They are used rather as a device for restricting imports without requiring onerous administrative control in import licensing and without giving large windfall profits to the fortunate recipients of import licenses.

What happens is that a big inflation of incomes and prices has made importing more attractive. Since costs have not risen so much as world market prices for particular exports, such as coffee and copper, a change in the export rate is not needed. But measures are necessary to restrict excessive imports. And the monetary authorities use the device of charging penalty exchange rates for imports of nonessential and luxury goods. The facts that in the category of nonessential goods we often find commodities consumed by people of very modest incomes, that at times 50 per cent or more of aggregate imports are subject to the penalty rates, indicate quite clearly that we are dealing not simply with a tax device but with a system for restricting excessive import demand through penalty exchange rates.

In my opinion we shall find that, in time, a system of multiple currencies originating in inflation tends to disappear, once the inflation is brought under control. In the later stages of inflation, costs continue to rise until they meet prices. Exports become unprofitable at rates of exchange that are too much below the penalty rates for imports. To induce the continued flow of exports there is a tendency gradually to extend to exporters the privilege of disposing of their exchange proceeds at the higher import rate. We see this, for example, in Chile where all exports, except copper and nitrates, are becoming unprofitable except at rates corresponding to free market rates roughly 50 per cent above the official parity.

For these reasons, I believe that as a practical matter multiple currencies, except where they are used for tax purposes, will in the course of time disappear. As a first condition it is important to halt the inflation which makes necessary the use of penalty rates to restrict imports. Furthermore, a change in world demand might reduce the exceptionally high prices received by some exporters and necessitate an adjustment in local currency prices of their products to enable them to continue to export. This combination of events—halting inflation and a change in the sellers' market—offers the most favorable opportunity for eliminating multiple currencies and establishing a new uniform parity, adequate both for encouraging exports and limiting imports.

### *Disorderly Cross-Rates*

A special aspect of multiple currencies has again become of importance since the end of the war. I refer to the fact that in some countries the rates of exchange that prevail for different currencies are at cross-rates that do not conform to the parities established by the Fund. In Italy, in Greece, in some countries in the Middle East, and now in France, where action was taken despite the objection of the Fund, so-called free markets prevail for dollars and for other currencies; the cross-rates of the quotations for the dollar and sterling are not within the limits established by the Fund.

It is easy to draw the mistaken conclusion that such exchange quotations represent realistic valuation of a currency. The fact is that under present conditions these so-called free quotations are wholly unrealistic. They are the result of an arbitrary determination by the monetary authorities to place a value on a currency in a so-called free market through the licensing system. The disorderly cross-rates that emerge are the normal consequence of a system of inconvertible currencies where coöperative action of the type represented by the Fund is not being carried out.

Suppose all currencies are inconvertible in the sense that they cannot be transferred by the exporters of one country to the importers of a third country. Then trade between any pair of countries must be balanced bilaterally, except to the extent that one of the trading partners is willing to use gold or dollars to meet its adverse balance with the other country. If, under these conditions, free markets are established for all currencies, exchange in each country will be quoted at a rate that will assure bilateral balance including capital transactions. Of course, import and export controls may act on the supply and demand for exchange in such a way that the rate is kept close to the parity established by the Fund. Failing such controls it would be normal to expect a pattern of exchange rates in which cross-rates do not conform to the parities established by the Fund. Furthermore, the pattern of cross-rates would almost inevitably differ from country to country.

The immediate harm done by disorderly cross-rates is perhaps not very great. But they can cause serious and unwarranted doubt regarding the future value of a currency, making more difficult the task of securing exchange stability with currency convertibility. They distort trade relations so that they no longer become suitable for multilateral trade with convertible currencies. What could be more ridiculous than to have a cross-rate of $2.60 for sterling in the Italian market and a rate of $4 for sterling in the American market? Such rates are an encouragement to Englishmen to export to Italy and import from the United States. Furthermore, disorderly cross-rates through commodity arbitrage can deprive a country of the dollar proceeds of exports of its own products and drain its limited reserves to pay for reëxport of dollar imports to other countries.

There is only one means of assuring the continuation of an orderly pattern of exchange rates among inconvertible currencies, and that is to have the monetary authorities buy and sell the currencies at the agreed parities. A number of devices can be used to secure the desired balance of payments under these conditions. The first is to use gold and U. S. dollars to settle adverse balances between countries with inconvertible currencies, whenever the monetary authorities are prepared to authorize an excess of imports over exports. This is what the United Kingdom does in most of its trade with the Western Hemisphere. The second is to have the creditor country accumulate moderate balances of the currency of the debtor country. This is what happens among most of the European countries with payments agreements. The third is to limit exports and encourage imports by the creditor country and to limit imports and encourage exports by the debtor country until the demand for exchange is in approximate balance with supply at the parities established by the Fund.

As a practical matter this third means of maintaining orderly cross-rates can best be made effective if the two countries whose currencies are involved will agree on an export and import policy between them which will permit, during the course of a year, a reasonable balance in their payments at approximately the parity of their currencies. Short period fluctuations could then be minimized by accumulating moderate balances of the currencies of the debtor or by utilizing moderate balances of the currency of the creditor. Perhaps such a solution for assuring an orderly pattern of rates among inconvertible currencies will seem unattractive to economists. It is, frankly, a device for assuring bilateral balance. But the fact is that the necessity for bilateral balance does not arise from the obligation to maintain the parities established by the Fund. The necessity for bilateral balance has its origin in the inconvertibility of currencies. The requirement for maintaining parities simply prescribes the exchange rate at which the bilateral balancing should take place. The reason why the Fund insists on the maintenance of orderly cross-rates based on these parities is that they are the essential condition for restoring currency convertibility and multilateral trade.

## *Prices in Trade Agreements*

I might perhaps mention a technique commonly used in European trade to secure balance at prescribed exchange rates, where the relationship of prices and exchange rates is not equally satisfactory in both countries. Some countries in Europe enter into agreements under which total trade in specified commodities is set out in detail. The trade in these commodities may be either at world prices (generally dollar prices) or at prices stated in the agreement. When stated in the agreement there is a tendency to relate the prices of the export goods to the prices of the import goods. For example, if Denmark buys wood pulp from Finland at inflated Finnish prices converted into Danish kroner at the overvalued exchange rate for the Finnish markka, Denmark offsets this by quoting to Finland higher prices in Danish kroner for Danish butter. Actually, Denmark does charge Finland, under its trade agreement, a considerably higher price for butter than it does the United Kingdom, Belgium, Poland, Russia, and other countries with whom it has similar agreements.

The solution to this unsatisfactory situation of multiple prices based on distorted exchange rates is obviously the restoration of a reasonable relationship between prices and exchange rates and the resumption of the inter-convertibility of nearly all currencies. Until that is done, we shall probably have to depend upon such trade agreements, domestic price equilization funds, and quite extensive state control of export and import trade in order to maintain an orderly pattern of exchange rates.

### *Direction of Exports*

Let us now revert to a question raised earlier. It was then said that the exchange rates accepted by the Fund would, on the whole, meet the practical test of permitting the exports of these countries to flow. In nearly every Western European country exports during 1947 rose steadily, approaching in many instances the 1938 volume of exports, and this was done at a time when a large part of the output of these countries was devoted to reconstruction and investment and when the use of resources by the government was at exceptionally high levels. But the fact that exports have increased is no final proof that these exchange rates are satisfactory. Unfortunately, the increase in exports of European countries has been relatively large in trade with each other. Exports from Europe to the dollar area have not kept pace with the general increase in European exports.

If we look at it from the other point of view, we find that in the United States total imports are considerably below the level that might reasonably be expected on the basis of national income and economic activity. Starting from the American position it is clear that United States imports fall short of what might have been expected on the prewar basis for a number of reasons. First, sources of United States imports have not yet fully restored production. This is true of the Far East; it is also true of Europe. In the case of Europe, even where production might be devoted to goods exported to the United States, relatively more resources are being used for domestic investment rather than export. Second, the war has brought important changes in technology and in the need of the United States for certain imports. Rubber and silk are such import commodities. Third, export prices within Europe, though not restrictive of trade, are still too high to be attractive to American importers. As European export capacity increases, the need may arise to adjust either prices or some exchange rates to make European exports attractive to dollar markets.

One possible misconception should be dealt with. Some people may feel that if European exchange rates and prices were properly adjusted, the dollar shortage which these countries are experiencing would be corrected. I think there is no basis for such a view. The shortage of dollars in Europe is very largely a reflection of the exceptionally great need for real resources in these countries. In part, this may be a consequence of inflation. Much more, it is a consequence of the urgency felt by these countries to restore their economies far more rapidly than they are capable of doing with their own output. Extremist politicians are prepared to promise the public increased production and a higher level of consumption if only the blessings of a state economy are adopted. Responsible politicians must compete with such impossible promises by pushing as far as they can reconstruction and modernization, while maintaining something approaching the prewar standard of living. Added to this have been the unfortunate crop failures and the difficulties of maintaining normal supplies of fuel.

In a number of countries the wartime inflation has been kept from manifesting itself in higher prices and costs through such devices as price and wage control, rationing, and subsidies. At some time in the future, it will be desirable for countries to abandon these measures in order to give the economy greater freedom in adjusting itself to changed conditions. Obviously, the restoration of a greater degree of economic freedom can best be undertaken when current production is adequate to meet current needs. At such a stage the latent inflation of the past may be consolidated or wiped out through permitting a rise in prices, through extraordinary taxes, or through the blocking of currencies as has already been done in a number of countries. With the new conditions, reconsideration of the parity of the currency would be desirable. In some cases, no doubt, a change in parity will be necessary to restore the situation created by the consolidation of wartime inflation.

A word of caution must be said against the widespread but dangerous assumption that all currencies, or at least all European currencies, should be devalued now and devalued substantially. That a large and general depreciation of European currencies might increase, to some extent, present exports to the Western Hemisphere cannot be denied. However, this would not provide a solution, to a significant degree, to the present dollar shortage. It might in some cases aggravate the inflation problem. Of course, not the present but the future balance of payments of Europe must be brought into equilibrium through an adjustment of parities as well as through other measures. In any instance in which a worth-while change in exports to the dollar area would result from an adjustment of parity, the feasibility of adopting such a measure should be considered.

## *Summary and Conclusions*

First, the Fund accepted the initial parities communicated by its members, with a number of countries withholding the determination of their par values. The main reason the Fund accepted the par values is that it believed that the parities would permit exports to flow from these countries during the first year or two.

Second, exchange rates in a number of countries will have to be changed in the future because they are interfering with the flow of exports. In some instances a change in parity is overdue but has had to be delayed in order to permit other measures to be taken.

Third, when a country is suffering from a progressive inflation a change in parity will not be effective in assuring the continued flow of exports. The proper policy is to have the change in parity preceded by a forceful program to stabilize the domestic economy.

Fourth, in countries where there is no immediate prospect of bringing a rapid inflation under control, a fluctuating exchange rate can be justified as a means of permitting exports to flow until the situation improves. Both the country and the Fund must, in the meantime, seek means for bringing the inflation to a halt and for restoring an orderly exchange system.

Fifth, multiple currency practices involving penalty rates on imports are a reflection of the difficulty, in time of inflation, of restricting imports through the exchange rate. As inflation is brought under control and costs catch up with prices, the establishment of a new parity at approximately the penalty rate for nonessential imports will make it possible to encourage exports and to limit imports adequately with the same rate of exchange.

Sixth, the inconvertibility of currencies has resulted in disorderly cross-rates in some countries where so-called free exchange markets exist. Such disorderly cross-rates can be overcome through coöperative action of the type contemplated by the Fund. The establishment of orderly cross-rates through coöperation is important for the purpose of maintaining confidence in established parities and facilitating the restoration of convertibility of currencies.

Seventh, exports to the dollar area have not been so large as might reasonably be expected. A general change in parities in order to meet the dollar shortage is not justified at this time; but where a worth-while increase in exports to the dollar area would result from an adjustment of the parity of a currency, such a measure should be considered.

Finally, there is no occasion to be complacent about the present pattern of exchange rates. It is far from satisfactory. Considerable help toward meeting future balance of payments problems can be derived from the adjustment of some exchange rates. There is no reason, however, why the Fund should embark on a general adjustment of parities, either now or later.

The adjustment of a parity to the international economic position of a country is a problem that the Fund can best deal with by taking into consideration the special problems of a country whenever conditions are favorable to a helpful change in the parity of its currency. The Fund will not hesitate to urge on countries domestic measures to assure that the parities they now have can be sustained without onerous restrictions on international trade. The Fund will be prepared to discuss with any country a change in parity that may be necessary to permit its trade to develop. The Fund will not insist on the empty shell of exchange stability if this would have the effect of hurting a country's economy and the expansion of world trade.

The Fund has a great responsibility in securing the establishment of exchange rates which will permit international trade to be restored and to grow. To perform this duty the Fund must be alert; it must not hesitate to speak frankly and to stand firmly for its ideals. In performing this duty the Fund needs the help of an intelligent public opinion which understands these problems and which will support the Fund in reasonable and realistic policies. Constructive criticism could be very useful in keeping the Fund aware of its duty and in urging the Fund toward a positive policy if and when it were inclined to let things slide.

# 12

## *THE INTERNATIONAL MONETARY FUND AND THE INTERNATIONAL BANK FOR RECONSTRUCTION AND DEVELOPMENT*

Allan G. B. Fisher[1]

To many of those who in the later stages of the war began seriously to speculate about postwar economic policy, "reconstruction" seemed at first sight an apt description of the objective which ought to be pursued. But, as many critics were quick to point out, the word might easily be taken to imply merely building up again the same things which had existed before the war. Many of these things, however, they had no desire to see restored. They wanted something new and better, and some were optimistic enough to believe that the very destruction and disruption of old habits of thought inexorably imposed by war offered an opportunity to start afresh on new foundations and to construct something which might offer some adequate recompense for the sufferings and the heroism of the war.

Intelligible as these aspirations were, some of the optimism of the late war period now seems a little naïve, when viewed in retrospect from the grim real world of 1948. But at least in one important and far-reaching field, that of international economic relations, it was in the nature of things impossible merely to "reconstruct." Here, particularly during the interwar period, had been the most marked deterioration, and if there was to be even a semblance of order in the international economic re-

[1] The views are those of the author and not of the International Monetary Fund.

lations of the postwar world, new institutions had to be created for the purpose. Especially in the years immediately before the outbreak of war it had often been difficult to discern anything resembling an orderly pattern in the patchwork of temporary stopgaps and emergency measures by which a substantial fraction of international trade was then carried on. There was little international movement of capital for normal productive purposes and much of the capital movement was motivated by political considerations which took little or no account of economic rationality. Everything was affected by a high degree of uncertainty, and no one would have regarded with satisfaction the prospect of a "reconstruction" of interwar conditions. In this field of activity the time had clearly come for a change.

In any event it was obviously impossible to expect that within any short space of time new and permanent standards of "normal" international economic relations could be constructed. The damage inflicted by the war upon customary trading and financial relations had been too far-reaching to permit any such hopes. Whether one liked it or not, it was not possible here to evade the obligation to start afresh. Even those who had persuaded themselves that the rough and ready trade and exchange devices harshly imposed by Germany upon the weaker countries, which had fallen under her control, might be capable of refinement and purification in the interests of a more stable order were usually at the same time prepared to pay deference, which was something more than lip-service, to the principle of international division of labor. It was, therefore, possible to assume general agreement, with qualifications expressed in varying degrees of emphasis, that, whatever else it might mean, starting afresh meant an endeavor to recreate conditions which would permit enjoyment of the benefits of a multilateral trading system. Some of the qualifications were, however, pressed with great pertinacity, and the story of subsequent developments cannot be properly understood unless these initial divergences of outlook, or at least of emphasis, are constantly borne in mind. It was, moreover, highly unlikely that, if each country were left to struggle by itself with its own peculiar postwar difficulties, there would be any spontaneous movement in the direction generally desired. The same breach of historical continuity which made it necessary to start afresh had also destroyed the conditions which were essential for the effectiveness of any informal non-institutional framework of international economic relations on the nineteenth-century model; the efforts of constructive thinkers—which were not confined to any single country—therefore gradually crystallized in a pattern of new international institutions, with constitutions more highly formalized and obligations more precise than the world had hitherto known.

The first formal step in this process was taken at the Bretton Woods Conference, when the Articles of Agreement of the International Monetary Fund and of the International Bank for Reconstruction and Development were adopted on July 22, 1944. Forty-five countries were represented at this conference, and the two Agreements were ultimately ratified by all but four of them. The two institutions came formally into being on December 27, 1945. Five countries not represented at Bretton Woods have been admitted to membership, making a total of forty-six. Negotiations for the construction of a parallel international organization with responsibilities for international trade policy began later and have been more prolonged; the provisional acceptance of a Draft Charter for an International Trade Organization has been delayed until the conclusion of the Havana Conference on March 29, 1948.

There has been some disposition in recent months to reproach the architects of these projects because, it is said, they failed to appreciate the complexities of the postwar world in which the new creations would have to operate. Their picture of the course of postwar development was somewhat as follows. The United Nations Relief and Rehabilitation Administration, which had already been set up in November 1943, was assumed to be adequate for dealing with the urgent immediate requirements of war-devastated countries, without running any risk of a repetition of the tangles of international indebtedness which had contributed so much to the troubles of the interwar period. At the conclusion of the relief period, some provision for long-term capital needs of a more normal kind would be necessary, and the International Bank for Reconstruction and Development was to be established for this purpose. Both these institutions had immediate practical tasks assigned to them. To establish a new and reasonably stable international order, however, it was also necessary to draw up and to administer "rules of the game," which would be accepted by the participants in international economic life as guides to their conduct in relation to each other. Here it seemed convenient to distinguish between monetary and foreign exchange relations, and international trade relations, though for most significant purposes these are merely two aspects of the same thing. For the former, objectives and rules were laid down in broad outline in the constitution of the International Monetary Fund and machinery was created for the further elaboration through consultation with members of the general rules which they had accepted. The Fund was "not intended to provide facilities for relief or reconstruction, or to deal with international indebtedness arising out of the war," but its members could, under specified circumstances, draw upon the funds with which it was equipped for financing current international obligations. The risk that these funds might be withheld from members was calculated to provide a useful stimulus for observance of the rules. Similar guiding principles for commercial policy in the narrower sense are set forth in the Draft Charter of the International Trade Organization.

Postwar history has failed to observe the timetable thus implicitly drawn up. In some countries the relief period is not yet ended, and the periods by reference to which the scope of these international economic institutions was provisionally outlined has overlapped in a highly intricate and disorderly pattern. The deficiencies of the timetable began to appear at quite an early stage of the story. Extensive supplementary finance, of which the Anglo-American Loan Agreement of December 1945 was a conspicuous illustration, was provided for a variety of purposes outside the institutional framework which was under construction. This has significantly affected the subsequent operations of these institutions, which will necessarily be further influenced by the European Recovery Program of 1948, which is the most recent response to the difficulties which have arisen.

That all the varied international economic relations of real life could be neatly classified according to the logical principles suggested by this fourfold differentiation of functions was, of course, unlikely. Some overlapping and arbitrariness were scarcely to be avoided. In particular, from the standpoint of economic effects, there is often little significant difference between trade controls exercised through the machinery of foreign exchange, which were to fall within the province of the International Monetary Fund, and controls applied directly to trade itself, which would be part of the responsibility of an International Trade Organization. Nor is it always possible to distinguish clearly between the field of operation of the Fund and the Bank. And even where the nature of any particular transaction is evident, so that no difficulty of classification arises, it is not always easy to be quite certain that funds allotted for one purpose will not in fact be used for another. If my banker makes me an advance for some purpose upon which in any event I should have felt obliged to spend some money, even the closest formal tie-up between the money which he has lent me and the purpose formally declared for the advance cannot entirely exclude the possibility that some of it may be used to finance my next summer holiday.

It would, however, be a mistake to make too much of these logical difficulties of classification. Once agreement was reached that orderly international economic relations demanded, after the unprecedented storms of the war, the construction of an institutional framework, mere practical convenience made some formal allocation of responsibilities necessary. It was inevitable that considerable anxious thought should be given to the precise definition of these responsibilities, and equally inevitable that, in the light of events which could not then have been accurately forecast, subsequent experience should show that the results of this anxious thought did not fit precisely the new situations which arose. It would be unfair to reproach the anxious thinkers on this account; behind every proposal for new machinery of government, whether national or international, must lie the implicit hypothesis that the machinery will ultimately be administered by men of reasonable intelligence, prepared in the discharge of their responsibilities to pay due attention to the changing realities of the world. Happily this hypothesis is not always fantastically over-optimistic, and the embarrassments arising from the necessity for interpreting constitutions in situations which were not and could not have been accurately foreseen when they were drawn up have been much less serious than might have been feared.

The principal declared purpose of the International Bank for Reconstruction and Development was "to assist in the reconstruction and development of territories of members by facilitating the investment of capital for productive purposes, including the restoration of economies destroyed or disrupted by war, the reconversion of productive facilities to peacetime needs and the encouragement of the development of productive facilities and resources in less developed countries." The authorized capital stock of the Bank is $10,000 million.

It was not, however, intended in the first instance that the Bank's operations should be confined to lending its own resources. "The chief purpose of the Bank," as the Secretary of the Treasury said at the closing plenary session of the Bretton Woods Conference, "is to guarantee private loans made through the usual investment channels"; it was only "when private capital is not available on reasonable terms" that the Bank would also "supplement private investment by providing, on suitable conditions, finance for productive purposes out of its own capital, funds raised by it, and its other resources." (Article I, ii.)

If, in the postwar world, resources were to be available for international investment, much the larger part would clearly have to be raised in the United States. Some of the smaller prewar international financial centers might indeed before long be able to resume, on a modest scale, some of their old lending activities, and a few other countries, hitherto without experience in this field, might also gradually establish their position as international creditors. But at best the amount invested internationally from all these supplementary sources was certain to be small, compared with the potential lending of the United States. In these circumstances, it would have been natural for Americans to inquire why it should be thought necessary to go through all the elaborate motions of setting up a complicated international organization in which, as they might have feared, the immediate beneficiaries would have more influence than was fair or reasonable in determining how the lending resources of the United States were to be used. The answer to this question was twofold. The need for international investment was certain to be no less pressing in the postwar world than it had ever been, and its satisfaction was to the interests of both the borrowing and the lending countries. During the preceding decades, however, a hesitant, and sometimes suspicious, attitude of mind had developed in many borrowing countries which, whether reasonable or not, might have unduly delayed the revival of international capital movements if there had been no alternative to revival according to prewar models. The fears of improper external control imposed by foreign finance were no doubt often exaggerated, but they were also real. Political uncertainties seemed likely, in any event, to postpone the resumption on any significant scale of ordinary private international investment; there was, therefore, a strong case for admitting right at the outset, in negotiations for international loans between governments, a substantial measure of genuine international responsibility and control. Actually the influence of the United States in the International Bank for Reconstruction and Development inevitably remained very strong. The distribution of voting power, and the dependence of the Bank for the time being upon the United States money market for any additions to its resources beyond the original capital subscriptions, necessarily meant that there could be no serious question of Bank policy running directly counter to United States policy. But the essential contributions which might be made to the recovery of the world economy by the revival of international investment were more likely to be forthcoming, if both the country without whose financial resources such investment would be impossible and the borrowing countries were effectively associated in its control. The constitution of the IBRD was designed to make this association possible. In the development of its lending policy, an institution of this kind could afford to take long views, and the provision that "the Bank shall impose no conditions that the proceeds of a loan shall be spent in the territories of any particular member or members" promised to be an important contribution to the revival of an effective multilateral system.

The association of a large number of countries of varied financial strength and at different stages of economic development also made possible another important feature of the IBRD which marked it as a genuinely new institutional invention. The resources of most of its members were insufficient to allow them to contribute much directly to international investment. The advantages which would flow from the successful operations of the Bank would not, however, be confined to the countries directly concerned either as borrowers or as lenders. To quite a significant extent, there was a common interest, in which every country shared, in the rapid rehabilitation of war-disrupted economies and in "the encouragement of the development of productive facilities and resources in less developed countries"; the constitution of the Bank made it possible for countries which were not in a position to participate actively in the provision of capital to associate themselves in a joint guarantee, in proportion to their holdings of the Bank's capital, against losses arising from Bank investments. Here, too, and especially in the early stage of the Bank's history, it was naturally the guarantee of the United States which investors were certain to take most seriously, but, as time went on, the guarantees of other countries would also have a favorable effect on the market for Bank securities, and make it possible for a widening of the Bank's range of investment at moderate rates of interest.

At the time of its foundation any estimate of the volume of Bank investments in the first year or two of its life could have been no better than a rough guess. The $10 billion figure represented by its nominal capital was unfortunately likely to give an inflated impression of what was practically possible within a short period of time. Members of the Bank are required to pay only 20 per cent of the total subscribed capital, the remainder being subject to call if needed to meet the obligations of the Bank. On October 31, 1947 the paid-in capital aggregated $1,640,105,000, of which $731,087,000 was in United States dollars, and the remainder in the currencies of other countries. The Bank's resources were further expanded by bond issues of $250 million floated in July 1947. By the end of 1947 $497 million had been lent to France, the Netherlands, Denmark, and Luxembourg. This was a substantial fraction of the resources which were at that time at the effective disposal of the Bank, though small in comparison with the original figure of $10 billion. Nothing has been done so far in the field of guaranteed loans; those private international investments that it has been found possible to negotiate in the disturbed political conditions of the postwar world have presumably been made for purposes and under conditions in which the added support of an IBRD guarantee was not necessary.

It is not surprising that some impatient borrowers have felt that the Bank loans might with advantage have been made available rather more liberally. When, however, the general financial and monetary conditions of the world, and of the United States in particular, are taken into account, it is difficult to believe that more lavish lending by the Bank in the first year of its existence would have made the world today a much better place. Some specific investment activities, though highly desirable economically, were no doubt held up during this period for lack of adequate finance, but for the most part their prosecution would have been at the expense of something else for which the economic justification was probably stronger. It is significant that some of the loans already granted have not yet been fully utilized because of supply inadequacies. The benefits to borrowers of a more active investment policy which had *inter alia* the effect of reinforcing inflationary trends might have been highly dubious. It is now being more and more widely appreciated everywhere that the effort to do too much too quickly is one of the most powerful influences lying behind the continued inflationary pressure, and the chronic shortages of raw materials, of labor, and of many other things, which stem from it. In these circumstances, it would be unreasonable to take a very harsh view of the cautious attitude so far adopted by the Bank.

A strong case might indeed be made out, in the interests of more rapid capital reconstruction elsewhere, for checking in some way the demand of the United States for the goods—particularly capital equipment—which are in short supply throughout the world today. But this is a good deal to ask, and when one reflects upon the dependence of many parts of the world on United States exports—the output of some of which could be maintained only with difficulty in the absence of substantial capital expenditure in the United States itself—the awkward nature of the dilemma which, in this connection, confronts the world becomes clear.

Even if too generous international financing might have dangerous inflationary consequences, great advantages certainly would be gained by knowing reasonably well ahead what resources were likely to be made available in the future; assurances of this kind might, by diminishing uncertainty, speed up current processes of production. But even when all the necessary qualifications have been made, the Bank's record to date has not been discouraging. If it has done less than was hoped at the time of Bretton Woods, the responsibility for the discrepancy falls much more upon general world conditions which are only to a minor extent under its control, than upon any peculiar defects or shortcomings of its own.

The Fund, like the Bank, is also an operating agency with funds at its disposal to be made available to members on certain more or less clearly defined conditions. In the long run, however, the more significant purpose of the Fund is to build up a set of principles, the general observance of which will permit its members to abandon the inevitably disorderly trading and exchange conditions of the postwar world, where ordinary economic rationality often plays a quite subordinate role in determining the flow of trade; and to establish a genuinely integrated world system, in which—to put the matter in the simplest terms—money would again play its normal part in facilitating the exchange of goods, without the delays, wastes, and frustrations that inevitably clog the wheels of commerce when barter and near-barter practices are widespread. The determination and maintenance of stable exchange rates, the avoidance of discriminatory currency practices, and the ultimate withdrawal of exchange controls, except those found necessary to keep movements of capital within proper limits, are the technical problems which have to be solved if this long-run purpose is to be achieved. The sale to members by the Fund of the currencies of other members "presently needed for making payments consistent with the provisions of the Agreement" might be thought of as incidental to the solution of these problems, something designed to protect members from falling into or remaining in conditions where they would feel that the maintenance of convertibility for their currency would impose an intolerable strain. The need for such sales was certain to vary from time to time, and the effectiveness of the Fund's operations would not necessarily be correlated at all closely with variations in the volume of its transactions in the currencies of its members.

It is possible to think of the Fund as eventually operating in a world where most national economies had achieved a reasonable equilibrium in their balances of payments, and where, therefore, the purpose of recourse to the Fund's resources would be merely to correct temporary disequilibria; the more or less automatic disappearance of these disequilibria would in due course permit the repayment of the currencies purchased from the Fund, and therefore the replenishment of its resources in time to afford protection against the next temporary upset. At the time when the Fund's machinery was formally established, the world bore little resemblance to this ideal picture, and the impediments in the way of any rapid movement toward its realization were clearly formidable. The architects of the Fund had never contemplated that, after it had been formally constituted, it should remain entirely passive, waiting for the emergence of the more "normal" conditions suitable for the performance of its ordinary functions. It was intended to be an effective instrument even during the transition period. The determination of the extent to which it should attempt, within the limits of its powers and financial resources, to assist actively in carrying the world through the transitional period to a newer stable international equilibrium, however, remained a difficult question.

The powers entrusted to the Fund were sufficiently wide and flexible to permit activities of this kind, and though risks were inevitably involved in assuming even a subordinate responsibility for helping the world through a "transitional" period, the precise length of which could not be confidently predicted, the decision was taken in favor of a role of modest activity. The first problem to be faced was the discharge of the Fund's duty to agree with its members the initial par values of their currencies. In the long run, exchange stability was an essential part of the international economic order which the Fund was charged with attempting to establish, at the same time recognizing the necessity for a reasonable degree of flexibility. But stable exchange rates are not to be imposed by any mere fiat. They are, in an important sense, merely the external manifestation of more fundamental and deep-seated economic conditions. If these fundamental conditions have not been realized, exchange stability must be precarious. At the end of 1946 the world was still very far from even an approximate realization of these conditions. Many of the rates at which exchange transactions were then taking place were based in part upon temporary and uncertain considerations which might later have little relevance to the equilibrium rates to be established when world conditions permitted a final determination of these issues. No simple rule of thumb calculations could be made to determine "correct" exchange rates, and, even if such calculations had been possible, conditions in some countries were so fluid that the results would soon have been out of date. The only sensible test available for judging the adequacy of prevailing rates was their effect upon the flow of exports. Unless there was evidence that current exchange rates were checking this flow, the common-sense step was to accept them; this the Fund did, with the execption of a few abnormally unstable currencies, and a few others where legal or administrative complications compelled further delay. At the same time it was made clear that the declaration of an agreed par value was not to be interpreted as involving any assurance by the Fund of confidence in the long-term stability of all the rates accepted. As circumstances changed, and in particular if cost and price relationships were found to be checking desirable movements of trade, some exchange rates would need reconsideration, and in such reconsideration the Fund was under an obligation not to interpret the claims of stability in any formal or rigid way. The Fund found itself unable to agree with the first proposal, that made by France, for the revision of an accepted par value, but its objections were not at all directed against devaluation as such, the necessity for which at the time of the proposal was clearly and formally recognized.

The second practical task of the Fund was to assist its members in discharging their obligation to avoid "discriminatory currency arrangements or multiple currency practices except as authorized under [the Fund] Agreement or approved by the Fund." The Articles of Agreement had already recognized the impossibility of making anything like an immediate clean sweep of such exchange practices, which were widely used and in some countries had been interwoven in the closest possible way with the national economic structure. The obligations of membership during the "Transitional Period" were so defined as to permit maintenance and at the same time to afford the Fund an opportunity of mitigating their most objectionable consequences and preparing the way for their gradual disappearance. It would, in any event, have been impossible seriously to think of getting rid of them merely by imposing a formal ban. Their adoption was not to any significant extent a manifestation of wickedness or malice on the part of the countries where they were used; they were much more often a response, and sometimes an unwilling response, to abnormal difficulties about which something had to be done without delay. The disappearance of the practices was to a large extent contingent upon the prior application of appropriate treatment to these abnormal difficulties.

The proper behavior of the Fund in relation to this problem raises questions of some delicacy. If it is not to content itself with vague empty generalizations, it must take a realistic view of the economic difficulties of its members, and therefore not attempt to insist on formal policy decisions which have little or no relation to the actual facts of the current situation. It may have to sit down with members and work out practical revisions of their exchange policies in ways which may give some color to superficial charges that it was actually encouraging exchange practices the elimination of which was one of its important responsibilities. At best progress is likely to be slow and unexciting. A direct frontal attack on discriminatory exchange practices is unlikely to have much success. They will much more easily be abandoned as effective steps are taken in other directions to remove or remedy the conditions to which their adoption has been a response.

In the meantime the Fund has been able to make significant contributions toward solving the difficulties of the transitional period by selling to its members the currency of other members (in all but one instance, the United States dollar) which they needed for the financing of current transactions. Apart from the quantitative limitations upon the volume of these sales, which were related to the members' Fund quotas, the Articles of Agreement had declared the right of members "to buy the currency of another member from the Fund in exchange for its own currency," subject to certain conditions, the most important of which was that "the member desiring to purchase the currency represents that it is presently needed for making in that currency payments which are consistent with the provisions of the Agreement." The period within which members should be required to restore to the Fund the currencies purchased from it is not specifically defined, but as contrasted with the Bank's interest in long-term investments, the Fund's transactions are expected to be for comparatively short terms. These conditions call for interpretation, and interpretation is most conveniently given as a by-product of the practical work of receiving and dealing with applications from Fund members. By the end of April 1948, ten members, Belgium, Chile, Denmark, France, India, Mexico, the Netherlands, Norway, Turkey, and the United Kingdom, had purchased the currency of other members to the aggregate amount of $606 million.

The exchange transactions of the Fund and its concrete decisions on specific issues are important events in its history. Nevertheless, in general the significance of its work is probably to be found more in the gradual evolution of techniques of consultation with its members from which, by a process of continuous adaptation, there should emerge agreed policy principles in the sphere of foreign exchange, which may serve as the foundation for a network of orderly and rational international economic relations. To the determination of these principles, economic analysis is, of course, highly relevant. The practical task of constructing them is, however, at least as much a problem of politics—and here the word politics is used without any disparaging intention. It is convenient, as a shorthand expression, to say, "The Fund has done this, or ought to have done that," but the too facile use of shorthand of this kind may delay a proper appreciation of the inevitable complexities of the political processes thus described. Economists should not slacken in their efforts to elaborate practical policies for the guidance of international institutions. But their disappointments will be less if they constantly remind themselves of the essentially political nature of the problem of getting their policies adopted.

It may confidently be anticipated that this reminder will be even more to the point when the time comes to survey the early operations of the International Trade Organization. We have already noted the obvious fact that even the complete elimination of all interferences with trade by means of exchange controls might have little effect in recreating a multilateral pattern in which trade would expand and real living standards rise, if at the same time each country were left free to do as it pleased with direct quantitative trade restrictions. "Quantitative restrictions cut across the distribution systems of the world, destroy world markets, and lead to economic self-sufficiency and isolationism." It may be going too far to argue, as some have done, that without a complementary organization to supervise and coördinate national commercial policies, the IMF would be a mere futility. But its effectiveness would certainly be limited, and the pattern of world trade which would eventually emerge would fall far short of what the best common interests of all countries demand.

The drafting of the constitution of the International Trade Organization has just been completed, and it has not yet been tested as a working instrument. Already, however, one point of the utmost importance for an understanding of the role to be played by international economic institutions in the modern world has emerged. The basic objective of those who have been most active in promoting the formation of these institutions has been the creation of conditions which would make possible the acceptance of a set of internationally recognized "rules of the game," designed to reduce commercial and financial obstacles to international commerce and to promote multilateral trading to the maximum possible extent. It would have been easy to set forth a body of principles so vague and general that every country could have subscribed to them without any perceptible changes in its actual practice. Little profit is to be gained from the devotion of energy to the elaboration of principles of this kind. If, on the other hand, rules were to be laid down which were to be taken seriously, all governments must of necessity scrutinize with the greatest care the tests to be accepted as an effective guide to their future policy. The restoration of trade on a multilateral basis is not the only objective to which they are devoted. For many countries the stability and adequacy of the volume of employment has been accepted as almost the primary end of economic policy, and, whether rightly or wrongly, the precautions justified by this objective have been taken to include many deviations from the strict practice of multilateralism. Other countries attach equal importance to other deviations which in their view are necessary to facilitate the more rapid diversification and development of their national economies. And over all is the clear impossibility, in face of the abnormal situation left by the war, of any rapid reversal of practices imposed by hard necessity. In these circumstances, any rules of international conduct which are to have a chance of general acceptance are necessarily highly complicated and untidy, and, after the International Trade Organization has been set up, the application of its rules to particular cases will necessarily be affected by the variations of emphasis placed by its members upon the various objectives which they have in mind. On the one hand, doctrinaire rules which failed to recognize the facts of the real world had to be avoided, while on the other care had to be taken lest the permitted exceptions and qualifications should in effect deprive of any real meaning the principles to which they were attached. The resolution of the general dilemma thus presented and of which this is an outstanding example is a process whose end will not be in sight for a long time.

For a general sketch of the evolution of these new international institutions, specific reference to the interests of any single one of the countries directly concerned is scarcely necessary. The individual reader will, however, naturally form his judgment in the light of his interpretation of the interests of his own country. The United States has played an active part at every stage of the story, so much so, indeed, that some jaundiced critics have gone so far as to represent these institutions as something imposed by United States pressure upon an unwilling world. This view is certainly unfair; the direct interest of the United States in the rebuilding of a relatively free multilateral trading world is, however, so great that, even apart from the ideological prepossessions which are dominant in United States public opinion, it is scarcely surprising that there has been more impatience there than in many other countries at the compromises which hard-headed negotiators have been obliged to accept. But if the United States has a strong interest in the healthy evolution of these institutions, it also has a weighty, though not an exclusive, responsibility for their development. If the kind of world which the United States would like to see is ultimately to emerge, it will be as the result of a series of responses by the governments of the world to the policy decisions of each other. United States policy cannot by itself create the conditions necessary for success. But without adequate action initiated in the United States in the fields both of capital investment and of commercial policy, the best efforts of other countries would be equally ineffective. And while adequate responses must also be registered in the policies of other countries, doctrinaire expectations here might be dangerous. There is everything to be said for a clear realization of the ultimate goal; this will, however, avail little unless it is combined with an equally clear understanding of the elements which inevitably slow down movement in the desired direction. For some years to come this movement is certain to be slow. Those who would recoil at once from anything which appears to compromise their doctrinal purity might run some risk of stopping it altogether.

# 13

## *GENERAL 'AGREEMENTS ON TARIFFS AND TRADE*[1]

Winthrop G. Brown

On October 30, 1947, in the Council Room of the League of Nations building in Geneva, twenty-three countries, representing among them approximately three-quarters of the trade of the world, authenticated the text of the General Agreement on Tariffs and Trade. This agreement established rules for the conduct of their trade with each other, and fixed the tariff treatment, item by item, for products which represented about half the world's international trade.

The General Agreement was the result of long preparation and seven months of actual negotiation. It is part of an integrated pattern of attack on the economic problems facing the world today. It looks to the future and yet has its roots firmly in the solid practices of the past. What are its origins? How was it achieved? What does it promise for the future?

After the second world war nations were faced with a world shattered economically as well as physically. The commerce which is the link and life blood of so many nations was disrupted far more deeply than was immediately apparent. Nations were short of goods for themselves and for export and short of the foreign exchange with which to buy abroad. Strong feelings of nationalism, strong desires for security, and a new surge of belief in government control and planning of trade were on the rise. National desires for self-sufficiency had been given a new impetus. And these forces had at their disposal techniques for

1 The views expressed are those of the author and not necessarily those of the agency for which he works.

the control and direction of trade which had been brought to a high degree of effectiveness under the necessities of a world war.

So under the pressures of desperate shortages, of anxiety as to where the next national meal was coming from, of fear for security, of national pride, and of new belief in the desirability and effectiveness of planning, trade was becoming increasingly canalized and directed and countries moved more and more in the direction of bilaterally balanced trade to make sure that the goods which they had to export would bring them the goods they needed the most and that their slim resources of foreign exchange would bring them at least the minimum of their essential needs.

Yet it was generally recognized that this was not the course which would hold out the best hope for the future; that in the long run it could not but result in a contraction of total trade to the detriment of all. High tariffs, quotas, subsidization of high cost and uneconomic industry, could give assurances for the moment, but ran up a bill which would have to be paid in the end.

The problem was too enormous, however, to be solved by the efforts of any one country or even of a few powerful countries. A concerted effort was necessary by many countries over a wide area of trade, so that the efforts and contribution of each would be buttressed by the effort and contribution of others, and each would see, as it started to take off a part of its economic armor in its own and the common good, that a sufficient number of others were taking off a sufficient amount of their economic armor to make the effort worth while. The vicious circle had to be broken simultaneously along a wide extent of its circumference.

Therefore, in December 1945, the United States Government, after consultation with the Government of the United Kingdom, put forward its *Proposals for the Expansion of World Trade and Employment,*[2] which have, through several

[2] The United Kingdom indicated its "full agreement on all important points" in the *Proposals* and accepted these as a basis for international discussion in the understanding on commercial policy reached by the United Kingdom and the United States in connection with the conclusion of the Anglo-American Financial Agreement of December 1945.

international meetings, been developed into the Charter for a proposed International Trade Organization, recently debated at Havana by representatives of fifty-eight countries. This charter would establish general rules for the conduct of economic relations between countries in the field of governmental and private barriers to international trade, intergovernmental commodity agreements, foreign investment, economic development, and employment, and would establish an international organization to deal with such matters, and to take its place with the International Bank and International Monetary Fund as a specialized agency of the United Nations. This charter and its significance are discussed elsewhere in this volume by Mr. Harry Hawkins.

At the same time that the *Proposals* were issued, the United States invited a considerable number of countries to negotiate with it and with each other for the reduction of specific barriers to trade such as tariffs, with the objective of complementing the adoption of general rules of economic conduct by concrete action. These invitations were accepted. The result is the General Agreement on Tariffs and Trade.

The enterprise thus launched was confronted from the outset by formidable practical difficulties. The trade likely to be involved in the negotiations was in excess of ten billions of dollars. Any idea of horizontal reduction in tariffs by a specified amount was out of the question. Therefore the problem had to be approached on a selective, product by product basis. A conservative estimate of the number of products that might require consideration was in the neighborhood of fifty thousand. Twenty-three separate customs territories would be involved in the negotiations. The experience of major nations in past trade agreement negotiations had been that almost a year was required to negotiate a single agreement between two major trading countries. Moreover, not only tariffs were involved, but the necessity of reaching agreement on a large number of general provisions essential to protect and give meaning to the tariff concessions, among countries representing a wide variety of points of view, governmental and trading systems, and states of economic development. And, finally, this project and the project for an International Trade Organization were closely related, and the relationship between the resulting agreements would have to be very carefully worked out. That these difficulties were overcome and agreement on all points reached in just under seven months was such a triumph of international mechanics as perhaps to justify some extended discussion of those mechanics.

Although the problem was to reach agreement among twenty-three countries on the tariff treatment of half the world's trade all at once, the approach adopted by each participant was in essence to act initially as though it was simply negotiating several bilateral trade agreements simultaneously. Country A, for example, looked over its trade figures and picked out the product of which country B was its principal supplier and the items of which it was the principal supplier to country B. It decided, according to its own domestic procedure, what concessions it would be able to offer or would like to request on those products. It did the same for countries C, D, E, and all the others at Geneva with which it had sufficient trade to justify a negotiation. It designated teams to negotiate these offers and requests with each of the other countries. Each country at Geneva did likewise.

To save time, requests by each country for tariff concessions were transmitted to the country on which they were made as long before the conference as possible, so a considerable number of countries arrived at Geneva knowing the requests made upon them. At the opening of the conference, or as soon as requests were received, each country presented to each other country the offers it was prepared to make, and the bargaining began. And for seven months, all over the Palais des Nations, little groups of men representing pairs of countries sat around the table and negotiated until they reached initial agreement on the concessions that each might be prepared to grant on items of principal interest to the other.

Although 23 countries were represented at Geneva, there were actually 19 separate participants in the tariff negotiations, since the customs unions of Belgium, Luxembourg, and the Netherlands, and Lebanon and Syria, negotiated as combined units, as did also India and Pakistan. Among these 19 participants, there could have been a maximum of 171 separate pairs of negotiations. In fact, in a number of cases the trade between certain pairs of the countries represented was not sufficient to justify a negotiation and certain countries in the British Commonwealth preferential system did not negotiate with each other. Nevertheless, there were over 100 initial negotiations between separate pairs of countries.

But this was only part of the negotiating process. For although no country participated directly in more than 18 negotiations, it was nevertheless keenly interested in the other 153. The General Agreement was to be a multilateral agreement, in which each of the parties was to obtain in its own right the benefit of all the concessions made by each of the others. Therefore, arrangements were made whereby each country was kept informed of all the offers made by each of the others, and no country agreed finally to the concessions developed in its initial direct negotiations until it was satisfied with the benefits which it would receive as a result of the 153 negotiations in which it did not directly participate.

When the initial negotiations were completed, and the results were known to all, each country combined the concessions which it had agreed to offer into a single schedule, which it offered to all of the others.

Thus, by using the traditional procedure of bilateral negotiation, a new form of multilateral agreement was developed—a form by which each country at Geneva secured for itself benefits in the way of tariff concessions far greater than it could have done in even a series of separate bilateral trade agreements made along traditional lines.[3]

Just as the multilateral tariff schedules of the General Agreement were patterned upon the schedules of the trade agree-

[3] One difficult problem which this procedure made it possible to solve was that of negotiating tariff concessions with a member of a preferential system, such as that existing within the British Commonwealth or between the United States and Cuba. Almost any tariff concession granted by a member of such a system would involve the reduction of a preference enjoyed by another member which would not be a party to a pure bilateral negotiation and would derive no direct benefit from it. In the multilateral negotiation, members of the preferential system can be parties and derive direct benefits which make it easier for them to consent to modifications in the preferential treatment which they receive.

ments negotiated by the United States in the past, so its general provisions were an extension and development of similar provisions in past trade agreements. Tariff concessions can be nullified by quotas or by discriminatory internal taxes, or by the maintenance or intensification of an "invisible tariff" in the customs house. So it was necessary to deal in the General Agreement with such matters as quotas and internal taxes, nondiscrimination, customs valuation and procedures, marks of origin, and the treatment of goods in transit.

The general provisions are based essentially on a few simple principles—nations should give each other unconditional most-favored-nation treatment in all their trade; barriers to imports should be imposed only at the customs frontier and in the form of tariffs; such barriers should be given the widest possible publicity and uniformity; the "invisible tariff" of customs administration should be lowered by simplification and the adoption of certain improved rules of practice; tariff concessions should not be impaired by changes in exchange rates, or customs valuation procedures, or customs classification; and there should be consultation, normally in advance, when action which might be deemed prejudicial to another's interest is considered necessary.

As they appear in the General Agreement these rules are of necessity qualified with exceptions and expressed in technical terms. A detailed discussion would unduly extend this article. But a brief summary of the more important provisions may be useful.[4]

The General Agreement incorporates the most-favored-nation clause in its unconditional and unlimited form, so that the tariffs applied by each party to the agreement to products imported from the other parties will not be higher than the tariffs which it applies to the same products when imported from any other country.

It continues the exception, made in past trade agreements, for certain well-established preferential systems, such as, for example, between the areas comprising the British Empire, be-

[4] This summary is based upon the "Preliminary Analysis of the General Agreement on Tariffs and Trade," issued by the Department of State, November 18, 1947.

tween France and its colonies, and between the United States and Cuba, but contains a new and important provision that no such preferences can be increased above the levels in effect on a specified date. This general prohibition of increase in preferences extends not only to products on which concessions have been granted in the tariff schedules of the agreement, but also to all products.

The most-favored-nation provisions also extend, without exception, to export taxes.

In order to ensure the elimination of internal excise taxes or other internal regulations which operate to protect home industries by laying greater burdens on the imported than on the domestic product, and to require that protection for domestic production be applied openly against imports at the time of importation, the General Agreement provides that all internal commodity taxes on imported products must apply equally to like domestic products; that internal regulations in general may not treat imported products less favorably than domestic products; and that any internal quotas or "mixing" regulations (which require the consumption of foreign or domestic products in specified amounts or proportions, and which can be as effective a device for restricting trade as absolute import quotas) must not restrict imports to an extent greater than they did on April 10, 1947 and must be subject to negotiation for their further limitation or elimination.[5]

The General Agreement provides for the free movement of goods and vehicles across national territories on routes convenient for international transit. It prohibits the imposition of special transit duties or other restrictions and requires that all regulations dealing with transit shall be reasonable.

[5] There is one important case in which measures applied at the customs frontier are not a suitable device to afford legitimate protection; and that is the case of motion picture films. Because of their economic peculiarities special measures are necessary to deal with them. As a counterpart of import duties, therefore, the General Agreement establishes for the film trade alone an approved protective device in the form of screen quotas which reserve a portion of screen time for domestic films. Such quotas are made negotiable in the same manner as tariffs. No screen time other than that reserved for domestic films may be allocated in any manner. A few existing preferential film quotas are permitted to continue, but their incidence may not be increased, and no new quotas of this type may be introduced.

It recognizes that many of the difficulties facing foreign traders lie in unnecessary or needlessly elaborate customs requirements and looks toward the removal of these obstacles at the earliest practicable date. Recognition is given to the principle that supplementary customs fees and charges should be limited to the cost of services rendered and should not represent a means of indirect protection to domestic industries, to the need for reducing the number and diversity of such fees and charges, for minimizing the incidence and complexity of import and export formalities, and for decreasing and simplifying import and export documentation requirements.

The General Agreement provides for nondiscriminatory application of marks of origin; it permits importers to mark their goods at the time of importation rather than at the time of manufacture or export; and proscribes marking requirements which may have the effect of damaging imported goods, materially reducing their value, or unreasonably increasing their cost.

The General Agreement provides for the publication of all laws and regulations affecting foreign trade in such a manner as to enable both governments and traders to become acquainted with them; for the official publication of any increased duties simultaneously with or prior to their application; and for the establishment or maintenance of customs courts or similar independent procedures to assure justice and fair dealing in the administration of trade regulations.

When goods are subject to *ad valorem* duties, the methods followed at the custom house in determining the value of the goods are as important to the foreign trader as is the rate of duty itself. If these methods are arbitrary, or result in fictitious valuations, a much greater burden on trade can result than would appear from the height of the duty. The General Agreement therefore provides that the values to be used shall be "actual" values and not arbitrary or fictitious values, and sets out a suitable definition of "actual" value for customs purposes. Internal taxes may not be included in the value of a shipment of goods if they have not in fact been paid on that shipment. In converting foreign currencies to arrive at the value of imported products, the par value of the currency involved, as established by the International Monetary Fund, must be used, except in cases where trade transactions are not in practice carried on in terms of the par value. Whatever the detailed method of valuation followed, the principle is established that valuation methods should be stable and should be given sufficient publicity to enable traders to estimate the value of goods for customs purposes with a reasonable degree of certainty.

The General Agreement also safeguards tariff concessions against adverse changes in methods of tariff valuation or currency conversion; against changes in tariff classifications; and against unwarranted increases in rates of specific duties in the event of currency depreciation.

Perhaps the most important provisions of the General Agreement, however, are those dealing with quantitative restrictions. These provisions are very extensive and highly technical.[6] Their net effect is to prohibit the use of quotas for normal protective purposes, but to permit their use, under carefully defined rules, when a country is forced to limit its imports because it is short of foreign exchange. The basic rule is that such restrictions may not be used unless necessary "to forestall the imminent threat of, or to stop, a serious decline in . . . monetary reserves," or (if the country has dangerously low monetary reserves) "to achieve a reasonable rate of increase in . . . reserves." Balance-of-payments restrictions must be gradually relaxed as the country's reserve position improves and must be completely eliminated when the reserve position would no longer justify their maintenance.

Rules are also laid down to ensure that restrictions imposed for balance-of-payments reasons will be operated so far as possible without discrimination as between sources of supply.

The General Agreement recognizes the special problems of underdeveloped countries which may need to use nondiscriminatory trade measures, otherwise forbidden, in order to encourage infant industries. Such measures may be used if the prior approval of the parties to the General Agreement is ob-

[6] Similar provisions appear in the Charter of the International Trade Organization and are discussed in more detail in Mr. Hawkins' article on the Charter at page 285 of this volume.

tained. Detailed procedures are provided to assure an adequate examination of the facts in each case and the expeditious and fair handling of applications for such approval.

The General Agreement also lays down rules for the conduct of state-trading enterprises. It provides that the principle of nondiscrimination shall apply to state-fostered enterprise, just as the most-favored-nation principle must be applied to measures taken by governments themselves to direct the flow of trade. Such enterprises must, insofar as their purchases or sales affecting exports or imports are concerned, act according to commercial considerations, and give the enterprises of other countries (whether private or public) an opportunity to compete for the international business of the state-trading enterprise "in accordance with customary business practice."

A government is, however, free to follow any policy it chooses in its purchases for the armed forces, for strategic stockpiles, or for similar purposes.

If a subsidy is used which increases exports or decreases imports of any product, it must be reported to the parties to the General Agreement with a statement of the reasons why it is necessary and the estimate of its effect on trade. The country granting the subsidy must, upon request, consult with the other parties concerned as to the possibility of limiting the subsidy.

Finally the General Agreement contains a number of exceptions which customarily appear in international commercial agreements, together with certain other exceptions growing out of the economic conditions peculiar to the transitional postwar period, and exceptions necessary for national security.

Throughout the General Agreement runs the theme that a country contemplating action which might adversely affect another should give notice, in advance if possible, and seek consultation in order to work out a mutually satisfactory solution of the problem. If such consultation fails to bring agreement, the CONTRACTING PARTIES (the term used to describe the parties to the General Agreement acting jointly on matters of common concern) may be appealed to. And if the country contemplating action is unable to accept their joint judgment, after full discussion and consideration, they may in many cases authorize the complaining parties to withdraw from the party taking the action the application of certain benefits which the complaining parties are bound to confer upon it.

The CONTRACTING PARTIES have no power to order action by any of the parties. But their collective judgment as to the merit under the General Agreement of a proposed action, and as to the limits of permissible retaliation for action taken which they consider improper, should be highly effective in deterring improper action and in preventing the spread of economic warfare in retaliation for some act considered injurious.

The multilateral structure of the General Agreement, as indicated above, brings to each party in its own right all the concessions granted to each of the others. This wholly desirable arrangement, however, results in a certain rigidity of structure, and gives rise to a number of new problems. Conditions in various countries and in different industries will certainly not remain static. Competitive conditions will change. The effect of a given concession may be quite different from what was foreseen when it was granted. Therefore it was necessary to provide machinery for changes in detail—in individual concessions—while at the same time preserving the bulk of the agreement. This was made possible in a number of ways.

In the first place, provision was made whereby a party could withdraw or modify a given concession as of right if, as a result of the concession and of unforeseen circumstances, imports should occur in such increased quantities and under such conditions as to cause or threaten serious injury to a domestic industry. If any country wishes to invoke this right, it is required, except under conditions of extreme urgency, to consult in advance with the country or countries principally interested in the concession, normally the principal suppliers with whom the concession was originally negotiated. If the concession were an important one, so that its withdrawal would seriously impair the balance of the bargain struck initially, adjustment would be sought by withdrawal of concessions of equal significance on the other side. Thus a country is free to take action to protect a domestic industry in case of need in a particular case, but must in equity pay a price for this impairment of its bargain.

The country would be the judge of the necessity for its action. The amount of the price to be paid would be determined either by agreement, or, if this proved to be impossible, by all the parties to the agreement, sitting as a group, that is, the CONTRACTING PARTIES. If the price thus determined was felt to be too high, the party initiating action would be free to withdraw from the agreement on short notice.

There might also be cases where no injury had been caused or threatened by a concession, but where conditions had changed. Let us say, for example, that it was desired to build up a new industry in the case of a product covered by a concession and to give it further tariff protection. The country concerned would in other respects be satisfied with the General Agreement. It is provided that after the initial three-year term of the agreement a country would be free to initiate negotiations with the countries principally interested for the modification or withdrawal of the concession and for compensation in the form of new concessions or withdrawal by them of concessions of equal value.

To keep the negotiations contemplated in these two situations within manageable bounds, the CONTRACTING PARTIES are authorized to determine what countries are substantially interested in the concessions involved and hence entitled to participate.

Finally, the multilateral form of the General Agreement presents special problems in connection with the accession of new parties. The General Agreement leaves these problems for future solution and merely provides that other countries may accede on terms to be agreed.

In Article 17 of the Charter of the International Trade Organization, members undertake to negotiate with each other, on request, for the substantial reduction of tariffs and the elimination of preferences. Bilateral tariff negotiations are not proscribed, but it is clearly contemplated that tariff negotiations by members of the organization will be conducted in the multilateral framework and their results incorporated in the General Agreement on Tariffs and Trade. Members negotiating outside the framework of the General Agreement must abide by the rules of the Charter not to increase preferences, and if a member fails to become a party to the General Agreement within two years after becoming a member of the International Trade Organization, other members which are parties to the General Agreement and which have requested it to negotiate for this purpose are no longer obligated to give it most-favored-nation treatment.

The CONTRACTING PARTIES may authorize a party to the General Agreement to withhold concessions under the Agreement from another party which has failed, without justification, to carry out negotiations of the type contemplated in Article 17 of the Charter.[7] This is to ensure that a country becoming a party to the Agreement cannot claim tariff benefits from any other party without negotiating fairly with that party.

Countries may become parties to the general provisions of the Agreement alone, but in such case may claim no benefits under the schedules of tariff concessions.[8]

One final procedural problem had to be solved in the General Agreement. The subject matter of its general provisions, involving as they did basic aspects of commercial policy, were also dealt with in the draft Charter for the International Trade Organization. The General Agreement was to be finally adopted and put into effect after Geneva. The draft Charter, as developed at Geneva, was merely a recommendation to a United Nations Conference at Havana, and the form in which it would emerge from that conference was uncertain. The possibility thus existed that a country which was a party to the General Agreement and a member of the International Trade Organization would find itself bound by two differing sets of rules with respect to important segments of its trade relations.

Moreover, a good many of the general provisions would require changes in the laws of the various countries—changes which it would be difficult to ask a legislature to make at the very time when a charter dealing with the same subjects and which the legislature would shortly be called upon to consider was being debated at Havana. A number of the parties to the

[7] Amendment to Article 25, agreed at Havana, March 24, 1948.
[8] Amendment to Article 35, agreed at Havana, March 24, 1948.

General Agreement had entered reservations to provisions of the Charter and expected to make a determined effort to get them changed at Havana. Moreover, certain countries felt that the provisions of the Charter dealing with employment and economic development were even more important than tariff concessions and rules with respect to trade barriers, so much so that they would be reluctant to enter into any lasting commitments with respect to trade barriers unless a Charter were adopted with satisfactory provisions in the employment and development fields. And to add complication to an already complicated situation, almost every party to the General Agreement had a different legislative or executive procedure which it had to follow to put the Agreement into effect. Some could do it by purely executive action, others had to get legislative ratification, and the legislatures of the last group all met at different times and required differing degrees of advance notice and consultation. Yet the General Agreement had to be made effective as soon as possible and over as wide an area as possible if it were to be made effective at all.

The solution of this rather terrifying aggregate of problems proved to be as simple as it was ingenious. All the countries signed a Final Act of the Conference which authenticated the text of the General Agreement and tariff schedules and provided that neither its signature nor the giving of provisional effect to the Agreement would prejudice the freedom of action of any signatory at Havana. Nine of the countries, accounting for over three-quarters of the trade involved, signed a Protocol of Provisional Application whereby they undertook to apply the Agreement provisionally and to the extent not inconsistent with their existing legislation as from January 1, 1948, with the right of withdrawal on 60 days' notice. Other countries could sign the Protocol at any time up to June 30, 1948. And the General Agreement itself provided that when the Charter of the ITO came into force, its provisions would automatically supersede the corresponding provisions of the General Agreement unless a party to that Agreement objected to the supersession of any particular provision. In case of such an objection the parties would meet to decide whether the provision of the

Charter or of the General Agreement, in existing or amended form, should apply.

Under this arrangement, on January 1, 1948, the General Agreement was made effective provisionally by Australia and Canada, France and the Benelux customs union, Cuba, the United Kingdom, and the United States.

The problems on which agreement was reached at Geneva ranged all the way from problems of broad policy to problems of minute detail, from general principles of future action to immediate action on tariff rates affecting the actual livelihood of individuals. The countries represented included the most highly industrialized in the world and some of those in comparatively primitive stages of economic development. Widely divergent philosophies of life and of government were represented. But there was a common desire shared by all; the desire to reach agreement. It is probably fair to say that if this desire had not been shared by all—if any important nation or group had wished to see the conference fail—it would have failed. But the fact of its success demonstrates dramatically the potentialities for international action if the desire to act in harmony is there.

The Geneva conference was a United Nations conference. The General Agreement is a United Nations document. It is a practical illustration of what the United Nations can do in the economic field. This does not mean that the Agreement could not or would not have been reached if there had been no United Nations. But it is indisputable that it was easier to reach because there was a United Nations.

One has often heard criticism of the United Nations, or of the Economic and Social Council because so much of their time is spent in discussing matters of machinery and procedure. People are apt to become impatient and ask why they do not concern themselves more with substance. But we are very apt to underestimate the importance of machinery. The facilities of the United Nations make it possible for a large group of nations to operate together in a manner hitherto almost impossible. Quite aside from everything else, the United Nations acts as host and does the housekeeping, and thereby lifts from the shoulders of the constituent nations a multitude of problems which, though unspectacular in the extreme, often present as great a hindrance to progress as basic problems of substance.

The United Nations acts as host. That means that international action has international sponsorship—the responsibility for international action is shared, and a project does not get launched unless a really substantial body of international opinion is prepared to support it. An impartial chairman is provided, and each nation is free to advocate its own point of view.

The United Nations does the housekeeping—and housekeeping in the family of nations is almost as important as housekeeping in the family of an individual. The Geneva conference probably brought together the largest group of tariff and trade experts ever assembled in one place. They would have accomplished nothing without the secretariat and services provided by the United Nations. The spoken and the written word were useless unless in two or sometimes three languages. The delegations and committees could not begin their day's work without the record of what had happened the day before. Each delegation had to know what the others were doing and had no time to tell them. The secretariat saw that they were kept informed. The delegations were free to concentrate on the substance of their work. International housekeeping is highly specialized, technical, arduous, undramatic, and terribly important.

Granted that the problems at Geneva were complex, granted that the area of agreement was extensive, granted that the General Agreement is one of the largest international documents ever signed—just how should it be evaluated? One might say that the rules it lays down are riddled with exceptions; that the principles accepted are too vague to be meaningful; that a mere promise to consult is not much guarantee of good behavior; that there has been no sacrifice of national sovereignty; that the tariff concessions made will not really hurt any domestic industry no matter how uneconomic; that to agree on principles of multilateral trade under present world conditions is to ignore realities and live in an ivory tower; that it was foolish to go to all this trouble under the appalling uncertainties of present conditions; that the wiser course would have been to wait until conditions were stabilized; until the shape of things to come could be more clearly discerned. All of these things could be and are being said, and each of them contains a modicum of truth.

But it can also be said that the deepest need of the world today is agreement and a sense of direction. Nations can no longer solve their problems alone. National boundaries have long since ceased to confine either depression or prosperity. When things are uncertain and confused, when there is a likelihood of nations working at cross purposes, when there is a common need and wide difference of opinion as to how to meet it, then is the time to reach agreement on the direction in which nations are to go. And the General Agreement set the direction of over three-quarters of the world's trade and took the first steps along the course thus charted.

This is a first step. It is part of a pattern of integrated attack on present-day economic problems. The establishment of the International Trade Organization will be the next step in fixing the long-term pattern of international economic relations. The European Recovery Plan is designed to deal with the shorter term. Its success is essential. If it fails, the General Agreement and the International Trade Organization will be of little use. But, by the same token, without the General Agreement and the International Trade Organization we would lack assurance that the benefits of the European Recovery Plan, the International Bank, the International Monetary Fund, and the Economic and Social Council of the United Nations would not be dissipated and nullified by policies of economic nationalism and economic warfare.

# 14

## *PROBLEMS RAISED BY THE INTERNATIONAL TRADE ORGANIZATION*[1]

Harry C. Hawkins

The creation of the organization and rules for international coöperation in the economic field is only partially completed. The means for dealing with monetary relations have been provided at Bretton Woods. The corresponding organization and rules for preventing conflict and promoting coöperation in the field of commercial policy have been exhaustingly debated at London and Geneva. They are still, at the time this is being written, under discussion at Havana, where the charter for an International Trade Organization is being considered by a United Nations conference on Trade and Employment.

Although a vast amount has been accomplished at these meetings in dealing with the problem of barriers to international trade, an internationally accepted trade charter, with its code of rules, has not yet been completed. This remains the most important piece of unfinished business of the United Nations in the economic field.

A brief description of this project and an examination of some of the issues which have developed in the long course of its discussion, will throw some light on the commercial policy aspects of our foreign economic policy and on the difficulties we are encountering in making that policy effective.

It should perhaps first be explained why, although three years have passed since the war, this project, which was conceived before the war ended, still remains in the category of unfinished business.

The explanation lies in the inherent difficulty of getting the

[1] The views expressed or implied in this article are the author's and do not necessarily reflect the views of the Government.

trade barrier problem under control. History is "strewn with the wreckage" of such attempts.

There are pressure groups in most countries who want protection from foreign competition. These groups are often politically powerful. Their influence is enhanced by the superficial plausibility of their case. Their proposition is that if imports were cut down, domestic production would fill the gap and domestic labor would be employed. The effects on the foreign relations, on the foreign trade, on consumers, and on the general prosperity of the country are considerations which it is difficult for the public to grasp. National administrations usually find that to avoid coming to grips with this problem is the path of least resistance in domestic politics.

There is, consequently, always pressure to obtain more protection—for trade barriers to rise; and, once they have risen, it is very difficult indeed to bring them down.

The trade barrier problem is formidable enough at any time. But, entirely apart from the influence of domestic pressure groups, there is a tendency at this time for governments to hesitate regarding commitments in this field. The emergencies which nations now face make them reluctant to take commitments which may impede their recovery efforts in ways they cannot foresee. Also, with the wartime difficulties of obtaining even essential supplies fresh in mind and still persisting, and with the state of international relations unsettled and the outlook uncertain, there is a tendency to seek greater freedom from the uncertainties of international trade by maintaining or building up production at home.

Despite these difficulties the work of formulating a charter for an international trade organization has been persistently carried forward. The aim is to create sufficient opportunity and stability in this field so that nations may more confidently coöperate to their mutual advantage; so that to a larger extent they may entrust their welfare to such coöperation rather than relying on purely domestic action which is often designed to shift as much as possible of the burden of necessary adjustments to foreign countries. Retaliation is the inevitable consequence, which intensifies the problem.

## *London-Geneva-Havana Trade Discussions*

The discussions on the charter for an international trade organization at London, Geneva, and Havana have dealt in detail with the kind of trade organization that should be established and the obligations that should be assumed by members.

Meetings of the Preparatory Committee of the United Nations Conference on Trade and Employment were held in London in the fall of 1946 and in Geneva in the summer of 1947. This Committee was established by the Economic and Social Council to draw up an agenda, including a draft convention, for consideration by a United Nations conference on this subject. The Preparatory Committee consisted of delegations of nineteen countries[2] selected with a view to obtaining representation of various geographic regions of the world, of various stages of economic development, and of different economic systems ranging from relatively free enterprise up to complete state trading. The Union of Soviet Socialist Republics was among the countries on the Preparatory Committee but did not participate in the meetings at London or Geneva, nor did it attend the world conference at Havana. The countries on the Preparatory Committee not only represented all systems, areas, and viewpoints, but accounted in the aggregate for three-quarters of the international trade of the world.

The London and Geneva meetings drew up a draft charter for consideration at a United Nations conference on Trade and Employment which met at Havana, Cuba, November 21, 1947. The Havana conference is, at present writing, still in session.[3]

## *The Draft Charter*

The draft charter for the International Trade Organization of the United Nations is a long and complicated document of a hundred articles. It is complicated because it goes far beyond

[2] Australia, Belgium-Luxembourg Economic Union, Brazil, Canada, Chile, China, Cuba, Czechoslovakia, France, India, Lebanon, Netherlands, New Zealand, Norway, Union of South Africa, Union of Soviet Socialist Republics, United Kingdom, United States of America.

[3] The London meeting created a drafting committee which met in New York and prepared a refined and improved text for consideration at the Geneva meeting. (The Havana conference ended in May 1948.—Ed.)

a statement of purposes and principles. This document, unlike many that emerge from international conferences in the form of general resolutions, is an international convention embodying specific and detailed undertakings which would be binding on member governments.

It would be impossible in an article of this length to describe the terms of the draft charter in any detail. But at the serious risk of oversimplification the bare essence of its various chapters can be stated.

What should be regarded as the core of the charter around which the other provisions center is something on which there is some difference of opinion. But since it is a trade charter designed from the outset primarily to deal with trade problems there is ample ground for saying that the heart of the charter is to be found in the provisions dealing with trade barriers in Chapter IV on Commercial Policy. In that fourth chapter the most important provisions are three: article 17 which would obligate members to negotiate for the reduction of tariffs and the elimination of tariff preferences; article 20 which would prohibit the use of quantitative restrictions for protective purposes; and article 16 which lays down rules designed to apply the principle of nondiscrimination in international trade.

Most of the other provisions of the charter, other than those setting up the trade organization, may be regarded as in greater or less degree qualifying or supplementing these provisions. The central idea in each of these other chapters is as follows.

Chapter V, dealing with Restrictive Business Practices (cartels), supplements the provisions on Commercial Policy. It contains elaborate provisions and procedure for preventing the frustration, by agreements between private or governmental enterprises, of governmental action for reducing trade barriers and eliminating discriminations. In an instrument which has as a major purpose the reduction or removal of governmental restrictions on trade, provisions designed to prevent such restrictions by private or governmental enterprises obviously have a place.

Chapter VI, which relates to Intergovernmental Commodity Agreements, permits deviation from certain of the provisions relating to trade barriers. It permits governmentally regulated trade as part of intergovernmental commodity agreements, such agreements being aimed at stabilizing production and trade in primary products, in which there is a tendency toward disequilibrium between production and consumption, the accumulation of burdensome stocks, and pronounced fluctuations in prices. This chapter lays down in detail the principles which must govern the use of such agreements and the principles to which they must conform.

Chapter III, relating to economic development, also qualifies the Commercial Policy provisions of Chapter IV. It permits the use of protective measures inconsistent with the trade barrier provisions in the later chapter, for purposes of promoting economic development, particularly in countries in a backward stage of such development. The Geneva draft requires, however, that such measures inconsistent with the commercial policy provisions of the charter may only be imposed with the prior approval of the Trade Organization. Other provisions of the chapter relate to measures for assisting in the economic development of underdeveloped countries, such as the provision of technology and treatment of private foreign investment.

These provisions relating to economic development have been, and probably still are, the major point of dispute, particularly the proposed requirement of prior organization approval for the imposition of trade restrictions for purposes of economic development. This issue is furtner discussed at a later point.

Chapter II, on Employment and Economic Activity, is supplementary to the commercial policy provisions. Delegates of some countries would consider the provisions for dealing with the trade barrier problem as distinctly secondary to provisions designed to maintain full and productive employment. They would argue that since a depression in a major country can have disastrous consequences to international trade and to the welfare of other countries; that since wide swings in business activity affect the volume of a country's imports more than any change in its tariff could do; the key to the problem of creating a flourishing and stable international trade is full employment in the countries of major economic importance. Compared with this, they would argue, the reduction of trade barriers is a secondary influence toward creating a healthy state of international trade.

There is, of course, no argument as to the relative effect of economic depression on international trade. But the difference between the problems presented is the difference between asking a man to obligate himself to remain prosperous and asking him to agree to a rule against deliberate attacks on the prosperity of his neighbors. If, moreover, he accepted both obligations, he might regard his obligation to be prosperous as one of somewhat higher order than his obligation not to attack the prosperity of his neighbors. Certainly protectionists who want to shut out foreign competition without heed to the effect on other countries would support the full-employment thesis more vigorously than a good-neighbor policy.

However, the effect of fluctuations in economic activity in important countries is so great that the question may appropriately find a suitable place in a charter designed to promote international trade. The obligation could not, of course, be as absolute as in the case of other matters which lie entirely within the volition and control of nations assuming the obligations of the charter. In the Geneva draft charter, the obligation imposed on each member is to "take action *designed* to achieve and maintain full and productive employment and large and steadily growing demand within its own territory through measures appropriate to its political, economic and social institutions." (The italics are mine.)

### *General Agreement on Tariffs and Trade*

At the Geneva Meeting the members of the Preparatory Committee also negotiated among themselves an instrument which may be regarded without any exaggeration as a landmark in the history of international commercial relations. This instrument, which provided for the reduction of trade barriers on a scale never before achieved in any single instrument, is the General Agreement on Tariffs and Trade.

In the discussions at London, Geneva, and Havana, the

United States has steadfastly pursued the policy of promoting the trade policies which were adopted by this country under the leadership of Cordell Hull and which were being successfully carried out in the bilateral trade agreements negotiated under the authority of the Trade Agreements Act. The General Agreement on Tariffs and Trade, signed on behalf of twenty-three[4] countries, is an enormous stride in the carrying out of this policy.

The method of negotiation employed was similar to that employed in the negotiation of our bilateral agreements, and the agreement was made effective on the part of the United States under the authority of the Trade Agreements Act. The duty reductions by each of the parties on products of interest to the others were made selectively; that is to say, reductions sought in the United States tariff, for example, were considered on a product-by-product basis and the concessions granted varied from a binding of an existing rate down through various degrees of reduction to the full 50 per cent permitted by the Trade Agreements Act. The other participating countries proceeded similarly on a selective product-by-product basis. The importance of the agreement is shown by the fact that the trade of the Contracting Parties on which concessions were made at Geneva represents, on the basis of 1938 values, more than two-thirds of their total trade, or a little under one-half of the total world trade.

Since each of the participating countries had to negotiate with each of the others, the negotiating process was one of great complexity. The negotiations by each pair of countries dealt with products which each was interested in exporting to the other. The schedule of concessions by each country annexed to the agreement is the result of all these bilateral negotiations. The final product, however, was a multilateral agreement in

[4] There were 18 countries on the Preparatory Committee which met at Geneva, the U.S.S.R. not attending. The discrepancy is sufficiently explained by listing the countries with separate schedules of tariff concessions: Australia, Belgium-Luxembourg-Netherlands customs union, Brazil, Burma, Canada, Ceylon, Chile, China, Cuba, Czechoslovakia, France, India, New Zealand, Norway, Pakistan, Southern Rhodesia, Syro-Lebanese Customs Union, Union of South Africa, United Kingdom, United States.

which the total schedule of bound and reduced rates of each country represented a direct obligation to all of the other parties to the multilateral agreement, in their own right. In other words the agreement is a multilateral agreement in the true sense; not a mere collection of bilateral agreements bound together in one cover.

During the thirties while the United States was carrying out a comprehensive program of trade agreement negotiations, other countries were negotiating relatively few agreements among themselves for the reduction of trade barriers on the basis of the most-favored-nation principle. The widespread negotiation of such agreements by foreign countries among themselves as well as with the United States, which had been a hope of American commercial policy in the thirties, was largely realized in one concentrated burst of activity at Geneva in the summer of 1947.[5]

The benefits resulting from such negotiations among other countries are not only that tariff reductions are obtained for a range of products of United States origin of which the United States is a secondary or minor supplier and which normally would not be made the subject of direct negotiations by us. More important than this is the fact that an increase in trade between other pairs of countries expands their purchasing power for goods of all countries, including ours.

### *Relation Between the General Agreement and the Charter*

The scope of the General Agreement on Tariffs and Trade is different from that of the draft charter which was being formulated simultaneously at Geneva. The General Agreement deals with tariffs, preferences, quantitative restrictions, and other barriers to and regulations affecting trade, and includes with such provisions the necessary reservations and exceptions. The qualifying provisions of particular importance are those permitting restrictions to safeguard the balance of payments and for encouraging development in underdeveloped areas. The draft charter, on the other hand, covers, in addition to the commercial policy matters just mentioned, Employment and Economic Activity, Restrictive Business Practices, Intergovern-

[5] Cf. Mr. Brown's essay where these negotiations are discussed at great length.

mental Commodity Agreements, some provisions on economic development which were not included in the General Agreement, and the creation of the International Trade Organization. In so far as the subject matter is the same the provisions of the General Agreement and the draft charter are substantially the same.

The plan under which these vastly important projects have been conceived and developed is that the two instruments would merge, the contracting parties to the General Agreement and the countries who accept the charter being bound by the same general provisions. One of the provisions of the draft charter would impose on members of the Trade Organization the obligation to negotiate for the reduction of tariffs and the elimination of tariff preferences. The parties to the General Agreement have in effect taken action in advance to comply with this obligation. When the charter comes into force all other members would be obligated to negotiate for admission to the General Agreement on Tariffs and Trade, that is to say, to offer tariff reductions in return for concessions by the parties to the General Agreement, and become parties to that agreement. The General Agreement, which was concluded by members of the Preparatory Committee who drew up the draft charter in effect sets at least the initial standard to which other countries should conform in respect of the obligation to take action on tariffs and preferences.

Although the General Agreement could remain in force among the contracting parties and others who might adhere, independently of the charter, the expectation has been that the provisions of the General Agreement will be superseded by the corresponding provisions of the charter when the latter comes into force. Provision is made, however, whereby the contracting parties to the General Agreement may decide that if a particular provision of the charter as adopted by the world conference is unsuitable, the General Agreement will not be superseded on that point.

### *Postwar Commercial Policy Issues*

The postwar commercial policy of the United States is a continuation of the prewar policy established under the leadership of Cordell Hull, and given effect in the Trade Agreements Act and the Agreements concluded under that authority. In the international discussions at London, Geneva, and Havana the aim of the United States representatives was to carry forward into the postwar world these same principles and to give them greater scope and effect.

The impoverished and disordered state of the world in the early postwar years is not, of course, conducive to the application of the same principles of commercial policy which are adapted to more normal times and conditions. Indeed, the actual reduction of barriers to trade can have little practical effect as long as production is so far short of demand that governments are more preoccupied with obtaining supplies of needed goods than with raising obstacles to their importation. Any international commitments which may be taken now must, during this reconstruction period, allow in practice such deviations from principle as the present chaotic state of the world may require.

Nevertheless the time is in one respect favorable to laying the foundations for future international trade; the people of the world are now particularly conscious of the consumer interest.

This psychology tends to make the task a little easier. Even under these conditions, however, governments negotiating the terms on which trade relations will be established have had their eye on the future when the emphasis will have shifted from buying to selling. Consequently the discussions at London, Geneva, and Havana have given an indication of the longer range developments and trends of thought which will shape the commercial policies of nations in the future. In the light of such indications some of the difficulties with which American policy is having and will have to contend are briefly commented on below.

### *The Handicap of our Economic Strength*

In the first place it may be noted that in so far as obtaining acceptance by other nations of our commercial policy ideas is concerned, our economic strength in a sense is a weakness. The disparity in this respect between the United States and most other nations is very great. The economic strength of this country in absolute terms is enormous, but to the nations whose productive facilities have been destroyed, disorganized, or crippled by the war it seems overwhelming. To foreigners who not only see our economic power but tend to exaggerate it, tariff protection by the United States presents a spectacle of an economic giant cowering behind tariff barricades. Consequently they tend to expect more from us in the way of tariff reduction than is practicable.

This economic strength also represents one of the obstacles to obtaining general acceptance of the policy of freer trade throughout the world, which is a chief tenet of the present economic foreign policy of this country. It gives rise to exaggerated fears of United States competition. It is feared that American production will swamp the markets of the world; that nations struggling back to their feet from the shock of war will be crowded out; that they will be unable to find markets for their exports which they must have if they are to be able to meet their import needs. All this tends to make other countries less receptive to our ideas of freer international competition than they otherwise would be.

### *The Growth of State Trading*

Another factor affecting our ability to give effect to our commercial policy is the growth of state, as distinguished from private, enterprise. If the parties to an international agreement, or any of them, have so-called planned or socialistic economies, the provisions affecting trade will be quite different than such provisions would be if production and trade were in private hands.

Our trade agreements, for example, reflect clearly our belief in and practice of the principle of private enterprise. The provisions of those agreements *reduce* government interference with the activities of traders. A reduced duty represents the reduction of a governmentally imposed obstacle to such activity. Whether trade expands under the provisions of such agreements depends entirely on whether private traders choose to take advantage of the improved opportunities afforded by the agreements. The Government does not control in any way the extent to which they do so. It does not know for sure when it negotiates an agreement how much trade will actually develop. It can only estimate what the results of a duty reduction will be.

The commitments of a government which has the trading operations in its own hands are quite different. Such a government agrees how much it will buy, at what prices, and on what terms.

If we are to have one world, in the economic sense, with one trade charter to govern international relations in this field, these different trading methods must be reconciled. The Geneva draft represents such an attempt. Under it each country keeps its own system, but rules are laid down governing the relations between countries with different systems. It is needless to say that this presents difficulties, and to the extent that state enterprise supplants private enterprise throughout the world the difficulties of giving effect to a trade policy of the kind we advocate are increased.

With the world in its present state of chaos and flux it is the sheerest guesswork now to estimate how serious a handicap this will prove to be. Whether the trend toward the management of economic activities by governments will continue cannot be known. With the world in its present state a large degree of state intervention in matters formerly left in private hands is to be expected. In times of serious national difficulty or crisis there is always a tendency for government to step in and take control of things. The more desperate the situation and the more doubtful the outlook, the more complete such control is likely to be.

Certainly the situation in many countries following the war is such as to cause an unusually high degree of government control and management. To some unknown extent some of this intervention represents a reasoned conviction and philosophy that government management is the best way to order human affairs, whether in times of tranquillity or crisis. But to some extent the tide of government control may recede with the recession of present economic emergencies. To the extent that it does recede the commercial policy of the United States, with its emphasis on greater opportunities for private traders, will have a better environment in which to thrive. Our policy, which seeks to reduce barriers to trade, to increase markets, and to provide opportunities for profitable production everywhere, itself serves to facilitate the return of such an environment.

*Industrial Development*

Another major obstacle to giving effect to our commercial policy is the understandable desire of countries which are in a backward stage of economic development to diversify and develop their production. At international conferences industrialization is now the rallying cry of the relatively underdeveloped countries throughout the world. It is an idea which sometimes tends to expand itself to the point of becoming an obsession.

The idea that greater industrialization of the underdeveloped countries is desirable, or even necessary, if we are to have the prosperous and peaceful world that statesmen seek, is based on solid common sense and cold logic. But the seriousness of the issue which it creates cannot be fully understood without a realization of the extent to which it has acquired an emotional content.

The idea becomes an obsession when the end is sought by any means, whether likely to be successful or not, and regardless of its consequences to living standards in the country concerned and in other countries. While it has been discussed dispassionately by many delegates at the international meetings at London, Geneva, and Havana, it has also at times lent itself to oratorical outbursts of a highly confusing and unenlightening sort. Inasmuch as it is simpler to analyze a complex problem of this kind in terms of someone else's being to blame for lack of progress, there is a tendency to cast the industrial countries in the role of oppressors, with the underdeveloped the oppressed, or at least the victims of indifference and neglect. It is the sort of problem that tends to become a cause.

These properties of the issue, and its real merits, are likely to cause the question of industrial development to occupy a prominent place on the stage, if not the very center of it, in every international meeting on economic subjects to be held for a long time to come. Industrialization is the battle cry in the world of economic relations.

Soberly considered, what is the real issue and where is the collision with United States commercial policy? What is the area of disagreement? It is *not* on the question whether the industrialization of underdeveloped countries is desirable. Most students of the subject thoroughly agree that it is. It is the policy of the United States to promote such industrialization on a sound basis by all appropriate means. The United States Government has applied this policy effectively in practice. It has lent millions to backward countries for development, and has given invaluable assistance in obtaining expert advice and needed technology. It has pursued this policy in the belief that to the extent that diversification of production and the development of industries is brought about there will be an increase in the wealth of the world in which all countries will share through the processes of trade. It has done so in the belief that the most serious limitation on the ability of the industrial and other producers of the world to sell their products is lack of buying power, not competition. To the extent that sound industrialization takes place this limitation is removed.

The issue is not *whether* industrialization should be promoted but *how* this should be accomplished. In the context of the London-Geneva-Havana trade discussions the issue arose because of the proposed provisions for reducing tariffs and other barriers to trade, and particularly the provisions prohibiting the use of quantitative trade restrictions for protective purposes.

The so-called underdeveloped countries argued that countries seeking to develop their industries should be free to restrict imports to encourage such development. Other countries contended that the use of such measures would in many cases not only fail to bring about the desired development, owing to the absence of favorable local conditions, but would raise prices to consumers and reduce living standards. They also pointed out that to permit the free use of protective measures would give free rein to protectionist pressure groups who always lurk in the background when national policies are made, and that unbridled economic nationalism would destroy the trade and the prosperity of the world. It was urged further that a free hand to restrict trade for development purposes would destroy or corrupt the charter, which instead of serving its purpose of promoting economic peace would provide international legal sanction for economic war. If the charter allowed a free hand in the imposition of restrictions on trade each country would, with the sanction of this international instrument, build up its own industries by tearing down those in other countries.

Those opposed to giving a free hand to impose trade restrictions for purposes of economic development conceded that in some cases, where a proposed industry showed promise, trade restrictions should be permitted for at least a long enough period to give it a start. They held, however, that any such action inconsistent with the commercial policy provisions of the charter should be permitted only with the prior approval of the International Trade Organization. Such a provision would insure more care and selectivity in the use of such measures. It would also give opportunity for some accommodation of the interests of the foreign exporting interests concerned, who might be seriously, or even vitally, affected.

In the course of exhaustive and exhausting discussions at three protracted international meetings this question came to be known simply as the prior approval issue. This issue more than any other has troubled the discussions at London and Geneva and was a source of disagreement during the discussions at Havana.

*Preferences*

Another issue troubling the Havana conference is related to the development issue. A number of underdeveloped countries felt that preferential arrangements might serve this end by giving industries in each country participating in such an arrangement sheltered markets outside that country. It was felt that if a group of small countries were to grant lower duties to imports from each other than applied to imports from countries outside the group, the larger sheltered market would serve as a stimulus to the creation of new industries.

Countries favoring the right to enter into such preferential arrangements objected to provisions in the draft charter which would forbid new preferences. They objected for the reasons indicated above, and also because they considered it unfair that countries not now using preferences should be forbidden their use while countries such as those of the British Empire, the United States, and Cuba, were allowed to retain their preferences until such time as they are eliminated by negotiation. A solution of this problem has not, so far as is known, been found as of this writing.

### *Substantial Accomplishments of London-Geneva-Havana Meetings*

There are, of course, many issues other than those discussed above which are raised in the attempt to frame rules of conduct which would obtain world-wide acceptance. Different countries have different problems, viewpoints, and methods. It is difficult to reach agreement on what measures should be outlawed or discouraged. The London-Geneva-Havana meetings have explored exhaustively the questions presented and have clarified the issues. This alone is of great value. If the Trade Organization is established, a satisfactory code of conduct will, because of this big start, more quickly evolve.

Whatever may come out of Havana, however, the General Agreement on Tariffs and Trade concluded at Geneva, which contains a large part of the code of rules to be embodied in a trade charter, represents a very solid achievement indeed. This Agreement, among countries carrying on the greater part of the trade of the world, is a landmark in the history of international commercial relations, and goes a long way in carrying into effect the commercial policy of the United States as established in the thirties under the leadership of Cordell Hull.

## PART IV

# *THE EUROPEAN RECOVERY PROGRAM*

# *INTRODUCTION*

Seymour E. Harris

Having dealt with the economies of important countries and with international agencies, we turn now to the ERP, which is an over-all approach to solving Europe's economic ills directly, and indirectly those of many other countries. Above all, the ERP is a political program developed in order to save Western Europe from the threat of communism, and incidentally to strengthen the political and economic ties of the Western democracies. Its success depends largely upon the attainment of the production and export goals set by the sixteen coöperating countries. In order to reach them, these countries will have to make the most of the large resources within the area, an achievement dependent upon improved trade, credit and exchange arrangements. Governments of sixteen countries will also have to provide, with the help of foreign aid, the food and other essential consumer goods without which adequate production is not possible; and to assure a distribution of these goods consonant with maximum output. It will not be easy for the socialist governments of Europe to strike a balance between consumption and investment, and between these and exports which will not unduly sacrifice the present for the future or vice versa, and will not stimulate excessive domestic use of factors at the expense of the export trade.

It is also imperative that the provision of goods required by the ERP should put the minimum burden on the United States. In the long run, the costs will largely fall upon the American economy; but in the short run, financial burdens (that is, the money costs) need not involve corresponding real burdens. When, for example, this country is producing excessively in relation to its resources (for example, oil) as compared with foreign ratios of output and resources, the correct policy is to force other countries to provide the supplies even though this country gives the dollars. It will be possible to achieve a time use of the dollars obtained for supplies purchased from abroad under the ERP which will reduce the burden on our economy. Furthermore, the goods purchased with these dollars will not be so scarce as those which might have been bought here had not this country under the ERP, shifted demands for goods which are in short supply here to other countries as far as possible. Through appropriate tax and other anti-inflationary measures, through the encouragement of development programs abroad, and *possibly* through the exportation of goods that otherwise would not have been produced, the sacrifices required of this country may be further reduced. Much will depend upon the skill with which the program is administered abroad and the courage with which corrective measures are taken in this country to deal with distortions likely to result from the execution of the ERP.

# 15

## *THE NEW APPROACH TO THE ROLE OF THE UNITED STATES IN EUROPEAN ECONOMIC STABILIZATION*[1]

Edward S. Mason

The character and magnitude of American interests in European economic stabilization quite obviously cannot be discussed without reference to our policy toward Russia. But the relevance of the current foreign aid program to our Russian policy needs to be carefully stated and explicitly understood.

To date we have attempted through negotiations with Russia to work out the basis of a stable postwar world. We have negotiated in the United Nations, in the Council of Foreign Ministers, in the Allied Control Councils in Berlin and Vienna, in the Far Eastern Commission, in Korea, and elsewhere. To say that these negotiations have been notably unsuccessful belongs in the department of understatement.

It is highly important, nevertheless, to diagnose correctly the reasons for this failure. Some say that our failure springs from the fact that Russia is obviously bent on world conquest. Others say that Russian actions to date can all be explained by her preoccupation with security. The Soviet Union, according to this explanation, is suffering from an acute case of encirclement psychosis. As far as American policy is concerned, both of these explanations add up to approximately the same thing. An acute preoccupation with defensive action can easily lead to action which is offensive in both senses of the word.

Both of these explanations are, however, in my opinion

[1] Revision of a paper delivered before the Academy of Political Science, November 12, 1947.

wrong, or, if not wrong, they are at least customarily stated in a manner that throws little light on appropriate American action. Our policy of negotiation has failed for altogether different reasons.

Whatever else the Russians lack—or for that matter anyone else trained in the Marxian school—they do not lack a sense of history. In fact they have, ready-made, a "scientific" interpretation of history which is not only equipped to explain the past but to predict the future. This interpretation of history tells them that time is working on their side. And if time is working on their side, why should they yield in negotiation today that which the inevitable course of events will bring them tomorrow?

What has happened in Europe, moreover, in the two and a half years since the end of the war against Germany, lends a certain credence to this view. The Soviet Union has made substantial progress in binding the former German satellite countries plus Poland and Czechoslovakia to the communist axis. In Western Europe, communist penetration to date has been less successful. But, if economic recovery in the West which, at least in the area of industrial output, has been substantial, is now checked, political instability, so obvious in France and Italy, is bound to increase.

Looking beyond the borders of Europe one also must take into account the fact that the depression in the United States still remains an imminent possibility in the Russian short-run forecast. And, over a longer period, Marxian ideology, of course, foresees a disintegration of capitalism everywhere. As long as events, in Europe or the world, appear to bear out this vision of the immediate future we may expect to get nowhere in negotiations with the Soviet Union on matters that seriously concern the shape of the postwar world.

Under these circumstances the only effective line of action open to us is to attempt, ourselves, to influence the course of events. To me this is the primary significance of the new approach in American foreign policy. If the Marshall program is successful and the participating countries are firmly established on the road tc recovery, we may reasonably expect to see the increasing stability and strength of democratic governments not only in Europe but elsewhere in the world. If and when this happens, we may also reasonably expect to see a change in the Soviet forecast, with a consequent improvement in the prospect of achieving agreement through the process of negotiation.

After all, this would not be the first time that Soviet truculence based on a faulty forecast has given way to sweet reasonableness once the falseness of the forecast had been demonstrated by the course of events. After World War I the leaders of the Russian Revolution expected revolution elsewhere in the capitalist world. Indeed, since it was widely held that the success of communism in Russia depended upon the success of world revolution, the communists in Germany, Hungary, and other countries were urged by their Soviet brethren to try out the formula. When the formula conspicuously failed, Soviet foreign policy changed 180 degrees. It was decided that communism could be made to succeed in one country after all.

If and when the short-run prospects for communist development west of the Iron Curtain hang fire and falter, the chances of a satisfactory European settlement will improve. There is then no incompatibility between the Marshall program and the continued attempt to reach agreement with the Russians through negotiation. In fact quite the reverse is true. Our best chance of reaching satisfactory agreement is through the success of the foreign aid program.

It is for this reason that to characterize the Marshall program as anti-Russian or as an attempt to by-pass the United Nations is particularly absurd. The United Nations will never be able to function as intended until the United States and the Soviet Union have settled by negotiation certain outstanding issues of which the most important are the international control of atomic weapons and the kind of peace settlement to be imposed on Germany. We shall never be able to settle these issues in a manner at all satisfactory to the United States so long as the Soviet Union foresees a course of events which, for her, makes negotiation unnecessary.

To embark wholeheartedly on the foreign aid program does not mean then that we should cease to negotiate with the Soviet

Union. Nor, I think, need we expect that the Soviet Union will break off negotiations unless and until it is sure that the course of events is moving so inexorably in its favor that further negotiation is unnecessary.

If the primary objective of our economic policy in Europe is to bring about a situation in which it will be possible to reach agreement with Russia on the main lines of a peaceful postwar settlement—and I believe this is a fair statement of the objective—it has certain implications, both domestic and foreign, concerning the way the program is conducted.

If we hope and expect later to be able to reach agreement with the Soviet Union, we will not attempt to convert the Marshall plan into an anti-Russian program. We will not ask the European countries to take sides for the inevitable war between East and West. We will not undertake measures which amount to the prosecution of economic warfare against Russia. Rather will we attempt to encourage so far as possible the exchange of goods between Western and Eastern Europe. In Germany, while taking the steps necessary to the economic recovery of the Western zones, we will not close the door to the unification of Germany. We will not bestow approval on Western European political parties and governments in proportion to the intensity and volume of their anti-Russian propaganda.

What we *will* do, if the foreign aid program is regarded as a necessary step toward a reasonable settlement among the great powers, is to focus attention upon the *economic* problem of recovery in Western Europe. We have the right and the duty to insist on such measures of coöperation from European countries as are clearly necessary to the promotion of economic recovery within the framework of established institutions. We have no right—nor will we be able—to impose conditions affecting the structure or functioning of political and economic institutions in the participating countries.

The domestic implications of the foreign aid program are equally important. If the program is merely a campaign in a so-called "cold war" against Russia, the domestic implications are of one sort; if, on the other hand—and as I believe—the promotion of recovery in Europe will lend aid and assistance to our attempts to negotiate with Russia, they are of quite a different sort. The hysterical overtones of some of the writing on Russia in certain sections of the American press certainly suggest the first interpretation of the program. Both this and the overzealous search for communist sympathizers in Washington and elsewhere may be condoned, however, if the European aid program is to be regarded as a lining up of allies for the inevitable struggle. They are hardly to be condoned on any other interpretation. If the foreign aid program is an attempt to promote European recovery in order to establish the basis for an equitable peace settlement, neither hysteria nor the loss of our civil liberties is called for.

Turning now to the character of the United States program in Western Europe it must be recognized that, if the course of events is to run contrary to the Soviet prognosis, what is called for is not merely relief but the laying of a solid foundation for economic recovery. Congress has proclaimed the end of "operation rathole." If the Marshall program is to accomplish its purpose, assistance from the United States henceforth must be justified primarily in terms of its contribution to economic recovery. And American assistance, if it is to be effective, must be rendered within an adequate framework of self-help by the European countries and of mutual assistance among these countries.

This is recognized in the Paris report of the sixteen countries which in its statement of principles and in its conception of the problem is an excellent document. When one turns from general principles to the detailed statement of requirements, the report, it is true, is something less than adequate. No one who has any inkling of the difficulties of negotiating among sixteen countries a schedule of estimated production, exports and import requirements, projected four years into the future, could have expected otherwise.

There is little doubt that a number of stated requirements will have to be scaled down either because of lack of availabilities in the United States or because of overambitious planning of the rate of industrial development and mechanization in Europe. But it is well to recognize that in other respects the

Paris report probably understates European requirements. The estimates of needed imports are frequently based on over-optimistic expectations of rates of local production. This seems particularly true in the case of coal, oil, iron and steel, and is probably true for certain other products. When one type of error is set off against the other, it seems doubtful whether the Paris report represents a serious overstatement of probable European requirements. Recognizing fully the difficulties of such a forecast, it would still be my opinion that the order of magnitude of European requirements stated in the report is roughly what will be required to set Western Europe on its feet again. Investigations by the President's Committee on Foreign Aid and the Executive Branches of the Government support the general order of magnitude suggested by the Paris Report.

While it is important to keep this order of magnitude in mind, it has little to do with the immediate problem. Congressional appropriations will be made on the customary yearly basis and there will be opportunity to review the operations of the program at a number of stages. What must be emphasized, however, is that unless appropriations for year one are made with the program for years two, three, and four in mind; unless, in other words, it is recognized that all parts of the program are interrelated and focused on a definite recovery objective, there is nothing to prevent this becoming another "operation rathole."

Congress has served notice that it is through with emergency appropriations and stop-gap aid. Is Congress ready to recognize the implications of an integrated foreign aid program carried through consistently to its final objectives? The answer to that question will be given not only in the halls of Congress but in the debate on foreign policy which should, and probably will, over the next few months, be carried to every village and hamlet in the United States.

One final remark on the new approach to United States foreign policy seems in order. Let us not expect too much from this program in the way of popular approbation abroad. Even if all the European requirements stated in the Paris report were supplied without question by the United States, I doubt whether we should be regarded as a generous big brother. The figure of Lady Bountiful is not an endearing one in literature. And when the position of Lady Bountiful is taken by a country which has half the world's industrial output and enjoys a standard of living unmatched elsewhere, it is too much to expect that she shall be voted the most popular member of the class. The one most likely to succeed, perhaps, but not the most popular.

European requirements, in fact, will not be supplied without question. And we shall find it necessary, if European recovery is to be effectively promoted, to lay down conditions which will be felt to be extremely onerous. Recriminations on both sides will, therefore, be inevitable. If our objectives are attained, however, and Western Europe once more stands on its own feet with governments both democratic and stable, that will be enough. We should not ask for more.

# 16

## *WHAT CAN EUROPE DO FOR ITSELF?*

Calvin B. Hoover

The first source to which one naturally turns for an answer to the question of What Can Europe do for Itself? is volume I of the *General Report of the Committee of European Economic Coöperation.*[1] This Report might indeed have been titled "What Sixteen European Countries Say They Can Do For Themselves In Order To Obtain Some Twenty Billion Dollars From The U.S.A."[2] The sixteen participating countries were well aware that they would have to make the utmost effort to demonstrate their willingness and ability to help themselves if they were to have any chance to obtain from one other country the means of paying for $20,000,000,000 worth of commodi-

[1] The data used are largely from volume I, *General Report,* and volume II, *Technical Reports, of the Committee of European Economic Coöperation* (1947), published by the State Department. When "the Report" is referred to in the text it is these two volumes reporting the work of the CEEC at Paris which are meant. Some data are from *European Recovery and American Aid, a Report by the President's Committee on Foreign Aid* (November, 1947), and from *Outline of European Recovery Program,* submitted by the Department of State for the use of the Senate Foreign Relations Committee (December 19, 1947).

[2] The total amount of aid to be furnished the sixteen participating countries and Western Germany during the period of approximately four years contemplated by the CEEC was estimated on the basis of the combined balance of payments deficit of these countries with the United States and with the rest of the American continent. The deficit with the United States was estimated to be $15.81 billions. With the rest of the American continent the deficit was estimated to be $5.97 billions, making the total balance of payments deficit $22.44 billions. Of this total it was estimated that financing by the International Bank or other credit operations would cover $3.13 billions, leaving $19.31 billions to be financed by the U. S. Treasury.

The State Department in its *Outline of European Recovery,* December 19, 1947, pp. 112-113, estimated that for the 4¼ years program from April 1, 1948, to June 30, 1952, new Treasury funds of from $15.9 billions to $18.6 billions would be required, in addition to $4.1 billions from other sources, including the International Bank. It was assumed that $1.7 billions would be furnished by other Western Hemisphere countries.

ties. Their need for presenting their case in the best possible light was of course accentuated on the one hand by the billions of dollars of aid which had already been advanced by the United States with no serious prospect of repayment, and by the circumstance that the prospects of repayment of any large fraction of the $20,000,000,000 of aid now to be requested is likely to be exceedingly remote. Consequently, when these sixteen countries stated what they were willing and able to do for themselves, it is obvious that they were putting their best goods in the showcase arranged under the most favorable lighting.

In the Report, Western Europe engaged itself to do the following seven things: (1) to develop its production to reach the targets, especially for food and coal; (2) to make the fullest and most effective use of its existing productive capacity and all available manpower; (3) to modernize its equipment and transport, so that labor becomes more productive, conditions of work are improved, and standards of living of all peoples of Europe are raised; (4) to apply all necessary measures leading to the rapid achievement of internal financial monetary and economic stability while maintaining in each country a high level of employment; (5) to coöperate with one another and with like-minded countries in all possible steps to reduce the tariffs and other barriers to the expansion of trade, both between themselves and with the rest of the world, in accordance with the principles of the draft Charter for an International Trade Organization; (6) to remove progressively the obstacles to the free movement of persons within Europe; (7) to organize together the means by which common resources can be developed in partnership. This list of seven undertakings or obligations ends with the statement: "By these means and provided the necessary supplies can be obtained from overseas, European recovery can be achieved."

## II

Almost all the things which Western Europe can do for itself could be summarized under the one heading of increasing production. The modernization of equipment and transportation, the attainment of financial and economic stability, the removal of trade barriers and, indeed, all the rest of the program have for their purpose increasing production. The first step in the process of trying to answer what Europe can do for itself is to analyze the CEEC program for increased production.

In general terms it is intended to achieve these results by 1951: (1) Restoration of prewar bread grain and other cereal production, with large increases above prewar in sugar and potatoes, some increases in oils and fats, and as fast an expansion in livestock products as supplies of feeding stuffs will allow. (2) Increase of coal output to 584 million tons, i.e. 145 million tons above the 1947 level (an increase of one-third), and 30 million tons above the 1938 level. (3) Expansion of electricity output by nearly 70,000 million Kwh or 40 per cent above 1947, and a growth of generating capacity by over 25 million Kw or two-thirds above prewar. (4) Development of oil refining capacity in terms of crude oil throughout by 17 million tons to two and a half times the prewar level. (5) Increase of crude steel production by 80 per cent above 1947 to a level of 55 million tons, or 10 million tons (20 per cent) above 1938. (6) Expansion of inland transport facilities to carry a 25 per cent greater load in 1951 than in 1938. (7) Restoration of prewar merchant fleets of the participating countries by 1951. (8) Supply from European production of most of the capital equipment needed for these expansions. These eight may be considered the basic targets of the European productive efforts. It is interesting to note that in the analysis of the process and the means by which these targets are to be achieved, the greatest possible stress is placed upon the coöperative efforts of the sixteen countries and Western Germany. To a considerable extent this emphasis on coöperation is part of the process of putting the best goods in the showcase under the most favorable possible light. In cold fact, the success of the program under present circumstances will really depend primarily on the sum total of the individual progress of each country. Nevertheless, aside from the specific examples of coöperation to which reference will be made later, the chance of success in attaining targets in each individual country will be tremendously enhanced simply if all the sixteen countries will strive toward goals which are consistent with each other instead of in conflict with each other.

## III

What can be said with respect to the realism of the production targets which have been announced? Are the goals capable of attainment? Are the goals such as to facilitate the all-important elimination of the deficit in balance of payments of the sixteen countries and Western Germany with the rest of the world and particularly with the Western Hemisphere? In sum, are the production goals consistent with a functioning economy in Western Europe which can be maintained without continuing special aid on a large scale from the United States after 1951?

There have been two official appraisals of the production targets set up by Committee for European Economic Coöperation. The first appraisal was contained in a report of the President's Committee on Foreign Aid, commonly called the Harriman Committee, made up of nongovernmental members from industry, labor, agriculture, and the universities. The second appraisal was embodied in the *Outline of European Recovery Program* submitted by the Department of State for the use of the Senate Foreign Relations Committee. The conclusions of the two appraisals with respect to the realism and feasibility of the production targets of the CEEC are in close harmony. The appraisal by the State Department drew upon the studies previously made by the President's Committee on Foreign Aid and in addition used data which later became available.

In summary, the appraisal of the State Department of the CEEC production program in its *Outline of European Recovery Program*, p. 82, is as follows:

> In broad outline, the following conclusions with respect to the CEEC production program have been reached:
>
> (i) CEEC food-production targets can be achieved and should be surpassed if the participating countries take the steps necessary to insure the most advantageous use of arable land, increased application of fertilizer, and efficient use of agricultural machinery. In estimating that the CEEC goals can be surpassed the assumption has been made that higher yields are possible of achievement.

(ii) CEEC coal-production targets, although they present a real challenge to the resourcefulness and enterprise of these countries, are believed to be technically attainable.

(iii) CEEC finished-steel-production targets will probably not be reached in 1948-49 even with vigorous steps to break the steel scrap, coke, and transport bottlenecks.

(iv) Even on the least favorable set of assumptions regarding finished-steel production by the participating countries, European industrial recovery will not be significantly impeded provided finished steel is directed to the most urgent uses; namely, the equipment-making and metal-fabricating industries producing durable capital goods. Anticipated shortages of finished steel will delay the rate of rehabilitation of the European economy, particularly in housing, and will slow down the expansion of exports of finished steel.

(v) Internal adjustments in the pattern of steel consumption such as those indicated above will reduce the production of consumer durables for indigenous consumption. On the other hand, world availabilities of raw cotton, hides and leather, and tobacco in 1948 and throughout the period of the European recovery program will provide a basis for improving living standards and stimulating labor productivity.

(vi) The direction of economic activity as well as the composition of output in the participating countries will deviate in many instances from programmed goals. However, the basic objectives of the European production program appear to be attainable and programmed levels of production of items essential to recovery can be reached.[3]

To begin with the most basic industry, are the announced targets with respect to agricultural production reasonable, and what are the prospects for their successful achievement? By 1951 Western Europe must be able to feed a population which it is estimated will be 11 per cent greater than prewar. This increase is in part due to natural increase and in part due to the movement of population from Eastern Europe to Western Europe, in particular the expulsion of German population from the area of Germany annexed by Russia and Poland east of the Oder-Neisse. It is in the light of this increase in population that the reasonableness of the target must be assayed.

[3] The conclusions in the remainder of the chapter are the author's, based upon his own analysis of the data. These conclusions are in general consistent with the two official appraisals to which reference has been made. The author was a member of the President's Committee on Foreign Aid.

In order to feed the assumed population, a diet is planned which would be by the end of the period about the same in total calories per capita as prewar, but of somewhat lower quality. In particular the quantity of meat available per capita is planned to be about 90 per cent of prewar. It is planned that the amount of all cereals produced is to be approximately the same in 1951 as it was in 1938. The amount of potatoes produced is to be greatly increased. These goals are certainly not too great in terms of human needs now as compared with prewar. Indeed, as will be pointed out, they are likely to be sharply inadequate in view of the actual import possibilities with respect to food and feedstuffs.

It seems probable that the targets for the production of cereals and potatoes as set forth could be achieved or even surpassed somewhat if initial quantities of fertilizer and agricultural implements are made available from the United States and if European production of these items can be increased as imports from the United States taper off.

On the other hand, even the reduced program for livestock production in comparison with 1938 is probably too ambitious. This is because the imports of feedstuffs which would be necessary for the planned levels of livestock production will not be available from overseas. Likewise, the quantity of foodstuffs which it is planned to import from abroad during the period probably cannot be obtained. Consequently grain produced in Western Europe must be reserved for human consumption to a greater extent than is planned. This means that whereas livestock production outside Western Germany was planned to be restored nearly to the prewar level, livestock production probably cannot be restored to prewar levels even outside Germany.

Even if the production levels, aside from livestock, are attained, an exceedingly serious problem in feeding Western Europe will still exist by 1951. During the prewar period, 1934-38, Western Europe imported annually on the average 25 million tons of grain, 3.2 million tons of fats and oils, 3.7 million tons of sugar, 1.7 million tons of meat and considerable quantities of other foods.[4] About 5 million tons of the grain com-

[4] *European Recovery and American Aid,* p. 41.

ponent of these imports was obtained from Eastern Europe, including Germany east of the Oder-Neisse line. In planning the food balance for 1951 it is assumed in the Report that food imports from this area into Western Europe will have been restored to their former level. This is a most optimistic assumption which is unhappily likely to be contrary to fact.

The CEEC countries expect to obtain 9 to 10 million tons of grain per year from the United States. During the 1946-47 crop year, the United States exported about 15 million tons of grain, of which the CEEC countries and Germany received about 9 million tons. But this was made possible by quite unusually good crops in the United States and by special measures to make this grain available for export. It seems unlikely that the quantity of grain expected from the United States during the life of the plan can be obtained, and it is likewise unlikely that the amounts apparently expected after 1951 can be obtained.

The total production of grain in Western Europe can probably be pushed during the four years only slightly above that planned in the report. The restoration of food consumption levels at a slower rate than planned and the development of food production in the dependencies of the CEEC countries would appear to be necessary. The first alternative, slowing up the rate of improvement in nutrition levels, which is the one which unhappily will probably have to be primarily depended upon, is closely associated with the necessity of keeping consumer incomes at levels low enough to permit the economic stability which is so essential to financial and monetary stabilization to which reference will be made later.

The report contains a reference to plans for expanding the production of oil-bearing seeds in British and French dependencies in Africa. The Harriman Report has pointed out the probable necessity for expanding this program, if need be by means of specially earmarked funds from the United States. The increased production planned (some 500,000 tons of nuts) is a good beginning, but is grossly inadequate in comparison with annual imports of fats and oils of 3.2 million tons before the war.

One additional comment needs to be made. The quantities of agricultural equipment, particularly of heavy tractors, which are requested from the United States in the furtherance of the production program, are larger than are likely to be furnished by the United States, and the total quantities of agricultural equipment planned to be produced for domestic use and imported together are probably in excess of those needed for the planned levels of production.

In sum, the CEEC countries have a production program in agriculture which is reasonably in line with their productive capacities in this field. Even if attained, however, it would not solve the food deficiency problem of Western Europe on account of the probable unavailability of adequate supplementary supplies from outside the area.

The production program for coal provides for an increase in output of about one-third above 1947 to 584 million tons. This would be about 30 million tons above output in 1938. No element in the whole production plan with the possible exception of foodstuffs is so vital to the CEEC program as is coal. During the past year some forty million tons of coal were imported into Western Europe from the United States. This coal has to be paid for in dollars at very high prices. Under anything like normal circumstances the importation of coal into Europe from the United States is an economic absurdity. The restoration of exports of British coal to Europe and the expansion of present exports of Ruhr coal would have an almost magically favorable effect upon the whole economy of Western Europe.

If the planned goals are achieved, coal production in Britain in 1951 would be about 8 per cent above the last prewar year, production in the Bizone of Germany would be about 6 per cent below prewar. Production in France would be increased about 30 per cent above prewar, but French production is relatively so much smaller than either British or German production as to be of much less significance than either. A larger proportion of Ruhr production would presumably be available for export on account of the lower level of German steel production envisaged in the plan compared with prewar.

The success of the coal program depends primarily upon

what happens in Britain and in the Bizone of Germany. Recent production data from both areas are encouraging. The production target of 200 million tons for the year 1947 in Britain was nearly attained. The incentive payments to miners in the Ruhr have raised *daily* production in that area to around 280,000 tons in November, 1947, from 229,000 tons per day in March of that year. By March, 1948, production had finally reached a level of 300,000 tons per day which had been the target for December 31, 1947. Any improvement in production or even the maintenance of this rate will depend upon the ability of the occupying powers to keep the food ration of the population in the Ruhr at least as high as the present low level. The Report states:

> The position in Western Germany calls for special comment in view of her importance as a producer of coal. The present low level of consumption cannot during the four-year period be raised to the prewar level, but it will have to be raised above present levels to enable the population to play its part in the production programme.

Closely connected with the production program for coal is that of electric power. It is planned to increase the output of electricity by 40 per cent over 1947. In terms of generating capacity the increase planned is about 65 per cent above prewar.[5] The electrical power program is one of the "show pieces" of coöperation of the participating countries of which the Report makes the most. The program includes a plan which combines the resources of six hydro-electric plants in Italy, France, and on the Austro-Italo-Swiss frontier, with two lignite thermal plants in Germany and one geo-thermal plant in Italy. It is commented in the Report that "These projects have been selected without regard to national frontiers and involved in some cases the coöperative development of resources cutting across frontiers."

The program for increasing oil refining capacity to two and one-half times the prewar level should probably be charac-

[5] The State Department, in its *Outline of European Recovery Program*, p. 79, doubts if the program for increasing hydro-electric generating capacity can be met within the assumed time period. It is estimated that one year more beyond the assumed time period would be required.

terized as grandiose in view of the probable availabilities of crude oil during the period. It is true that a large part of the crude oil might be obtained from sterling areas but it is doubtful nevertheless whether total world supplies will be such as to warrant so large and rapid an expansion of oil refining capacity in Western Europe.

The steel production program is likewise vital to the general plan. It is planned to increase steel production by about 80 per cent above 1947 which would mean an increase of about 20 per cent above 1938, although this production would be only about the same as the total of the best prewar production years of each of the participating countries and the Bizone of Germany. At the present time steel production in Western Europe outside Germany is somewhat above the prewar rate of production. In the Bizone of Germany on the contrary it is at a rate of about 3.5 million tons per year or about 1/5 the prewar annual production rate. The planned program would allow for a per capita rate of consumption of steel in Western Europe about one-third that of the U.S.A.

A very substantial import of scrap and semifinished steel is planned for in the Report. It is intended that the imported semifinished steel or its equivalent would be reëxported from Europe as fabricated goods, and it is apparently expected that this would continue even beyond 1951, since there is little "tapering off" provided for. This part of the program has been strenuously opposed by the steel industry of the U.S.A., where scrap is very short and where exports of semifinished steel would accentuate the scrap shortage.[6]

It is striking, however, to notice the profound changes in the proportion of steel production planned for the sixteen participating countries on the one hand and the Bizone of Germany on the other between 1938 and 1951. According to plan the production of Western Germany would be reduced almost by half in comparison with 1938. The production of the 16 participating countries would be increased by two-thirds above that of

[6] The State Department in *Outline of European Recovery Program,* p. 82, estimates that the quantity of finished steel available for consumption in the participating countries and Western Germany might be some six million tons below the CEEC estimates during the first two years of the program.

1938. That is, production outside the Bizone is to *increase* from 27.7 million tons per year in 1938 to 45.4 million tons in 1951. In the Bizone production is to *diminish* from 17.8 million tons to 10 million tons on the same base. Steel production of France would, according to the plan, become greater than that of Western Germany. This represents a most important geographical shift in this vital industry.

Since limitations of time prevent devoting a separate section of this chapter to Germany, it is perhaps admissible to draw from the Report a brief comment or two with respect to the relation of the Bizone to the economy of Western Europe.

In the Report references are almost always to "the sixteen participating countries and the Bizone of Germany." In appendix B—*Problems Relating To Germany,* the opening sentence reads,

> For the purpose of drawing up a European balance sheet of resources and requirements, it is indispensable to take account of Germany, since that economy has been, in the past, and by the nature of things will remain, closely tied up with the economic systems of other European countries. . . . Considerations of security demand also that both the rate and nature of her economic recovery should be carefully controlled.

Under the circumstances it was inevitable that no representatives of the German people were to be present at the Paris Conference. Representatives of the occupying powers of the combined British and American zones were there to furnish statistical information but they did not participate in formulating the Report.

In dealing with coal, steel, food, balance of payments, and indeed with almost every aspect of the economic four-year plan, the participating countries took account of the German economy and made every effort to incorporate the Bizone into the program. Even in the case of consumer goods it was necessary to take account of German industry. The Report states:

> An excessive concentration of the production in Western Germany of consumer goods traditionally supplied from other countries might create in those countries almost insoluble problems of adjustment, and this factor must be borne in mind when working

out the rehabilitation of Germany along peaceful lines consistent with security.[7]

The production and balance of payments plan for Germany which was incorporated into the Report was based upon the new Level of Industry Plan adopted for the combined British-American Zones by their Commanders in the summer of 1947. In the case of steel this involved a production rate of 10 million tons per year in 1951, compared with a permitted ceiling on production of 10.7 million tons per year, although it was noted that it was doubtful whether more than 7 or 8 million tons could actually be produced.

Turning to transportation, the CEEC planned to expand inland transport facilities by 1951 to 25 per cent above 1938. Merchant fleets of the participating countries are to be restored to the prewar level by 1951. There is some doubt as to whether steel in exceedingly short supply should be used in a merchant ship building program on this scale. Instead a greater number of American Liberty and other ships might be furnished to make up the deficiency.

Finally it is noted that most of the capital equipment needed for the expansion of production facilities planned is to come from European production. This emphasizes the degree to which the goods required from the United States under the plan would be in large part food and raw materials. These are essential to the European program of capital equipment construction, but most of the actual manufacture of this capital equipment would take place within Western Europe itself.

## IV

All during the Paris Conference the United States was pressing hard both at Paris and at Geneva for the removal of barriers to international trade. At Paris this took the form of using the influence of the United States towards bringing about a European Customs Union. Once more the process of putting the best goods in the show case is represented in the part of the Report dealing with the removal of barriers to trade among the CEEC countries. Quoting from the Report,

[7] From recollections of negotiations in Berlin in 1945, the writer would wager that a British hand penned those particular lines.

> To achieve the freer movement of goods the participating countries are resolved: (1) to abolish as soon as possible the abnormal restrictions which at present hamper their mutual trade; (2) to aim, as between themselves and the rest of the world, at a sound and balanced multilateral trading system based on the principles which have guided the framers of the Draft Charter for an International Trade Organization.

This declaration of intention is then considerably elaborated upon.

Recognizing the enthusiasm of the United States for a European Customs Union, every effort was made to make progress in this direction appear as substantial as possible. The Benelux agreement to form a Customs Union is presented with pride, although of course its formation antedated the Paris Conference and the Marshall Plan idea. The action of Denmark, Iceland, Norway, and Sweden in declaring, after a meeting of their foreign ministers in Copenhagen in August, in favor of examining the possibilities of a Customs Union is noted favorably. The French Government announced its willingness to consider the possibility of the formation of a Customs Union with any countries "whose national economies are capable of being combined with the French economy in such a way as to make a viable unit." The Italian Government associated itself with this statement by the French Government. The Governments of Austria, Belgium, Denmark, France, Greece, Ireland, Italy, Iceland, Luxembourg, the Netherlands, Portugal, the United Kingdom, and Turkey announced their intention of creating a Study Group to examine the possibility of the formation of a Customs Union or Customs Unions.

As further evidences of economic coöperation, the participating countries note that they are seeking to increase the efficiency of production through the standardization of equipment, particularly mining and electrical supplies and freight cars. It is intended also to work out pooling arrangements for freight cars between the countries. Arrangements have been made to permit motor trucks to cross international boundaries and thus avoid the previously existing necessity for unloading and transshipment of goods. Arrangements are also mentioned for interchange of information between countries of their programs for the modernization and extension of their steel industries so that each country in developing its program may take account of the plans made by the others. Finally, it is stated in the Report that measures are to be taken to facilitate the free movement of persons between countries to the end that surplus labor in countries such as Italy may be transferred to labor deficit countries such as France.

## V

Probably of even greater importance than the reduction of trade barriers is the program of internal economic financial and monetary reform to which the participating countries have pledged themselves. There can be no doubt of the immensely favorable effect upon production which such a program would have if successfully carried out. Increases in production of goods and financial and monetary reform have a decidedly "chicken-and-egg" relation to each other. Both would be greatly facilitated if they could be carried out simultaneously. Neither could succeed in the event of substantial failure of the other.

In countries such as the Bizone of Germany, where a pound of butter on the black market is reported to bring as much as a ton of wheat at governmentally fixed prices, the distortion of agricultural production which is thus encouraged is of serious proportions. Similar situations exist in France and Italy. Indeed, in Germany, prices nominally stabilized at the 1936 level are practically without meaning except for rationed foodstuffs. The monetary reform of June 1948 may improve matters.

The stimulating effect of the reëstablishment of truly functional cost-price relationships between goods and services and between these and producer-consumer incomes cannot be doubted. Currency stabilization, balancing of budgets, elimination of black markets, restoration of a rational price structure, revaluation of currencies in the direction of purchasing power parities, are all part of an economic mosaic in which the absence of one of the principal pieces can largely nullify the fitting together of the others. The Report shows that this was quite adequately realized by its framers.

The participating countries express their resolve to balance their budgets as soon as humanly possible. They likewise resolve to render their currencies convertible at appropriate rates of exchange as defined in the Articles of Agreement of the International Monetary Fund.

They state however that "The quick success of stabilization will to a very large extent depend upon adequate foreign assistance being available during the period in which stabilization is being achieved." They then expressed the belief that in order to provide the necessary gold reserves for internal stabilization and international convertibility, the sum of 3 billion dollars of outside aid would be required. There is considerable ambiguity about this amount, however. It is conceived of in some sense as outside the total of aid otherwise sought for. At another point in the report it is implied that if the aid granted could be properly planned the 3 billion dollars would not necessarily be an additional sum but comprehended within it.

It is stated clearly that "External Aid must be used in such a way that by the end of the period national income in its widest sense will cover national expenditure. The main aim should clearly be to reduce inflationary pressure where it exists." It is further stated,

> For example, the local currency received by any government concerned as the result of such assistance [from the United States] which directly or indirectly takes the form of imported goods, should be used, as circumstances make it appropriate, to put an end to the recourse to Banks of Issue to cover budget deficits, to repay advances already received from Banks of Issue, or to reduce the resort to other inflationary budget devices.

## VI

In summary, what are the prospects of success for this three-pronged program of Western European self-help, involving as it does great increases in production, the removal of trade barriers, and monetary and financial reform and stabilization? The difficulties which this comprehensive and ambitious program are certain to encounter can be partially visualized by noting the assumptions in the Report upon which the plan for eliminating the deficit in balance of payments for Western Europe by 1951 are based:

These include the assumptions that their production will increase greatly, that the imports required for this will be available, that a state of full employment and full use of productive resources will be continuously maintained, that an increasing part of the needs of the participating countries and Western Germany can be obtained from Eastern Europe and from South-East Asia, that the goods which the participating countries can produce for export can be sold to the American continent and to the rest of the world, that there will be a progressive reduction in the price of imports in relation to the price of exports, and that non-participating countries will so far as necessary be able to pay for such goods in dollars.

The levels already attained by industrial production in Western Europe in 1947 augur well for the success of the production program for the four-year period ahead. By the middle of the year, except for Italy which lagged behind the remainder of Western Europe at 65 per cent of prewar and for the Bizone of Germany where production levels were little above 40 per cent of prewar, the 1938 level of industrial production had been nearly achieved or even surpassed.

By May of 1947, Jean Monnet, head of the Planning Commission, estimated that industrial production in France had reached 106 per cent of the prewar level. In Britain industrial and agricultural production both surpassed prewar by substantial margins. Only coal and textiles lagged, but coal production during the fall of 1947 increased substantially. Steel production in Britain is at an annual rate of 14 million tons compared with 10 million tons before the war. In Scandinavia, notably in Sweden, the level of industrial production is substantially above that of the period before the war. In Belgium and the Netherlands industrial production is now at a rate which nearly approaches prewar levels.

The optimistic auguries for the future which may be drawn from this recent record of industrial production must be tempered by two significant circumstances. First, as has been shown by recent events in France and Italy, industrial production is exceedingly vulnerable to politically induced interruptions to production. Second, the level of production reached has been dependent to a large degree upon the import of food and raw materials obtained from abroad through loans or gifts.

This latter point emphasizes the crucial nature of the problem of balance of payments.

The answer to whether the CEEC program will succeed or fail will be largely reflected in the balance of payments position of Western Europe. If the deficit in balance of payments is to be eliminated by 1951 the production goals aimed at must be achieved. The maintenance of a real balance between exports and imports will also depend upon increased productivity made possible by new capital investment provided for in the Plan. Somewhat paradoxically, however, it is essential that the increase in new capital investment should not be greater than that which can be supported by real savings plus imports. If too grandiose a program is attempted, it will have an inflationary effect and will reduce the volume of capital construction which can actually be completed. There is some danger that the program of capital construction planned is too ambitious and that it should be reduced.[8]

Closely connected with the limits on capital construction is the volume of exports attainable.[9] Out of total national income produced plus imports, there must come consumption plus exports plus net additions to capital equipment. Particularly in view of the current domestic political difficulties in Europe, enhanced ten-fold by the bitter opposition of Soviet Russia to the Marshall Plan, it will prove exceedingly difficult to keep the components of total consumer income within limits which will permit monetary and financial stabilization.[10] This problem, so different from that faced by governments in the depression-ridden thirties, confronts practically all countries. Our own difficulties in this field enable one to understand the far more difficult position in which the governments of Western Europe find themselves.

Finally two factors beyond the control of the CEEC coun-

[8] The State Department in *Outline of European Recovery Program* concludes that "The C.E.E.C. program probably implies a rate of capital formation that is excessive from the standpoint of the participating nations themselves," p. 72.

[9] The State Department also concludes that the volume of exports could be increased somewhat above that planned. *Outline of European Recovery Program*, p. 73.

[10] "So rapid an improvement in the standard of living in Europe cannot in fact be achieved." *Outline of European Recovery Program*, p. 74.

tries will condition their ability to eliminate the deficit in balance of payments. They must be able to sell greatly increased quantities of goods and services abroad and particularly in the United States. In this respect our foreign trade policy will be of great importance. Even if the CEEC countries can sell their goods abroad, they must be able to purchase food stuffs and raw materials on barter terms of trade consistent with a real balance of payments. In this field the future course of prices in the Western Hemisphere and the absolute availability of supplies give reason for substantial concern.[11]

The conclusion reached after examining the CEEC Report drawn up by the representatives of the sixteen countries is that they have done extraordinarily well in presenting the evidence of their will and ability to help themselves. If they have, as suggested at the beginning of the chapter, placed their best merchandise in the show case under the most favorable lighting, the samples are nevertheless reasonably representative. In some cases where the planned results seem unduly optimistic, we have ourselves largely to thank—as when the CEEC reduced the prices assumed for imports in order to diminish the total aid suggested to a sum more likely to be acceptable to the United States.

Whether all that these countries can do to help themselves, plus whatever aid they may receive from the United States will actually enable Western Europe to attain self-sufficiency is another matter. Certainly the result of failure on our part to extend large-scale aid to this great coöperative effort at self-help would produce most serious consequences.

There has been no attempt to deal in this chapter with the political aspects of the problem under discussion. There can, however, be no doubt that even if the economic obstacles to recovery could be surmounted, political events might still destroy Europe. The declaration by Soviet Russia, through the Cominform, of her intention to defeat the Marshall program at all costs removes all doubt in this matter, if any still existed.

[11] Professor Seymour Harris points out that prices which the CEEC countries must pay for imports are more important than the barter terms of trade. This is so largely because so much of the trade is not covered by real barter but must be covered by loans and/or gifts and returns on investments.

Soviet policy, to be successful, needs to attain no constructive ends. If strikes and other forms of economic sabotage can succeed in disorganizing the economies of France and Italy to the point where the Congress of the United States becomes convinced that the Marshall Plan is becoming "operation rathole," Soviet Russia will have won a most important battle in the "cold war." Congress needs to be tough-minded and strong-nerved if it is to support a foreign policy appropriate to this situation in which the Soviets, as always, fight without any concern for Marquis of Queensberry rules.

# 17

## *AMERICA'S RESOURCES IN RELATION TO EUROPE'S NEEDS*

Kirtley F. Mather

Granted that there is widespread desire in the United States to render all possible aid to the less fortunate people of war-devastated lands, it is nevertheless well recognized that the ability of even so richly endowed a country as ours to make contributions to the material welfare of others is definitely limited. It would be folly, in seeking world prosperity, to deplete America's resources to such an extent as to endanger our own future as a great industrial nation. World economy cannot be established on a just and stable basis unless the United States is able to continue indefinitely on a high level of industrial and commercial prosperity.

The foundation upon which the industrial economy of any region must rest may be likened to a tripod, each leg of which must be strong and of appropriate length. In the long run, the leg of that tripod representing the human resources is the most important. At the moment, the intellectual ability of scientists, engineers, and technicians, the potential industriousness of men and women who work with hand and brain, the emotional and spiritual qualities of its citizens, constitute America's greatest asset. But the best people in the world—and I do not mean to imply that Americans are unquestionably that—cannot accomplish what they might like to do unless adequate material resources are available.

The second leg of the tripod might be designated as the agricultural resources, if in that category we include all the products derived from the growth of plants and animals. The quantity of such resources is limited by the extent and nature of the soil and the factors characterizing climate. Thanks to modern techniques of soil conservation, plus recently developed methods for utilizing the inexhaustible stores of nitrogen in the atmosphere as food for plants, the resources of the plant and animal kingdoms may now be considered as potentially renewable. Wisely used, they remain in the category of annual income. For them the earth is a factory rather than a storehouse. There need be no fear of future depletion of this type of resource, provided the factory is managed in accordance with procedures now available to men of intelligence and goodwill.

In striking contrast, almost all the resources of the mineral kingdom are nonrenewable. The geologic processes responsible for their presence in the outer shell of the earth operate so slowly, in relation to man's haste in extracting them from the ground, that for all practical purposes the earth must be considered as a storehouse of mineral wealth rather than as a factory. When petroleum and coal, iron and aluminum, copper and tin, are extracted from wells and mines, we are drawing upon stored capital. These and many other mineral resources, essential to life in an age of science and technology, are being exhausted at an increasingly rapid rate. This third leg of our symbolic tripod is therefore the one that at the moment gives us most cause for worry. Will the depletion of America's mineral wealth, in the endeavor to assist other nations in their efforts at postwar rehabilitation and reconstruction, be such as to endanger our nation's future industrial development?

To answer that question it is necessary to review available information concerning the current consumption and remaining reserves of certain critical minerals, both for the United States and for the world as a whole. Although the data are not nearly so complete nor precise as one might wish, they nevertheless suggest certain fundamental principles of global and national economics that may well serve as a guide to public policy and private action.

Foremost among these nonrenewable resources is petroleum. Both as fuel and as raw material for chemical industries, it is of prime significance in the economics and politics of almost every nation. Between 1859, when the first oil well was drilled in the United States, and January 1, 1948, the world production of petroleum has totalled approximately 54 billion barrels. Of that total, about 32 billion barrels were produced in the United States. At present, American consumption of petroleum products is in almost perfect balance with American production and requires an annual supply of 1.8 billion barrels of crude oil. If present trends continue, the average annual requirement of petroleum products in the United States for the next ten years will be the equivalent of about 2 billion barrels of crude oil.

The proved reserves of crude oil in the United States are reliably estimated to be 21.5 billion barrels, as of January 1, 1948. In addition there are probable, but as yet undiscovered reserves, that are estimated to total between 20 and 30 billion barrels. Although this looks like an adequate supply for the next twenty or twenty-five years, the mechanics of oil recovery are such that it will prove quite impossible to get the oil from depleted reservoirs as rapidly as it is needed. The prospect for the future is inescapable: although the United States is now enjoying the greatest petroleum production of all time, our domestic production will fall far short of our needs within five or ten years from now. Thereafter the gap between demand and domestic supply will increase year by year, even though it will be at least a century before all the oil is completely exhausted from the ground.

There are two alternative sources from which this deficiency in supply can be met: imported petroleum from foreign oil fields, and synthetic petroleum products derived from oil shale, coal, and natural gas. The known reserves of oil shale and coal in the United States are almost unbelievably extensive. They are quite adequate to provide the equivalent of 2 billion barrels of petroleum products every year for at least a thousand years. Although the techniques of synthesizing all of the more important petroleum products from those carbon-rich rocks are already known, it is a physical and economic impossibility to construct and equip the necessary plants in time to meet the deficit that looms so near in the future. Synthetic gasoline and other petroleum substitutes can hardly be available in sufficient quantities to balance our petroleum budget in less than ten or fifteen years. In the meantime we will have to depend more and more upon crude oil imported from abroad.

The distribution of the world's major known reserves of crude oil is shown in the accompanying table, in which the estimates are given as of January 1, 1948, and the percentages of production are for the year 1946.

World Reserves and World Production of Petroleum[a]

| | Estimated Proved Reserves *Billions of Barrels* | Estimated Proved Reserves *Per cent of Total* | *Per cent of World Production* |
|---|---|---|---|
| United States | 21.5 | 31 | 62 |
| Soviet Union | 9.5 | 13.8 | 5.7 |
| Kuwait | 9.0 | 13 | 0.25 |
| Venezuela | 7.5 | 10.9 | 14 |
| Iran | 6.0 | 8.7 | 5.25 |
| Iraq | 6.0 | 8.7 | 1.25 |
| Saudi Arabia, Bahrein and Qatar | 5.0 | 7.2 | 2.5 |
| Netherlands East Indies | 1.0 | 1.5 | 1.5 |
| All other countries, no one of which is credited with as much as 1 billion barrels of proved reserves | 3.5 | 5.2 | 7.55 |
| Totals | 69.0 | 100 | 100 |

[a]Based upon data in *Petroleum Report* issued by De Golyer, E., and H. W. MacNaughton (New York, 1947).

When using the above data for a comparison of the petroleum resources of the various countries, it should be noted that the relation between proved reserves and probable but yet undiscovered reserves is markedly different in different regions. Exploration for oil and development of discovered fields have advanced much farther in the United States than in almost any other country. Whereas the total reserves—proved plus probable—are little if any more than twice the figure given above for American proved reserves, the total for other countries is three or four times the amount indicated above. It is quite probable that the total crude oil resources of the earth approximate 250 billion barrels at the present time and that America's remaining share is only about 20 per cent of the world's oil.

The fact that in recent years we have had to produce 62 to 65 per cent of the world's annual production of crude oil in order to meet our needs for petroleum products, combined with the fact that we possess far less than 30 per cent of the world's oil resources, leads unerringly to the conclusion that we cannot afford to share any appreciable fraction of our dwindling stores of oil-in-the-ground with other nations. Even so, we will doubtless find it desirable to continue to export considerable quantities of petroleum products to Canada if for no other reason than because of our dependence upon that neighboring Dominion for nickel, cobalt and uranium.

The data summarized above indicate also how favorable is the opportunity for supplying American petroleum needs from foreign oil fields, pending the shift to significant dependence upon oil shale and coal as substitute sources of liquid hydrocarbons. At the present time, American interests control 75 per cent of the proved oil reserves of South America, 42 per cent of those in the Middle East, and 28 per cent of those in the Far East. All told, about 57 per cent of the world's known oil is American controlled, a figure that probably approximates very closely the percentage of the world's production that will be needed to satisfy American demands during the next decade.

None of the sixteen nations associated in the European Recovery Program can meet its needs for petroleum products from its own production. Nor is there any hope that oil resources, adequate for current needs, may be found within their areas. Intensive search, guided by the best scientific information, has resulted in the development of new fields in England and Germany in the last ten years, but these are very small and contain relatively trivial quantities of petroleum. Prospects are favorable in certain parts of Denmark, Holland, and Belgium for additional slight production. New pools may be discovered in Italy. But the nature of the recent surveys and the results obtained to date only confirm the conclusion that the highly industrialized nations of central and western Europe must depend upon foreign sources for a large fraction of the petroleum products essential to their prosperity.

Alternative domestic sources such as the oil shales of Scotland and Sweden have already been exploited almost as completely as possible. The lower grade coals of Germany, Belgium, Luxembourg, and France may eventually provide considerable quantities of liquid and gaseous hydrocarbons, but that is a development of the future rather than of the present. Great Britain's coal reserves amount to only about 160 times the recent annual extraction, whereas the coal reserves of the United States are about 5,000 times as great as our annual production. It would be unwise to allocate any considerable fraction of Britain's dwindling coal reserves to a program for synthetic petroleum products.

The picture is all too clear. The "Marshall Plan" must provide for the importation of considerable quantities of petroleum products from sources outside Europe. But the crude oil must not come from American oil fields. The Middle East is the logical source, with South America as a less desirable second choice. Some of the oil may possibly be processed in the United States but that will probably prove to be unnecessary. If the United States will finance the operations for a few years, the reserves in the Middle East and the equipment necessary for the production, refining, and transportation of that oil will prove to be fully adequate to meet European needs. Furthermore, inasmuch as American oil interests have such extensive holdings and investments in that region, a large fraction of the American funds allocated for petroleum supplies will actually be used to support American business enterprises and will stimulate profitable returns to American investors. Perhaps this is a modern variation of the ancient theme about "casting bread upon the waters."

Crowding close upon petroleum for leadership in importance among the nonrenewable resources is iron ore. The same questions pertaining to percentages of world production and world reserves should be raised concerning it. Unfortunately for our present enquiry it is not possible to answer those questions with the desired precision, but at least the orders of magnitude may be ascertained.

One difficulty accrues from the impossibility of defining an ore. The minimum percentage of iron oxides in a rock necessary to make it useful as an ore depends upon many factors. Costs of mining, transporting, refining, and smelting the ore are very different for various geologic and geographic occurrences. With improved methods of beneficiation, large bodies of rock that today cannot be considered as a profitable source of iron tomorrow may be valuable ore. It is therefore necessary to consider not only discovered ore and inferred ore, but potential ore as well. With reference to the last mentioned, however, one must be cautious against overoptimism, both with respect to the success of experiments now under way and to the time required to put new procedures into practical, large-scale operation.

As for oil, so for iron, American production and American consumption have been in close balance over the years. During the war years, the annual production of iron ore was of the order of 100 million tons, reaching a peak of 105 million tons in 1942. Unlike petroleum, the production and consumption of which was greater in 1947 than in any preceding year, the production of iron ore has fallen off appreciably since the close of the war. Presumably the average requirement for the next few years will be of the order of 75 or 80 million tons per year. That would be about 15 or 20 million tons greater than the average for the decade 1922-31.

The world's richest and most economically exploited iron ores are in the Lake Superior region, largely in the United States. The Mesabi Range alone, in northeastern Minnesota, has produced to date more than half of our domestic supply of iron. Next in importance to the Lake Superior ores are those in the vicinity of Birmingham, Alabama. Then come the magnetite deposits of the Adirondack region and the various ore bodies in the western, central, and Gulf states. Probably all the really significant iron ore bodies within the continental limits of the United States have already been located, although the dimensions of several of them have not yet been determined even within broad limits.

The reserves of discovered ore—"measured" plus "indicated" ore, in the parlance of the geologists and engineers—are computed to be approximately 3.4 billion tons, as of January 1, 1948, for the continental United States as a whole. That would be better than a forty-year supply at the average rate of exploitation suggested above as probable for the next few years. In addition, there are reserves of inferred ore totalling 1.7 billion tons as well as approximately 63 billion tons of potential ore.

This is a very different picture from that which has frequently been presented of late by several individuals on various occasions. It is quite true that the discovered ore remaining in the Lake Superior region is now less than half the amount already mined there. It is also true that the reserves of high grade ore in that region are only about thirteen or fourteen times the amount extracted annually during the war years. But those statements, with their gloomy portent, tell only a part of the whole story. The wartime production was at a peak from which we have already receded, and the experience of those years cannot be taken as indicative of the future trends. Moreover, the Lake Superior reserves comprise only a third of the total discovered reserves of the country as a whole. Mining of iron has been concentrated in that region, and was greatly accelerated there during the war because of the favorable economic and geologic factors, but the ore bodies elsewhere are far better from every point of view than many of the iron ores that have long been the base of industrial developments in several European countries.

Prior to 1940, there were several years during which a few million tons of high grade iron ore were imported into the United States from Chile, Cuba, Sweden, or other countries. In that way the steel corporations filled the gap that opened at various times, for one reason or another, between the supply of domestic ores and the demands for iron and steel. Little or no thought was given to the possibilities of utilizing the vast reserves of potential ore that were known to be present, especially in the Lake Superior region. Since that year, however, several corporations have established and are supporting well-designed programs of research concerning methods of beneficiation of those ores to make them available as needed in the future. In the meantime, however, it would be well to base our policy with regard to the exportation of iron and steel upon the facts pertaining to the types of iron ore upon which we have long depended for this strategic metal.

The United States percentage of world production of iron ore is currently about 35 per cent. In the 1930's it averaged about 25 per cent and will probably be less than 30 per cent during most of the next ten years. No trustworthy data are available concerning world reserves of iron ore, except for a very few countries. There can be no uniform standard by which to distinguish actual ore from potential ore, nor the latter from rock too lean in iron to permit its exploitation. Nor are the methods of measuring and estimating the dimensions of ore bodies uniform in the different countries. The best estimates that have been made for many important regions are indicative only of the order of magnitude of the iron ore reserves, not of their precise tonnage. It would appear, however, that the United States reserves constitute about 25 to 30 per cent of the total world reserves.

The picture for iron and steel is therefore very different from that for petroleum. The American percentage of world annual production is closely similar to the American percentage of world reserves. Moreover, iron ore reserves in the sixteen associated European countries are very extensive. They likewise bear a similar relationship to total world reserves as does the normal consumption of iron ore from the mines within that portion of Europe to the total world consumption.

In the present emergency the United States can safely afford to export some but not very much of the iron and steel derived from its domestic ores. The emphasis in the European Recovery Program should therefore be placed upon the shipment of machine tools and mine equipment. These should be used by the European recipients to fabricate from their own ore bodies the tools with which to process the output from their own mines into consumer goods. The use of United States ore as a source of consumer goods for Europe should be kept to a very low minimum. Locomotives, freight cars, and other means of transport, including the rails for the railroad lines, should as promptly as possible be manufactured in Europe with the machine tools shipped from the United States and from the iron and steel secured from European iron ore. Thus the draft upon the exhaustible iron ore reserves of the two regions will be balanced as fairly as possible, and the European economy may be rehabilitated without danger to the future stability of the American economy.

The farther we proceed in "The Air Age," the more important become the light metals aluminum and magnesium. Science and technology have succeeded in placing the latter in the category of inexhaustible resources, by developing practical procedures for extracting it from sea water where it is present in practically limitless quantities and from the magnesium salts in certain sedimentary rocks where the quantity is literally beyond computation. But no such miracle has yet been performed for aluminum, despite the fact that it is the third most abundant element in the earth's crust.

Nearly all the aluminum fabricated to date has come from the ore mineral bauxite. Deposits of bauxite are high grade ores if they run better than 50 per cent alumina (aluminum oxide) and are rated as low grade ores if they contain between 35 and 50 per cent of alumina. The reserves of high grade ore in the United States, known in 1941, were estimated in November of that year as amounting to little more than 18 million tons. Had it been necessary to rely exclusively upon those reserves to meet the tremendous increase in amount of aluminum required during the war, they would have been completely exhausted by this time. Actually, a large fraction of the aluminum fabricated in the United States each year since 1923 has been derived from bauxite imported from abroad, principally from the Guianas. Although imports were stepped up to nearly a million tons per year, as the average for the five-year period 1941-45, an intensive campaign of geophysical exploration was pursued in the hope of finding additional deposits in the United States, and steps were taken toward perfecting the processes of recovery to make available the low-grade ores. Research was also directed toward the utilization of non-bauxitic aluminous materials, such as the high-alumina clays, the aluminous laterites and such minerals as alunite and leucite.

So successful have been these applications of science and technology to the problem of supplying increased amounts of aluminum that the position of the United States with regard to that metal has been completely changed in the last five years. The known reserves of bauxite ore, commercially usable by the improved methods of treatment that have been developed, are currently about twice the amount of available bauxite estimated in 1941, in spite of the large withdrawals that were made since then. In addition, there are enormous reserves of lower grade bauxite, high-alumina clay, and other mineral deposits, most of which should still be considered as potential rather than actual ore, even though the commercial exploitation of certain deposits of clay in Oregon and Washington has already been started. Although it is still cheaper to import high grade ores from foreign sources than to extract aluminum from low-grade domestic ores, the latter constitute a reserve of aluminum, adequate in an emergency to supply the entire national requirement for a considerable period.

It is practically impossible to forecast the probable withdrawal of aluminum from domestic sources in the United States during the next few years. Annual consumption will undoubtedly be less than during 1941-45 and greater than during 1936-40, but it is not even safe to assume that it will be near the average of all ten of those years. Account must also be taken of the fact that aluminum is not necessarily as expendable as the readily oxidized metals such as iron. In 1944, the recovery of aluminum from scrap was equivalent to 42 per cent of the production of virgin metal. The huge backlog of scrap aluminum now available will have a large but not accurately measurable effect upon the future consumption of the reserves of ore. The only statement, therefore, that is justified at this time is the very conservative one that the outlook with regard to aluminum for the United States is not nearly as serious as it appeared in the early days of the war.

When considering the attitude that should be taken toward sharing our aluminum resources with the war-ravaged people of Europe, the principle developed in connection with petroleum and iron should of course be applied. Unfortunately, any quantitative appraisal of the world's aluminum resources must be even less precise than that for iron ore reserves. It is certain, however, that the percentage of United States production in relation to world production is appreciably greater than the percentage of United States reserves in relation to world reserves. In the global perspective, therefore, it is only fair for the United States to conserve its own aluminum resources for its own use; only the dire emergency of our time would justify the exportation of appreciable quantities of aluminum. On the other hand, the fact that large quantities of aluminum ore are now entering the United States from British Guiana and Surinam provides Great Britain and the Netherlands with a perfectly valid argument in favor of any claims they might make for aluminum refined in the United States from reserves which legally belong to them. Once more, mineral interdependence rears its lovely head in economic councils!

Inasmuch as there are extensive reserves of aluminum ore in France and elsewhere within the territory of the sixteen nations associated in the European Recovery Program, the same conclusion is appropriate for aluminum as for iron. Assistance from the United States should be concentrated upon increasing the ability of those nations to exploit their own aluminum resources, and shipments of consumer goods fabricated in whole or in part from aluminum should be kept to the absolute minimum made necessary by emergency conditions. Such assistance will involve both equipment and technical knowledge of the new procedures developed in the United States during the war. The latter is in some respects even more important than the former, and it is a resource the sharing of which involves no depletion of the supply.

Although iron and aluminum are quantitatively the most important metals in our machine age, the mechanical devices upon which depend the kind of life that we call civilized would be impossible without lesser but equally necessary supplies of a large number of other mineral resources. For some of these, such as nickel, tin, the platinum metals, chromite, and manganese, the United States is nearly or completely dependent upon foreign sources.

Successful administration of the Marshall Plan may facilitate access to the reserves of tin in British Malaya and the Netherlands East Indies, but it may possibly result in curtailment of the movement of the platinum metals, metallurgical chromite ore, and ferro-grade manganese from the Soviet Union to the United States. Prior to 1934, the Soviet Union was the principal source of platinum and palladium, but since that year Canada has been the world's largest producer. Since 1938, the United States has ranked fourth in world production, with about three quarters of its domestic supply coming from southeastern Alaska. It would be difficult, but not impossible to meet American needs from sources outside the Soviet Union. Similarly, there are alternative sources of metallurgical chromite ore in Rhodesia, Turkey, and New Caledonia, if supplies from the Soviet Union should be cut off. There seems to be no likelihood of developing adequate domestic sources, although United States production was temporarily increased during the war. Less than 10 per cent of United States requirements for manganese ore, used in steel making, is obtained from domestic sources and a large part of the imports of this essential material has come from the Soviet Union. There are, however, alternative sources, probably adequate for our needs, in the Gold Coast, Cuba, Brazil, Chile, and elsewhere. Possibly knowledge of the fact that the United States is not irrevocably dependent upon the Soviet Union for its supply of these three materials may cause that country to continue existing export-import arrangements despite the antipathies of recent months.

There are several minerals, including cobalt, copper, lead, mercury, tungsten, tantalum, and zinc, for which the United States is partially dependent on foreign sources. So far as can now be foreseen, the operation of the European Recovery Program will have no deleterious effect upon the quantity of any of these that would be available for domestic use in the United States in the near future. World reserves of these metals are apparently adequate to meet the requirements of all the industrial nations for a long time, and their sources are so widely scattered that access to them seems to be assured. Moreover, for each of them there is good expectation that domestic production may be significantly increased through new discoveries or improved techniques of exploitation.

Accepting, as inevitably we must, the fact of mineral interdependence of all technologically progressive nations, it would appear that the kind of coöperation envisioned by Secretary Marshall may well result in a significant improvement in the prospect for future supplies of mineral resources for the United States. The dynamic program of research and exploration, so successfully carried out during the war, resulted in very great expansion of the known reserves of many important materials. Only a small part of those results have been mentioned in the foregoing pages, and the limits of accomplishment along those lines have by no means been reached. It is unthinkable that the program should not be continued indefinitely in the future, here in the United States. But it is also imperative that similar exploration should be extended throughout the world and specifically in the regions occupied by the sixteen associated European nations and their far-flung dependencies.

Perhaps the most important contribution the United States can make to the welfare of Western Europe will be not the food and clothing, the machine tools and industrial equipment, but the knowledge of new techniques and the stimulation of research and exploration, resulting from American experience during recent years. Proof is abundant that the application of science and technology can vastly increase the available stores of nonrenewable mineral resources and thus lengthen the third leg of the symbolic tripod upon which the prosperity and security of every nation must be based. The more is known about the mineral wealth of other lands and the more efficiently that wealth is put to the service of mankind, the more certainly will the United States be assured of adequate sources of the raw materials essential to American prosperity for the long run of future centuries.[1]

[1] For further readings, see Collier, James E., "Aluminum Resources of the United States," *Economic Geography*, v. 24 (January, 1948), pp. 74-77. Dewhurst, J. Frederic, et al. *America's Needs and Resources* (New York, 1947). Hotchkiss, William O., *Minerals of Might* (Lancaster, Pa., 1945). Leith, C. K., J. W. Furness, and Cleona Lewis, *World Minerals and World Peace* (Washington, D. C., 1943). Mather, Kirtley F., *Enough and to Spare* (New York, 1944). Mather, Kirtley F. "Petroleum, Today and Tomorrow," *Science*, v. 106 (December 19, 1947), pp. 603-609. Staffs of the Bureau of Mines and Geological Survey: *Mineral Resources of the United States* (Washington, D. C., 1948).

# 18

# *OPERATING PROBLEMS AND POLICIES UNDER THE EUROPEAN RECOVERY PROGRAM*

Lincoln Gordon[1]

In the public and official discussions surrounding the development of the European Recovery Program, attention has been focused primarily on the problems of the European economy, the reasons for American support to European recovery, the necessary scale and character of the program, its impact on the American economy, and the form of organization which should be established to carry it out. Less dramatic, but of at least equal importance to the successful completion of this unprecedented peacetime venture in international economic coöperation, is the solution of a series of major problems of operating policy, many of which will arise promptly upon enactment of the authorizing legislation.

The sound solution of these problems will require a unique combination of talents and personnel of the highest competence, not only in the two principal positions in Washington and Europe, but also in each of the participating countries and down through the administrative structure as a whole. These talents must be found and operating policies determined without loss of time, for it would be tragic to sacrifice the momentum gathered by the program's initiation. The years 1948 and 1949 may well mark a critical turning point in European economic and political affairs.

[1] Although the author is a consultant to the Department of State and to the Economic Coöperation Administration, this article is solely his responsibility and does not necessarily represent the official views of either agency.

The determination of sound operating policies will depend not only on the judgment of those immediately charged with the program's administration, but also on the maintenance of an informed and constructively critical public opinion. This article outlines some of the principal issues and suggests the type of considerations which must be brought to bear on their solution.

## *Programming the Available Aid*

The ERP involves an extremely complex problem of program making, which finds no precise parallel in any of the previous programs of American foreign aid. The broad outlines of American support authorized by Congress must be translated into specific terms of commodities, properly distributed as among countries, individual items, and sources of supply, all within limitations set by the appropriated funds and by shortages in available supplies. The program must be equitable as among countries and must take into account their sometimes divergent interests and their varied traditions and attitudes. It must make the maximum contribution to European economic recovery at the least cost to the United States.

By contrast, the lend-lease program, although far from free of operating difficulties, enjoyed virtually unlimited funds and shaped its policies under the relatively simple governing criterion of military victory. The British loan was also an entirely different type of project, intended to tide over a supposedly temporary balance-of-payments deficit in the sterling area and not tied to specific commodities or specific measures of self-help. The operating procedures of the ERP will be more akin to those of the relief assistance and interim aid programs of 1947-48. In these cases, however, the countries have been few; the commodities have been largely confined to the basic relief items of food, fuel, and fertilizer; and the test of assistance has been the prevention of human suffering and economic retrogression. Under the ERP, the basic test must be the most rapid possible achievement of Western European self-support.

The necessary economic recovery effort is primarily a European affair to which the program of United States assistance will make a crucial, but yet only a marginal, contribution. The total Western European national product is in the neighborhood of $100 billion a year, which will be supplemented by less than $6 billion from the United States. Of the capital goods required for the program, the great bulk will be produced in Europe itself, the United States supplying only a comparatively small volume of key items. Even within the more limited area of imported supplies, the United States Government is expected to finance during 1948-49 only about three-eighths of the total imports into Western Europe (or about four-sevenths of the imports from the Western Hemisphere), the rest being covered through current exports, aid from the International Bank, private investments, and credits and other aid from other nations. In subsequent years, the proportionate role of American aid will become even smaller. Without American support, European recovery would be impossible, but that support is basically only a supplement to the efforts of the European countries themselves.

It follows that the initiative in developing specific programs of proposed imports and financial support must rest with the Europeans. The principle of European initiative so strongly stressed by Secretary Marshall when he set the program in motion is even more vital in the ERP's operations. But the proposals for American aid thus initiated will almost certainly exceed the available funds and supplies. The ERP Administrator will therefore face a most difficult task of rationing. The program of $6.8 billion for the fifteen months ending June 30, 1949 (or $5.3 billion for the twelve months ending March 31), even if fully matched by appropriations, contains no cushion. When originally computed, this program involved in physical terms more than a 20 per cent reduction in the amount of assistance sought by the Committee of European Economic Co-operation, and subsequent price increases have magnified the cut. The program assumes the achievement of ambitious European production and export targets, making no allowance for organized interference or sabotage pursuant to the avowed Soviet opposition. The most authoritative impartial independent analysis, that of the International Bank, sets the fifteen-month needs from $800 million to $1 billion above the official estimates. The Harriman Committee's estimates lead to substantially the same net results as those of the Administration, despite important differences of judgment on components within the balance-of-payments computations; both were set on an intentionally conservative basis. Any reduction in appropriations would intensify the difficulties of the rationing task.

What standards can be established for screening proposed programs? There will be issues of equity as among the several countries. There may be a tendency to rely on restoration of prewar levels as the measures of justifiable aid. Such a test would be self-defeating. For those nations which have lost major prewar sources of foreign exchange, prewar production and export levels are obviously inadequate. Nor can the relative prewar standards of living among the several countries be accepted as valid for all time. A successful program demands forward-looking rather than backward-looking standards. Difficult though it may be to translate into specifics, means must be found to put into practical terms the general test proposed by the CEEC itself—to work as quickly as possible toward a standard of living and a pattern of production and foreign trade, both intra-European and extra-European, which is capable of maintenance after 1952 without abnormal outside assistance. This is the fundamental criterion for the ERP, which corresponds to the wartime test of contribution to military victory.

The application of this general test will require far more intensive analysis of the conditions of long-run self-support than has thus far been made. The program clearly does not envisage an integrated European "four-year plan" blueprinting every phase of economic development. Yet there must somehow be developed a broad and flexible pattern, at least for the key industries, as a guide for measuring the validity of specific requirements and projects in relationship to each other and the general goal.

Important segments of the programming task are readily soluble. Food and coal, for example, have been under international allocation since the end of the war. The principles developed by the International Emergency Food Council and the

European Coal Organization have withstood the test of time and above all have met the pragmatic standard of general acceptability. For most raw materials there is no similar body of recent experience, but guides can be established based on processing capacity, other available supplies, and contribution of the fabricated goods to essential domestic needs and particularly to expanded exports.

It is in the field of capital reconstruction and expansion that the greatest difficulties will arise. This is the area most fertile in potential disagreements among the participants and most subject to emotional ardor for rival national development plans. The far from successful American wartime experience bears witness to the difficulties of systematically programming capital development, even in a single country and under the pressure of military necessity. Under the ERP, the focus must be on the contribution of proposed projects to the prompt alleviation of the international payments deficit, taking into account the time required for getting into operation, the relation of returns to cost, and the need for ultimate balance on a country-by-country basis as well as for the area as a whole. Projects will also require rigorous technical screening, in many cases on the spot. The ERP Administrator can be greatly aided in this task by joint arrangements with the International Bank and with private investors, as well as by special missions of competent technicians. To the greatest possible extent, moreover, the invidious burden of decisions among rival national claimants should be shifted to the Europeans, by obtaining recommendations from specialist subgroups of the newly-formed Organization for Economic Coöperation or where appropriate from the UN Economic Commission for Europe.

In reviewing proposed programs submitted from Europe, the ERP Administration will also have to be fully informed as to the proposed use of other dollar resources available to the recipients of American aid. The program is designed to meet a balance of payments deficit with the Western Hemisphere, but only a residual deficit which assumes the elimination of unessential imports and the most intensive promotion of exports. The selection of particular commodities for financing with

United States Government funds is essentially arbitrary, and the wise and efficient use of other dollar earnings is of equal importance to European recovery and to minimizing the cost to the United States. On the other hand, it is neither possible nor desirable for the United States to substitute itself for the international trade and foreign exchange control authorities of sixteen sovereign nations. A reasonable and workable compromise must therefore be found providing full information on the proposed use of other dollar earnings and adequate assurance against their dissipation, as well as assurance of vigorous domestic measures to maximize exports, while refraining from undue interference in individual cases which are essentially matters of European policy.

### *The Financial Program*

A sound commodity program must be matched by a sound financial program. This involves not only the proper division of aid for each country as between loans and grants, but also decision on the terms of any loans, integration of loan policy with lending by the International Bank, and stimulation of private investment, either with or without the help of a partial government guaranty.

As stated in the Act, the primary test to determine the division of ERP assistance between loans and grants is "the character and purpose of the assistance and . . . whether there is reasonable assurance of repayment."[2] This test was adopted in preference to a division by types of commodities favored in many quarters. The principle followed by the Congress appears sound, since, as indicated above, the selection of particular European imports for ERP financing is necessarily arbitrary; the repayment of a dollar loan is a charge on a nation's entire future foreign exchange position; and the character of particular commodities now imported with American financial assistance bears only a very indirect relationship to the future over-all capacity to repay. In one country, for example, imports of capital equipment may make the greatest such contribution, but in another, imports of food may release local resources

[2] Foreign Assistance Act of 1948, Section 111 (c) (1).

from uneconomic marginal food production and make them available for producing current exports or capital goods to expand future exports. Subject to the primary test, it is agreed by all that grants should so far as possible be assigned to the financing of imports of "relief type" items and loans to capital goods and perhaps to industrial raw materials.

Translating the general test into specific practical country-by-country application is a task of no mean proportions. In principle, it requires forecasting each nation's balance-of-payments position over some twenty or thirty years. Moreover, the decisions should be made early and be subject to revision only for excellent cause, since frequent redeterminations might discourage the very steps necessary to achieve "ability to repay." The situation would appear to call for a series of rough and ready decisions, based upon the best available judgment as to the prospective economic strength of the various countries concerned.

The terms of the loans and their relation to International Bank and private financing are matters of no less complexity. The program should be so designed as to encourage the maximum contribution from sources other than the United States Government during the life of the ERP and to permit these sources—notably the International Bank and private investors—to assume the burden of any balance-of-payments deficits which may continue beyond 1952. Onerous terms for ERP loans would lessen the ability to repay and therefore the scope and volume of such loans, but unduly easy terms would encourage their use in preference to nongovernment sources. Moreover, the ERP Administrator, with his responsibility for the over-all program, must adjust his plans to the possibilities and prospects of other financing. It will be essential to work out with the International Bank a division of responsibility and to obtain from private capital as large a contribution as possible.

One means of broadening the scope of loans in the program would be the use of contingent terms, making interest and amortization payments dependent upon the balance-of-payments position when they fall due. There is a precedent for this device in the British loan. On the whole, it would appear undesirable to build into the structure of international indebtedness a large volume of contingent liabilities. Difficult questions of priority of repayment would be raised in relation to other debts and the existence of contingent liabilities might prove a serious impediment to developing a normal flow of private capital. On the other hand, it might be desirable to give to International Bank loans a preferred position over those of the ERP Administrator.

The guaranty provisions in the Act [Section 111 (b) (3)] are properly limited in scope, and it is impossible to foretell accurately how much use will be made of them. They require that each guaranteed investment be approved both by the European Government concerned and by the ERP Administrator as falling within the purposes of the program, and the guaranty itself is limited to conversion into dollars of foreign currency derived from the project only up to the original dollar investment. Only a vigorous and persistent stimulation of these sources of aid in preference to the use of government funds will ensure their proper part in the program as a whole.

### *Relation to the American Economy*

In developing a specific program, the ERP Administrator will have to give constant attention to American supply considerations and means of minimizing the impact on the domestic economy. At least during the first year, the bulk of projected American supplies to be financed under the program will be under formal allocation by the Departments of Agriculture and Commerce. Even within allocated quantities, however, the scheduling of procurement will require the best possible business judgment.

Presumably agricultural purchases will continue to be made by the Commodity Credit Corporation, and virtually all others by private European importers or by European government missions. To obtain a smooth flow of supplies will require broad contacts with American industry and skill in devising revised specifications and finding substitutes where supplies are unusually tight. Similar activities will be required in connection with inland transportation and overseas shipping. These are essentially advisory and facilitating, rather than directing functions, but effective catalytic action in obtaining timely deliveries of the needed goods may well mark the difference between success and failure in the program.

Fulfillment of the program may occasionally require application of formal controls of the type developed during the war. Despite the large scale of the projected financial assistance, it is doubtful that such controls will be needed substantially, if at all, more frequently than during the past year or two. The ERP does not involve a radical shift in the 1947 pattern of American exports to Europe, either in magnitude or in commodity distribution. From the viewpoint of American supplies, it is primarily a means of financing a continuing flow rather than generating large additional exports. Nonetheless, it is vital that the scheduled commodities move promptly and in the requisite quantities. A key bottleneck item may sometimes mean a difference of months to a capital project of high urgency. The continued reserve authority for "spot" export priorities is an important means of insurance against undue delay, but the Administrator will doubtless seek its use sparingly.

For a very limited group of items, perhaps including certain steel products, farm machinery, and freight cars, it may prove necessary to arrange on an industry-wide basis to set aside a specified share of output for export to Europe. Such arrangements run counter to the long-run goal of unregulated private trade and can be justified only by the existence of severe shortages and the need to spread the impact of the European program. For the most part, such "set-asides" should be attainable through voluntary agreements, but the existence of reserve compulsory authority may prove helpful to the Administrator in his negotiations.

Export licensing has an important part to play in implementing allocation decisions and should assist the ERP both through limiting exports to non-European destinations and through insuring that the best use is made of European quotas. The licensing function has been closely associated with decisions on the suballocation of quotas among individual countries. The ERP Administration will of course have a decisive, if not the exclusive, voice in such decisions with regard to Western Europe, and arrangements will have to be worked out to assure the conformity of license issuance with the ERP programs. In some quarters it has been felt desirable to expand the scope of export licensing to nonallocated commodities in order to help conserve European dollar resources. On the whole, it would seem wiser to leave this function to the exchange control authorities of the Europeans, subject to such general understandings as may be reached in connection with approved programs of American assistance. In any event, a number of difficult operating problems will arise in adjusting the apparatus of export control to the special requirements of the European program.

### *Supplies from Other Sources*

By far the most effective means for reducing the impact of the program on the United States will be the securing of supplies in the tightest categories from other nations. In the official projections, over one-third of the ERP funds are estimated to be so used during the initial year and an even higher proportion subsequently. Such "off-shore" procurement would of course not relieve the total burden on the American economy if the dollars were immediately spent for Latin American and Canadian purchases in the United States. These expenditures, however, would fall more heavily on items in easier supply and their impact can where necessary be controlled and partially deferred through export licensing. At the same time, these purchases will provide a means of furnishing the supplying countries with badly needed dollars which they cannot now obtain from Europe, thus maintaining the channels of traditional inter-Continental triangular trade.

Securing supplies elsewhere does not generally imply United States Government procurement. In most cases, European governments would be reimbursed for expenditures by them or by their nationals. Nonetheless, the ERP Administrator will obviously be greatly interested in the terms of such purchases. He will have to develop special techniques of coöperation with both the receiving and the supplying governments, doubtless involving a series of trilateral or broader multilateral negotiations. Moreover, the degree of coöperation enlisted from other suppliers will depend in part on American policy on licensing exports and on possible financial assistance, as well as on other aspects of relationships with the United States. It is clear that such policies should promote maximum coöperation on the part of other supplying countries in making their contribution to the European recovery effort.

A special case is posed by procurement under the program from one participating country on behalf of another. In the report of the CEEC financial experts, it was proposed that a portion of the available American funds be set aside and geared to a European multilateral clearing scheme so as to assure the convertibility to dollars of net balances in intra-European trade.[3] While not accepting this proposal in full, the program as enacted does make possible the financing of procurement for one participating country from another. Under this authority, for example, part of the deficit of Bizonal Germany with the Western Hemisphere might be financed by supplying dollars to France for the purchase of Ruhr coal, the dollars then becoming available for Bizonal purchases from the Western Hemisphere. Employment of this authority clearly has great potential influence on intra-European trade. Apart from moving temporary surpluses, its prime advantage would lie in promoting trade patterns which can endure beyond the limited period of special aid. Determining specific programs in this regard is a particularly difficult matter which will require the closest possible European coöperation in working out specific proposals both equitable to the parties concerned and clearly in the interests of sustained recovery.

### *Strategic Materials*

It is widely felt that in connection with the ERP, the United States should be given an opportunity to improve its position in regard to exhaustible raw materials. This is the outstanding

[3] See Committee of European Economic Coöperation, *General Report* (Volume I), Department of State Publication 2930, Government Printing Office (Washington 1947), p. 134.

respect in which our contribution to the recent military victory was disproportionately large in comparison with the other allies. Undeveloped availabilities are substantial, particularly in the overseas dependencies of certain of the participating countries. The development of such resources is also to the interest of the countries themselves, since it affords one means of improving the long-run European international payments position, although it must be recognized that from the purely European viewpoint the same funds might in some cases be more advantageously devoted to other types of development.

Consideration of this question has been confused by the issue as to whether supplies of such materials to the United States should be paid for by additional dollars, or whether they should be a direct *quid pro quo* for a part of our current assistance. It is generally recognized that raw materials supplied "free" during the life of the program would directly and proportionately increase the cost of the program itself, but it has been widely argued that such repayments might be made over a term of years out of production beyond the normal commercial requirements. If the principle discussed above of establishing the proportion of loans to grants on the basis of ability to repay is adopted, however, and if future potential sales of strategic materials for stockpiling are taken into account in estimating the ability to repay, the argument becomes academic, since any requirement for repayment in materials will reduce the ability to repay in dollars and thus necessitate an increased proportion of grants to loans.

Far more important to the United States than the method of accounting is the matter of the best means of obtaining maximum supplies. On this issue there can be little question but that the greatest results will flow from payment in dollars at the time of purchase. Such payments would provide a continuing spur to exploration, development, and expanded production, and they would permit direct negotiation with private producers rather than the less satisfactory intergovernmental negotiations. The alternative of contingent repayment in materials, with additional dollars to be supplied if the balance-of-payments position of the supplying country is unfavorable, would be particularly unsatisfactory. It is both subject to the general disadvantages of any form of contingent loan and unlikely to draw out the desired supplies.

The substantive issues of operating policy relate to means of finding new sources of supply, promoting exploration and development, and insuring availability of adequate quantities on reasonable terms. Opportunities must be sought for exploration and development rights on a nondiscrimatory basis. In some cases, purchase on reasonable terms may require overcoming obstructions posed by producers' cartels. Obtaining satisfactory solutions will require a rare combination of tact and hardheadedness in negotiation.

### *European Self-Help and Coöperation*

The issues discussed thus far have to do primarily with the program of American assistance and the direct relations between the United States and the individual participating countries. The crucial determinants of success in the program, however, will be the actions taken in Europe, both individually and collectively, which look toward the achievement of economic self-support. The pledges taken by the participating countries during the Paris Conferences of 1947 are far-reaching. If implemented in full, they would lay the foundation for a radical change in the economic face of Western Europe. Since the Conference submitted its report, moreover, there is evidence of increasing recognition in Europe of the need for even more intensive measures of self-help and particularly of the need to move in the direction of further economic and indeed political integration.

The war-induced changes in the European economy, coming on top of several decades of progressive economic deterioration, make the task of achieving genuine recovery within a few years a most difficult one at best. The necessary short-run actions are clear: currency stabilization; control of inflation; expanded production of key resources and their allocation while still scarce to the best uses. Middle-run needs are also evident, although more difficult to satisfy: the reduction of trade and financial barriers to European economic intercourse. Most difficult are the long-run measures: the development of resources and productive techniques to make it possible for this congested area to become truly self-supporting at decent standards of living and to maintain its position as a major creative factor in Western civilization.

The area as a whole now contains 198 persons per square mile compared with 44 in the United States. Its poverty in natural resources can be compensated only through the fullest exploitation of its richness in human skills. Development in the colonies, especially in Africa, of new sources of food and raw materials affords one promise, but it will be only slowly realized at best. More immediately important is the restoration of sufficient comparative advantage in industrial production and in management and marketing techniques to provide the means for financing the enormous volume of permanently necessary imports.

There is little question that a greater degree of economic and political integration would make a vital contribution toward this goal. Its political consequences in terms of a powerful aggregation of free peoples in an area of unique strategic importance are so obviously important and desirable as scarcely to require comment. The ERP affords a unique opportunity to foster such integration. But it would be foolish to expect too much too quickly. The European position is in no sense really analogous, as is often argued, to that of the thirteen American colonies in 1775 or the thirteen States in 1787. The difficulties of accomplishing European economic integration overnight may be vividly brought to mind by considering the obstacles to the far less ambitious project of a mere customs union, to say nothing of a more general economic union, between the extremely closely related economies of Canada and the United States. In Europe, differences of national tradition, economic and social institutions, interests, and language are far more extensive and deeply rooted. And Soviet opposition, while perhaps a stimulant toward integration in some of the countries, operates in others as a powerful deterrent.

A large degree of economic integration has of course been a fundamental characteristic of the European economy for the last century or two. Its further development will be at best a slow and often painful process. Even the relatively simple step of creating the Belgium-Netherlands-Luxembourg ("Benelux") customs union required years of negotiation, and while the union is now in operation, a host of transitional production quotas and other devices will defer the full realization of its economic benefits for additional years to come. The situation calls for boldness in initiative and leadership, but also for patient and laborious step-by-step negotiation of detailed coöperative measures.

The working out of many such measures will extend far beyond the projected life of the ERP. The leadership must be European, but American participation and encouragement are vital. The wise provision of such encouragement will be the sternest test of economic statesmanship on the part of the ERP Administration.

One key will be our participation in the new organization of the European participants. The precise functions of this organization cannot be blueprinted in advance, but they may range from recommending international allocations of certain commodities in short supply to the negotiation of multilateral trade and financial arrangements and the planning of international projects for the development of natural resources. Above all, the very existence of such a forum should create a *point d'appui* for bringing to bear persuasion and encouragement toward additional measures of coöperation.

At the same time, it would be most unfortunate if the encouragement of economic coöperation among the participating European countries were to foster any notion of Western European autarchy or to create a bloc economically antagonistic to the outside world. Without extensive continuing international trade, the very physical survival of Western Europe at anything close to its present population levels, to say nothing of other elements in a desirable standard of living, would be impossible.

Of particular importance in such continuing international trade is that between Western and Eastern Europe. The present program has assumed not merely the avoidance of discouragement to East-West trade but its positive expansion to almost prewar levels. Such trade is not absolutely indispensable to Western

Europe, but its elimination would make recovery both slower and more costly and would require difficult adjustments to obtain extra-European markets and supply sources in place of those lying close at hand. It is clearly not desirable for the West to take any initiative in curtailing trade with the East. Hence the need for a careful balancing of the activities of the new joint Western European organization with those of the United Nations Economic Commission for Europe, which affords a forum for promoting continuing economic coöperation with Eastern Europe. Moreover, maintaining a political "open door" toward the East, if it is possible to do so, is no less important than maintaining healthy economic relations.

At the same time, it is evident that the trade policies of the Eastern nations, no less than their political conduct, are wholly subject to Soviet dictation. It must be anticipated that Soviet control may be exercised not merely to drive hard economic bargains, but also to sabotage the success of the ERP in any way and at any time that seems advantageous to the makers of Soviet policy. It would be folly to risk the failure of the program by being unprepared to take remedial measures promptly against such sabotage in any form. Thus a major political dimension is added to the many and diverse economic factors which the ERP Administration must take into account. To fulfill all these conditions in the presence of universal good will and coöperation would be sufficiently difficult; to do so in the face of declared and organized Eastern European opposition to the success of the ERP is a most formidable undertaking. It must be confessed that economic warfare seems a simple matter indeed when compared with the waging of economic peace in these circumstances.

### *Local Currencies*

In connection with the promotion of European self-help, one peculiarly difficult problem of operating policy is posed by the management of blocked accounts of local currencies which are to be established in quantities corresponding to American supplies furnished as grants-in-aid. For certain of the countries these local currency funds will be of enormous magnitude.

Their disposition can be a major factor in the fiscal affairs of those countries. It would be most undesirable for the United States to take title to these funds or to exercise initiative in their use. So great an interference in internal economic affairs might entail the withdrawal of some of the most important countries and would raise the issue of sovereignty in its most naked and unpleasant form. Indeed, if the choice were between full control and no control, the United States would be well advised to eliminate entirely the proposal for establishing special blocked accounts. It would be a most invidious burden for any American to exercise such far-reaching responsibility for the economic life of a foreign nation. On the other hand, the funds will arise by virtue of American assistance and their sound disposition may vitally affect the program's success. Hence the provision that their use be agreed between the recipient governments and the United States—a plan which calls for American concurrence and potential veto but not American initiative.

The first issue of operating policy in this connection is the extent to which such funds should be used to reduce government debt or be permanently withheld from circulation, rather than being spent for any purpose. It is sometimes argued that the withholding of these funds cannot serve as an effective anti-inflationary device, since their effect can readily be counterbalanced by corresponding increases in government borrowing. It must be said however, that there are often significant institutional barriers to such borrowing, sometimes in the form of specific parliamentary authorization of any increase in the public debt. Even a slight additional weight may be important in the closely balanced complex of political forces which surround the efforts of any government, and especially a weak government, to combat inflation. At any rate, there is a clear net advantage in making further inflationary borrowing overt rather than available as an easy temptation to a Minister of Finance in chronic budgetary difficulty.

The local currency funds should presumably not be used to finance ordinary government expenditure. To the extent that they are spent at all, they should be devoted to reconstruction and development and other uses contributing directly to the goal of economic self-support. Defining these areas is another difficult task of administration, similar but even broader in scope to the problem of screening capital projects requiring direct dollar support under the program.

*Western Germany*

High on the list of factors contributing to Europe's present economic discontents is the economic void of western Germany. It is there that production is relatively the lowest, currency reform the most urgent, suppressed inflation the most rampant, economic demoralization the most severe. And by a singular paradox, pressure on the military government to save dollars has tended to make Germany economically the most nationalistic. At the same time, the potential contribution of western Germany to total European recovery is among the greatest. The conditions of four-power control, the extraordinarily complex administrative arrangements in the Bizone, the uncertain degree of German participation in economic direction, the changing policies as to the level of industry, the reparations issue, and the general physical and psychological state of a defeated people all combine to make the effective reintegration of western Germany into a working European economy without a restoration of military potential a peculiarly difficult but also a peculiarly necessary aspect of the program as a whole. The general lines of policy have fortunately been steadily clarifying and the administrative arrangements adopted early in 1948 should simplify the task, but it remains a major test of effectiveness in joint effort among the Western occupying authorities, the Germans themselves, and the ERP administration.

There will be complex problems of administrative relationship between the ERP administration and the Bizonal (or, it is to be hoped, the Trizonal) authorities. Clearly western Germany should so far as possible be treated for ERP purposes in the same manner as the other participating nations. Such treatment would be facilitated by increased responsibility for the Germans and by ECA participation in the exercise of American governmental responsibility. But the relationship cannot be precisely parallel with that elsewhere, for western Germany is not a genuinely sovereign body and its international economic relations are closely affected by international political considerations. Even after a treaty of peace is negotiated there may well be provision for continuing supervision and possibly control of certain segments of the economy as a safeguard against rearmament. The Bizonal authorities themselves must be prepared to promote German economic integration with the neighboring countries more actively than in the past. Provision must be made for effective participation on behalf of western Germany in the continuing European organization of the participants, and it is to be hoped that Germans may be able to participate along with and ultimately in place of the Bizonal authorities.

With an apparently indefinite stalemate on general economic unification of Germany, the ERP will crystallize the issue of effective economic recovery in the western area. Without closing the door to the East, means must be found for creating a viable place for Germany in the Western European economy without a perpetual drain on the occupying powers.

### *Conclusion*

Even this brief review of outstanding issues of operating policy will make it evident that the ERP poses a unique challenge to its Administrator and to the American Congress and public from whom he must draw his support. Much printer's ink and many words have been wasted on the debate as to whether this is a "business" or "diplomatic" job. Surely it is both and neither. The wise programming and smooth provision of American assistance to the best effect, and the furnishing of technical assistance to economic stabilization and improved production are functions involving elements of business judgment, but this will be no ordinary business task. Negotiation and collaboration with the participating countries in stimulating their own efforts and promoting economic and political integration will require tact and understanding, knowledge of foreign ways and interests, and experience in international affairs, but this will be no routine diplomatic task.

Even in purely economic terms, a coöperative endeavor for the economic reconstruction of a highly developed continent would be a major test of administrative resourcefulness. But this program will not be conducted in an economic vacuum. Like all public economic policy in all countries, it must also take account of public desires, hopes, fears, and ambitions, in this instance magnified in geometric progression by the diversity of national policies involved. And even more important, it must be carried through to success despite Soviet opposition which may be manifested through an arsenal of weapons of sabotage, ranging from the manipulation of Eastern European trade to the use of political strikes within the participating countries. In such circumstances and with the stakes at issue so high, the task calls not merely for a combination of business and diplomatic experience, but even more for imagination, flexibility, and adaptability to the needs of an undertaking literally without precedent.

# 19

## *EUROPE'S NEEDS AND PROSPECTS*

Sidney S. Alexander

### *American Interest in European Prosperity*

The United States is vitally interested in the prosperity of Europe because a depressed Europe is likely to become a fascist or communist Europe. If this should happen another war would be probable, and we would certainly be involved.

That prosperity in Europe contributes to prosperity in America is a valid argument, but one that has frequently been exaggerated, especially by Radio Moscow. It is of limited importance to us. Our economy can get along very well even if Europe is poverty-stricken, provided our domestic economic policy is well designed. We need European prosperity for political rather than for economic reasons.

On the other hand, European prosperity does depend on ours. Over the next few years our high production will provide aid for European recovery. In the long run our prosperity will help maintain, directly and indirectly, markets for European exports. These markets are required because Western Europe specializes in manufacturing and therefore needs trading partners with surpluses of agricultural and mineral products to exchange for its manufactures.

### *Why Europe Needs Aid*

Europe needs help because it depends heavily on imported food, fuels, and raw materials. With production reduced by the war, Europe cannot pay for its normal imports, and its needs are greater than normal. If imports are not maintained, production will fall still further. If Europe gets sufficient imports and an opportunity to readjust its production processes, it can produce enough to pay for its imports.

Just after VE day output in Europe was very low. Since then the people of Europe, aided by relief, principally from the United States, have raised the level of industrial production well above the depths of 1945, as shown in Table 1.

TABLE 1

INDUSTRIAL PRODUCTION RELATIVE TO PREWAR CONDITIONS[a]

| | Date | Industrial Production % of 1937 | Date | Industrial Production % of 1937 |
|---|---|---|---|---|
| Norway | Jan. '45 | 46 | Nov. '47 | 124 |
| Denmark | Ave. of '45 | 74 | Jan. '48 | 123 |
| United Kingdom | Dec. '45 | 93[b] | 2nd Qr. '47 | 110–120[c] |
| Netherlands | Ave. of '45 | 31 | Oct. '47 | 110 |
| Sweden | Ave. of '45 | 88 | June '47 | 109 |
| France[d] | Ave. of '45 | 48 | April '47 | 95 |
| Belgium | Ave. of '45 | 31 | April '47 | 88 |
| Greece | 3rd Qr. '45 | 35[c] | 2nd Qr. '47 | 76[c] |
| Italy | 1st Qr. '46 | 28[c] | 3rd Qr. '47 | 72[c] |
| Austria | Ave. of '46 | 41[e] | Mid-'47 | ca.50[f] |
| Germany: | | | | |
| U. S. Zone | 1st Qr. '46 | 26 | July '47 | 52 |
| U. K. Zone | Jan. '46 | 27 | Nov. '47 | 40 |

[a]Data, unless otherwise specified, from United Nations, *Monthly Bulletin of Statistics.*

[b]Represents employment in manufacturing rather than industrial production.

[c]United Nations, Department of Economic Affairs, Economic Report, *Salient Features of the World Economic Situation, 1945-47* (Jan. 1948).

[d]1938 = 100. This is the older series, not adjusted for number of working days.

[e]1938 = 100. Source: Senate Committee on Foreign Relations Staff, Committee Print, *Basic Documents and Background Information* (November, 1947).

[f]United Nations, *Salient Features of the World Economic Situation,* p. 133: "Not much above half of prewar."

In some countries industrial production has recovered so well as to raise the question of why further aid is needed. There are three parts to the answer. First, there is a food crisis because the bad weather of 1947 has reduced agricultural production far below prewar, so that maintenance of even minimal diets requires continued large food imports. Secondly, the maintenance and extension of such recovery as has been achieved depends on continued imports. Finally, and most significant of all, not nearly enough exports are yet available to pay for required imports.

## *Why Consumption is Low*

The 1947-48 production of grain in Western Europe[1] was about 15 million tons below the average prewar level, and imports, in spite of the emergency programs, will in 1948 be about 5 million tons below normal. Consequently there is currently available in Western Europe about 22 per cent less grain to feed a population about 7½ per cent larger than prewar. Without overseas shipments, there would be 44 per cent less grain than in prewar years.

The resulting food shortage is of much greater importance than is indicated by the values involved. The 15 million ton deficit of grain production at current prices represents about 1¾ billion dollars compared with a prewar national product of Western Europe in the neighborhood of 100 billion dollars. But when food is short, people can think of little else, and they are not inclined to measure the difference between the normal diet and the short rations in terms of money. So even though the decline in national incomes attributable to the low levels of food production is only moderate, the absolute impact on the well-being of European consumers is tremendous.

To the extent that a large portion of the national output is going into investment goods rather than into consumption, the present standard of living is somewhat lower than would be implied by the production statistics. Thus in France, although about 88 per cent of the 1938 volume of goods and services was available in 1946, investment and governmental activities took a larger share in the later year, leaving consumption only 81 per cent as great in 1946 as in 1938.[2] Of course the sharpest drop of all was the 25 per cent decline in consumption of food, even before the effects of the poor crops of 1947 were felt.

In addition to these real factors depressing European consumption, the abundance of money relative to goods makes the

[1] We shall mean by Western Europe the sixteen countries participating in the Marshall plan, plus western Germany. These countries are: United Kingdom, Austria, Belgium, Denmark, France, Greece, Iceland, Ireland, Italy, Luxembourg, Netherlands, Norway, Portugal, Sweden, Switzerland, Turkey, as well as the three western zones of Germany.

[2] Figures from United Nations, Department of Economic Affairs, *Survey of Current Inflationary and Deflationary Tendencies* (September, 1947), pp. 39-40.

shortages seem more acute. We in the United States should clearly understand this—we had a meat shortage at a time when we were consuming more meat than ever before in our history: the shortage was generated by our eagerness to buy even more. European consumers also have the money to buy more goods than they can get, so the real shortages are accentuated by the unsatisfied monetary demand.

### *The Measure of Needs*

The willingness of the American people to extend aid to Western Europe is based both on sympathy and on anticommunism. Because we share cultural ties and common ancestry with the peoples of Western Europe we are moved by their hardships. We also recognize the threat to our security of an extension of communist power over Western Europe. A certain amount of aid is required for the direct service of these ends—the relief of distress and the support of noncommunist, preferably democratic, governments. But the principal measure of the aid a country needs is neither hardship nor the imminence of the Communist threat; it is the amount required to restore the country's productive activity to a high level which it can then maintain.

There are accordingly three important components of need for aid: relief, political support, and recovery. These three are rarely distinct but are usually intermingled. For example, relief itself is required for recovery. If people can be fed and clothed they can contribute a great deal toward the reëstablishment of their productive activities. Much of the recovery which has so far been achieved in Europe is of this sort. Foreign aid, principally American, was available to help keep people alive, and they themselves reorganized their shattered economies and raised their production well above the low levels to which it had been reduced by war. Though European recovery since VE day has been remarkably rapid, at least until the middle of 1947, the full elimination of the disorganization of war will take some time, especially in agriculture, coal mining, and other key industries.

The political component of our aid program operates sometimes more subtly, sometimes more directly. To a certain extent the political requirements are satisfied by the operation of the other components. Baldly stated, communism may be driven off by relief and recovery aid which will strengthen the natural resistance of the body politic of the Western European countries. But in some countries, as in Greece, political differences may reach the point of open warfare, and one cannot then expect economic recovery to settle these differences. Our government may then give aid directly for political and military uses. In such countries the problem is primarily political: how to obtain a government worthy of our support. Only after such a government is in power can we hope for much political gain from improved economic circumstances.

The European Recovery Program may possibly be impaired by a transfer of emphasis from recovery aid to direct political and military support. The latter, like relief, should be a short-run measure, appropriate in some countries until recovery is achieved, when neither relief nor political and military support should be any longer required. Only economic recovery will bring about a successful conclusion of the aid program. If, then, political and military support is strengthened at the expense of recovery measures, the aid program may no longer be self-terminating, and the Marshall Plan may degenerate into a direct bolstering of European governments by goods and by force. The great virtue of the European Recovery Program is its reliance upon the beneficial effects of prosperity rather than upon the use of force of arms or of wealth. Economic recovery must accordingly have first priority if the aid program is to succeed.

A gradual improvement of the functioning of industry and agriculture can be expected to reinforce the aid program. This is the silent partner of the Marshall Plan. It explains why big things are expected of a program which, although large compared with any previous peacetime effort at international aid, is small compared with the scheduled increases in European production. Two factors operate to magnify the effect of the aid. First, each object supplied sets to work idle productive powers already available in Europe, awaiting the scarce factors to be imported. Secondly, each step toward recovery supports a better organization of production and an increase of output that makes the next step easier.

Coal furnishes a clear example of both factors. Each ton supplied by the United States permits the manufacture of products worth many times the cost of the ton of coal. But even more important, a restoration of normal conditions in Europe will permit an increase of coal production much greater than the imports. Once the European countries are given aid in meeting the needs of their daily existence and in restoring their productive equipment, their own recuperative powers can carry them forward.

The use of recovery needs as a measure of aid raises two very important questions: What level of ultimate production is appropriate as a recovery target? How well or poorly shall the people of the country live during the period of recovery? The needs of Europe depend on the answers to these questions. No final answer can be expected, but these questions will continue to plague the operation of the European Recovery Program.

### *Official Recovery Targets*

The goal of the United States is the achievement of that degree of well-being in a self-supporting Western Europe which will furnish the basis for a peaceful, stable, and democratic political and social system. This objective cannot easily be translated into a quantitative target for European recovery. Only subjective judgments can be formed of the production and consumption necessary to maintain peace and stability. Such judgments were implicitly made by the Committee of European Economic Coöperation (CEEC, or the Paris Committee) in the formulation of its report on the European Recovery Program.[3]

Instead of asking what level of recovery is required for peace and stability, the Paris Committee asked: what is the best recovery we can plan for over the next four years? Furthermore, recovery was not projected in terms of over-all production, or national income, but attention was concentrated on the key items: food, fuel, steel, timber, and transport.

The substitution of maximum achievable recovery for the

[3] Committee of European Economic Coöperation (CEEC), v. 1, *General Report,* and v. II, *Technical Reports,* Washington, Division of Publications, Dept. of State (Sept. and Oct., 1947).

vaguer concept of the level required for political ends reduced the problem to more workable terms. Each nation drew up a schedule of the key items it could produce if raw materials and equipment were available. Schedules were also drawn up of the raw materials, equipment, and consumption goods needed to support these programs. From these schedules there was then derived a combined program for European recovery, providing for the satisfaction of the food, raw material, and equipment needs from European resources up to the limit of those resources, and the uncovered items constituted the Paris Committee's estimate of European requirements from outside sources. These import requirements were then broken down according to their presumed availability from the American continent or from other non-European areas, roughly constituting the dollar and the nondollar sources respectively.

The requirements so computed were scaled downward at Paris to take account of the limitations of world supplies. The resulting import program was transmitted to the United States Government in September, 1947. Various American committees investigated the United States situation with respect to foreign aid and suggested modifications of the Paris program in the light of American conditions.

Then the staffs of many Washington bureaus and agencies went to work on the report of the Paris Committee, compared it with the suggestions of the presidential and congressional committees, and constructed a new schedule of aid based on a screening of the European proposals and a study of the American supply situation, with due regard for the American interest in economy in the operation of the program.[4] The aid program constructed by the executive branch of the United States government is basically similar to that proposed by the Paris committee, but quantitatively revised in the light of American information or evaluations, as shown in Table 2.

The distribution of aid among the various countries can be

[4] "Commodity Requirements of European Recovery and the Cost of United States Assistance," printed in: 80th Congress, 1st Session, Committee Print of Senate Committee on Foreign Relations, *Outline of European Recovery Program, Draft Legislation and Background Information,* U. S. Government Printing Office (Dec. 19, 1947).

TABLE 2

ESTIMATED IMPORTS OF THE 16 PARTICIPATING COUNTRIES AND WESTERN GERMANY (INCLUDING DEPENDENT AREAS) FROM THE AMERICAN CONTINENT, AND BALANCE OF PAYMENTS[a]

(*Millions of Dollars at 1947 Prices*)

| | CEEC Estimate 1948 | Executive Branch Estimate Fiscal year 1948–49 |
|---|---|---|
| Food, Feeds, and Fertilizer | 3650 | 3529 |
| Coal and Solid Fuels | 369 | 297 |
| Petroleum | 577 | 531 |
| Iron and Steel Products | 370 | 261 |
| Timber | 266 | 267 |
| Key Commodities | 5232 | 4885 |
| Agricultural Mchy. and Tractors | 353 | 158 |
| Industrial Equipment (excl. Petroleum eqpmt.)[b] | 549 | 315 |
| Petroleum equipment | 175 | 225[c] |
| Key Equipment | 1077[d] | 698[d] |
| Minus dependent areas' share of above | −430 | n.a. |
| "Other imports" (excl. dependent areas) | 3286 | n.a. |
| Total Imports (excl. dependent areas) | 9165 | 8695 |
| Exports to American Continent | 2159 | 2382 |
| Net position of dependent areas with American Continent | −455 | +105 |
| Net position on invisible account with American Continent | −574 | −168 |
| Deficit in Current Account with American Continent | −8035 | −6376[e] |

[a]Sources: CEEC, v. I and II, and *Draft Legislation and Background Information*, p. 100, and *passim*.

[b]Includes equipment for coal mining, electrical, rail transport, iron and steel, and timber industries; does not include motor vehicles.

[c]Figure supplied by author. Executive branch estimated 4-year imports between 850 and 950 million dollars.

[d]Not given in source, obtained by addition.

[e]Given as 6303 in source, presumably in error.

expected to be roughly in proportion to their net deficits in balance of payments as estimated by the executive branch and shown in Table 3. The four largest countries will get the lion's share of the aid, but less in proportion to their prewar national incomes than many of the smaller countries. The estimated deficits reflect the respective countries' requirements for relief

TABLE 3

ESTIMATED NET DEFICITS OF EUROPEAN COUNTRIES[a] WITH THE AMERICAN CONTINENT APRIL 1, 1948 THROUGH JUNE 30, 1949 COMPARED WITH PREWAR NATIONAL INCOMES

(*Millions of Dollars at 1947 Prices*)

| | Net Deficit[b] 15 Months | Prewar National Income—Annual Average (1925–34)[c] |
|---|---|---|
| United Kingdom | 2,200 | 30,500 |
| France | 1,600 | 17,400 |
| Western Germany | 1,007 | 16,000[d] |
| Italy | 977 | 7,420[e] |
| Netherlands | 864 | 3,660 |
| Belgium and Luxembourg | 520 | 2,830[f] |
| Greece | 195 | 1,280[g] |
| Austria | 194 | 2,240 |
| Denmark | 192 | 1,400 |
| Eire | 152 | 1,150 |
| Norway | 90 | 840 |
| Sweden | 76 | 2,410 |
| Portugal | 50 | 1,170 |
| Iceland | 13 | n.a. |
| Turkey | ? | n.a. |
| Switzerland | — | 2,660 |

[a]Including dependent areas' deficits, minus dependent areas' surpluses.

[b]Executive branch estimates. Source: 80th Congress, 2d Session, Committee Print (Senate Committee on Foreign Relations) *The Role of ERP Countries in European Recovery and Their Need for United States Assistance* (February 16, 1948. U. S. Government Printing Office), *passim*. Net deficit is defined as total imports from the Western Hemisphere minus exports to the Western Hemisphere plus or minus net balance on shipping and other invisible items. These net deficits may be met not only from U. S. aid but from other sources of dollar funds such as International Bank loans, or private loans.

[c]Source: Colin Clark, *The Conditions of Economic Progress* (London, 1940), p. 40. Clark's figures in "International Units" were roughly converted to 1947 prices on the basis 1 I.U. = $1.39. These figures are of course only roughly accurate, and are used with great reservations.

[d]Estimated as 65 per cent of all Germany on basis of percentage of Germans gainfully employed in this area in 1939.

[e]Average of 1927 and 1931.

[f]Belgium only.

[g]Average of 1924, 1929, 1934.

and recovery aid, except that Germany is probably scheduled for less than would be consistent with a rigid application of the principles mentioned above. Its recovery and consumption are being placed behind that of our former allies.

It was found that the European countries did not in general ask for more than they needed, but their import programs sometimes had to be cut because of the strain on American supplies. It was obviously impossible to measure just how much reduction of American consumption is justified by the needs of Europe. The American consumer was given the benefit of the doubt by a broad margin. Highly urgent European needs were left unsatisfied in order not to cut American consumption of a more nearly frivolous sort.

The executive branch estimates of needs accordingly are based on the same concept as are the estimates of the Paris Conference. The planned level of recovery is the highest believed practical of attainment under prospective conditions. This concept is logically imprecise because it depends so much on the estimator's evaluation of "practicality" and "prospective conditions." What it amounts to is a rough and practical judgment of a good recovery program.

For example, if more coal, steel, and equipment were allotted to France, French production by the end of 1951 might quite possibly be higher than it will be under the present schedule. Such larger allocations were not made because it was believed that France could not make the required internal adjustments fast enough to take full advantage of increased allotments. Or perhaps it was not judged desirable to take more steel away from American consumers; or it was decided that Italy needed steel as a raw material for her metal-working industries more urgently than France for expanding its industrial capacity.

Judgments such as these can be made only roughly, and those who administer the European Recovery Program will have to make a great number of such rough decisions. The principle of maximum possible recovery will furnish them with valuable guidance within the practical limits in which they will operate. Ultimately, of course, that principle will give no answer at all until the amounts we are willing to take from American consumers and the European standards of living we are willing to help support are specified.

### *Consumption, Exports, Investment, and Foreign Aid*

The second basic question "How well or poorly shall the people of Europe live during the period of recovery?" was also approached by the Paris Committee. Any definite specification of the standards of living to be sought in each country was strictly avoided. No attempt was made to compare the distress of different countries, or to use hardships as a measure of need. Instead, the principle was adopted that no nation should seek a higher standard in 1948-51 than it could support after 1951; and a gradual return to a standard of living which presumably could be supported after 1951 was scheduled. In short, the extra production of European recovery is to be used partly to increase exports and so reduce the need for aid, partly to raise consumption toward a level which may be considered postwar normal, and partly to furnish investment to support increased production.

In view of world scarcities, extravagant imports for consumption into the participating countries are unlikely. However, domestic consumption may, if too high, impede the recovery program by limiting exports even if it does not swell imports. There is a tremendous demand in European countries for all sorts of manufactures that the people have long done without. These products can profitably be sold domestically so that the stimulation of exports will be difficult.

This difficulty is already evident in Britain where production is above prewar. It seems to the British people that everything desirable made in Britain is earmarked for export. Abstaining from the consumption of exportable goods is generally believed to be part of austerity; it is nothing of the sort, it is merely foregoing exported goods in order to have more imported goods. A country can get the imports and keep the exports too only if it can finance a payment deficit, and that Britain is now doing as well. The aim of American policy must be the steady reduction of such deficits, but the European governments will find it hard to restrict consumption sufficiently to provide exports to approach self-support.

Furthermore, domestic consumption may conflict with domestic capital formation. This is the occasion for austerity, since by limiting consumption resources may be spared for building up the country's productive capacity. The more resources that are channelled into rebuilding factories, railroads, and mines, the sooner will the country be able to be self-supporting. But the Economic Recovery Program cannot support vast schemes of capital construction any more than it can support high levels of consumption. It is paradoxical that although a country's recovery will be advanced by new plant construction, the administrators of the aid program must discourage ambitious plans for expansion of capacity except in key industries.

Extensive investment programs will greatly increase the cost of the aid program to the United States. This is true whether the investment goods are imported or are produced domestically. Much of the labor and materials needed to make the investment goods might otherwise be used to produce consumption goods or exports and so the need for aid can be reduced by foregoing capital formation. Certain investments in key industries may lead to increased production of goods for export or for replacement of imports within the period of the aid program, and so are well worth the present cost. Other investments, however, may increase production only much later or in lines which will not help Europe become self-supporting. These will be useful in maintaining a higher ultimate standard of living, but will not contribute to the recovery program. The aid program cannot afford the luxury of ambitious investment projects that do not promise early contributions toward self-support. The principle of maximum recovery must be tempered by a limitation of the recovery targets so as not to overburden the aid program by excessive investment.

Mr. Roy Harrod has argued that a major part of British need for foreign aid is the result of an overambitious program of new investment,[5] and the transfer of productive powers from the digging of tunnels and building of plants and houses to the production of currently consumable commodities would make more goods immediately available, either for consumption or for export. His numerous opponents, besides pointing out that factors other than investment account for a major part of Britain's foreign payments deficit, reply that if Britain is to maintain a high standard of living, more rather than less investment is required. This is a conflict in preferences rather than in eco-

[5] Roy F. Harrod, *Are These Hardships Necessary?* (London, 1947).

nomic analysis. The familiar choice of classical economics is open to Britain and the other European countries: to sacrifice present availability of goods and services for a higher future availability through the increase of productivity by investment. Mr. Harrod is willing to settle for a lower recovery target in order to get a higher interim consumption. His opponents are not.

The two determinants of the amount of aid required are, accordingly, the ultimate recovery target and the interim standard of living. A high ultimate target requires large investment which must come either from a reduction in the interim standard of living or from an increase in foreign aid. A high interim standard can be achieved only at the expense either of the recovery target or of foreign aid.

Since the need for aid depends on the interim living standards and the investment programs, it seems that the United States must enforce some limits on these quantitics. But the participating countries will hardly welcome such interference in their domestic affairs. Fortunately a simple solution of this dilemma is possible. The United States, with the help of the continuing organization of the participating countries, can decide how much aid each country will be given on the basis of specified interim standards and recovery targets. The aid being granted, there can be no objection if any country resolves to consume less than scheduled in order to build a more productive economy for the future. But if a recipient country chooses to consume more than scheduled at the expense of its recovery target, then the United States' interest will be adversely affected. The United States may appropriately require commitments that certain minimum investment programs be carried through; no limitation need be imposed on the amount by which scheduled investment may be exceeded. But the requirements of overambitious recovery targets and the investment programs they imply cannot be accepted as the basis of need for aid.

### *Suppressed Inflation vs. Exports*

Almost everywhere in Europe today there exist strong inflationary forces. In many countries these forces are successfully held in check; there have been no sharp price rises recently reported in Britain, Scandinavia, Switzerland, Belgium, or the Netherlands except in certain commodities largely as a result of price increases in the United States. In other countries, such as France, the price level continues its upward climb, sometimes interrupted but not yet really checked by government effort.

Even a partially suppressed inflation, so long as there is money purchasing power ready to be spent and unable to find objects of expenditure, greatly increases the difficulties of encouraging exports. Domestic demand is so strong that exports can be achieved only by governmental measures to set goods aside out of the reach of domestic purchasers. If exchanges and prices were set free, the automatic operation of supply and demand would encourage exports or discourage imports. Most European governments fear that the resulting rise in prices would disastrously disorganize their economies.

The disorganization would be the direct result of the way a free market operates to close the gap between imports and exports. If markets are freed and all foreign aid terminated, the domestic prices of urgently needed products, such as food stuffs, will be bid up sharply. The prices of less urgently required goods will not be bid up quite so high since the high prices of food and other necessities will take so much of the consumers' money that the other goods will no longer be so eagerly demanded. Meanwhile, if the foreign exchanges are free to move in response to supply and demand for commodity transactions, the currency will decline relative to the dollar, roughly reflecting the increase in domestic prices.[6] The less urgently needed goods will then be available to foreign purchasers at lower costs to them, while the domestic demand for these goods will be weaker. Thus, goods formerly taken by the domestic market will be exported.

Not only will more be exported, but less will be imported because the rise of the domestic prices of imports will prevent some former buyers from continuing to purchase. The domestic demand for imports may be so strong that the decline in imports, at least over a certain range of price rise, may be slight. Or possibly foreigners cannot be induced to spend more of their

[6] It is assumed that strict controls are maintained over capital movements.

money on the country's exports by a cheapening of the exports through depreciation of the country's currency. If both these conditions hold (inelastic demand, both foreign and domestic) then the depreciation of the currency and the rise of prices will be so much the larger, continuing until a point is reached where the domestic prices are high enough to discourage imports or the dollar value of the currency low enough to encourage exports. In either case, from the point of view of the domestic consumer, something has to be given up because of the price rise; either a foreign import must now be foregone, or a domestic product, formerly consumed, must now be exported. Much of these sacrifices will fall on the workers.

If the workers resist the reduction of their real incomes caused by the price rise and demand higher wages, then a further spiral of rising wages and prices will be initiated. How the burden of the reduction of the availability of goods will finally be distributed depends on the developments of the ensuing inflation. The chain of events described above is a "solution" of the foreign deficit problem, but hardly one that will appeal to European governments. Free prices and free exchanges will wipe out the foreign trade deficit by forcing certain people to consume or invest less, but the burden is likely to fall on those least able to bear it. Furthermore, production will be disrupted by the runaway inflation.

In order to avoid such chaotic developments, governments will prefer to control foreign exchanges, domestic prices of necessities, and possibly other aspects of the economy. The principal hope in this situation is that as production increases a significant part of the increase may be exported or substituted for imports, and so the foreign payment deficit may be reduced. There is a presumption that at the present low levels of consumption the workers in Europe will resist any cuts in their real incomes and will demand increased wages if prices rise, but as production increases the workers will not demand the full amount of the increase so that greater exports will be possible.

If prices and foreign exchange remain under control, the government must take specific measures to stimulate exports—either through direct controls such as allocating scarce materials preferentially to export industries, or through price concessions or favored exchange rates. The latter methods will be ineffective if domestic prices keep pace with the export prices, as they can be expected to do unless directly controlled.

The stimulation of exports is therefore an onerous and unpleasant task which no government anxious for popular support will push farther than it has to. How far each government of Western Europe has to press its export program depends principally on how much aid it can expect from the United States. Only a crisis can force a government to take the drastic and unpopular measures necessary to attain the maximum level of exports. The availability of American aid averts such a crisis. The responsibility then falls on the aid administration of gradually building up the same pressure to export as would be exerted by the operation of a free market in the absence of foreign aid. If the aid administration fails in this, Europe may still need aid in 1952.

## *The Long-Run Prospect*

### RECOVERY AND PRODUCTIVITY

The immediate economic goal in Europe is the recovery of production. That recovery depends first upon key imports, which are scheduled to become available in supply that is not abundant, but probably adequate to support recovery.[7] The next requirement is an enterprising and able government in each country to make the most of the opportunities for recovery. Such governments exist in northwest Europe, but in France, Italy, Greece, Austria, and Germany, external or internal political developments may prevent a high level of efficiency in recovery. At best those countries may muddle through. As recovery proceeds, however, the political situation may be stabilized, and the governments will be capable of more effective economic policies.

Beyond the next few years looms the long-run problem of the adjustment of the European economy to that of the rest of the world. Given short-run recovery and skillful, stable govern-

[7] Cf. Ch. 16.

ments, the productive capacity of Europe will depend largely on the energy with which improved techniques are adopted and on the availability of new capital for the new techniques.

Britain and Germany are probably as efficient in manufacturing as any of the countries in Europe. Yet the average productivity per worker in manufacturing in those countries in 1935-37 has been estimated as about half the corresponding productivity of American workers.[8] There is therefore a possibility of greatly increasing productivity in the European countries. The rate of improvement of efficiency in Europe must depend on a number of subtle factors whose effects cannot easily be quantitatively evaluated. Probably most important of all will be government activities to stimulate investment and to improve techniques. Much can be hoped for provided the governments themselves are stable and skilled, which in turn will probably depend on whether sufficient recovery is achieved in the short run to make these governments secure.

### *The Need for Imports*

Europe's import requirements are not expected to decline as European conditions improve; in fact, they will probably grow. Food imports, for example, are expected to rise, although the additional imports are scheduled to come from the nondollar areas. Similar developments are probable with respect to many other commodities. A decline is anticipated only in coal, in equipment, and in iron and steel products. As a result, aggregate imports in 1951 (measured in constant prices) will probably be slightly larger than in 1948, although a smaller part of those imports is expected to come from the American Continent.

This means that the recovery of European self-support requires an increase of exports or a change in the terms of trade in favor of Europe. Exports from Europe are at present very low. Nor are they scheduled to recover very rapidly.

The Paris Committee estimated exports from the sixteen countries and western Germany to the American Continent at about 2.2 billion dollars in 1948, rising close to 4 billion dollars

[8] Rostas, L., "Industrial Production, Productivity, and Distribution in Britain, Germany and the United States, 1935-37," *Economic Journal*, v. LIII (1943), p. 46.

by 1951. Unless the terms of trade alter in favor of Europe (as CEEC estimated with an optimism born largely of American pressure to keep down the amount of aid requested), that will still leave Western Europe with a deficit balance with the American Continent in 1951 of about 4.6 billion dollars as compared with 7.6 billion dollars estimated for 1948.[9] The executive

TABLE 4

ESTIMATED IMPORTS (CEEC) OF THE 16 PARTICIPATING COUNTRIES AND WESTERN GERMANY (EXCLUDING DEPENDENT AREAS) 1948 AND 1951[a]

*(Millions of Dollars at 1947 Prices)*

| | From all Non-Participating Countries | | From American Continent | |
|---|---|---|---|---|
| | 1948 | 1951 | 1948 | 1951 |
| Food, Feeds, and Fertilizer | 5,245 | 6,135 | 3,308 | 3,385 |
| Coal | 597 | 492 | 342 | 27 |
| Petroleum Products | 512[c] | 550[c] | 512 | 550 |
| Iron and Steel Products | 413 | 337 | 370 | 303 |
| Timber | 519 | 665 | 266 | 208 |
| Key Equipment[b] | 1,081[d] | 586[d] | 1,081 | 586 |
| Other imports | 5,497 | 5,591 | 3,286 | 3,123 |
| | 13,864 | 14,356 | 9,165 | 8,182 |

[a]Source: CEEC, v. I, p. 118, and p. 114.

[b]Includes agricultural, electrical, coal mining, rail transport, iron and steel, petroleum, and timber equipment.

[c]From dollar sources only; sterling source petroleum is considered as coming from a participating country.

[d]Not specified in source. It is here assumed that all scheduled equipment from nonparticipating sources comes from U.S.

branch of the U. S. Government has suggested that a somewhat larger export program is possible and projects a deficit in the balance of payments of the participating countries of $3.3 billion in the fiscal year 1952 on the basis of 1947 prices.[10]

Just how much the exports of the participating countries can be raised is the most uncertain part of the whole Marshall Plan. There is little doubt that under favorable political circumstances production can be greatly increased in Western Europe.

[9] CEEC, v. 1, pp. 127 and 119: Deficit of 3.54 billion for 1951 given on p. 127 assumes an adjustment of 1.02 billion for change in terms of trade, so the deficit would be 4.56 if there were no change in the terms of trade.

[10] *Draft Legislation and Background Information,* p. 113.

A very large part of the increased production should be available for export, and the problem will then arise of finding markets for these goods.

### *The Need for Markets*

The most obvious opportunity for improvement of productivity in Europe is through the further development of manufacturing, thereby increasing European dependence on international trade for raw materials and food. An increase of the value of agricultural production is of course also possible, as for example, by feeding more livestock on imported feedstuffs. Mechanization of agriculture would probably increase yields per man, but not necessarily yields per acre. On the whole not a great deal is to be expected by way of freeing Western Europe from dependence on foreign sources of agricultural products, even though some increase of Western European agricultural production is to be anticipated. An increase of population may also be expected at least over the next few decades, although a long-run decline is possible in Western Europe.

Consequently the principal hope is for greater industrial production and greatly increased exports. Such a tendency characterized the Western European economy in the nineteenth and early twentieth century, but since 1913 there was a leveling off and even a decline in the volume of exports of manufactured goods from Europe. The slackening of exports after 1913 was mitigated not only by Europe's earnings from shipping and overseas investments, but also by the fact that Europe obtained from 20 to 50 per cent more imports for its exports after the first World War than in the preceding twenty-five years.[11] Now the terms of trade are somewhat less favorable to manufactures than in the period between the wars. British exports in December 1947 purchased only 93 per cent as much imports as in 1938, but still about 128 per cent of what they bought in 1913 and 140 per cent to 150 per cent of what they bought from 1890 to 1913.[12] However, a decline in agricultural prices is widely ex-

[11] See Colin Clark, *Conditions of Economic Progress,* p. 453, quoting Dr. Schlote.

[12] Dec. 1947 import and export price indexes from U. K. Board of Trade, quoted in *Economist,* Records and Statistics Supplement (Feb. 7, 1948), p. 116.

pected in the near future, although this decline will not necessarily restore the interwar relation to manufactured goods.

Can Western Europe find export markets for manufactured goods much larger than prewar? It should be prepared to give terms of trade considerably more advantageous to the raw material producing countries than the prewar terms. Will these be sufficient to stimulate export sales so that Europe can buy more abroad than before?

If prices alone governed the flow of world trade, it would be safe to predict an increase in European exports of manufactures. But in a world of tariffs and quotas, predictions are not so easy. Many raw material producing countries such as the Argentine and New Zealand stand to gain by exporting agricultural products for manufactured goods because in those countries productivity is probably higher in agriculture than in manufacturing, even at 1937 prices. If in the future, agricultural prices are higher, relative to industrial prices, the comparative advantage of these countries specializing in agriculture will have increased.

The case for the United States is not so clear, but it should certainly be advantageous for us to trade some of our raw materials and manufactures for European manufactured goods. However, our manufacturers will certainly resist large imports of European goods. Similarly, in the raw material producing countries, industrial aspirations may not be so closely calculated on relative advantage that industrialization schemes will be abandoned because of the more favorable terms of trade offered by countries exporting factory products. Consequently, even though Europe will offer attractive bargains to many countries of the Western World,[13] most of these countries will probably be prevented from accepting them by their ambitions for industrialization, however uneconomic.

A world-wide adoption of multilateral free trade might well solve this problem, but it should not be counted on. Bilateral or multilateral agreements may approach the same end from an opposite direction. Through them the European countries may

[13] In this context the Western World includes not only the Western Hemisphere but Africa and the Pacific areas as well—in fact all the non-European world outside the control of the Soviet Union.

offer their suppliers better terms of trade than exist in the world market in exchange for an assured volume of sales. The fundamental basis of profitable world trade exists in the fact that the rate of exchange of agricultural for industrial products is more favorable to agricultural products in Europe and to industrial products in the great agricultural countries. The unresolved question is whether obstacles to free exchange will in the future be great enough to choke off world trade to prewar proportions.

Traditionally the countries of Western Europe traded principally among themselves and westward. Further growth of their manufacturing could be well adapted to the needs of the Western World, but may run into trade barriers which will be supported by influential interests in the countries of the Western World. So Western Europe may be forced to turn eastward.

In the past, East-West trade in Europe has not been of major importance. In 1938, less than 17 per cent of German trade, and less than 9 per cent of the international trade of the seven other major trading nations of Western Europe, was transacted with Russia and the areas now under Russian domination, excluding the Russian zone of Germany.[14] There is currently a tendency to exaggerate the importance of normal East-West trade, partly based on a desire to blame Russia for the economic difficulties of Western Europe, and partly based on the fact that certain commodities prospectively forthcoming from the East, such as grain, coal, and timber, are urgently needed now. After the recovery of world production, the special importance of these commodities will subside, and their significance will be measured by their value as a very small part of the imports of Western Europe. Of course, the trade between eastern and western Germany was of vital importance to both parties and may be expected to be resumed unless prevented by the split of Germany between East and West.

In Eastern Europe the governments are quite likely to welcome the manufactured products of Western Europe, machinery

[14] Source: League of Nations, *Network of World Trade,* 1942 (Series II, Economic and Financial, II. A. 3) Annex III, quoted in *Preliminary Report Twenty of the House Select Committee on Foreign Aid,* U. S. Government Printing Office (March 7, 1948), p. 9. Also *Statistisches Jahrbuch,* 1941-42, for the German figures. The seven Western European countries are: United Kingdom, France, Italy, Belgium-Luxembourg, Netherlands, Sweden, and Switzerland.

and developmental products, in the immediate future, and possibly light manufactures later. The communist-dominated countries can easily adjust the future development of their economies to the receipt of manufactures from Western Europe. The greatest difficulties faced by the countries of Eastern Europe in this connection will be the production of adequate surpluses of agricultural products and raw materials. Their own plans for industrialization may reduce their willingness to accept manufactured goods, but there are in fact great opportunities for Eastern Europe both to industrialize and to develop trade with Western Europe.

Western Europe may accordingly turn its trade either eastward or westward. The real conditions are most favorable westward, but governmental policies in the West are likely to hamper such trade. The immediate real difficulties beyond the prewar level of trade are greatest eastward, but governmental policies in the East may possibly be favorable. The ultimate challenge to the Marshall Plan will accordingly be not only the task of reviving Western Europe's production, but of opening up the channels of trade in the Western World so that the European economy can fit into it well. If we fail in this, even though we have succeeded in reviving European production, we may fail in our aim of keeping Western Europe free and democratic and out of the control of Russia.

### *Summary*

The short run recovery of Europe requires our goods in aid. In order to economize on these goods we must see that they are used most effectively to promote recovery. Our efforts will be very powerfully aided by the inherent recuperative powers of the countries of Europe.

The need for aid is to be measured by the requirements for recovery, which in turn depend on the projected recovery targets and the interim standards of living. A delicate balance must be preserved among consumption, capital formation, and exports. Exports may be limited not so much by the level of production, but by the strong domestic demands of the countries of Western Europe, unchecked by the normal operation of supply and demand according to the laws of classical economics because of the controls on prices and foreign exchange.

If in five or more years exports are forthcoming, they are likely to face unreceptive markets outside Europe because of protectionist policies in the Western World. Unless these policies are modified, either by multilateral free trade or extensive trade agreements, Western Europe's trade may be forced eastward and the economy of Europe may, though with difficulty, be unified under the leadership of Russia. The ultimate success of the Marshall Plan is to be measured not only by the recovery of European production, but by the integration of the European economy into that of the Western World.

PART V

# *PROBLEMS OF INTERNATIONAL EQUILIBRIUM*

# *INTRODUCTION*

Seymour E. Harris

It remains only to concentrate on some theoretical issues. The outstanding international economic problem is the excess of dollars wanted on the exchange markets relative to the supplies available, the problem of international disequilibrium to which so many economists are now turning their attention. This is the subject matter of Part V. First, there is the problem of discovering the presence or absence of disequilibrium. The orthodox approach is to observe exchange and gold movements. Interwar experience of some countries whose exchange rates—and gold and exchange reserves—were relatively stable suggests that these indexes of disequilibrium are not reliable. In these countries, there appeared large amounts of unemployment over long periods, in part associated with disequilibrium exchange rates, or (and) reduced standards of living associated with curtailed trade. In Great Britain disequilibrium was concealed by maintaining reserves through imposing restrictive monetary policies on the country and, with them, unemployment. In other countries the way out was a rigid control of supply and demand for foreign exchange; instead of allowing the exchange rates to move in response to, for example, the excessive demands for foreign currencies, the free market was abolished and supply and demand controlled. Restriction of trade and higher costs of production were the price paid for a specious equilibrium.

Few will deny the prevalence of disequilibrium today; our main question relates to the causes and cures. Despite the numerous and varied controls, the outside world is short of dollars. There is no over-all analysis nor an over-all cure for all countries, varying as they do in symptoms and economic conditions. They all have indulged in the luxury of inflation; and surely a moderation in the price rise, and a fortiori a decline, would discourage excessive purchases abroad and encourage sales. All would agree. Again, in many cases adjustments of exchange rates would help reduce the adverse balance. Unfortunately, the rate which might be appropriate as a catalyst for exports might also serve as a depressant for essential imports and thus cause a further domestic inflation. It is not easy, furthermore, to agree on the extent or even direction of adjustment of exchange rates. The practitioner who seeks advice from the economist will find support for monetary and fiscal reform; and he will also find authority for adjustments of exchange rates, and even for exchange control and other quantitative restrictions. How much reliance should be put upon one or the other will be the difficult problem. Depending upon where they seek such advice, they will find answers not always in agreement as to the importance of political as against economic causes of dollar shortage; of mistaken policies as the cause of these distortions; of the contribution that can be made by multilateral trade and United States leadership.

# 20

## *FUNDAMENTAL DISEQUILIBRIUM*[1]

Alvin H. Hansen

Professor Haberler in his illuminating article concludes that the term "fundamental disequilibrium" should be interpreted in terms of an objective, unambiguous, and observable criterion. Such a criterion he concludes could only be an actual deficit in the balance of payments, but he suggests that it must be left to the judgment of the managers of the Fund to decide how large the deficit must be and how long it must last before the disequilibrium can be regarded as fundamental. (See Chapter 21.)

I am not convinced that an actual deficit, or its absence, in the balance of payments is a satisfactory criterion on the basis of which to determine the presence or absence of a fundamental disequilibrium of a character requiring a change in the exchange rate. My skepticism is no doubt related to serious questioning that, in many if not most cases, a deficit in the balance of payments can in fact be cured by a change in the exchange rate. I do not deny, however, that along with other measures a change in the exchange rate may, in certain specific cases, help.

A wrong exchange rate may not reflect itself in a deficit in the balance of payments at all. As Mr. Nurkse has pointed out and as Professor Haberler has reiterated, there was no deficit in the balance of payments in England in 1925-1930. Yet the judgment of most competent students is that the pound was overvalued. The overvalued pound was reflected not in a deficit in the balance of payments but in a serious deflationary pressure upon prices and wages, especially in the export industries, and in widespread unemployment. Similarly, in the period 1931-1933,

1 This chapter is a revision of an article in the *Review of Economic Statistics,* 1946.

the depreciation of the currencies of many countries had no significant effect upon the American balance of payment position, but exerted a downward pressure upon American prices. American industries competing with import industries took their licking by meeting the price competition of depreciated currencies. But they held their own in the market. American imports did not rise.

The essential point I think is that the price elasticity of exports and imports is frequently not very great. Exchange depreciation can improve the balance of payments only in so far as the price elasticity of exports and imports is relatively high.[2] An incorrect exchange rate often creates a disequilibrium not so much in the balance of payments as in the internal cost-price structure of the country in question. An overvalued currency has a deflationary effect on prices, distorts the cost-price balance, and contributes to unemployment. On the other side, while an undervalued currency reduces the price competition of foreign competitors, nevertheless the volume of internal investment may be so low as to create internal deflation and depression despite the favorable exchange rate. The favorable exchange rate does however facilitate a program of planned expansion, if such a program is undertaken by the government.

It seems to me, therefore, that there is a far greater core of truth in the "purchasing power parity" theory than either Mr. Nurkse or Professor Haberler admits. I should rather state it in terms of "cost structure parity," since admittedly the purchasing power concept is too loose and ambiguous—for reasons that have been adequately discussed in the literature of the last two decades. An exchange rate may be regarded as correct if it affords no "artificial" advantage in international competition. This means that when all of the productive resources of a country are fully employed, the exchange rate should not divert productive resources artificially to the foreign market. A correct exchange rate is one in which only those productive resources of the country are employed on exports which have a comparative advantage in the foreign markets on the basis of an eco-

[2] In this connection, the condition of high levels of employment in the export markets would facilitate the stimulation of exports.

nomic world-wide allocation of resources. The exchange rate of a country should be adjusted so that its cost structure will tend to be pushed neither downward nor upward by an artificial exchange rate. An equilibrium exchange rate is therefore one that represents a "parity" in the cost structure of the different countries.[8]

It should not be very difficult to discover serious departures from an equilibrium exchange rate if all countries really enjoyed full employment. Under these conditions the "pull" of the foreign market in the case of an undervalued currency, or the price-depressant effect of foreign competitors in the case of an overvalued currency, would be fairly easy to detect. In the case, however, of varying degrees of employment in different countries and in various phases of a violently fluctuating business cycle, the cost-price structure relationship within any one country and the cost-structure relationship between countries may be more seriously affected by internal than external factors.

It is a question whether variation in the exchange rate should be used as a means to remedy artificial price competition from foreign countries caused by the cycle behavior of different countries. As a means of meeting cyclical distortions it may be that temporary exchange control is a more appropriate remedy. At all events, neither short-run cyclical fluctuations in exchange rates, nor the imposition of exchange control at certain phases of the cycle, could give us a satisfactory international economy. Merely to mention such remedies only underlines and stresses the urgent necessity of coördination of internal policies to maintain full employment and to reduce cyclical fluctuations in all important countries.

If a country is under continuous and strong price deflationary influences from the outside world, it can, I think, be concluded that the country's exchange rate is out of line and should be adjusted. This is a case of a fundamental disequilibrium. It may, however, not be suffering a deficit in its balance of payments. As

[8] See the excellent article by J. J. Polak on "Exchange Depreciation and International Monetary Stability," *Review of Economic Statistics*, August 1947. In this article Mr. Polak argues that "price disequilibrium" between countries presents a case of fundamental disequilibrium which justifies a change in the exchange rate.

business is organized under modern conditions, the consequences of a foreign exchange rate which is out of equilibrium may not be a deficit in balance of payments but price deflation and unemployment. This is the kind of case which, I think, may not uncommonly come before the Board of the Monetary Fund.

In determining whether this condition is caused, or at least intensified, by a wrong exchange rate, judgment must of course be applied with respect to various matters. The country may be depressed by reason of a low volume of internal investment. It should not be utterly impossible to distinguish between the depressional effect on prices flowing on the one side from inadequate internal outlets for investment and on the other side from pressures from the outside. Mere price deflation and unemployment are no proof of a disequilibrium in the exchange rate.

Consider now the case of a country that has a deficit in its balance of payments. This condition is by no means proof that its exchange rate is out of line. Its balance of payment position may be due to a reduced demand for its exports in a foreign country which normally is its best market. If this condition is cyclical[4] in character, the problem is a short-run one; if it is secular in character, the exporting country affected thereby will need to take appropriate measures to improve its position. Again the deficit in its balance of payments may be a chronic one owing to an unbalanced structure of production. In either case, a change in the exchange rate might not prove of any significant value. What is needed is a realistic study of the structure of the country's imports and exports. Following such a study, it should be possible to find ways and means of developing the natural resources of the country, the required human skills, and the capital facilities necessary to alter the structure of the imports and exports so as to promote a balance in its international account. If the fundamental structure of a country's imports and exports is seriously out of balance, enormous changes in the exchange rate would be required to bring about equilibrium. The balance brought

[4] See Robert Triffin, *International Monetary Policies, Postwar Economic Studies,* No. 7, Board of Governors of the Federal Reserve System. Dr. Triffin distinguishes between cyclical and fundamental maladjustments, and also between temporary (i.e., export crop failure) and fundamental maladjustments.

about by a change in the exchange rate might indeed merely tend to perpetuate a serious distortion in the structure of the economy. A thorough survey of the potential resources of the country, both human and material, the possibility of diversification of its agriculture and its industries in a broad developmental program, is certainly a more meaningful and realistic solution than reliance upon the weak reed of a change in the exchange rate.

The conclusion which I reach, so far as the cycle is concerned, is that a solution must be found by a direct attack upon the problem of full employment and parallel programs of economic stability in the leading industrial countries, and not by juggling the foreign exchange rate. And the solution of a chronic deficit in the balance of payments in many countries is to be found in resource surveys and developmental programs.

A country may, however, in fact be suffering from a fundamental disequilibrium caused by an inappropriate exchange rate. The real basis for determining whether such a disequilibrium exists is to be found in divergencies of the exchange rate from what I would call the "cost-structure parity." The evidence of such disequilibrium would be the pressure of an artificial competition in prices from abroad causing deflation and unemployment.

# 21

## CURRENCY DEPRECIATION AND THE INTERNATIONAL MONETARY FUND[1]

Gottfried Haberler

It is unavoidable that the Agreements of Bretton Woods should leave many important questions unanswered and reserve their solution for future amendments to the pact or for the policy decisions of the two international agencies. This is especially true of the International Bank Agreement which breaks new ground. The International Monetary Fund, when it begins to fill in the details of the picture outlined in the international agreement, will be able to draw upon the maxims of a more or less well-established Central Bank tradition and an extremely rich literature. But in many cases the answers derivable from these two sources are far from clear and unequivocal.

One such case is discussed in the present paper. It concerns the provisions of the Fund Agreement on currency depreciation (Art. IV, Sect. 5, "Changes in par value"). The pact of Bretton Woods provides, as is well known, that a change exceeding 10 per cent of the initial par value of any currency can be made only with the approval of the Fund. And the Fund shall approve "if it is satisfied that the change is necessary to correct a fundamental disequilibrium. In particular, provided it is so satisfied, it shall not object to a proposed change because of the domestic social or political policies of the member proposing the change" (Art. IV, Sec. 5, f.).

The question immediately arises, what is a fundamental disequilibrium? The Fund Agreement refrains from giving any

[1] This chapter is a revision of an article in the *Review of Economic Statistics,* 1946.

definition, thus leaving the question to the judgment of the managers of the Fund.[2] This is probably a wise thing to do. But it certainly makes a discussion of how to define "exchange equilibrium" or "equilibrium exchange rates" (which otherwise might be regarded as a dull and pedantic exercise) a very timely and important task.

Negatively it can be argued that a loss of gold and/or foreign exchange (including, of course, credit facilities with the Fund)[3] due to capital exports should not be regarded as a symptom of fundamental disequilibrium, for the Fund Agreement envisages exchange control for the purpose of preventing capital movements and discourages the use of the Fund's resources for financing capital exports.[4]

But does it follow—positively—that "fundamental disequilibrium" should be defined as a serious and protracted loss of gold due to a persistent deficit in the current balance of payments?[5] This is certainly the standard case of disequilibrium on which all experts would agree.[6] One difficulty here, which we may men-

[2] In the meantime, it has been revealed by R. F. Mikesell, who had access to "the unpublished minutes of the pre-Bretton Woods negotiations," that "the principal criterion for rate alterations in the minds of the authors of the text of the Fund agreement was the existence of a disequilibrium in the current international accounts of the member requesting a change." "Although fundamental disequilibrium is not defined in the Fund's *Articles of Agreement,* it was evident from the discussions which preceded the formal drafting of the agreement that the term refers to a sustained imbalance in a member's current international accounts." Mikesell, "The Role of the International Monetary Agreements in a World of Planned Economics," in *Journal of Political Economy* (December 1947), p. 503, footnote 14.

[3] For the sake of brevity, gold will from now on stand for international reserve.

[4] This seems to be clear as far as the law laid down in the Agreement is concerned. *De lege ferenda,* however, it must be questioned whether this rule should be applied to normal long-run capital movements for developmental purposes from rich to poor countries. Suppose an "old," wealthy country which habitually exports capital to "new," industrially backward countries loses gold. Should it be denied a devaluation and forced to undergo an internal deflation or else give up its capital exports?

[5] Disequilibrium could not be defined as a deficit in the current balance as such, because that would include the case of a country importing capital for developmental purposes.

[6] The question could be raised as to whether a protracted loss of gold due to unsound financial policies (chronic failure to balance the budget) should not be regarded as an exception. In other words, should not the Fund refuse permission to depreciate in such cases? The clause cited above forbids such a refusal in the case of "domestic social and political policies." This also practically excludes refusal in the case of "financial policies" because they can always be construed as

tion in passing, is the exact definition of international reserve. The standard definition is "gold plus equilibrating or accommodating[7] capital movements." The difficulty consists in giving an operational definition to the term "equilibrating capital movements." They cannot be identified with short-term capital movements, as is sometimes done. For, on the one hand some short-term capital movements are of the spontaneous (disequilibrating) kind,[8] and on the other hand long-term capital movements—at least if they are defined according to the nature of the credit instruments involved—are frequently of the equilibrating kind.[9]

This problem is evidently again one on which the managers of the Fund will have to exercise their judgment. Assuming, however, that a satisfactory solution has been found, the question still remains whether a country could not claim, under certain circumstances, the existence of a fundamental disequilibrium even though its balance of payments on current account is in equilibrium.

That this possibility cannot easily be dismissed will become apparent if we consult what Ragnar Nurkse in his authoritative study, *International Currency Experience: Lessons of the Inter-War Period,*[10] has to say about the meaning of the terms over- and undervaluation of a currency.[11] "The standard to which [these terms] relate is the equilibrium rate of exchange" (p. 124). Mr. Nurkse first defines the equilibrium rate as "that rate which maintains the balance of payments in equilibrium without any net change in the international currency reserve." He

---

adjuncts of social and political policies. Moreover, the term "political policies" is not a very precise one and can easily be construed so as to include financial policies.

7 The latter term was introduced by F. Machlup, *International Trade and the National Income Multiplier* (Philadelphia, 1943), p. 130.

8 They can again be subdivided into (a) "hot money" (disequilibrating in a strong sense) and (b) spontaneous movements of the ordinary sense—from capital-rich to capital-poor countries.

9 On these various classifications and criteria, compare Carl Iversen, *International Capital Movements* (London, 1935), C. P. Kindleberger, *International Short-Term Capital Movements* (New York, 1937), and F. Machlup, *op. cit.*

10 Prepared with the assistance of S. K. Fong and published by League of Nations (Columbia University Press, 1944).

11 Some people think it fortunate that these terms are not used in the Fund Agreement. But the term "fundamental disequilibrium" evidently implies over- and undervaluation of currencies.

then explains why "attempts to define the equilibrium rate in terms of a 'purchasing power parity' have been unsuccessful" (p. 125). To this I would add that purchasing power parity calculations should not be regarded as a definition but rather as one symptom (indicator) among others of exchange equilibrium or its absence.[12] It is true that the thing indicated—equilibrium or disequilibrium in the current balance covered by gold flows or equilibrating capital movements—is in most cases easier to ascertain than the indicator—purchasing power parity—itself. There is, however, one important exception: When there is no trade or when it is on a barter and government basis as in wartime, purchasing power parity calculations can give a rough and approximate idea about what the equilibrium rate is likely to be at the reopening of the trade channels. Moreover, even when there is trade and the absence of equilibrium can be observed directly, purchasing power parity calculations may give an idea of the *degree* of the over- or undervaluation.

But it is certainly true that purchasing power parity is a very inaccurate and unreliable guide which must be checked and supplemented by other kinds of evidence. These difficulties are difficulties of judging a concrete situation rather than difficulties of definition and ambiguity of policy objectives.[13] But let us go back to the fundamental criterion of equilibrium.

Mr. Nurkse points out that if "balance of payments equilibrium were the sole criterion of the equilibrium rate of exchange, there might be little justification for regarding the pound sterling in the years 1925-1930 as overvalued. For there was little sign of disequilibrium in the British balance of payments" (p. 125). According to him, there was no gold outflow during the period before July 1931 and no evidence of a continuous influx of equilibrating short-term balances.[14]

[12] Another indication would be the state of employment in the export industries.

[13] See H. S. Ellis' statement, "To define the equilibrium rate formally is one thing; to determine its height or probable behavior in a given situation, another. Precisely the latter and infinitely more complicated task must be performed . . . by the monetary and trade authorities who *have* to determine the extent of devaluation." "The Equilibrium Rate of Exchange" in *Explorations in Economics* (New York, 1936), p. 27.

[14] See *op. cit.* for further details.

"A country may have a rate of exchange such that its balance of payments can be kept in equilibrium only by a contraction of total domestic income and demand; and if wages and prices are rigid, such a contraction must operate through unemployment. This seems to have been the situation in the United Kingdom during the period 1925-1930 (though of course there were various other factors at work, such as an adverse shift in demand for certain articles of export and probably a relative lag in technical advance). The external accounts were kept approximately in balance, but only at the cost of large-scale unemployment and depressed business conditions in comparison with the outside world. Thus balance-of-payments equilibrium alone is not a sufficient criterion; at different levels of income and employment, equilibrium in the balance of payments can be secured at different rates of exchange. It may be better therefore to define the true equilibrium rate as one that maintains the balance in equilibrium without the need for mass unemployment at home, or at any rate without a degree of unemployment greater than in the outside world."[15]

This is certainly a most important case which deserves the closest attention. It would be easy to find other examples, especially among the gold bloc countries (France, Belgium, Netherlands, Switzerland) whose situation in the thirties conformed to that pattern. To be sure, the British situation arose largely because of the ill-advised appreciation of the pound sterling after the war, and the predicament of the gold bloc countries was the result of the beggar-my-neighbor depreciation of sterling and dollar and other currencies. Such acts should not be allowed under the new scheme. But we cannot be quite sure that the same situation will not occur again and that similar situations may not arise from other causes.

How should the Fund act in such cases? Should mass unemployment, especially in export industries, be regarded as sufficient proof of the existence of a fundamental disequilibrium or, more specifically, of overvaluation? In general, that rule cannot be followed. For in periods of worldwide depressions (for example, in 1931) all currencies would have to be regarded as over-

15 *Op. cit.*, p. 126.

valued. Only if one country or a small group of countries is in a badly depressed state and the rest of the world prosperous, or if during a worldwide depression one country is in especially bad shape, can depression conditions be regarded as good reasons for a depreciation of the currency. But even in that case there are weighty objections against permitting depreciation in the absence of a current balance of payments deficit.

The main objection is that depreciation will improve the balance of payments for the depreciating country.[16] Therefore, if the starting point is an even balance, depreciation will lead to a gold outflow from other countries which, under the balance-of-payments criterion, would constitute an overvaluation of other currencies. This suggests the conclusion that permission for depreciation should be given only if there is an actual balance of payments deficit. It is interesting to recall that this was the position of the original Keynes plan, which provided that a country should be entitled to depreciate its currency if its debit balance exceeded a quarter of its quota for at least two years, on the average.[17,18]

[16] Under improbable, though not impossible, elasticity conditions with respect to exports and imports, the balance may deteriorate rather than improve because of a depreciation. But this case can be dismissed as practically impossible when one country or a small group of countries is considered as against the rest of the world.

[17] *Proposals for an International Clearing Union:* Sect. (8). A 5 per cent depreciation was to be permitted, under the above conditions, without consent of the Governing Board of the Clearing Union, and more only with permission. In practice, these provisions would have been too rigid in my opinion. But this is another matter which need not be argued here.

[18] Arthur I. Bloomfield in his interesting paper on Keynes's views concerning "Foreign Exchange Rate Theory and Policy" (chap. 22 of *The New Economics*, edited by S. E. Harris, New York, 1947) reminds us that Keynes, at an early date, discarded the purchasing-power-parity theory and "substituted the simpler and more direct balance-of-payments criterion" *(op. cit.*, p. 296). Keynes's definition of an equilibrium rate of exchange as quoted by Bloomfield *(loc. cit.)* runs as follows: "We have to consider, on the one hand, a country's balance of payments on income account on the basis of the existing natural resources, equipment, technique and costs (especially wage costs) at home and abroad, a normal level of employment, and those tariffs, etc., which are a permanent feature of national policies; and, on the other hand, the probable readiness and ability of the country in question to borrow or lend abroad on long-term (or, perhaps, repay or accept repayment of old loans), on the average of the next few years. A set of rates of exchange which can be established without undue strain on either side and without large movements of gold (on a balance of transactions), will satisfy our condition of equilibrium." *(Lloyd's Bank Review,* October 1935, p. 528.)

See also the discussion of Fundamental Disequilibrium in my Comments on R.

However, before this rule is accepted two possible objections should be considered. It has (a) been denied that depreciation must in all cases result in an improvement in the current international balance of the depreciating country, and (b) it has been said that if a country has an insufficient international reserve it should be allowed to develop a favorable balance in order to accumulate a sufficient reserve.

Let us dispose of the second point first. This point does not really imply an exception to the balance of payments criterion. For it must be remembered that the International Monetary Fund will have supplied a sufficient international reserve to all its members. Therefore, if a country finds itself with an insufficient reserve, it must have lost the monies supplied by the Fund, i.e., its balance of payments must have been unfavorable. In that situation the country would qualify for depreciation on the balance of payments criterion. Apart from that, if a country with an insufficient reserve finds itself in a depressed situation, it can claim that it could not embark on an expansion unless it were allowed either to depreciate in order to acquire a sufficient international margin or to introduce import controls.[19] The latter possibility is clearly less satisfactory. If the acquisition of gold through an export surplus by a country with an insufficient reserve is regarded by other countries as a beggar-my-neighbor policy, the answer is, first, that such a country is, in fact, a beggar,[20] and should be accorded the privileges of its status; secondly, the "rich" neighbors have it always in their power to provide "poor" countries with an international reserve by means

---

Triffin's paper, "National Central Banking and the International Economy," in *International Monetary Policies, Postwar Economic Studies,* No. 7, September 1947, Board of Governors of the Federal Reserve System, p. 99, and my article "The Choice of Exchange Rates after the War," *American Economic Review,* vol. 35, June 1945.

[19] The classical possibility of cutting prices and wages, which, if it could be done, would eventually provide the required international margin is disregarded here because it is precisely the method which the new plans wish to avoid. Moreover, if gold were drained from other countries by means of an internal deflation, the classical method of adjustment would be just as much a beggar-my-neighbor device as a depreciation.

[20] If its reserve is really insufficient. What is to be regarded as sufficient or insufficient cannot be discussed here. It may be remarked, however, that if capital movements can be effectively controlled, the required reserve is much less than in an uncontrolled system.

of credit operations through the mechanism of the International Monetary Fund or other channels, if they dislike being subjected to a gold drain (import surplus). Precisely one of the functions of the International Monetary Fund is to provide countries with an international reserve, thus obviating the necessity of bringing about an export surplus for that purpose.

The other objection mentioned above, which states that a depreciation need not necessarily result in an improvement of the balance of payments, requires more careful consideration. The argument runs as follows: If a relatively depressed country expands to full employment (or at any rate to a higher level of activity), its balance of payments will become unfavorable. A certain depreciation is therefore necessary to equilibrate the balance at full (or fuller) employment; if this degree of depreciation is permitted, no disturbance in the balance of payments will occur.

The answer to this argument is that at best it explains the eventual equilibrium position. But the question of how the equilibrium is reached is just as important. Take *first* the case where the expansion is brought about by internal measures (easy money policy, spending, etc.). In that case the balance of payments will become unfavorable and the country should be entitled to a depreciation. But should the depreciation be granted *in anticipation* of the planned expansion and the expected deficit in the balance? In the author's opinion a wise policy on the part of the Fund would be not to attempt to cross the bridge before it is reached; in other words, it would be wise to follow the provision of the original Keynes plan and permit a depreciation only after there is objective evidence of a deterioration of the balance of payments.

A second case is where an expansion is brought about (or intensified) by a stimulation of the export industries. If a depreciation is demanded for that purpose it should be refused, because it is a typical beggar-my-neighbor policy, although in the end when the expansion has proceeded far enough the balance will certainly correct itself. This beggar-my-neighbor effect will also occur if a depreciation is granted in anticipation of a domestic policy of expansion which is slow in developing.

Since it is impracticable to time the various measures so nicely as to keep the balance on an even keel all the time, it will be better to defer depreciation until an outflow of funds occurs. After all, one of the main objectives of the new monetary plan is to provide a sufficient buffer and thereby to minimize the necessity of frequently making disturbing currency revaluations.

Our conclusion then is that "fundamental disequilibrium" should be interpreted in terms of an objective, unambiguous, and observable criterion. Such a criterion can be only an actual deficit in the balance of payments. But even if this rule is accepted much will be left to the judgment of the managers of the Fund. For they will have to decide how large a deficit must be and how long it must have existed before the disequilibrium can be regarded as sufficiently *fundamental* to justify a change in the value of the currency.

I should also like to take this opportunity to discuss some points raised by Professor Hansen in his discussion of disequilibrium in Chapter 21.

Professor Hansen raises a most important issue when he questions the efficacy of changes in the exchange rate to redress the balance of payments. I did not go into this question, but assumed the elasticities of demand for exports and imports to be great. The opposite assumption is now very fashionable, but I confess that I still believe that Marshall was, and still is, substantially right when he said: "It is practically certain that the demand of each of Ricardo's two countries for the goods in general of the other would have considerable elasticity *under modern industrial conditions*,[21] even if E and G were single countries whose sole trade was with one another. And if we take E to be a large and rich commercial country, while G stands for all foreign countries, this certainly becomes absolute."[22]

This is not the place for a thorough discussion of the arguments and evidence for and against that proposition. Only a few observations can be made here. First it should be clearly understood that what Professor Hansen must assume is not that the

[21] Italics in the original.

[22] *Money, Credit and Commerce*, p. 171.

price elasticities of exports and imports are *small* but that they are *unity*.[23,24] For if the elasticities were smaller than unity, a change in the exchange rate would influence the balance of payments, though in the opposite direction: A depreciation would deteriorate and an appreciation improve the balance rather than the other way round as in the usual case. In a free market this would lead to instability, because the demand and supply mechanism would work the wrong way. But if the exchanges are fixed and changed by government decision, no difficulties arise, provided the authorities are aware of the elasticity situation and, when gold flows out, appreciate the currency instead of depreciating it. (It should even make things easier and more pleasant, because an appreciation will be associated with an improvement in the terms of trade while a depreciation would reduce their value.) Now, it looks to me rather improbable, to say the least, that the elasticities could be precisely unity.[25,26]

Take a case of full employment. Suppose there is a disequilibrium in the balance of payments and gold flows; money income and prices are allowed to rise in the country which gains gold. Can there be any doubt that "under modern industrial conditions" (to use Marshall's phrase) the country will import more in value terms?[27] Suppose next that instead of letting prices and

[23] More precisely, that the sum of the two elasticities is unity. For a simple demonstration of this see Abba P. Lerner, *The Economics of Control* (New York, 1944), p. 378. If exports and imports are not equal, the *weighted* sum must be unity, the weights being the values of exports and imports.

[24] Dr. Albert Hirschman in an unpublished memorandum suggested this formula for clarifying the effects of devaluation upon the balance of payments. If we denote elasticities of demand for imports and exports by $t_i$ and $t_e$, respectively (and assume that the elasticity of supply is infinite), a devaluation will have a favorable effect on foreign balance provided: $t_e + \frac{I}{E} t_i > 1$. (I and E are the value of imports and exports, respectively.)

For a more elaborate discussion of these relationships, compare J. Robinson "The Foreign Exchanges," in *Essays in the Theory of Employment* (2d ed., 1947), and J. Polak "Exchange Depreciation and International Monetary Stability," in *Review of Economic Statistics*, August 1947.

[25] It is true they need not be unity over a large range. It is sufficient that the elasticity below the point of unitary elasticity is smaller, and above greater, than unity. But why should it not be the other way round?

[26] The following should, however, be noted: If the elasticities are greater than unity but are not very large, a devaluation would, it is true, improve the foreign balance, but at the cost of a deterioration of the terms of trade.

[27] It should be remembered that the elasticity of a country's demand for im-

money wages rise in the gold importing country we raise prices in that country, compared with the other country, by appreciating its currency. Why should the effect on imports be different than under the first method? The reason why in this case the price effect on imports is hardly subject to doubt is that by assuming full employment we have eliminated possible income effects in the upward direction—real income cannot rise any more. (It should be observed that income elasticities of international demand are defined in real, not in money, terms.) If there is much unemployment, the price effects may be smaller but the main difference, I suspect, is that they are swamped by income effects.

Professor Hansen says that over- or undervaluations of currencies (brought about by changes in the exchange rate or through other factors) are likely to show themselves in a price distortion resulting in unemployment and low activity level rather than in a disequilibrium of the balance of payments. If that statement is based on a denial of the efficacy of a change in the exchange rate to influence the balance of payments, I would not accept it for the reasons given above. It need, however, not imply that. It may be interpreted to mean that a comparatively small balance of payments deficit will quickly bring about sufficiently large income effects to correct the balance. In other words, it may be based on the supposition that the foreign trade multiplier[28] works so rapidly and efficiently, raising income in one and lowering it in the other country, that a small loss in the international reserve is sufficient to correct the balance. This hypothesis I find much more promising.[29]

---

ports is determined not only by the elasticity of demand of its consumers for the products of foreign lands but also by supply conditions, that is by the adjustability of production. That is what Marshall meant by "modern industrial conditions." I have the impression that those who question the likelihood of highly elastic reciprocal demands forget that vital element although Marshall laid great emphasis on it. Recognition of this fact suggests at once that the time element is important. Adjustments in the supply situation take time and can be impeded by tariff quotas, etc.

28 Here we think of the multiplier in a somewhat broader sense than the ordinary technical sense, comprising measures of "secondary" credit expansion and contraction taken in the gaining and losing countries respectively under the spur of the gold flow. In fact, the multiple credit system has been criticized for operating too efficiently in that respect. Cf., e.g., Hayek, *Monetary Nationalism and International Stability* (London, 1937), *passim*.

29 Anticipated income effects may be so strong as to blot out price effects for

Professor Hansen wishes to substitute for the purchasing power parity criterion, which is too "loose and ambiguous," a "cost-structure parity." I am afraid that this concept is even more ambiguous and loose than purchasing power parity. At any rate, it could be shown that the former is subject to exactly the same objections as the latter.[30]

This being so, I cannot share Professor Hansen's optimism that it will be easy to discover departures from an equilibrium exchange rate. Before we can detect them we surely must know what we are looking for.[31] I still believe that the managers of the Fund would be wise if they followed the rule of the original Keynes plan and granted permission to change the value of a currency only after a certain loss of gold has occurred, although it may also be good policy not to lay down publicly in advance any hard and fast rule to that effect.

Whether a loss of international reserves due to a cyclical depression abroad should be regarded as a fundamental disequilibrium and justify a currency depreciation depends on several circumstances. If the authorities are confident that it is a short-run difficulty, they should wait and, in the meantime, cover the loss, if it is of a manageable size, by credit. Temporary exchange control I would recommend only if it were stripped of all discriminatory features and steps were taken to prevent the

---

a while or even give the impression of a perverse price effect. Nurkse gives the following striking example: "Belgium . . . chose a rate [of depreciation] (28%) designed to leave a margin for an expansion. . . . This expansion materialized, and in consequence demand for foreign raw materials increased to such an extent that the first twelve months after the devaluation witnessed a sharp rise in the import surplus." *(International Currency Experience,* p. 128.) These raw materials were largely needed in export industries. Contrary to the first superficial impression, what happened does not support the hypothesis of perverse price elasticities. The case illustrates the pitfalls of a mechanical analysis in aggregate terms.

30 "Cost level" is after all also a price level, only a level of a different set of prices. Moreover, the set of prices to be included is not well defined. In that respect the "cost parity" is much inferior to the "purchasing power parity." The objection against any kind of price parity is not that there does not exist an equilibrium relationship under any given set of circumstances but that it is difficult to know what it is, because in general it is neither equality of a level at a point of time nor covariation over time, but some more complicated relationship.

31 The following definition might satisfy many: The equilibrium exchange rate is that rate which equilibrates the balance of payments under conditions of high (or full) employment everywhere. This definition is theoretically attractive, but for several reasons not suitable for policy purposes.

appearance of unearned windfall profits, because such profits would help to perpetuate the controls.[32] An exchange control, however, which answers these specifications comes very close to a thinly disguised depreciation.[33] But something can be said, it seems to me, in favor of a temporary, partial, *de facto* depreciation (in the form, for example, of a flat import tariff and export bounty) confined to commodities and services but not applicable to capital items and interest transfers.

[32] A type of nondiscriminatory exchange control which could be also described as a partial and temporary currency depreciation has been proposed by Dr. R. Triffin. See his article "National Central Banking and the International Economy" and my "Comments" in *International Monetary Policies, Postwar Economic Studies,* No. 7, September 1947, Board of Governors of the Federal Reserve System.

[33] Let me remind the reader that "deficit in the balance of payments" does not mean "deficit on current account." This follows, of course, from what was said above when it was pointed out that I use the usual definition of a deficit, viz., a decrease of the international reserve of a country. It is necessary to stress this once more in view of the fact that Dr. Thomas Balogh in the *Review of Economic Studies* (vol. XIV, 1946-47, p. 83) has completely misunderstood my definition. He says that I define as equilibrium rate that rate which "maintains the balance in international payments on current-account," although (cf. p. 385), I expressly say that "disequilibrium cannot be defined as a deficit in the current balance" and give reasons for this statement. Because of his misunderstanding, Dr. Balogh's strictures fall to the ground as far as I am concerned.

It is true, however, that Keynes in his posthumous article on the U. S. balance of payments in the *Economic Journal* uses the current balance as criterion of disequilibrium. (In an earlier article he used the same definition as I use. See on that point footnote 18 in the present article.) Although I do not accept Keynes's definition, I would not call it "odd," as Dr. Balogh does. What is really odd (and a source of many confusions) is the inability of Dr. Balogh and some other ultra-Keynesians to distinguish (a) the current balance (which is equal in size—although opposite in sign—to the combined gold and capital balance), (b) the gold balance, (c) the capital balance in the narrow sense (short- and long-term capital movements), and (d) the balance of gold plus equilibrating capital movements. Each of these balances is important for certain purposes. In the present context the distinction between (a) and (d) is relevant. See my chapter on "Dollar Shortage" in the present volume for further discussion of these matters.

# 22

# DISPARITY IN POSTWAR EXCHANGE RATES

Paul A. Samuelson

## *I. Introduction*

There are admittedly numerous theoretical weaknesses of the purchasing power parity doctrine, as enunciated by Gustav Cassel and others. Still, something of a pragmatic case can be made for its consequences when applied to the dislocated exchange rate situation of (1) the immediate post-World War I period, and (2) the depressed 1930's.

In the hands of Cassel one of the most important functions of purchasing power parity was the defense of *de facto* postwar exchange rates against the almost unthinking demand of some economists and bankers for a return to prewar mint parities. To a first approximation, purchasing power parity's great virtue was its implicit recognition that price levels could not be easily "rolled back" to prewar levels—in short, its defense of the *status quo* as against the *status quo ante bellum*.

In the years after 1929, purchasing power parity played a minor role in economic discussions. But, generally speaking, the influence of purchasing power calculations was in the direction of causing those countries which had devalued their currencies least to depreciate their currencies. There are exceptions to this, but the Belgian case and that of the gold bloc provide important illustrations.

As a result, therefore, by the time the world had experienced considerable recovery in the middle and late 1930's, we found ourselves back at almost the same relative exchange rates as before the crash[1]—but, of course, with all currencies devalued

[1] League of Nations, *International Currency Experience*, p. 129.

in terms of gold. While no one can prove that this pattern constituted an optimal result—and certainly its time path of realization was far from ideal—still it is not a *prima facie* indefensible one.

## *II. Purchasing Power Parity and Present Exchange Rates*

Let us grant therefore that purchasing power parity calculation did not lead to too bad results in the two major periods of international crisis prior to World War II. What then of its import for the present postwar period? What will the consequences be of neglecting its testimony, as has been done recently in setting the initial Monetary Fund exchange rates on the basis of the immediate *status quo?*

Broadly speaking, the initial exchange rates accepted by the Fund yield exchange rates for the rest of the world that are "overvalued" and a U. S. dollar that is apparently "undervalued."[2] That is to say, exchange rates abroad had not fallen by as much as their prices had risen in relation to ours. Was this neglect of purchasing power a grave mistake?

Now in a sense it is quite possible to argue that the Fund authorities had little discretion in the matter, it being necessary in terms of political expediency to accept the wishes of its member nations relative to the *status quo*. There is much to this; for example, one can immediately envisage the difficulties at the time of getting the United States to lower its buying price of gold. But let us leave these political considerations aside. Should not the member countries, if more enlightened, have desired a nearer approach to purchasing power parity?

I, for one, have not the courage to answer this question dogmatically. There is nothing sacred about the *status quo,* but the strong burden of proof must be thrown onto any doctrine that favors an extreme, and generally unpopular, departure from the prevailing state. Neither purchasing power parity nor other theoretical doctrines of international trade equilibrium

[2] See Lloyd A. Metzler's article in *International Monetary Proposals, Postwar Economic Studies* No. 7 of the Federal Reserve Board (1947), pp. 25ff. The U. K. is an apparent exception to this generalization. Her prices have been so well controlled relative to the rest of the world that her index gives a seeming picture of "undervaluation" of the pound.

have at this time, and as applied to present abnormal conditions, the theoretical or empirical validity necessary to justify strong conviction in favor of a drastic and radical gamble—which is what extensive revision of exchange rates would imply. And it is part of my diagnosis that such allegedly corrective action would have to be quantitatively fairly drastic rather than moderate. It is only reasonable to expect further revision of rates in the future; but the fulfillment of this expectation will not be proof that present rates were a mistake.

To put matters bluntly, purchasing power parity works best when *no substantive changes* in the world have taken place, but only "fictitious scale changes in price levels." One has only to look at the devastation and disorganization wrought by the war, the permanently changed pattern of international indebtedness, and the sweeping alterations in political and social structures, to realize that the essence of the present-day problem is an important substantive change in the whole international trade situation. One can hardly argue convincingly that the very real problem of "universal" dollar shortage arose primarily out of differential price level movements of the usual sort. The reverse is, in my opinion, more nearly true.

### *III. Elasticity of Demand?*

I should go farther and argue that there are reasons to doubt the efficacy of correcting the present abnormal situation by exchange rate variations and relative price movements of the classical type. Among other things, the classical pattern of adjustment rested upon the empirical faith of very strong elasticities of reciprocal international demands. For example, if the U. S. export surplus is equal to about one-half of our total exports, minor exchange rate variations of not more than 10 per cent could only wipe out the surplus if the "net" elasticity of reciprocal[3] demand were very great indeed. A net demand elasticity of 2.0 or 3.0 would require a tremendous relative exchange rate and price change to wipe out the enormous postwar unbalances.

For an instant let me grant the extreme possibility that the

[3] As defined in section V of this paper.

dollar-shortage areas all have great net elasticities of international demand. To bring out an important element almost completely neglected in recent discussions, I shall even suppose that this elasticity is infinite, so that practically no deterioration of the terms of trade is needed to "rectify" any given import surplus. From many current discussions, one would be tempted to infer that such a rectification would then be almost completely costless!

Of course, nothing could be farther from the truth. Suppose Marshall Plan aid of, say, 5 billion dollars per annum ceases a few years from now. The loss to Europe will necessarily be a loss of at least that much worth of goods and services. She will have at least that much less of output available for domestic consumption or capital formation.

At the end of World War I, economists discussing reparations at first naïvely concentrated solely on the "primary burden" of a unilateral international payment, only gradually becoming aware of a possible "secondary" burden involved in the deterioration of terms of trade caused by the transfer. After World War II, economists have become so sophisticated as to push to the background of the discussion everything *but* the secondary burden.

Great elasticity of demand will, at best, moderate the secondary burden involved in rectifying present universal unbalance. The primary burden—which, if the optimistic classical theory were correct, would be the more important cost—would still remain. Over and beyond the real aspect of the primary burden, there is also the inflationary pressure induced by a reduction in available domestic output.

The secondary burden must now be examined. If we lump the rest of the world facing the United States into one unit, it becomes no longer a question of a single small country facing an elastic world demand. On the contrary, considering the war-induced urgency of world need for our products, the scarcity and inelasticity of foreigners' domestic supply, and the character of U. S. importing, we cannot be even sure that the net demand elasticity is greater than one. Therefore, we cannot even be sure that lowering the value of an already overvalued currency will make the situation any better at all. If the net elasticity is in a fairly wide range around the critical value of unity, no feasible exchange rate depreciation change would appreciably affect the discrepancy in the balance of U. S. trade with the rest of the world. But if the exchange rate variation is even to begin to work as envisaged by classical theory, it will succeed in turning the terms of trade substantially against Europe—for if it does not work in this direction, the classical remedy is licked to begin with. Even where a considerable net elasticity of international demand occurred, exchange depreciation would to some degree further impoverish the impoverished and increase the strain on Congressional generosity.

There remains the possibility that in the present state of trade between the United States and the rest of the world, net international demand is very inelastic. In this case the cure for so-called overvalued currencies is more overvaluation. Perhaps the United States should then be asked to raise its buying price of gold and to make the dollar cheaper to foreigners. Theoretically, a new free exchange rate might be found at which the dollar shortage would disappear. However, such an intersection of international supply and demand curves would be an "unstable" one,[4] so that any momentary departure from equilibrium would be self-aggravating and cumulative. Orthodox stabilization fund operations would encounter difficulties in maintaining exchange rate stability in free markets at such an unstable intersection, and in all probability recourse would be had to supplementary exchange control methods not unlike those now prevailing.

On the whole, therefore, the case of inelastic demand does not provide much comfort for us economists who personally favor a maximum of freedom in international trade. We cannot recommend to authorities—Go thou and adopt an equilibrium rate of exchange. At the least we must definitely tell them—depreciate your currencies; or appreciate them. And I have not yet encountered many liberal economists who are willing to stick their necks out in favor of the latter.

[4] See the discussion of Joan Robinson's analysis in section VI below.

### *IV. Agriculture Versus Industry*

The probable elasticity of demand between the United States and the rest of the world is a difficult question of fact, concerning which it would be dangerous to make dogmatic assertions. There is some weight of theoretical authority in favor of the view of considerable elasticity; but there may be an element of wishful thinking in this position, and the extraordinary character of the postwar scene may rob customary relations of their usual validity.

On the other hand the testimony of practical observers and so-called experts seems usually to be in favor of the view that demands are rather inelastic. But the few of these whom I have interrogated on the matter have not been able to advance any very elaborate arguments in favor of their opinion, having had instead to fall back upon their best intuitive view of the situation.

Perhaps it will help bring the question into perspective if we consider the problem, not simply as one between regions, but as one between prices of agricultural foodstuffs and raw materials and prices of industrial products.[5] Agricultural staples are notoriously of short-run inelastic supply, or even in some cases of negative elasticity of supply. Their demand is usually considered to be of rather low price elasticity. When both supply and demand are rather inelastic a free price system works least well, and prices are prone to considerable amplitude of fluctuations as a result of even small shifts in the schedules. If we add to this basic fact the wartime reductions in supplies from many regions of the globe and the higher demands for food resulting from an increase in postwar money income and from equalitarian programs all over the world, the expected result can be a tremendous increase in food and raw material prices, a tremendous redistribution of real and money income as between urban and rural families, a tremendous increase in the economic rents from farming and mining.

[5] This comparison is suggestive rather than rigorous. Many agricultural countries also have their dollar shortage problems. But in part—as the case of Canada so well illustrates—this is due to the failure of multilateral convertibility of their favorable balances with such "soft currency" countries as the U. K.

Our theoretical expectations are fully matched by the quantitative revolution in the prices of staples. As compared to depression lows, the price of wheat has increased tenfold. The cost of food has more than doubled so that the percentage of disposable income spent by American families on food has significantly increased. Net farm cash incomes have more than tripled.

The end is perhaps only now coming into sight, and the wonder is that the process did not go farther than it actually did. The reason is not hard to find: throughout the war almost universal rationing and direct controls served to hold in the demand for staples so as to keep free market forces from bidding up the imputed rents of factors of production inelastic in supply. At the moment the United States has abandoned most of its direct controls; but exchange controls and internal direct controls all over much of the rest of the world are still holding in a tremendous volume of demand for basic necessities of life. One can scarcely doubt that a simultaneous release of these forces of extra demand would—other things equal—result in a further increase in basic materials' prices, in further redistribution in favor of agriculture, and a tendency toward further adverse balances of trade on the part of European countries.

If the present supply-demand situation were to be permanent, some serious problems of basic policy would be raised. Shall nations continue direct controls permanently in order to keep competitive forces from raising basic prices against them and thus reducing their real standards of living? This is not unlike the reverse problem of seemingly chronic agricultural surpluses in the years before the war. The answer rests upon considerations of administration, politics, and even ethics.

But if the problem is one simply of the next few years, the scales will be tilted more in favor of a rather gradual relaxation of exchange and direct domestic control.[6] Such a solution is by no means ideal. Leaving out the problem of over-all inflation

[6] On balance it might still be a good thing to abolish direct controls because of their detrimental effects upon productivity at a time of "suppressed inflation." Questions of fact, of economic analysis, and of political philosophy must be weighed in arriving at a decision on this question. Judgment is made all the more difficult by the fact that the cure for many of the evils of suppressed inflation may be *either more or less controls*—a halfway house being the worst possible situation.

that might result from relaxation of all controls, and concentrating only on relative prices and well-being, we can argue that the world would be better off to let the food-producing countries receive higher prices and, if desirable, make gifts to the impoverished countries to compensate them for the deterioration of the terms of trade. But I am afraid that this is utopian and irrelevant; there are very real political limitations on gifts, and already the world has probably reached its limit in this respect.

## *V. Technical Problem of Interpretation*

I have intentionally glossed over a few technicalities. The equilibrating efficacy of exchange rate variations does not depend upon each of the two countries' having an elastic demand. The critical question is now recognized to be whether the sum of the two elasticities—the "net elasticity"—is greater or less than unity.

It is also necessary to distinguish between (1) the elasticity of real exports and imports with respect to a real change in the terms of trade, and (2) the elasticity of the trade balance with respect to exchange rate variations. Thus, suppose that real international reciprocal demands are actually very elastic with respect to the worsening of the terms of trade of a debtor nation. But suppose that exchange depreciation intensifies the inflationary spiral within the debtor country so as to cause prices and costs to rise by as much as the exchange has fallen. The terms of trade will not have fallen at all, and the resultant elasticity of the trade balance with respect to the exchange rate will give the appearance of being exactly unity, so that exchange variations will not improve the balance of payments. An omnipotent slide-rule parity theorist would keep adjusting the exchange rate downward only to find that prices move so as to make the exchange always overvalued, with the result an endless exchange spiral.[7]

This cooked-up illustration is in many ways entirely germane to the present scene. Much of the world is in the throes of ex-

[7] The early 1948 experience with the devaluation of the French franc may provide an illustrative case, although it is still too soon to say.

plicit or held-in inflation, and this is not simply the result of a wanton diarrhea of money on the part of Treasuries and Central Banks. People as a whole want what they cannot have in the postwar world, and, if uncontrolled, free market forces would lead to inflationary spirals. Nor does it help much to proffer smug advice concerning Spartan fiscal and monetary measures to governments already on the brink of political disaster. But to pursue this line of thought would lead us into the more remote fields of politics and sociology.

However, there does still remain one related technicality concerning some of the current interpretations of purchasing power calculations. Many writers tend to regard purchasing power parity as, under certain conditions, a truism; and, under other conditions, as definitely untrue. When a truism it is thought to be useless; but when untrue, the doctrine becomes potentially useful. This is a case of capitalizing with a vengeance on a theory's inadequacies and weaknesses; a case where the exception not only proves the rule but improves it as well.

If one has already made the error of falsely identifying purchasing power parity with a narrow theory of spatial price relationships, there is some justification for this paradoxical belief. Two wrongs can be nearer the truth than one. But even in this context possible confusion is involved.

Let me illustrate by considering the present situation where universal exchange control cloaks overvaluation of exchange rates. Prices abroad are too high compared to U. S. prices, at least in terms of free market forces. Now let us drop the crutch of exchange control. Something will have to give way. But can prices abroad and here be expected to remain constant so that it will be the exchange rate that will have to give all the way? Something like this is assumed by the usual quantitative calculation of parity.

If we still believe, as did Cassel, that Central Banks can, and do, easily control the quantity of money and, through the Quantity Theory, the level of prices, there would be something to be said for this bold assumption. But when we have come to believe that John L. Lewis has more to do with prices than does the Federal Reserve Board and that the 1948 rainfall in the wheat belt may have more lasting effects on the index of wholesale prices than interest rate policy, doubts creep in.

Even more specifically, we must realize that one-sided obstacles to trade are themselves substantive changes in international trade, and their removal is also a substantive change. Their removal will directly lower the spread between foreign and domestic prices. Any parity exchange rate calculated from data gathered while the restrictions are in force cannot be extrapolated to the restrictionless situation except with modifications and caution.[8]

To sum up by repeating the almost obvious: it is illegitimate to take price relationships as given and to assume complete passive adjustment of exchange rates. The problem is one of mutual determination, and especially complex under present abnormal conditions. Temporary controls and distortions of price relationships do not make purchasing power more valid; they simply make the exchange rate problem more significant—which is not to say less difficult.

## *VI. The "Dollar Shortage"*

Disequilibrium in the balance of payments can arise from many reasons. Many of these are of a temporary nature and easily jibe with the simple formulations of the orthodox international trade mechanism. But the problem of the so-called chronic "dollar shortage" is something else again. Precise descriptions of what is meant by this concept are hard to find. Indeed if one interprets the classical theory of comparative advantage in a narrow sense, such a chronic unbalance will appear to be an impossibility.

[8] That most writers are at least dimly aware of this difficulty is seen by their concern with the artificial character of many official price statistics, since these represent prices of rationed commodities not freely obtainable at the stated prices. Yet sometimes it is almost argued that it is the controls and imperfections of the price series that alone make the parity theory "interesting." "Under wartime conditions calculations of purchasing power parities are, from one point of view, more useful than under normal conditions . . . Because the war has interrupted international trade, wholesale prices in the various countries can move independently. Therefore their relative change provides a better measure of comparative price level changes than in peacetime." G. Haberler, "The Choice of Exchange Rates," *American Economic Review*, vol. 35 (June 1945), p. 313.

However, from a broader view of the pure theory of international trade, such a chronic condition can certainly exist as an actual possibility. For example, it is simply not true to say that the theory of comparative cost proves that one country cannot continue to "undersell" another in every commodity. If one assumes only simple barter to be possible, then *ex definitione* goods can only be exchanged against goods. But this is a postulate, not a theorem. The question has been begged not proved.

To do justice to the pure theory of international trade, we must be willing to admit the possibility of capital movements. In this case, it is perfectly possible for one country continually to export more than its imports, the difference being made up by securities or I.O.U.'s. In this sense, one country may undersell another in every line of activity. More than that, it is possible for each country in a sense to be underselling the other *at the same time:* namely, when each is giving away exports to the other for I.O.U.'s which will later be repudiated.

There is nothing then in the pure theory of comparative cost that prevents the rest of the world from continually obligating itself to pay (in the future) for more American goods than it can pay for by barter. There is nothing in the theory from preventing such one-way borrowing from leading to periodic financial collapse—to be followed by a renewal of the same process after confidence and gullibility have been restored. Note that (1) no flow of gold need be induced by the process; (2) no exchange rate depreciation need result; and (3) no self-correcting specie-price mechanism or (4) income-multiplier mechanism need be set up by the process so as to put off the evil day of general financial collapse. The fact that the I.O.U.'s might be long-term securities rather than short-term would not alter the process, or its aftermath, even though many of the recent definitions of exchange equilibrium (à la Nurkse and Haberler)[9] would seem to regard the situation as an equilibrium one up to the moment of revealed bankruptcy.

[9] R. Nurkse, "Conditions of International Monetary Equilibrium," *Princeton Essays in International Finance,* No. 4, Spring, 1945; see also Haberler's Comments in the previously cited Federal Reserve *Postwar Economic Studies,* No. 7, pp. 99-102.

If the authorities of both the debtor or creditor countries are free to pursue any coöperative policies, and if they wish to end the chronic dollar shortage, there is much they can do about it. But they are not free. And the measures they take to "correct" the situation will have repercussions on (a) unemployment, on (b) inflation, (c) on terms of trade, (d) on available national output, and (e) on relative exchange rates. I put the word "correct" in quotation marks because there is nothing in the analytical theory of welfare economics—new or old—that assures us that the so-called equilibrium situation *sans* dollar shortage is "better" or "fairer" than the "uncorrected" situation. The equilibrium situation is perhaps in a sense more permanent and maintainable. That is all.[10]

So far I have been talking in generalities. I have shown that the possibility of a chronic dollar shortage or surplus is perfectly consistent with theory. Let me now turn to the empirical reasons for the dollar shortage both in its chronic aspects independently of the war, and also in its immediate postwar context.

The United States is the richest country in the world. Also, it is the pace-setter in technological progress, and increasingly in setting fashions of standards of life. It is natural for the poor to want to borrow from the rich. It is also natural for the rich to have the surplus income to lend to the poor. If the rich man has had trouble—however caused—in finding investment outlets for his money, the case is that much more probable.

It is also natural for the poor often to default on their obligations to the rich. And in the absence of international bailiffs who can "attach" the property of the poor, it is natural for the rich to go unpaid even when the poor are not totally devoid of assets.[11]

[10] For even this to be true, the current definition of equilibrium as involving the absence of short-term capital and gold movements needs careful reformulation, after which it will be dangerously near to a tautology incapable of empirical application.

[11] Historically within the United States, the frontier West has experienced a chronic dollar shortage in its relation with the East; but nationalism and sovereignty have not impeded the problem of creditors in receiving their due. See also P. A. Samuelson, *Economics* (McGraw-Hill, 1948), pp. 367-368.

It is not unnatural for the rich to tire of this game of "hold the bag"; when the poor country cannot find private investors who will accept I.O.U.'s, the exchange rate must fall. The debtor country offers its I.O.U.'s (currency, etc.) at lower and lower prices. So long as foreign lenders remain adamant and net commodity demands inelastic, there is no end to the process. It becomes cumulative and self-aggravating.

Recently Mrs. Robinson has argued[12] that "it can be shown that, from a formal point of view, this objection [of perverse inelasticity of demand] is not fatal to the classical analysis."[13] I do not disagree with the spirit of her remarks, but they do seem to require three modifications in their application to the present discussion.

The first qualification is within the realm of the purest formal theory and can be relegated to a footnote.[14] The second point to be noticed (as Mrs. Robinson is clearly aware) is that the existence of an elastic range of the curves beyond the prevailing region of inelasticity means that the quantitative adjustment of exchange rates and relative price levels must be very drastic indeed. The balance of trade gets worse before it gets better; therefore, the terms of trade must deteriorate to a tremendous degree. This could be elaborated upon in greater detail by the use of the concept of arc elasticity.

Thirdly, as soon as we drop the assumption of pure barter of goods against goods, the doctrine of eventual elasticity of demand sufficient to wipe out any deficit in the balance of payments not only fails to be formally true as a universal generalization, but in addition the empirical exceptions become more likely. To see this, imagine that both rich and poor countries

[12] J. Robinson, "The Pure Theory of International Trade," *Review of Economic Studies*, vol. XIV (1946-47), pp. 100-102.

[13] *Ibid.*, p. 100.

[14] From a rigorous mathematical viewpoint, her formal proposition seems to be incorrect. At the critical point in her argument she assumes as obvious what is not universally necessarily true. She says "at some point the goods become so expensive relative to world money incomes that demand turns elastic . . . and there is some level . . . at which exports fall to zero." I grant that it is customary to draw demand curves so that at high prices they touch the price axis and become elastic. Probably, this is realistic. But it is not universally necessary as a matter of logic. It is easy to specify indifference curves such that demand is *always* inelastic.

produce and consume only a single homogeneous commodity, say chocolates. Under barter assumptions, differences in (opportunity) cost are obviously meaningless since there is only one commodity, and the simplest neo-classical theory of comparative advantage tells us that trade is an absurdity. Admitting now the possibility of capital movements, suppose that the poor country has an initial amount of non-producible non-augmentable gold or an equivalent line of credit upon which it can draw over a period of time.

Is there any permanent cheapening of its relative prices that will necessarily cause it not to run an import surplus? If there were a central decision-making authority in the poor country, it would realize that regardless of the exchange rate the poor country could currently consume all of its domestic chocolates and import as well. Depending upon time preference, a deterioration of the terms of trade between gold and imported chocolates might indefinitely speed up the value of imports.

Assuming atomistic competition in both countries and more than one commodity forces us to reëxamine the above result. Consumers in either country feel that they can acquire more of either home or imported goods at going market prices. If their demands for the product of the poor and rich country are relatively elastic, then exchange rate and terms of trade changes will tend to reduce the import surplus of the poor country. But with capital movements possible, we require more than that there be elasticity of demand. There must be enough elasticity of demand of commodity balance to outweigh the previously desired capital movement. There is no geometrical or empirical reason why there should ever be that much elasticity of demand.[15]

To illustrate this argument, consider the hypothetical question: is there any permanent increase in American prices relative to England that would necessarily make the American loan to Britain last *longer?*

The above theoretical discussion of the dollar shortage is

[15] In technical terms if one or both of the Marshallian international offer curves are shifted by capital movements, then, even if they are of normal shape, they need never intersect.

meant to be suggestive rather than exhaustive. Very briefly now, I should like to point out a few reasons why the current postwar shortage of dollars is especially acute. Monetary mismanagement and clumsily suppressed inflation are certainly part of the story, but I suspect far from all.

The wartime devastation and loss of European foreign assets is of course very great. Perhaps even more important is the war-induced disorganization of production. Europe is an *off-balance* economy, full of petty shortages which spread in vicious circles. Things in themselves not important become important in such an environment. Steel is short, but it takes steel to make steel; it takes coal to make calories and it takes calories to make coal. Inept price controls are partly to blame (witness the case of Germany), but the alternative would often be open inflation of sizable proportions—and, paradoxically, in going from barely tolerable suppressed inflation to open inflation might involve in the process riots and worse.

Commodity stocks in Europe are at a low ebb. Needs and demands accumulated during the war are at a high level. Military expenditures are economically costly. Equalitarian programs add to the excess demands of those who previously were in a superior economic position and who still have considerable liquid and non-liquid assets.

All this leads to an especially acute current dollar shortage. By 1951, it may not be easy to wean Europe of American aid but conditions should be much more favorable.

## *VII. Conclusion*

Bigger issues than those of international trade mechanics are involved in the question of free exchange rates. Many nations all over the world have forsaken the paths of liberalism in favor of governmental planning. In the Fund and International Bank, we have pledged ourselves not to force our economic doctrines on the rest of the world, much as we would recommend them. But the question of exchange control necessarily cuts across this domestic ideological problem. If a socialist government abroad wishes to supplement its income tax structure with a policy of curbing imports of luxury goods in favor of necessities or capital equipment, then we may privately disapprove. But without risking the charge of supporting imperialism and being a propagandist, we cannot raise objections. Yet that is what insisting upon free exchanges comes close to doing. Or what insisting upon financial belt-tightening measures abroad often appears like to foreign eyes.

There remains no valid alternative but to proceed cautiously, compromising, if one wishes to put it that way, with evil, but not thereby forgetting that unnecessary distortion of an efficient international division of labor does represent an evil for all parties concerned. However—fortunately or unfortunately—this does not qualify for the top rank of evils that the world faces today.

# 23

## *EXCHANGE CONTROL AND EQUILIBRIUM*

Robert Triffin[1]

The very title of this paper—"Exchange Control and Equilibrium"— is testimony to the changes that have taken place in our economic thinking over the last decade. Until very recently, even the most representative and eminent studies on international economics and finance could dismiss the whole problem summarily with the observation that exchange control is the most harmful of all interferences with freedom of trade, because it prevents the operation of normal reëquilibrating forces, and tends to perpetuate, rather than correct, the potential balance of payments maladjustments which call forth the adoption of the controls.

Lesser writers would be carried further by their arguments and demonstrate easily the superiority of free and stable exchanges over any system of exchange control, destructive of international trade. This, of course, is irrelevant when any of the practical alternatives to exchange control—barring an indefinite piling up of deficits in a country's international transactions—must also involve of necessity a reduction in imports and other expenditures abroad.[2] The fact that exchange control achieves this result should, in such cases, be counted as a virtue rather than a vice.

Any practical discussion of exchange control techniques must therefore assess their advantages and disadvantages, as com-

[1] The author is a member of the staff of the International Monetary Fund, but the views he expresses are entirely his own and do not in any way reflect the views or policies of the Fund.

[2] There remains, of course, the possibility of eliminating the deficit by expanding exports, but such a solution often lies beyond the practical possibilities of the deficit country. See below, pp. 417ff.

pared to other methods—all painful and undesirable, but none the less necessary—to finance or eliminate a balance of payments deficit. The following alternatives come immediately to mind: 1. The financing of the deficit through the use of accumulated reserves, or the receipt of loans or grants from abroad. 2. The deflation of domestic prices and costs, in order to stimulate exports and curtail imports. 3. The devaluation of the currency, with the same objective in view. 4. The institution of quantitative import controls. 5. Increases in tariffs. Other, and less obvious, alternatives may lie in various fiscal measures designed to encourage exports—tax remittances or subsidies—or to curtail imports either directly—for example, through excise taxes on articles which are largely of foreign origin—or indirectly—through high taxation of incomes most likely to give rise to foreign expenditures.

This classification of alternative techniques, however, can only serve as a starting point for our discussion. While useful from an institutional or descriptive point of view, it tends to confuse the real issue, that is, the comparative effects and incidence of alternative policies on the balance of payments and, indeed, the whole economy of the country.

From this point of view, we should differentiate:

1. Between general controls of an undifferentiated character, and selective controls whose incidence is directed more precisely toward certain categories of transactions. Deflation or devaluation would generally belong to the first group, and tariffs, import quotas, exchange control, and fiscal measures to the second.

2. Between corrective measures, and stopgap—often called "conservation"—measures. Here, devaluation, deflation, fiscal policy, and tariffs would definitely belong to the first group.[3] On the other hand, and contrary to the view which seems to dominate discussions of the subject, import controls and especially exchange controls may belong to either group, depending on the exact techniques adopted.

[3] The financing of the deficit through the use of reserves, loans, or grants also falls in part in the first group if automatic deflationary effects are not offset by opposite monetary and fiscal policies.

We touch here on a fundamental defect of most discussions of the problem, that is, the tendency to argue words rather than facts, and the failure to realize the extraordinary diversity of techniques cloaked under the same term "exchange control." The last section of this paper will return to this problem, but first we should discuss briefly the first distinction mentioned above, that is, general versus selective controls.

### *General versus Selective Controls*

The main advantages of deflation—whether automatic or induced—and devaluation as remedies for balance of payments deficits are that they constitute the lesser interference with economic freedom and motivations, and that they may resorb the deficit not only through their incidence on imports, but also through stimulating exports. Their main shortcomings, on the other hand, are their lack of selectiveness and the fact that while increasing the volume of exports, they may well *decrease* export receipts through deterioration of the country's terms of trade.

Because of its lack of selectiveness, devaluation curtails indifferently essential as well as nonessential imports. During, or immediately following, a process of domestic inflation, it may even affect the first more than the second, because of the inflationary distortion of incomes from the lower to the higher income groups, and of expenditures from essentials to luxuries. More important, however, is the fact that the necessary contraction in imports, especially in the case of inelastic demand, will depend in part on the decline of real national income. Since only a fraction of a country's total income is spent abroad, the income contraction required to curtail import expenditure may be several times the size of the needed import cut. From this point of view, deflation fares even worse, because of the additional discouragement to business activity associated with the slow and painful process of downward price adjustments.

Selective controls, on the other hand, make it possible to concentrate the main burden of the restrictions on luxuries or, at least, less essential imports, and to bridge the gap in the balance of payments without the multiple income contraction mentioned above. They involve, however, a greater or lesser degree of interference with the freedom of income recipients to spend it as they wish. The choice involves here the basic problem of evaluating the actual distribution of incomes in the country concerned. If this distribution is generally deemed satisfactory and desirable, selective controls should be resorted to only as a temporary expedient to tide the country over a passing emergency. They should be rejected if the disequilibrium is of such a fundamental character as to require permanent measures to correct a persistent tendency toward balance of payments deficits.

A tendency to overimport may go hand in hand with an excessive distortion in income patterns. This is a problem of many undeveloped countries—in Latin America, for instance—in which an extremely uneven distribution of national income is one of the factors leading to a weak balance of payments position. Increases in national income tend to accrue first to the richer groups and to create balance of payments difficulties because of these groups' propensity to import luxuries from abroad and to keep their savings or even bank balances abroad. As a result, national income is prevented from rising as much as it might, because of the resulting balance of payments pressures and their deflationary repercussions on the national economy. The problem becomes all the more acute when development programs are undertaken, involving both larger imports and increased domestic incomes. It then becomes especially necessary to increase savings and to direct them toward useful employment at home rather than capital absenteeism.

In any case, wherever selective controls are deemed preferable, the nature of the controls should be chosen in such a way as to minimize administrative interference with individual choices of action. From this point of view alone,[4] tariff increases or other fiscal measures would be superior to import quotas, and exchange taxes or multiple exchange rates to quantitative exchange restrictions. Rather than assign import or exchange licenses through bureaucratic action, all necessary restrictions

[4] Less philosophical arguments strongly reinforce this conclusion. See below, pp. 422ff.

can be operated through the price mechanism, leaving importers free—but at a cost—to import *whatever they please from wherever they please.*

The second advantage of deflation or devaluation over most exchange and import control systems is that their effect is not only to contract imports and other expenditures abroad, but also to stimulate exports, tourist receipts, etc. There is little doubt that lower domestic prices, or a lower valuation of the currency, will tend to encourage the volume of exports and other activities productive of foreign exchange. If the demand for the country's exports is fairly elastic, export proceeds will increase and permit a readjustment of the balance of payments at a higher level of imports and foreign expenditures than would be the case otherwise.

On the other hand, if foreign demand for the country's exports is inelastic, devaluation will decrease export proceeds, measured in foreign currencies, even though the volume of exports is increased. If the elasticity of demand is unity, export proceeds will be unaffected, but the country will be giving up a larger volume of goods without improving its foreign exchange receipts.

Devaluation, therefore, will be advantageous from the export point of view only if the world demand for the country's exports is substantially larger than unity. We must be careful, however, not to exaggerate the impact of this argument. Some people have seen in it a condemnation of devaluation as entirely futile for agricultural or raw material producing countries, because the demand for such commodities is usually relatively inelastic. The fact that demand for coffee is probably inelastic does not mean that the demand for a single country's coffee exports is also inelastic. On the contrary, a reduction in the dollar price of Colombian coffee, for instance—consequent to a devaluation of the Colombian peso—would probably increase the demand for Colombian coffee very considerably, not so much because of an increase in over-all demand, but through its redirection toward the cheaper supplier.

The real obstacles to the stimulation of a country's exports are of a different character. First of all, the competing countries which suffer an inroad on their exports may retaliate and devalue their currency also. In this case, it is the over-all demand and its elasticity—rather than the demand for the exports of that particular country—which become significant. In the 1930's, the nearly simultaneous depreciation of most coffee-producing countries was probably one of the factors in the catastrophic decline of coffee prices, and curtailed, rather than expanded, export proceeds. Devaluation, to be successful, must not be widely imitated by competing countries. It is most likely to be so imitated, and most likely to fail, if it is adopted as a remedy to an export contraction resulting from an economic crisis engulfing all, or a large group of, countries. It is least likely to evoke retaliation, and most likely to succeed, if it is adopted by a country as a corrective for export difficulties arising from a localized inflation of prices and costs which has priced the country's exports out of the world markets.

A second obstacle to an expansion of export proceeds through devaluation of the currency may be the inability to increase the export volume itself. In the absence of stockpiling and price maintenance policies, many agricultural countries sell all their exportable production at whatever prices the market may bring. Devaluation, in that case, cannot expand exports, although it may be useful to restore domestic profit margins.

The most extreme, and most recent, example of the same difficulty was recently faced by the International Monetary Fund when establishing par values for its members in December 1946. Many countries were admittedly in a situation of fundamental disequilibrium, but of a structural character which could not be affected immediately or decisively by a mere devaluation of the currency. Until reconstruction policies had had time to take effect and bring about an improvement in production, balance of payments deficits would continue and would have to be financed in part, and in part reduced, by direct control measures rather than by devaluation. As compared to selective controls, a readjustment of the balance of payments through currency depreciation might have involved intolerable suffering and driven down the exchange rate far more than was necessary or useful in the long run.

In some cases, the problem of the structural deficit was accompanied by currency overvaluation in terms of comparative prices and costs and the currency would have to be devalued at some future time. The timing of this devaluation, however, was of paramount importance. In the sellers' markets then prevailing exports were, in many cases, held in check by production difficulties rather than price considerations, and no amount of devaluation could have increased their level substantially. The result of devaluation would then have been to increase inflationary pressures at home, without any immediate benefits, but with long run positive harm, to the balance of payments position. The proper timing for devaluation, when needed, would rather be the time when sagging world prices, or increased domestic costs, would begin to squeeze out exporters' margins and act as a break upon exports. The parities were thus accepted with the warning that many of them would have to be changed at a later date. In the meantime, exchange or import controls were again necessary to limit the flow of imports and keep balance of payments deficits within manageable proportions.

The substitutability of controls for devaluation, in such cases, is clearly of a limited character. There comes a point when the attempt to ward off exchange readjustments through exchange controls decreases exports by reducing production, or by diverting it toward alternative domestic uses, including hoarding. Such a point will be reached sooner in the diversified economies of Western Europe than in monoculture countries where export goods or resources have no alternative domestic outlet.

In conclusion, the choice between devaluation (or deflation) and other more selective measures to readjust the balance of payments is a very complex question, the solution of which depends on the particular circumstances of the concrete problem at hand. In general, we may say that devaluation will be more justified to correct difficulties arising in a single country from monetary factors, for example, a previous inflation which has distorted prices and costs in relation with foreign countries. On the other hand, the appropriateness of devaluation will be more doubtful in the case of structural disequilibrium or of a generalized economic crisis engulfing a large number of competing countries. In such cases, the deterioration of the terms of trade, implicit in currency devaluation, may affect export proceeds unfavorably. Moreover, whenever the volume of production is limited by other factors, devaluation may cause useless increases in domestic prices and aggravate domestic inflationary forces without profit to the balance of payments. Selective control measures which avoid such results may then prove preferable, especially if the difficulties are of a temporary rather than a permanent character.

Other considerations of many kinds will, of course, qualify these generalizations in each concrete case. Some of them will be considered in the following section.

### *Corrective versus Stopgap Measures*

Devaluation (or deflation) lowers domestic prices and costs in relation to foreign prices and costs, and tends to restore the competitiveness of national production both in the domestic and in the world market. Quantitative restrictions, on the other hand, fail to improve the cost position of the country and to correct any tendency toward a fundamental deficit of the balance of payments.

This defect may, however, turn into an advantage if the deficit is due only to temporary, rather than fundamental factors. If the difficulties originate in a bad crop, or in a cyclical depression in foreign markets, it may be counter-indicated to reinforce the resulting deflationary influences through deliberate monetary policy. Even from an international point of view, a readjustment of the exchange to eliminate a *temporary* deficit will leave the currency *fundamentally* undervalued, and will become a further source of international maladjustments when the short-lived factors prompting the deficit have ceased to act. This objection to devaluation as a method of adjustment to an international depression of foreign origin reinforces the conclusions reached in the previous section, and based on the likelihood of devaluation proving ineffectual in that case.

On the other hand, if the balance of payments troubles

originated in a disequilibrium between domestic prices and costs compared to foreign prices and costs, a fundamental readjustment is needed to eliminate the root of the difficulties. In this case, deflation or devaluation may become a most logical, or even indispensable, means of correcting the deficit at its source. Again, if the measures taken are limited to the restoration of a previously disturbed equilibrium between the country in question and the outside world, retaliation should not be necessary, and devaluation may attain its objectives. It is interesting to note in passing that this was basically the case assumed in the classical discussion of balance of payments disequilibria. Classical writers examined, in general, the problem of price and cost equilibrium of a single country versus another, or versus the rest of the world. They were not normally concerned with the balance of payments effects of world-wide cyclical disturbances, acting primarily, or at least initially, through incomes rather than prices.

The best case for devaluation, therefore—whether from a domestic or an international point of view—is that of a country which has suffered from inflation to a greater extent than other trading nations, and especially than its competitors in world markets. Even if devaluation is then admitted in principle, however, there remain important problems of its desirable timing and extent.

From the point of view of domestic stability, it would be preferable to time the devaluation so as to coincide with a decline in the country's export prices in world markets, and to offset in part the effects of such a decline on the prices and profitability of exports expressed in local currency. On the other hand, if, in spite of cost inflation, export prices and profits are still high owing to the prevalence of sellers' markets, it would be undesirable to add still more through devaluation to the exporters' profits and to the domestic inflationary trend. And still, it might be necessary to limit at the same time excessive imports resulting from inflationary incomes and liquidities. In other words, it would then be indicated to correct the balance of payments deficit through measures which act exclusively on imports, and not on exports. Such a situation is by no means theoretical; on the contrary, it has been characteristic of many countries, especially in Latin America, since the end of the war.

Quantitative import or exchange restrictions are not, however, the only, or even the best, answer to the problem. Excessive imports can be checked through the price mechanism as well or better than through administrative action. Tariff duties, excise or exchange taxes, etc., can be used to cut down import demand or other exchange expenditures, without the heavy, and often arbitrary, mechanism of import or exchange quotas and licenses. A proper assessment of such duties or taxes should make it possible to curtail the different categories of transactions to the desired levels,[5] and to reach, in a much simpler and more liberal manner, the same effects that would otherwise have to be enforced through administrative quotas or licenses. It is true that consumer prices will rise as a result, but in the absence of domestic price controls and allocation, the artificial scarcity of the restricted import goods would also tend to raise prices to a corresponding degree if mere quantitative restrictions were applied. The only difference is that the price increases would, in one case, be translated into windfall profits for the licensed importers and middlemen, while in the other they would be recouped by the State.

Quantitative restrictions make more sense if complemented by effective price controls and rationing. In this case, the scarcity profits accrue to the consumers themselves.[6] In some circumstances this may be highly desirable, especially if the balance of payment difficulties are of a very short-run character. The question is somewhat akin to that of subsidies designed to maintain artificially low prices for domestically produced goods. The dangers are that such price subsidization encourages consumption—or imports—which the State is then forced to compress through rationing or licenses, and that the forced savings thus realized by the consumers tend to spill over into

[5] When a very precise curtailing is needed, and when difficulties of calculating the necessary taxes are too baffling, licenses could be sold by auction. See Robert Triffin, *National Central Banking and the International Economy, Postwar Studies* No. 7, Board of Governors of the Federal Reserve System (Washington, 1947).

[6] In the case of devaluation, the scarcity profits pass instead from the importers to the exporters and may help to restore exporters' profit margins.

other non-controlled areas. Thus, if the system is long maintained, there may arise a need to extend gradually the controls to a larger and larger sector of the country's economic life.

The advantages of controlling excessive foreign expenditures through pricing methods rather than quantitative restrictions are especially marked when the situation calls for a policy of monetary contraction. I have said earlier that corrective measures, such as devaluation, may then be more adequate and promising than quantitative controls. The extent of the devaluation needed to correct the disequilibrium, however, will vary, depending on the domestic monetary and fiscal policies adopted. In any case, of course, new inflation must be arrested. It would also be agreed by many that a real deflation policy, involving a lowering of wages and salaries, would be extremely difficult to pursue in most countries today. These two considerations, however, still leave a large margin of choice for the extent of the devaluation necessary to correct the disequilibrium. One of the reasons for this is the distortion in the pattern of prices and costs which accompanies a period of inflation. This distortion will tend to disappear gradually once the generating forces of inflation have been arrested, but the new balance may be reached through an upward movement of the lower price sectors or a downward movement of the higher ones. Since wages, in general, will have lagged behind prices, it will often be possible to bring down the more highly inflated prices to the level of the more rigid ones, including wages, or at least to avoid adjustment at the highest level.

These were the considerations behind the monetary purges undertaken after the war by several European countries. Where such drastic policies prove impossible or inadvisable, similar—though usually less immediate and extensive—results can be sought through contractive monetary and fiscal policies of a more traditional character. The proceeds of the duties and taxes mentioned above as an instrument for checking excessive imports and other foreign expenditures can be sterilized and earmarked for this purpose. Such a policy was recently adopted by Ecuador in June 1947, with a marked degree of success. By the end of the year, money supply was down by about 12 per cent, as against an increase of about the same order of magnitude in 1946 and much larger ones in the preceding years. Most of the decline was due to an extraordinary amortization of the Government debt to the Central Bank, by about 25 per cent in seven months.

### *Conclusions*

The battle which has been raging for some years between the protagonists and the opponents of exchange control is too often a sort of shadow boxing over words rather than over the real and concrete issues of exchange administration. One of the paradoxes resulting from this verbal tournament is the preference granted in the ITO Charter to quantitative restrictions over tariff controls or other market methods of checking a balance of payments deficit. Such direct administrative interference with the economic mechanism involves far greater departures from a free economy than many of the alternative methods working through the price mechanism, against which the Charter and the accompanying tariff agreements have directed most of their fire. The large loophole open for quantitative restrictions as a method to combat balance of payments deficits seems to me the most unfortunate choice among several types of unavoidable evils.

Selective controls over foreign trade and exchange are in part the inevitable projection in the international field of the tremendous growth of planning in the field of domestic economic activity. In part, they are also the reflection of the profound disturbances and dislocations bequeathed us by the great depression and the second world war.

The cure for the abuses of exchange control and economic nationalism does not lie in legal commitments to abolish such controls over night. The futility of this approach to the problem was never more clearly demonstrated than by the recent return of sterling to inconvertibility in spite of the solemn undertakings to the contrary in the Anglo-American Financial Agreement. Convertibility lasted five weeks. It could have lasted longer, but no amount of legal commitments could have stood against continuing balance of payments deficits and the exhaustion of the U.K.'s gold and dollar resources. Agreement or no agreement, either the stability or the convertibility of sterling would have been wiped away in a matter of months. This outcome was, indeed, so evident that hardly a murmur was heard in Washington when, on August 20, 1947, the brief experiment was terminated by Britain.

Exchange freedom or stability cannot be established by mere legislation or agreements. Burying our heads in the sands of legal commitments will not protect us from the inevitable consequences of international maladjustments and balance of payments disequilibria. If we wish to restore a workable international economic order, we should speak a little less about enforcing stability and convertibility, and work a little more toward recreating conditions under which they will become possible, and indeed attractive, to members of the Fund or of the ITO.

In the meanwhile, exchange and import controls should be "exorcized" rather than "excommunicated." This calls especially for a clear recognition of their international character and incidence. External controls over trade and exchange are a matter affecting, and affected by, more than one nation. Nationalistic measures of control will react unfavorably upon the international community itself, and may be defeated or offset, even in the country which initiates them, by warranted, or unwarranted, reactions abroad. The very success of external planning, therefore, depends on the international integration of national decisions. External planning must also be international planning, if it is not to degenerate into international chaos.

# 24

## *DOLLAR SHORTAGE?*

Gottfried Haberler

The layman, banker, statesman, any reader who is not a professional economist, will raise his eyebrows when he notices the question mark in the title of this paper. Can there be any question that practically the whole world is desperately short of United States dollars?

In a way this is of course true, not only in the trivial sense that many countries cannot earn as many dollars as they like to spend and try to spend more than they earn (in this sense, dollars are scarce also for most Americans); but it is true also in the somewhat less trivial sense that in recent years, at the existing exchange rates, the demand for dollars has exceeded the supply in almost all countries except Switzerland, Portugal, and a few others. Dollar scarcity is, thus, another word for a disequilibrium in the balance of payments, that is to say, a balance-of-payments surplus of the United States and a balance-of-payments deficit of the rest of the world. The balance-of-payments deficit is usually supposed to find its expression either in an outflow of gold or "equilibrating" capital movements (such as borrowing from the International Monetary Fund) or in the necessity of restrictive exchange and trade controls.[1]

[1] There is a certain lack of precision in this definition for two reasons: First, the concept of short-term capital movements which are equivalent to gold flows, that is, of "equilibrating" or "accommodating" capital movements is not quite clear-cut and very difficult to apply. Secondly, certain types of exchange control are indistinguishable from, or are close substitutes of, ordinary protectionist measures designed to reduce or prevent imports. Suppose, for example, a country loses gold and hence is said to have a balance-of-payments deficit. If it introduces exchange control of the rationing type, we still say it has a potential deficit, a disequilibrium. But suppose it restricts imports by means of import duties. Shall we say it still has a balance-of-payments deficit? If yes, would we

In that sense, then, we may say the "dollar shortage" is a "fact." But all those economists who use the term with the more or less explicit allegation that it is a novel phenomenon which has never been contemplated in international trade theory and requires some new, unorthodox explanation, are not or should not be satisfied with merely pointing to that brute fact. They wish to imply that there is a persistent balance-of-payments problem which is not curable by orthodox measures, that is, by changes in prices or exchange rates, or that such a cure would have intolerable consequences. Only a balance-of-payments disequilibrium of a high degree of malignancy deserves to be called a dollar shortage in the strict sense. But before we go into these questions of causation and remedy, let us have a closer look at the alleged "fact." How long has there been a large surplus in the United States international balance?

## II.

It is not surprising that there has been a surplus ever since the outbreak of World War II and that the war threw its shadow at least a couple of years before it. But according to many writers the dollar shortage goes back to the outbreak of the great depression and according to some has existed in a more or less severe form throughout the interwar period.

An inspection of the United States balance-of-payments statistics for the interwar period[2] yields the following results: we find really massive gold imports of more than $1 billion each year only during the years 1934 to 1939; during the period of 1919 to 1933, gold movements were much smaller; only in 1921 was there a gold import of more than $500 million; during the other years the movements were much smaller, sometimes positive and sometimes negative; over the whole period of 1919 to 1933 the net import was $832 million. (See the summary in Table 1.)

During the period of the heavy gold inflows, 1934-1939, the gold inflow was largely due to, and offset by, large capital

---

not also have to say that any country that has a high tariff wall has a balance-of-payments deficit, because it would lose gold if it reduced its tariff?

At present, however, the situation is so clear in most cases that we may disregard difficulties of classifying borderline cases.

[2] Cf. *The United States in the World Economy*, U. S. Dept. of Commerce, 1943.

inflows. It will be remembered that this was a period of capital flight from Europe. The question may be asked whether such a situation should be regarded as a balance-of-payments surplus indicating a dollar shortage. The Department of Commerce,

TABLE 1

United States Balance of Payments[a]

*(In millions of dollars)*

| | Balance of all current transactions[b] | Net gold movement[b] | Long-term capital movements[c] | Short-term capital movements[c] | All capital movements (3 + 4)[c] | Unexplained items (1+2+5) |
|---|---|---|---|---|---|---|
| | (1) | (2) | (3) | (4) | (5) | (6) |
| 1919 | +1498 | +164 | −384 | ——[d] | −384 | −1278 |
| 1920 | +2687 | + 50 | −832 | ——[d] | −832 | −1905 |
| 1921 | +1594 | −686 | −592 | ——[d] | −592 | −316 |
| 1922 | +642 | −235 | −815 | ——[d] | −815 | +408 |
| 1923 | +548 | −295 | − 45 | − 33 | − 78 | −175 |
| 1924 | +975 | −216 | −700 | +119 | −581 | −178 |
| 1925 | +709 | +102 | −570 | −106 | −676 | −135 |
| 1926 | +454 | − 72 | −726 | +419 | −307 | − 75 |
| 1927 | +721 | +154 | −1037 | +585 | −452 | −423 |
| 1928 | +1027 | +272 | −847 | −348 | −1195 | −104 |
| 1929 | +786 | −120 | −278 | − 4 | −282 | −384 |
| 1930 | +735 | −278 | −298 | −479 | −777 | +320 |
| 1931 | +175 | +176 | +194 | −637 | −443 | + 92 |
| 1932 | +159 | − 11 | +225 | −446 | −221 | + 73 |
| 1933 | +108 | +173 | + 77 | −419 | −342 | + 61 |
| 1934 | +341 | −1178 | +200 | +222 | +422 | +415 |
| 1935 | −156 | −1720 | +436 | +1072 | +1508 | +368 |
| 1936 | −218 | −1147 | +777 | +431 | +1208 | +157 |
| 1937 | − 31 | −1271 | +521 | +356 | +877 | +425 |
| 1938 | +967 | −1657 | + 97 | +344 | +441 | +249 |
| 1939 | +732 | −3018 | + 27 | +1470 | +1497 | +789 |

[a]From *The United States in the World Economy*, Dept. of Commerce, 1943.
[b]An "export" surplus is +; an "import" surplus is −.
[c]"Capital exports" are −; "capital imports" are +.
[d]Not available.

in its publication, *The United States in the World Economy*, simply adds gold flows, short-term capital movements, and unexplained items and calls the sum "net movement of balancing items" or "the excess of dollars used (demanded) over dollars supplied." This series of figures has been much advertised and quoted and is very often taken as a measure of the imbalance of the U. S. international accounts, and is supposed to prove the existence of a persistent "dollar shortage."[3]

There are, however, very serious objections to this procedure. First, "unexplained items" are without question regarded as consisting entirely of unrecorded short-term capital movements, although they consist in reality of the sum of all errors and omissions relating to *all* items. Secondly (and this is the more serious objection), the statistical distinction between short-term and long-term capital transactions is not the same as the one between autonomous and induced or equilibrating capital movements. During the period under consideration (1934-1939) both short-term and long-term capital transactions were largely of the "autonomous" type, more particularly they reflect that kind of autonomous capital movement which we call "capital flight" or "hot money flows." There was probably little if any of the equilibrating kind of capital movement.[4]

There seem to be two possible interpretations of this situation. One choice is to take seriously the usual definition of a balance-of-payments surplus, that is, as gold plus equilibrating capital movements. In that case we would have to try to ascertain the magnitude of equilibrating capital flows. On the plausible assumption that they were small or non-existent during the period under consideration we would take the gold flow alone as a measure of disequilibrium.

The other possibility is to say that capital flight should not be permitted and that therefore that part of the gold imports which is due to the inflow of flight capital should be ignored in the calculation of the balance-of-payments surplus. It follows that, since the capital imports into the United States during those years were without doubt predominantly in the nature of capital flight (rather than of normal capital flows from capital-rich to capital-poor countries), the capital should be deducted

[3] See, for example, Professor Harris' interesting article "Dollar Shortage" in *The Economic Journal* (June 1947), p. 165.

[4] Statistically this finds its expression in the fact that during this period (1934-1939) the capital movements (on short- and long-term) were of the opposite sign from the gold movements. Gold movement (imports) being negative, capital movements being positive—capital imports. Equilibrating capital movements which are close substitutes of gold movements should have the same sign as the gold movements.

from the gold imports in calculating the balance of payments disequilibrium. This amounts to saying that the degree of disequilibrium should be measured by the balance on current account, for the current balance is equal to the combined gold and capital balance (assuming that the "unexplained rest" which, by the way, was quite substantial during those years, consists mainly of unrecorded capital transactions).

It will be observed that neither of these two approaches is identical with the one adopted by the Department of Commerce study. Indeed, there is no justification whatever for taking gold and short-term capital as the measure of disequilibrium. One can take gold alone or the gold plus all capital transactions, which is equal to the current balance.

The rationale for the first alternative, that is, for taking the gold inflow as criterion of disequilibrium, would be this: We accept the political and economic factors (currency disorders, rising fear of war, revolution, and occupation by Nazi Germany) which were responsible for the capital flight from Europe to the United States and then the capital flows themselves as a datum to which the balance of payments has to adjust itself by developing an import surplus. In other words, the wish of foreigners to move capital to the safe haven of the United States constitutes demand for dollars. If, then, the surplus on current account fails to materialize, in other words, if there is no increase in the supply of dollars to match the increased demand and hence gold flows in, we speak of a dollar shortage. That there was a dollar shortage in that sense no economist, classical or otherwise, would deny.[5]

It seems to me, however, that the second criterion of disequilibrium, namely, the current balance, is more appropriate for this particular period, for dollar shortage theorists rest their claim, as we shall see, upon the alleged intractability (by orthodox methods) of the current balance. Keynes, too, takes the current balance as the measure of disequilibrium,[6] and this interpreta-

[5] However, how to deal with such a situation is another question. Should capital flight be prevented by exchange control? Can it be prevented effectively? If not, would it be possible to transfer large sums by developing a favorable trade balance? I cannot go into these questions at this point. Some of them are discussed in my *Theory of International Trade* (1936), Chapter 6.

[6] "The Balance of Payments of the United States," *Economic Journal* (June 1946), pp. 172-173.

tion is also suggested by the Bretton Woods agreements which obligate members of the Fund to prevent capital flights.[7]

If we inspect the figures of the current balance, we find that they are not large during the critical years except in 1938 and 1939. That it was large in those two years is not surprising in view of the mounting preparations for war. For the years 1935, 1936, and 1937, the United States current balance even shows a deficit (an import surplus). Hence, if we take the current balance as criterion, an unmanageable disequilibrium indicative of a dollar shortage simply did not exist, except in years of intense preparation for war which were also depression years in the United States.

Throughout the twenties until 1933 there was a surplus in the current balance in every single year. That it was large immediately after the war until 1921 is again easy to understand. It was much smaller from 1922 on, and until 1929 it was largely due to long-term capital exports, which during that period were predominantly of the ordinary "approved" kind, neither flight capital nor of the equilibrating variety.[8] There is, therefore, again no question of a large and supposedly unmanageable disequilibrium.

[7] It should not be forgotten, however, that the rationale of using the current balance as a measure of disequilibrium breaks down if the capital movements are of the ordinary, desirable variety from capital-rich countries to capital-poor areas. That is to say, it would be a pity if a balance of payments deficit of rich, capital-exporting countries were simply cured by stopping the capital exports. But this is not relevant during the period under review.

These considerations, it will be observed, illustrate the conventional or normative character of the concept of disequilibrium. It all depends on what one takes for granted and considers desirable. One might very well say that capital flight is an unavoidable evil (to some varying extent this is surely true for many a country), but some people may not regard it as an evil at all. On that basis the gold balance would be regarded as the measure of disequilibrium.

[8] It can hardly be said that the capital exports from the U. S. during the 1920's were of the equilibrating kind. It was quite natural that war-impoverished Europe imported capital from the U. S. It was a capital flow from a capital-rich to a capital-poor area.

This is entirely compatible with the fact that the rather abrupt cessation of the U. S. capital exports in 1928-1929 caused balance-of-payments troubles and was a factor in bringing about the depression.

Professor Harris, in his introductory essay to the present volume, takes the position that there was a dollar shortage in the twenties because there were large capital exports. At the same time he speaks of a dollar shortage in the thirties although the large gold imports were largely offset by capital imports. The capital exports in the twenties may be said, according to Professor Harris, to indicate

These were also Keynes' conclusions in his above mentioned article, but as far as the middle and later thirties are concerned there is a serious objection to this reasoning. It could be objected, and has in fact been said, that in those years the balance could be maintained only by means of all sorts of drastic trade restrictions (exchange control, quotas, and so on) and/or by permitting a serious depression and unemployment to develop. In that sense it might be said that a disequilibrium did exist. There is much prima-facie force in this argument, although to make the case for a persistent dollar shortage complete it would be necessary to prove that more orthodox methods of adjustment, if they had been tried, would not have worked and that the trouble was more than a passing difficulty due to a severe depression in the United States.

Summing up, we may say that there is no striking prima-facie evidence of an unmanageably large surplus in the United States balance of payments except during years of severe depression, war preparation, and war. We now turn to questions of cause and remedy.[9]

## III.

What are the basic reasons for the present excess demand for dollars, and is there any truth in the contention that it is more than a temporary phenomenon and that it is unmanageable

---

a dollar shortage "in view of subsequent history which showed an inability on the part of foreign countries to finance the credits of the twenties."

I would deny that history did show inability to pay. What it did show is that the war loans were repudiated. Moreover, Germany not only repudiated reparations but also defaulted to a large extent on her private debt. But in view of the enormous sums which Hitler spent on armaments and other unproductive purposes, can anybody seriously question that Germany could have easily serviced her private debt and paid reparations in addition?

It may be admitted that during the worst years of the depression the transfer would have been difficult or impossible. (At any rate, a country which allows a large part of its own resources to be wasted in idleness in a severe depression has no right and should not be permitted to exact reparations and debt repayments from abroad.) But from that it does not follow that during the prosperous years of the twenties equilibrium could not have been maintained without the capital exports from the United States.

9 See, e. g., T. Balogh, "The U. S. and the World Economy," in *Oxford Statistical Bulletin,* Oct. 1946.

For further discussion see my paper "Some Economic Problems of the European Recovery Program," *American Economic Review,* September 1948, and below, Ch. 25.

except by direct controls of a very severe nature? In order to get some perspective of the problems we must distinguish degrees of scarcity. Take first the case of Germany, Austria, Greece, and, to a much lesser extent, Italy—defeated countries which have the privilege of living on or along the Iron Curtain. These countries are, or were until recently, on the verge of starvation. If they were cut off from foreign aid, if they could import only what they can pay for by exports, they would sink into chaos, and hundreds of thousands might die of starvation.

There is, secondly, a group of countries in Western Europe, including Great Britain, which were in a similar position when hostilities ended. But these countries have made great strides towards recovery and are in a different class now. To be sure, if they were compelled to balance their international accounts at short notice, if they were no longer able to finance an import surplus by grants, loans, sales of gold, and other assets, in other words, if they had to live within their present means, on their current output, they would have to undergo a considerable reduction in their standard of living. In some of these countries this would surely impair output and lead to a social upheaval and revolution. But a distinction must be made between three factors: first, physical difficulties of the transition to a balanced trade position; second, social and political difficulties of the transition; and, third, the permanent level of production and consumption which could be sustained after the transitional difficulties to a balanced trade position have been surmounted.

Nobody denies that whatever the eventual income level obtainable, there would be physical, economic, and social difficulties of transition. Export industries would have to expand, certain investment projects undertaken with foreign aid would have to be abandoned, curtailed or postponed, export channels would have to be opened by an initial sales effort and price concession, and so on. It would be necessary to increase taxes in order to check inflation, the fight against which had been aided by the import surplus. (This is, of course, only another aspect of the fact that by running into debt or selling foreign investment a country can live on a higher level than otherwise.) It would also be necessary to reduce real wages and other incomes, lengthen the work week, and to give up or postpone programs of social reform and public investment.

Nobody can deny that all this would be painful and might put an intolerable strain on the social and political structure of some of those countries. But it seems to me equally clear that the over-all level of production in most Western European countries, particularly in Great Britain and Scandinavia, is by now high enough to support a standard of living which would make the smooth functioning of their economies possible, if the transitional difficulties can be overcome. It is economically very fortunate and socially and politically imperative that through the Marshall Plan the transition to a balanced trade position be prolonged or postponed for some time, but economically speaking for Western Europe, foreign aid (or loans) is no longer a question of life and death as it is for the first mentioned group of countries.

There is a third group of countries where it cannot well be doubted that they can maintain their customary living standard within the limits of their present national product but which have nevertheless in recent years or months developed a balance-of-payments deficit and have started to complain about a dollar shortage—Sweden, Canada, Australia, Argentina, and other Latin American countries. These countries suffer from a balance-of-payments deficit *pur et simple,* uncomplicated by the alleged impossibility of living within their means. Hence it is here that the idea of the dollar shortage as an economic problem finds its clearest expression.

Let us look now at the problem from the therapeutic point of view. There are two extreme schools. The first we may call, for want of a better word, the orthodox or classical school, although in a sense it should appeal to Keynesian economists and is in fact championed in strong language by so eminent a Keynesian as Roy Harrod.[10] The other school consists of the be-

[10] It should appeal to Keynes of the *General Theory* because it runs in aggregative (macroscopic) terms and abstracts from price effects. It is true, however, that to Keynes of the reparations discussion (with Ohlin in the *Economic Journal,* 1929) the opposite view is more akin. Whatever one's view there is always a Keynes to whom one can look for support!

See Harrod's pamphlet *Are These Hardships Necessary?* (London, 1947). He

lievers in the dollar shortage who like to regard themselves as a group of innovators and heretics.

According to the first, the necessary and sufficient condition for restoring stable equilibrium in the balance of payments of any country is to stop inflation and to adjust the exchange rate.[11] It is, of course, realized that in the first group of countries which we distinguished above this cannot be done, except on a starvation basis, unless large import grants are forthcoming. Also in the second group to stop an open or repressed inflation is an extremely difficult job, a socially and politically almost impossible task, unless for some time longer an import surplus can be financed by loans, grants, gold sales, and so on.

But this school insists that the dollar shortage is merely a consequence of the fact that many countries are unwilling or unable for one reason or the other to live within their means. The propensity to spend and to inflate is so strong that the equilibrium in the balance of payments is constantly upset. Under such conditions, if the exchange market were free, the value of the currency would fall continuously. Since few countries are willing to put up with the consequences of freely fluctuating exchanges, drastic controls of international payments supported by trade controls through quotas and licenses is the result.

The opposite view, the theory of the dollar shortage in the

---

says of the "dollar famine" that it is "one of the most absurd phrases ever coined" (p. 42). "This allegation of a world 'dollar shortage' is surely one of the most brazen pieces of collective effrontery that has ever been uttered" (p. 43).

[11] Professor Harris in his introductory essay asks whether I would "suggest that planned economies of the forties and fifties can and should succeed in bringing about equilibrium through use of orthodox weapons, when the unplanned economies of the twenties and thirties under much more favorable conditions failed."

As to the fifties, one can only hope that if there is to be planning it will be more efficient than planning in the forties which can be aptly described as "planning for chaos." There was surely not much planning in the twenties and thirties. But one can hardly agree with Professor Harris that economic policy in the thirties was led astray by doctrinaire adherence to orthodox methods. Indiscriminate and reckless currency depreciations of the beggar-my-neighbor type, bilateral clearings, discriminatory exchange control, quotas, and so on, which are the characteristic policies of the thirties cannot well be regarded as "orthodox weapons." Also the major mistake during the twenties in the field of international monetary policies, the disastrous revaluation of sterling after World War I, was a flagrant violation of orthodox teaching. As is well known, Ricardo himself had warned that it would be unwise to return to the prewar parity if it involved a substantial appreciation of the currency.

strict sense, is often expounded in an extreme form in which it is entirely fallacious. In this form it states that, even if it were possible by draconic measures to avoid inflation, no equilibrium may be possible in a free exchange market. It would not be necessary to waste time on this theory, if it were not for the fact that it is sometimes to be found in the writings of reputable journals and well known economists. *The Economist* a few years ago put forward the theory in a surprisingly crude form. In an article on "The Dollar Problem" (December 4, 1943, pp. 750-751), it came to the following conclusion:

> It may be, in fact, that the [dollar] problem should not be regarded as the fruit of aberrations of policy . . . but that it should be looked upon as the result of a set of economic circumstances never contemplated by the textbooks—namely, the existence of a country which, all policy apart, needs so little from the rest of the world, while the rest of the world requires so much from it, that an equilibrium of accounts can be brought about by no means available to a free, or even a tolerably free market.

Evidently even in the land of Adam Smith, Ricardo, Marshall, and Keynes it is necessary to point out again and again that trade is governed by comparative not by absolute cost! But we should perhaps not be too severe with the editorial writer of *The Economist.* For even an economist of the distinction of Thomas Balogh comes dangerously close to propounding the fallacy under consideration. Dr. Balogh is frightened by the prospects of a bad United States depression which indeed would be most unfortunate from many points of view.[12] Naturally he was in 1943 much impressed by the much advertised danger of oversaving—

[12] It is interesting to observe, however, that many of those who a few years ago were praying for continuous full employment in the U. S. and thought that such a condition would solve practically all economic problems, are beginning to realize that there are a few other things left to worry about. One can now frequently hear the thought expressed that an American depression (presumably if it did not get too severe) may be, after all, a more desirable condition for Great Britain and other industrial countries than the present state of full or over-full employment because they could expect better terms of trade and could presumably protect themselves against infection with the depression bacillus. There is much to be said for this view, provided in a depression an outbreak of protectionism in the U. S., like the Smoot-Hawley tariff of 1930, can be avoided. Hence the tremendous importance of the ITO for countries like Great Britain.

a ghost which in the meantime has been effectively buried—at least until the next depression![13] But in addition to this he thinks that even if, against all expectations, by "prodigious investment activity in the U. S.," a depression were effectively prevented, the dollar problem would not be solved, because these investments would "increase the competitive power [of the United States] faster than productivity elsewhere."[14] According to Dr. Balogh an equilibrium could be achieved only if "U. S. savings were used for foreign investment . . . or if United States business activity were maintained by social reform or 'non-productive' government expenditures."[15] But our gloomy economist is still not satisfied. The criminal, that is, the idea that things may work themselves out without being completely planned, must not only be hanged, but also quartered and beheaded: "Even in these cases—given the initial startling superiority of the U. S. and the aggressiveness of its managerial leadership—it is likely that technical progress will be faster in the United States than in other countries." Dr. Balogh is afraid that "even in agriculture where she [the U. S.?] is relatively less efficient [?, compared with whom?] the U. S. seems to be gaining ground."

The meaning of this somewhat cryptic passage seems to be that there is grave danger that the United States will out-compete and undersell the rest of the world all along the line.[16] This is, indeed, high praise for the productive power of capitalism

[13] Perhaps I should point out that there may be a depression—and I personally am sure there will be one sooner or later—without prior oversaving. But once a depression has developed, "oversaving" is one of its regular features, in the sense that in a depression not all savings are invested and therefore a high rate of saving tends to intensify the depression.

[14] Thomas Balogh, "The U. S. and the World Economy," *Oxford Statistical Bulletin* (October 1946), p. 321.

[15] "The U. S. and the World Economy." On an earlier page, Dr. Balogh suggests another solution: "Only a continuation of strikes without limit would produce a situation in which foreign countries would be safe from U. S. competition" (p. 316). Dr. Balogh feels, however, that it would be unduly optimistic to assume that this solution will be adopted.

[16] Although I tried hard, I could not think of any other interpretation, at least none that makes sense. Did Dr. Balogh perhaps want to say that rapid technological progress in the United States will lead to continual changes in the comparative cost situation and so throw a burden of adjustment on other countries? If so, he did not make his point.

and free enterprise. But the economics is unacceptable none the less!

Let us sketch a few further problems arising from technological progress. It goes without saying that rapid technological progress is bound to change the comparative cost situation, irrespective of the relative speed with which different countries take part in the advance. Suppose, however, for argument's sake, that in the United States progress is faster than elsewhere. It is, of course, entirely fallacious to say that this will lead to a continuous underselling of the rest of the world by the United States. What it means is, first, that the comparative cost situation changes and that a new equilibrium must emerge.

It may, however, also mean—but that is by no means necessary but depends on special circumstances—that there will be difficulties of transition. It may furthermore mean—this again depends on the special direction which technological progress takes, not on the mere assumption that the United States economy progresses faster—that the new equilibrium is less favorable than the old for the rest of the world.

To take up the second problem first, it is possible that country A is hurt by progress in B. If, say, synthetic nitrate and rubber are developed, Chile and British Malaya *may* be permanently injured. But it is, of course, just as well possible that technological progress in B is such that it benefits A. This will be the case if progress takes place predominantly in B's export industries rather than in industries competing with A's exports, or if A can find some other lucrative exports. Obviously all sorts of things may happen and reference to the possibility or probability that progress in the United States will be faster than elsewhere is entirely irrelevant for judging the final outcome (the nature of the new equilibrium). Unfortunately, nobody can tell where future progress is likely to be concentrated, and even if we had a hint that it will be of a nature unfavorable for A it would be hard for country A to do anything about it. On the other hand, it would be easy to cite examples where in the past dire predictions to the effect, say, that the industrial countries as a whole would be placed in a difficult situation by technological progress in the industrially backward countries, have proved to be entirely wrong. That may be conceivably different in the future, but there is no evidence that Dr. Balogh had such long-run changes in the comparative cost situation to the detriment of some particular countries in mind when he expressed fears of the growing American superiority. In fact, he does not betray any awareness of the real issues involved.

As far as transitional problems are concerned what happens depends, in addition to the factors mentioned in connection with the long-run problem, on monetary policies, mobility of labor, and the flexibility of prices and wages. There may be transitional difficulties either in the rapidly advancing country (the United States in our hypothetical example) or in the comparatively stagnant country (rest of the world), depending on the concrete constellation of the various factors mentioned. Then transitional difficulties may take the form either of structural unemployment in particular industries ("technological unemployment") in the United States or in the rest of the world, or of inflationary or deflationary spirals. It is impossible to go into these questions within the limit of an article. But two things can be said with assurance. First, there is no presumption that the transitional difficulties will be usually or mainly concentrated in the slowly advancing country rather than in the more progressive one; all depends on the precise point of where and how the technological progress takes place, on the elasticities of demand and similar factors.[17] Second, even if in a particular case, in view of the concrete circumstances, the transition to a new equilibrium takes the form of causing an export surplus of the United States and so implies a temporary deflationary pressure on the rest of the world, it is always possible successfully to counteract, to offset, and to cut short the deflationary phase by monetary and fiscal policy, currency depreciation, fostering labor mobility, and similar measures designed to facilitate and hasten the emergence of a new equilibrium, without

[17] Suppose, for example, that technological progress makes an American export article cheaper. If the foreign elasticity of demand is less than one, the value of United States exports will fall, that is, the United States balance of payments will become unfavorable. If the elasticity of demand is greater than one, the value of United States exports will rise. Technological progress in A may also increase A's demand for B's raw materials. Atomic development in the United States increases demand for uranium from the Belgian Congo.

resorting to crude protectionist policies which, even if they succeeded in alleviating transitional strains, would do so only at the cost of permanently impeding the international division of labor and preventing the optimum allocation of resources.

## IV.

Before turning to a more sensible version of the dollar shortage theory, I should like to say that I am concerned, not with Dr. Balogh's pessimistic forecasts, but with his economic analysis. As a prophet of doom he has quite an impressive record, and he may well be right again, but let us remember there is such a thing as to be right for the wrong reason.[18]

As an illustration of how easily things can be mismanaged by those who wish to restore multilateral trade take the failure of the short-lived policy of sterling convertibility, in the summer of 1947. This failure is often referred to triumphantly as a proof of the dollar shortage theory and a refutation of the opposite view.

In reality it is nothing of the sort. In a state of repressed inflation with a fancy exchange rate, convertibility could not work. As soon as the door to the British market was opened a little bit to the exporters from the continent of Europe and elsewhere, commodities were bound to pour in in excess of British exports.[19] An economy under inflationary pressure, with excess demand at current prices, absorbs commodities like a sponge. The mistake that was made by making the pound prematurely convertible was the same as was made in the early thirties in Germany, Austria, and elsewhere. When after the onset of the depression the gold standard had collapsed and trade had come, in some cases, to almost a complete standstill (because countries like Austria and Germany had lost almost all their gold or were unwilling to part with any that was left) it was thought that trade could be easily revived by organizing bilateral clearing

[18] Let me add that Dr. Balogh was often right for the right reasons, especially in his writings on war economics at the beginning of the war.

[19] In addition to this factor it seems that substantial capital sums, which were previously accumulated, escaped during the short period of convertibility. In the short run this may have been even the more important leak.

arrangements at the old exchange rates. The immediate consequence was that imports into the soft-currency countries, via the clearing, exceeded exports and that the clearings were soon hopelessly choked by large balances in favor of the hard-currency countries. (The fact that the clearings were all on a bilateral rather than a multilateral basis was aggravating but not the essential factor.)[20]

Similarly now with convertibility. The whole episode is nothing but a close analogy of the phenomenon described by Gresham's Law: Bad money drives out the good. If "soft" currencies are made convertible at fixed rates, excessive exports from any one country will be diverted to the soft currency areas, earning pounds instead of dollars, unless special measures such as elaborate export and import licensing systems are taken to direct them into other channels.[21]

Far from disproving the classical theory of international trade, the failure of convertibility could have been deduced in advance from the most elementary principles of classical or even pre-classical (Sir Thomas Gresham, 1519-1579) economics.

## V.

I turn now to the milder version of the dollar shortage doctrine which is at least theoretically defensible, although in my opinion it is based on untenable factual judgments and assumptions.[22]

It is one of the troubles with economics that a proposition can be as absurd as you wish, it is almost always possible, by comparatively moderate qualifications, to find a similar proposition which, although perhaps quite wrong, is extremely

[20] Schacht used, as is well known, this mechanism to extract involuntary loans in the shape of unpaid clearing balances from unwary countries.

[21] Difficulties of preventing export leaks into soft currencies seemed to have been responsible for the inability of France and the International Monetary Fund to come to an agreement in the recent case of the French devaluation. It has been reported that the IMF proposed to France to permit any devaluation, even a fluctuating franc, so long as the official cross rate between dollar and pound was preserved. One of the reasons why the French did not accept that proposal seems to have been that they were afraid that they would accumulate a lot of inconvertible pounds.

[22] Maybe Dr. Balogh had that version in mind. If he did, it is a pity he did not say so.

hard to refute for the reason that complicated questions of fact are involved.[23]

It is difficult or even impossible to find a clearly reasoned statement of this milder, theoretically tenable dollar shortage theory. But it can be formulated as follows: If a free market equilibrium in the trade between the U. S. and the rest of the world were established, the terms of trade would have to shift sharply in favor of the U. S., against other countries. This would involve in some of the other countries, especially in Great Britain, a socially and politically (if not physically or economically) intolerable fall in the standard of living. If an attempt were made to impose that kind of equilibrium, it would be impossible to resist demand for higher wages and salaries which either would lead to renewed inflation, again upsetting the equilibrium in the balance of payments and recreating the dollar shortage or, in case inflation were resisted by monetary policy, would produce unemployment and severe depression.

It is impossible within the short space of an article to deal adequately with the issues involved in this view. This is the more difficult because we found it necessary to create our own adversary in view of the inadequacies and extravagances of the usual statements of the criticized doctrine. (The reader will observe that this procedure is the exact opposite of the usual practice of setting up a straw man which can then be easily knocked down.) Only a few observations can be offered at this point.

First, in view of the tremendous wastes caused by the current policies of trade and exchange control,[24] it would be necessary to prove that a free market equilibrium (which is not intended to imply free trade in any strict sense) would result in an equally large deterioration in the terms of trade.

Secondly, it is quite wrong to look at the problem as a contest between the dollar as against the rest of the world. What

[23] This is the reason why economics cannot be taught "in one lesson." See Mr. H. Hazlitt's book *Economics in One Lesson*.

[24] It should not be forgotten that the actual policies are not the optimal ones that are contemplated in the theory of control and planning. Actually these policies are carried out by people completely innocent of the "Economics of Control." For numerous examples of the absurdities of the present trading methods and a general evaluation, see the report of the *Economic Commission for Europe, A Survey of the Economic Situation and Prospects of Europe*, 1948, Part 4, Chapter II.

is going on in reality is a *bellum omnium contra omnes*. The dollar-starved world is divided against itself.

Thirdly, the fact that so many countries of entirely different economic structures, different policies, different economic development all suffer from a dollar shortage weakens the case for the criticized doctrine instead of strengthening it. We have industrial countries on the one hand—Great Britain, Western Europe—and predominantly agricultural export countries on the other—Canada, Argentina, and others; there are war-ravaged countries on the one hand, and on the other hand there are neutrals like Sweden or war-enriched[25] countries like Canada, again Argentina and others—all suffering from a scarcity of dollars. It is mathematically inconceivable that restoration of a free market equilibrium should turn the terms of trade against all of them.

Fourthly, it would be an entirely different matter if we had a division of, say, industrial as against primary producing or agricultural countries. In severe depressions something like that division usually develops. In such a case it is good theoretical economics, although difficult or even bad practical politics, for primary producers to band together and present a monopolistic front against the rest of the world (including the urban population of their own countries). The economics (although in only few cases the actual practice) of buffer stocks, raw material restriction schemes is unassailable. But the division in the dollar market, between dollar-rich and dollar-poor, surplus *and* deficit countries, soft and hard currencies cannot be reduced, even approximately, to the division between industrial and primary producing or agricultural or undeveloped countries. The first division cuts across all the others.

I conclude then that the dollar shortage theory, even in its well considered form, claims altogether too much; the case should be sent back for better preparation, if not definitely thrown out of court because of flagrant *plus petitio*.

[25] Meant in an absolutely non-derogatory sense.

VI.

Our general conclusion is that the classical, inflation theory of the dollar shortage is substantially correct. It is necessary, however, to elaborate a little bit to guard against a serious misunderstanding. It might be said that the inflation formula is too simple. Many readers will ask themselves: Can it be true that to stop inflation and adjust the exchange rate is all that needs to be done to balance the international accounts of any country? Is the actual situation not infinitely more complex than that?

The answer to these questions is, that it would be a serious misunderstanding to believe that the problem is simple or easy to solve, because we have reduced it to a short formula.

The causes behind the inflation are, of course, manifold and complex. War losses of all sorts, actual devastations, large public debt, losses of foreign investment and investment income, and so on play their role. Internal political troubles, losses of foreign markets, and similar factors are obviously involved. To stop inflation is surely not an easy task.

There are special problems involved in countries like Great Britain and, still worse, Germany that suffer from latent or repressed rather than from open inflation. A galloping open inflation is, of course, worse than a mild repressed inflation, but a strong repressed inflation is the worst of all. The trouble with repressed inflation is that it seems to be almost impossible for a country to extricate itself from it and to return to a free economy without going through a stage of open inflation first. Take the case of Great Britain. If controls were abolished, the present artificially low price level would certainly have to go up sharply. To avoid that, in other words, to validate the present controlled price level in a free-market economy, it would be necessary to mop up or freeze a considerable portion of the accumulated liquid purchasing power and to deflate labor cost. Since that is not practical politics (and perhaps even poor economics), a sharp rise in prices can be hardly avoided in the transition to a free economy. (One of the functions of the price rise would be to reduce the real weight of the debit burden.) The only alternative is to perpetuate indefinitely the state of repressed inflation with all its wastes and misallocation of resources. In fact, experience has shown that the latter concomitants of repressed inflation necessitate more and more drastic interferences (see, for example, recent developments in Great Britain and earlier ones in Nazi Germany). Those economists were victims of a grave illusion who thought that in a year or two the British economy could shed its wartime controls of prices, rationing, and so on, as easily and painlessly as a snake slips out of its old skin.

Another extremely serious complication is the drastic redistribution of income which has taken place under the cover of repressed inflation. The impoverishment of the middle classes in favor of labor and agriculture, if perpetuated, is bound to have grave social and political consequences, even in Great Britain.

Many other aspects of the problem remain which cannot be mentioned, let alone adequately discussed, within the space of this article.

# 25

## THE UNITED STATES AND INTERNATIONAL ECONOMIC EQUILIBRIUM

Thomas Balogh

Judgment on the implications of the postwar agreements for international economic reconstruction based on the restoration of "free" market economies rests primarily—though not entirely—on the estimate of the future trends in, and the implications of the dominant position of, the United States in the world economy. The present article attempts to analyze the consequences of the rise of a power to a uniquely strong economic position on the customary theory of foreign trade and more especially on the conclusion that a return to uncontrolled nondiscriminating multilateralism would result in a maximization of real income all around, in accordance with the principle of comparative costs. The nonapplicability of classical tenets does not necessarily indicate that the rejection of the Final Act of Bretton Woods nor of the proposals for an International Trade Organization is indicated. Their acceptance might still be regarded as the lesser evil—*politically*. But the recognition that they are basically unfavorable for every other smaller and poorer country is of utmost importance if we wish to mitigate their evil effects by pressing for suitable interpretation of the objectionable and unjust clauses.

### *I. General Considerations*

The rigid formulation of the comparative cost principle, which is the basis of the rules for policy, rests on two sets of assumptions—though this division was not made by the "classical" authors as they contemplated a self-adjusting equilibrium system in which dynamic phenomena, such as cumulative movements, occurred mainly as unimportant frictions (statics being conceived in terms of unchanging capital intensity). The first category of assumptions, conveniently termed "static," was as follows:

1. Given tastes and technical knowledge. This should be interpreted in the widest possible sense: differences between countries must be due solely to immutable or slowly changeable factors, such as the existence of natural resources, the differences in climate, and so on, and not to factors which can more quickly be influenced by conscious policy (involving the scope of international trade), such as skills, capital equipment, etc.

2. Free competition in the world markets, that is, within each member country and each industry. Thus, the law of decreasing returns must generally operate, there must be no advantage in size—especially in the size of markets. Moreover, there must be free mobility of factors, that is, no difference in efficiency remuneration between broad categories of occupations within each country.

3. The relation between social and private costs (which must be proportionate in accordance with Section 2) must be uniformly influenced by the existence of foreign trade, i.e., the riskiness of enterprise must not increase.

Even if we concede these—in practice highly unlikely, not to say impossible—assumptions, the trouble for the policy-maker is by no means ended. There is a further set of dynamic assumptions:

1. The system is supposed to contain *given* physical resources which are fully employed.

2. The balance of current payments must be in equilibrium in the sense that income and outlay are equal.

The full employment of resources is not a criterion from the point of view of the countries which are not subject to depression.[1] That is to say that if the depression does not result in

[1] The depressed country could of course increase her real income by protective measures if from her point of view comparative costs are vitiated. It stands to reason, however, that the proper policy is not a beggar-my-neighbor attempt to create an export surplus but domestic plans to increase effective demand.

balance of payment difficulties to other countries (condition 2), it does not invalidate the theory of comparative costs for other countries. In this sense a *stable* though low level of employment is not a danger to other countries. The failure of maintaining full employment would, however, vitiate the principle of comparative costs for countries on which depression is being imposed by the depression dumping of other countries leading to unemployment (because of the specificity of factors of production) which cannot be effectively cured by domestic measures, that is, without such decrease in productivity over time (taking slumps and booms together) as would be greater than the decrease produced by the absence of foreign trade. Thus fluctuating employment (rather than stable though possibly widespread unemployment) is the real danger to third countries—at any rate in theory. In practice, however, it is improbable that mass unemployment will be compatible with balanced trade over a period.[2] Wage cuts or other measures to relieve unemployment by pushing exports are very likely to be enacted if a domestic program of increasing effective demand is opposed on political grounds. As the demand for imports will also be at a low level, the danger of an excess of exports will be appreciable.

The orthodox school in applying the general principles to particular problems disregarded, first, the fact that if unemployment is imposed from abroad there is a strong case for protective measures to maximize real income, and secondly, that under these conditions readjustment "conformable" to market economies, that is, devaluation, would probably fail in the sense that there would be no level of exchange which would both balance the country's international payments and permit the maintenance of domestic full employment. The first fallacy was due to the fact that in most cases the assumption of full employment was not conscious, and hence the analysis was never carried beyond; or, if it was, the importance of business cycles was consistently played down.[3] The second came from

[2] The British case, 1925-1931, where unemployment was aggravated by rigidities combined with an overvaluation of the currency, is not likely to be repeated.

[3] Cf., e.g., the treatment in Haberler's *Theory of International Trade*.

the habit of treating these problems on the basis of regarding each country as equivalent to every other country, and very small in comparison to the world economy as a whole. This is of course implicit in the assumption of free competition. Thus the high elasticities demanded by an equilibrating system were implicit in the assumption.

We shall first inquire into the consequences of dropping the assumption of full employment. Secondly, we shall turn to the problems which arise from neglecting the lack of validity of what we have called "static" assumptions.

### *II. Stability and the Rise of the United States*

We have seen that, once the possibility of a serious deflationary instability in an important member country of the system is admitted, multilateral schemes cannot a priori be expected to secure optimum progress for all members of a world system. It is exactly the "multilateral" character of the system which is responsible for the *spread* of the depression if there are no means to stop it by international action. Once a slump starts, the depressed country will be a good market to buy from and a bad market to sell to. Unless it is isolated, i.e., discrimination introduced, it will absorb the liquid reserves of the other members of the system and force them to deflate.

The "secondary" action by the affected countries, that is, either competitive devaluation or deflation, will reduce world income and demand in terms of gold or whatever currency remains "stable." Under these conditions it is in the highest degree misleading to assume a given world demand and its elasticity. We are confronted not with a "pure" oligopoly situation, i.e., a limited number of sellers competing for a *given fixed demand,* but with a family of (short-term) demand curves each of which will correspond to a specific income position in the world system as a whole (and each of the constituent members). The statistically observable "demand" will lie on the points at which the (short term) "supply curves"—corresponding to those "demand curves"—cut the latter. The price "elasticity" of these historical curves is certain to be exceedingly low except under certain conditions for necessities: the income effect will in all other cases swamp the substitution effect.[4] The question then arises: (a) whether a considerable degree of instability should be expected and what means can be devised to minimize it; (b) what measures are needed to isolate other countries from its effects?

The decision on the policy of single countries (or a group of countries) will have to depend—on an economic plane—on the extent of the instability on the one hand, and the potential loss of productivity—if any—due to the limitation of the international division of labor on the other hand.

Thus we are driven to consider the factors which in a world system will determine the degree of instability, that is, the problem of the determinants of international employment. We can no longer assume that the *size* and *wealth* of the members of a world economic system are of no importance in determining the course of events. We cannot assume, as it is palpably fallacious, that international trade merely differs from internal trade by the fact that the mobility of certain factors, especially labor, is not perfect.

Even in the nineteenth century the countries were far more positive in their action than to provide a "framework" within which individual entrepreneurs conducted trade—not otherwise influenced or inconvenienced as by political regulations, that is, hindrance to the movement of populations. But on the gold coin standard identical gold movements take place between and within countries. The establishment of central banks must, from the "liberal" point of view, be regarded as the first step to "state interference." The really logical followers of that school, of whom Professor Mises may be mentioned, in fact advocate "free banking" linked by gold automatism. Central banking, by enabling a variation of internal monetary conditions contrary to gold flows or at least a variation of gold reserve ratios, represented the most important break with the automatic functioning of the system.

[4] For a more detailed discussion of this problem, cf. my essays, "The International Aspects of Full Employment" in *The Economics of Full Employment* (Oxford Institute of Statistics, Oxford, 1944), and "Devaluation and International Economic Readjustment" scheduled to appear in the *Review of Economics and Statistics,* November 1948.

But, apart from the regulation of the flow of money, the imposition of tariffs and the regulation of wages (negatively the prevention of trade unionism) affect entrepreneurs in one country as a unit differently from another. As the number of these units is limited, variations in one country can no longer be assumed of no importance for the system. Dynamically these differences will determine the essential features of the business cycle.

If we apply the modern theory to the balances of payments we must immediately recognize how vastly important is the size and especially the relative size of units. For small countries, even if they suffer large excesses or deficiencies, cannot influence the level of business activity of their rich neighbors, especially if the latter are blessed with relatively large gold reserves. On the contrary, instability and the competitive position and the policy of the dominant power will have decisive effects upon smaller countries (especially such extensively depending on foreign trade). The degree of leadership will depend partly on the size of the country (or rather of its industries) relative to the rest of the world, and partly on the size of its reserves relative to its foreign balance of payments (strictly speaking, to the variations of the balance). In a favorable position an inflow or outflow of gold will not enforce a change in monetary policy. Nor will the income effects which give rise to these gold movements, or are caused by them, significantly alter, or cause a country to alter, its own national income because of its preponderance in the total world money income.

Indeed, this is the point from which a properly conceived general theory of international employment and exchange should start to explain the concrete patterns of all historic economic fluctuations. This method will give us a clue why, for example, economic development before World War I, in France, was slower yet more even than in the "English orbit," including Germany. It will reveal, for example, why a world system in which England was the "leader," though also suffering from sharp fluctuations, could be expected to recover more quickly and with less damage to the "peripheries" than the new system in which the United States is the "leader."

The degree of instability in a multilateral and nondiscriminating system will depend mainly on the stability in the "leading" country and its relationship to the world economy: (1) on the decline in demand in the leading depressed country relative to its national income; (2) the fluidity of its costs (determining the probable course of business); (3) the size of the surplus in its balance of payments and its relation on the one hand to domestic saving (determining whether the slump can be cured by an export of unemployment) and on the other to total world demand, determining the pressure abroad.

The size of the country's export surplus will depend *initially* partly on its own foreign trade multiplier and the relative domestic elasticities of demand and supply, partly on those of foreign countries. Once the export surplus has materialized, the further course of events will depend on the reaction of foreign countries. This again in its turn will be influenced by a host of factors, the most important of which is whether the foreign country is *able* to "carry" the deficit, i.e., on the size of liquid reserves relative to the balance which developed, and whether it is *willing* to do so, that is, whether the "leading" country's own policy is "orthodox" in following the "rules of the game," or whether it tries to attempt to stabilize its employment. These competing waves of action and reaction will determine a family of world demand curves which are interrelated and determine the position of world conditions at any one moment. The larger the "leading" country and its national income relative to the world, the greater its own instability relative to that of the world, the more fluid its cost structure and the more important its products, the greater will be the instability of the system as a whole.

If the "leading" member has no employment policy and is insensitive to outside influences, while the "weak" members have no reserves, the resultant oligopolistic system (in which balances in international payments and the level of employment play a role similar to that of prices and quantities of sales in the theory of duopoly)[5] will be unfavorable for the latter: the

[5] That is, the central bank of the smaller country either can minimize unemployment or the deficit in the balance of payments.

weak countries must try to maintain exports at, and reduce imports to, their old level, i.e., restore the balance, at all costs, if the leading country experiences a slump. And this will involve (apart from the automatic "deflationary" income effect of the emerging export surplus of the leader on the others) a conscious "secondary" deflation in the weaker members, which will hit *all* countries and not merely that in which the slump originated. The resulting shrinkages in income and/or counter measures will bring the whole system to a point where the leading member's savings are sufficiently reduced to provide a stable basis for recovery as opportunity for investment increases.

## *III. The United States in the World Economy*

### A. THE TRANSITION PERIOD

The problems of the transition period should be dealt with on a different basis from the long-term problems, otherwise they might prejudice the establishment of a stable system—as was the case after 1920. While their effects on the balances of payments are similar, their solution must differ considerably if not diametrically. It is fair to assume that in all countries which have not adopted tightly centralized plans the present shortages will sooner or later bring about a deficiency of international currencies in stable values. Then and only then can plans which are based on international liquidity come into their own. For any premature program of this character unaccompanied by rationing and other direct controls would cause "true" inflation even in the best-supplied countries. The resistance against such programs—unless based on purely political motives —will therefore be considerable.

But in the transition period itself there will be a formidable monetary strain between countries which were able to preserve some equilibrium between money demand and productive capacity without direct controls because they escaped devastation, and those where decontrol would result in a violent inflation. This strain will be similar to that which might appear later when one or more countries are depressed while others are still in the midst of a reconstruction boom. And it will produce considerable unfavorable balances in the war-weakened countries. A multilateral solution to the probable longer-run problem (i.e., of deflation) is—at least theoretically—easy, because the cure would merely imply bringing back into production the unemployed capacity of the richer countries. Because the richer countries are themselves fully employed, this procedure, it should be noted, is not practicable in the transition period without international planning and controls. The poorer areas will then have to curtail their intercourse with one another even while there is no chance of obtaining additional supplies from the surplus areas (themselves fully employed) except at the cost of violent price movements which are likely to retard rather than to help their reconstruction. From this point of view, the exceptions provided to the rule of absolute multilateralism and nondiscrimination in the Bretton Woods Final Act and the ITO Charter for the transition period are wholly insufficient. The period contemplated for the transition period, moreover, already very short, was further shortened by the financial agreements which the United States concluded with European countries. It can already be seen that those were right who warned that nondiscrimination under postwar conditions will have a restrictive rather than an expansionist effect on trade. The breakdown of unrestricted convertibility enforced by that agreement, preceded by a period of indiscriminate restrictionism in the vain hope to obtain dollars which reduced trade unnecessarily, should be a warning. Unfortunately, the attempt was pushed so far that its breakdown left Britain bereft of reserves and enforced a restrictive bilateralism instead of an expansionist controlled multilateralism.

The Marshall Plan and the attempt to harmonize a consciously planned coördination of Western European countries with their special ties to overseas areas complementary to them represents a most welcome though all too belated break with earlier trends of policy embodied in international postwar agreements. Nevertheless, it is to be feared that it will not lead to a reconsideration of the basic problem of Europe[6] *but merely to a stopgap aid which will mitigate the severity of the present*

[6] See below p. 478.

*crisis but not produce a new equilibrium position which is a precondition of the applicability of the classical principles on which the postwar agreements are based.*

### B. THE LONG-RUN PROBLEM

This apprehension is increased if we contemplate the prospective pattern of the world's economic system. Our considerations so far have made it clear that the likelihood and degree of instability of the world system will be increased by a growing inequality of wealth between and within countries. The two wars and more especially the second one have destroyed large areas of the Eastern Hemisphere, continents where poverty was already very acute. This has resulted in the loss of foreign assets and foreign markets by countries the maintenance of whose population at a tolerable standard of life was dependent on those markets and income. At the same time the last war has increased the productive capacity and commercial influence as well as the power to grant loans of the Western Hemisphere, especially North America.

Indeed, the United States has achieved a far more overpowering position in the world currently than Great Britain at any time of her industrial and commercial supremacy.[7]

A number of interesting calculations have been made in the United States and elsewhere about that country's prospective position in the world economy as a whole. The remarkable analysis of the United States Department of Commerce—*The U. S. in the World Economy*[8]—has put the share of the United States in the 1927-28 consumption of nine principal raw materials at 39 per cent of the total for the fifteen most important commercial nations.[9] So far as the volume of industrial production is concerned, the importance of the United States in 1925-1929 was 48 per cent (excluding the U.S.S.R.). American national money income equalled that of twenty-three foreign countries together, including Britain, France, and Germany. If we

[7] "The U. S. and the World Economy," *Oxford Institute of Statistics Bulletin*, vol. 8, No. 10, 1946.

[8] Reprinted by H. M. Stationery Office (London, 1944).

[9] *The U. S. in the World Economy*, p. 29, on the basis of calculations of the U. S. Department of Agriculture.

were to investigate the investment capacity of the United States at full employment, that is, the flow of voluntary savings at full employment level, we should find its share was even higher, hardly less than two-thirds of the total. No doubt all such international comparisons are subject to many doubts. But we are interested here in the importance of the United States in market relations and, in that respect, the order of magnitude of its share is, on the whole, beyond dispute.

Since then (1925-1929) Germany has collapsed, French manufacturing output has declined by at least 30 per cent, and that of Europe has, in general, suffered a relapse of hardly less than 40 per cent. The Far East has partly gone back to medieval conditions and partly been reduced to a fraction of its former importance; in the meantime, gross output in the United States almost doubled. One would not go far wrong if one were to estimate the present share of the United States national money income and manufacturing output at some two-thirds of the world total, outside the U.S.S.R. and China, with an investment capacity which can hardly be less than three-quarters of the total. What this means can best be demonstrated by reference to the calculation of the League of Nations of the percentage distribution of the world manufacturing production in earlier periods.[10]

As can be readily seen—especially if agricultural production and services are taken into account, in which America's relative importance has also spectacularly increased during World War II—countries outside the U.S.S.R. are faced with a position for which there is no parallel, at any rate since the days of the Roman Empire. Even the paramountcy of the United Kingdom in the final period of the Industrial Revolution—1840-1860—was less complete than the present economic weight of the United States.[11]

10 *Industrialization and Foreign Trade,* 1945, p. 13.

11 Professor Haberler, one of the strongest protagonists of the classical school of thought, attacks—rather ingenuously—the British "heretics" because they apostatize at the moment when the U. S. at last was converted to the Truth. (*Economic Reconstruction,* Ed. S. E. Harris, 1945, p. 327). He should ponder the "coincidence" that England in 1846, just as the U. S. in 1946, was persuaded that "free trade" was as good morals and economics as it was good business. The resistance then in the U. S. and Germany and now in England to this rather simple approach cannot astonish anybody who has some historical sense.

Thus should the degree of employment in the United States fall below the critical level (i.e., when efficiency wages become sensitive to pressure from abroad), the maintenance of employment elsewhere will become extremely difficult, as the impact effect of the depressed U. S. industry, because of its overwhelming magnitude, especially in the most sensitive field, capital goods, cannot easily be counterbalanced, at any rate in third markets, under the "multilateral rules of the game." At that low employment level, moreover, the U. S. price-elasticity of demand for foreign goods is likely to be rather low, and the pressure on the part of both employers and labor to eliminate foreign "dumping" or "slave-sweated" competition becomes irresistible. If, of course, the depressed country could be forced to take the consequences of its depression on itself and maintain its net international demand by a large appreciation of its currency, without in turn upsetting each of the smaller countries and starting a number of separate deflationary spirals, the situation might be different.[12] It is thus not true that it is *merely stability* in the United States (and other large economic units) that is required for a smooth working of a multilateral international system, *but stability at high employment.*[13] A long depression in one country—if the country is big enough—

TABLE 1

MANUFACTURING CAPACITY[a]

*World = 100*

| Period | U. S. | U. K. | Germany | France | Russia (U.S.S.R.) |
|---|---|---|---|---|---|
| 1870 . . . . . . . | 23.3 | 31.8 | 13.2 | 10.3 | 3.7 |
| 1881–1885 . . . | 28.6 | 26.6 | 13.9 | 8.6 | 3.4 |
| 1896–1900 . . . | 30.1 | 19.5 | 16.6 | 7.1 | 5.0 |
| 1906–1910 . . . | 35.3 | 14.7 | 15.9 | 6.4 | 5.0 |
| 1913 . . . . . . . | 35.8 | 14.0 | 15.7 | 6.4 | 5.5 |
| 1926–1929 . . . | 42.2 | 9.4 | 11.6 | 6.6 | 4.3 |
| 1936–1938 . . . | 32.2 | 9.2 | 10.7 | 4.5 | 18.5 |

[a]From: League of Nations: *Industrialization and Foreign Trade*, 1945, p. 13.

[12] Cf. *Economics of Full Employment*, p. 142.

[13] Stability even at low employment—if it were possible—would be preferable to violent swings.

is a perpetual menace to the world economic system, because of the direct and indirect (psychological) pressure it exerts on other countries.

Moreover, not only has the share of the United States in total effective demand increased and thus the absolute concentration of wealth in the United States and the shortage of (commercial) investment opportunities elsewhere relative to the investment capacity of the United States at full employment, but the possibility of influencing the United States level of employment by export surpluses has practically vanished. The United States, unlike nineteenth-century Britain, is a relatively self-sufficient continent. Hence the existence of a relatively large surplus in her balance of payments will hardly have any effect on her internal position.

TABLE 2

NATIONAL INCOME, SAVINGS, AND FOREIGN TRADE[a]

| | U. S., 1947 million $ | U. K., 1911 million £ |
|---|---|---|
| Gross national income | 215,000 | 2,173 |
| Depreciation | 12,400 | 185 |
| Net national income | 202,600 | 1,988 |
| Net investment | 24,100 | 414 |
| Exports | 16,022 | 454 |
| Imports | 6,047 | 577 |
| Balance of trade | +9,975 | −123 |
| Balance of payments | +8,700 | +194 |

[a]British figures are taken from Professor Bowley's estimates; American figures are those of the Department of Commerce.

Table 2 tries to bring out the great difference between the basic economic relationships of pre-1914 Britain and post-1945 United States.

In the immediate postwar period the critics of the postwar international agreements entertained grave fears about the chances of maintaining employment in the United States.[14]

Europeans live in areas devastated by war and many still suffer from reduced standards of living. Their misfortune is their opportunity. The "backlog" of investment and consump-

[14] "The U. S. and the World Economy" (written in the summer of 1946).

tion in these areas will persist for at least a decade, and, even if only part of the reforms decided upon or discussed are realized in practice, demand in these territories will tend to outstrip supply. *Our* problem is to try to find *sufficient savings,* that is, reduce consumption to permit such investment as we must undertake if we are to restore productive capacity.

The United States, on the contrary, succeeded not merely in colossally increasing her capital equipment, but also in raising her civilian consumption during the war, and even more since the war.[15] Nearly all restraints against speculative excesses have been abolished in that country. This has not been reflected in an exuberance which usually characterizes the upward swing in the United States. On the other hand, few, if any, of the legislative reforms proposed by the progressive school of economists in order to mitigate basic instability, have been accepted or have any chance of being accepted in the near future. The postwar relief in taxation largely benefits savings rather than consumption and, if this is fitting in the transitional period of inflationary tension unrelieved by controls, it does not augur well for social peace and national unity. It is not likely in these circumstances that the trend of the tax measures adopted can be promptly reversed when increased productive capacity necessitates a relative stimulus to consumption rather than saving. A fraction only of the social measures declared necessary to arrive at a distribution of the national income compatible with greater stability (especially those favoring a redistribution between the States of the Union in favor of the poorer and backward areas) has been passed. The 'backlog' of pent-up consumer purchasing power, which was to sustain demand, has melted to relatively small proportions: not less than 60 per cent of all liquid assets was found in the possession of 10 per cent of the spending units, and 87 per cent in that of 30 per cent, 70 per cent of the people holding not more than 13 per cent.[16] The sharp rise in prices since July 1946, incompletely followed by a rise in wages, must have

[15] These statements do not intend to deny the role of the United States in winning the war—on the contrary.

[16] *Federal Reserve Bulletin,* June 1946, pp. 574f.

further reduced the importance of this stabilizing after-effect of war. At the same time reconversion proceeded far faster than anyone predicted and, at the moment, employment is at an all-time high level for peacetime. Only a prolonged series of strikes could produce a situation in which foreign countries would be safe from United States competition. This is at least unlikely, especially in view of the trend of Congressional opinion.

The last few paragraphs and several below follow closely an article written in 1946. Most of the fears expressed in them have proved unjustified up till now, but no complacency is justified on that account. Instead of an anticipated Federal Budget of about $25 billion, expenditure was maintained at some $40 billion and shows all signs of rising toward $50 billion. Apart from this fundamental change there was an unexpectedly high private investment program, amounting to about $60 billion in 1946 and 1947, the effects of which (very much like after World War I) have not yet shown themselves generally, though productivity, not merely in some branches of manufacture but also in agriculture, has increased over 1939.

Nevertheless at the end of the first half of 1947 and again at the beginning of 1948, signs were multiplying that the prodigious productive capacity of the United States was overhauling the "pent-up" demand bequeathed by the war. On both occasions a certain hesitation was discernible which might well have resulted in a definite downturn. The catastrophic crop failure in Europe in the summer of 1947, the abrupt worsening of the international situation which accounted for the European Recovery Program, and the anticipation of huge United States Government expenditure on armament has, if one might put it in these words, "saved the day." Net foreign investment rose from $4.8 billion in 1946 to the colossal total of $8.7 billion in 1947. The excess of receipts over payments on current account was $11.3 billion.

Lord Keynes, in his review of the prospects for the United States balance of payments,[17] put forward the conclusion "that

17 Published posthumously in the *Economic Journal,* June 1946. There is a persistent tendency—not attributable solely to a comprehensible sense of grief

the chances of the dollar becoming scarce over the next five or ten years are not very high."

I continue paraphrasing material from my article which was published in the *Bulletin* of the *Oxford Institute of Statistics* in October 1946.

He based this conclusion on two propositions: The first was that the development of the balance of payments of the United States since the depression of 1931, and more especially since the war, does not justify the apprehension that the United States will denude the world of its international reserves and, under the 'multilateral' 'rules of the game,' impose deflation on other countries. His second proposition was that the United States proposals for commercial policy 'represent a magnificent objective approach which a few years ago we should have regarded as offering incredible promise of a better scheme of things.' This "better scheme of things" is to be brought about by the "fundamental" forces described in classical theory. These forces are expected to make the United States a 'high living and high cost' country and thus banish the fear of deflation. The United States—just as Britain in the last century—will become a staid creditor country.

The first proposition, that is, that the United States is not likely to deflate the world by absorbing international liquid reserves, rests on two arguments. The first of these is the well-known fact that, in 1930-1938, the balance of payments of the

and piety at his premature death—to rewrite the history of Keynes's last great labors within the terms of the apostolic succession and dogma. Thus it is implied that he would have disapproved of the partial freeing of blocked sterling balances (Professor Robbins, Letter to the London *Times*, Oct. 28, 1947). In point of fact, evidence is available that Keynes proposed to free a much larger proportion of balances than were made convertible by the Treasury in 1947. This is also borne out by the undue optimism of the forecast on the dollar. His sudden reconversion to the effectiveness of the "hidden hand" (*ibid.*) is interpreted (by Mr. Roy Harrod, *Are These Hardships Necessary?*, London, 1947) as an adherence to "free trade" principles and hostility to "bilateralism." As a matter of historical truth he made the famous pun—referring to the representatives of the nineteenth-century dogma in the British Delegation to Washington—that what the British team needed was a "bit of un-Liesching and un-Shackle-ing." He was a great admirer of Schacht (not realizing perhaps that Schacht was an ultra-"liberal" in the toils of armament-full-employment) and thoroughly opposed to ITO. The contradictions between the tenor of his statements in Britain and the United States show that he was trying to persuade himself as others of the adequacy of his schemes.

United States on current account did not show a large positive balance. The pressure on other countries' reserves was exercised by the violent movements of "hot money" which not merely need not but positively cannot recur under the Bretton Woods plan which enjoins borrower countries to supervise and prevent capital movements. But the mere fact that the American current balance of payments did not show a large excess between 1930 and 1938 does not suffice to show that under different conditions a vast excess would not materialize. Since because of a flight of capital (hot money) and the withdrawal of previous United States credits the debtors had no reserves, the United States balance of payments on current account could show no excess as there was nothing with which to pay for it.

To elucidate the causal inter-relations, let us look at the data supplied by the United States Department of Commerce. The annual total supply of dollars made available to foreign countries decreased between 1929 and 1932 by some $5 billion. The decrease of the supply originating in current transactions—imports and services—accounted for no less than $4 billion of this reduction. To avoid losing more gold or other reserves than they lost during the period of acute financial confidence crisis in 1930-31, the other countries of the world deflated, suffering the unemployment of millions of their workers (and in weak countries a breakdown of democratic parliamentarism), devalued by much more than the 10 per cent permitted without consultation of the Fund, increased tariffs, and instituted exchange control, multiple-currency practices and reciprocal purchase, payments and clearing agreements, soon no longer to be permissible. In fact, in face of the American maelstrom, they did precisely the things which they now have pledged themselves never to do again. Nevertheless they could not avoid an appalling volume of unemployment. It is somewhat astonishing that precisely the experiences of the 1930-1938 period should be advanced to assert the lack of damaging effects to America of the undertakings which we have signed or to which we have given our assent.

Nor is it possible, on the basis of these statistics, to argue that there is no reason to suppose—as some of us have done—that the United States balance of payments on current account is likely to be favorable when there is a depression in the United States. It is difficult to understand how the statistics relating to the period of 1929-1932 can prove or disprove this proposition, because, as we have already pointed out, every possible restrictionist and deflationist device known was practiced in that period and the raging deflation abroad could not be stopped. On the other hand, the data for 1937-38, when the United States suffered a violent setback, which, however, the growing political tension abroad and the accompanying armaments prevented from spreading elsewhere, show that exports did increase relatively to imports—despite the fact that preferences, quotas, discriminating purchase agreements, and exchange restrictions were maintained, almost as strict as during the great depression, and all countries, except Germany and the U.S.S.R., suffered from *some* unemployment.

What the United States excess of exports would have been had there been no unemployment abroad nor recourse to the restrictionist and autarkic devices now outlawed I do not pretend to know. I am sure it would have been many times greater than that actually experienced—that is, if the other countries had had the necessary gold or dollar exchange reserve to permit a deficit of such magnitude. It is precisely the vastness of the probable United States export surplus in conditions like these that led some commentators to urge that even the original Clearing Union plan (not to mention the White plan adopted as the basis of the Final Act of Bretton Woods) was insufficient to permit the maintenance of full employment internationally, unless some supranational device were incorporated in the scheme in order to bring about equilibrium.[18]

Let us now turn to the argument that the balance of payments of the United States during the war augurs well for the future. But an analysis of the United States balance of payments during the late war cannot be used for predicting its future develop-

[18] Cf. M. Kalecki and E. F. Schumacher, "New Plans for International Trade," *Oxford University Institute of Statistics, Bulletin,* Supplement, 1943.

ment. The United States had become a large-scale debtor. Her short-term obligations amounted in October 1945, to no less than $6.4 billion. On top of this, foreign countries held $4 billion of gold under earmark and possessed another $4.6 billion worth of marketable United States securities (and further direct investments). To this must be added the funds made available by the United States indirectly through her contributions to the Monetary Fund and the Bank, as well as direct loans through the Export-Import Bank, or (as in the case of the British loan) by the Treasury and by private bankers. The world's potential reserves of dollars had never been so high as in 1945. Unfortunately, a large part of these reserves had been used up by early 1948.

No doubt many European economists—in their preoccupation with the prospective position of their own countries—have been guilty of underestimating the very real changes in the international position of the United States capital account during the war. But even if they committed this oversight (and most of them did not), surely a venial offense only can be charged to them. The United States during the war not merely achieved over-full employment—a condition not likely to persist for long—but, robbed by the Japanese attack of essential supplies and hindered by the German submarine campaign in the access to others, she also invested on a lavish scale in alternative sources of supply abroad—a process which is unlikely to recur. She placed at the disposal of her allies Lend-Lease supplies of about $42.5 billion, supplies which consisted not merely of warlike stores but those necessities of life the continued production of which on a massive scale is one of the main reasons for the strength of the United States' international economic position in peacetime. She initiated purchasing schemes in South America in order to maintain the loyalty of those countries to the cause of hemispheric defense. She bought silver, and put large amounts at the disposal of these and other countries through the Export-Import Bank. Altogether she put at the disposal of foreign countries vast amounts of money. The balances and other assets now advanced to foreign countries in the United States are but a small reflection of the gigantic activity of the United States Government during the war. Yet this vast activity was accomplished with relative ease.[19]

No one has thrown any doubt on the proposition that, if the United States Government could be induced to act in peace as it acted during the war to achieve a common aim, and if that common aim were the maximum economic progress of the world at large, we should really enter a New Era. But can anyone maintain that this is at all likely? And if (as I think most people would venture to say) it is not likely, the figures for the dollar reserves of foreign countries no longer look very impressive.

First of all, the distribution of the short-term reserves is very unequal. If Canada, some South American countries, and the two rich European neutrals have international reserves, that does not help the countries impoverished through the war and whose reconstruction would offer the best avenue of approach to a truly international policy of full employment. Instead of fearing the United States dollar as the sole currency potentially scarce, we merely have to begin to think of several scarce currencies. Moreover, most countries with these potential secondary scarce currencies have large visible surpluses towards the weaker European countries and deficits towards the United States, and so contribute to the threat of a "multilaterally" induced deflation upon the "weak" currency countries. By 1948, moreover, even Canada and Latin America have become short of reserves.

Nor should we forget that figures for foreign reserves which look impressive in a world of established international equilibrium are not so decisive in a world which has suffered from the devastation of a second World War. The French Government alone proposed a reconstruction program involving a deficit of some $6 billion over the years 1947-1952. Moreover, because of the monetary troubles experienced in most countries, some of the gold and dollar reserves cannot be drawn upon, especially in Europe, as 'confidence' has to be maintained. I do not venture to estimate the size of these 'blocked' reserves."

[19] Data for 1939 can be found in *The United States in the World Economy*, for the following years in *Foreign Commerce Weekly*, March 10, 1945.

The events of the last years have borne out this pessimistic interpretation. Although total United States aid in the two years ending June 30, 1947 was more than $15 billion,[20] the reserves

TABLE 3
ANALYSIS BY COUNTRIES OF FOREIGN BANKING FUNDS IN U. S. A. ON OCTOBER 31, 1945[a]

| | $ million | |
|---|---|---|
| Europe | | |
| U. K. | 740 | |
| France | 360 | |
| Netherlands | 228 | |
| Switzerland | 284 | |
| Belgium | 196 | |
| Norway | 183 | |
| Sweden | 213 | |
| Other European | 341 | |
| | — | 2545 |
| Canada | | 1552 |
| Latin America | | |
| Brazil | 179 | |
| Cuba | 145 | |
| Mexico | 164 | |
| Argentine | 77 | |
| Colombia | 83 | |
| Panama | 64 | |
| Chile | 90 | |
| Venezuela | 40 | |
| Other Latin America | 248 | |
| | — | 1098 |
| Asia | | |
| China | 592 | |
| Netherlands East Indies | 104 | |
| Other | 312 | |
| | — | 1008 |
| All Other Countries | | 194 |
| | | 6397 |

[a]Source: *Federal Reserve Bulletin.*

of practically all European and most other countries have been exhausted. American imports have fallen relative to the prewar "normal" to three-quarters in terms of national income.[21] While

[20] National Advisory Council Report to Senate Committee on Finance, *Foreign Assets and Liabilities of the United States,* 1948, p. 168.

[21] *Survey of Current Business,* March 1948, p. 19.

to some extent this reflects the extreme difficulties of extra-American countries to restore their production (and their partial failure to promote exports), nevertheless is it not probable that the vast improvements in America's productive and advertising technique and the interruption of the flow of non-American goods to the United States market have created a situation which it will be extremely difficult to reverse?

Is it not quite clear that the United States net balance of payments will bear a relationship to the flow of savings at full employment altogether different from that in pre-1914 Britain? Even if we take a low figure for net savings at full employment and a very high figure for exports and imports, it seems clear that the former will be several times higher than the latter. To affect America's internal position, foreign loans on a very large scale would be needed, especially relative to the wealth of foreign countries and the prospects for repayment. These loans would be large relative to potential excess savings. The pre-1914 British case was in complete contrast to this. Foreign trade was much greater than the volume of total savings at full employment. An alteration in the foreign balance thus had an immediate and considerable effect in Britain, setting in train an offsetting cumulative process. This inter-dependence of foreign and home trade was the factor which provided the mechanism tending to restore equilibrium without which "free multilateralism" implies an intolerable strain. That the situation is no longer the same is not surprising. The United States is a continent; Britain was a small country where relative wealth depended on foreign trade. The United States must not be 'blamed' for this disharmony. It is nothing but the foreign aspect of a well-merited prize which falls to those who successfully organize a large area under a common economic system. But it behooves those who were not as successful to beware lest they should be even further penalized.

The rise of the United States to a position unparalleled since the Roman Empire has placed the world in a dilemma unless indeed, as we shall argue below, conscious measures are taken to restore equilibrium. We either have to envisage prodigious investment activity in the United States which increases the competitive power of that country faster than productivity rises elsewhere and thereby *leads to periodic pressure abroad and probable breakdowns,* or continued depression which makes nonsense of the classical mechanism of adjustment towards a 'creditor position.' The only escape to be found from this dilemma would be that United States savings be used for foreign investment—a case with which we shall deal presently—or that United States business activity be maintained by social reform or 'nonproductive' Government expenditures. But even in these cases—given the strong initial superiority of the United States and the aggressiveness of its managerial leadership—it is likely that technical progress will be faster in the United States than in other countries adhering to the 'classical' rules of the game. The old theory is based on the "seesaw model" of full-employment economics combined with (simultaneous) inflations and deflations in the respective countries. It never envisaged a state of oligopolistic competition in international trade largely dependent upon relative money wage levels determined by the relative bargaining power of trade unions and employers' associations. There is no reason to suppose that trade unionism in America will be relatively stronger than its European counterparts."

The dilemma has been temporarily resolved by the Marshall Plan and rearmament. But in the long run we cannot build a tolerable solution on continued foreign aid of such proportions or on continued armament in the United States. Unless the political tension which gave rise to these measures abated, a shooting war and the destruction of the Eastern Hemisphere including Western Europe would have to be envisaged. If, however, these expenditures should cease after three or four years, then the problem would be posed again and with renewed force. After all, up till now we in Europe did not have to contend with a depression in the United States nor with the consequent increased competitive pressure and efficiency of her reorganized industries.

It would, to say the least, be foolish to expect that the problem would be much less severe once reconstruction has progressed some way in Britain and continental Europe, and if the

United States suffers from a slump. In that case, both the International Monetary Fund and the Bank are only too likely to prove as insufficient and irrelevant to the solution of the problem as they have proven at the present juncture. Unless internal social measures (the acceptance of which is not made probable by recent economic trends in the United States) provide for stability at high employment and unless the breathing space is used for a basic reorganization of Western Europe and its related, complementary territories, the outlook for the future remains uncertain if not grim. It shows considerable lack of realism to say in this context that "It is precisely this situation which the International Fund is so well organized to meet."[22] The total of the quotas of the potential debtor nations is at most some $4½ billion. Twenty-five per cent available each year represents some $1⅛ billion. The surplus of the United States balance of payments in 1946 was over $7 billion, and, in 1947, about 9 billion—in the midst of an unparalleled boom in which domestic gross *investment* rose to some $30 billion, despite the vast pent-up *consumer* demand which was rapidly being supplied. The reader is left to make his own guess as to what surplus would develop in the United States balance of payments if the latter suffered from a severe depression while the European and Asiatic countries were trying to maintain full employment. I doubt whether he will share American optimism (or the illusion of most of the British negotiators at the Bretton Woods Conference) that the scarce-currency clause would protect the new "peripheries" in the *first* year of a United States depression.

The "liquidity approach" to multilateral full employment,[23] i.e. schemes "which permit single countries to maintain full employment irrespective of the consequences of this policy on the balance of their international payments by creating and placing at their disposal internationally acceptable means of payment," must be on a much vaster scale than the International Monetary Fund, much vaster even than the original "Clearing Union" plan of the late Lord Keynes. But then such schemes involve

[22] Dr. Triffin "National Central Banking and International Economy," *Review of Economic Studies*, 1946-47, No. 36, p. 65.

[23] Cf. my essay, "The International Aspects, etc.," *Economics of Full Employment*, p. 159.

grave dangers. "To allow depressed countries to run up export surpluses which would permit the maintenance of full employment policies everywhere, has the drawback that the cumulative debt balances would be distributed haphazardly. Unless they are periodically forgiven they would tend to force mature deficit countries to adopt deflationary policies, as such countries will not in the long run tolerate a growing indebtedness, however vague the obligation to 'repay' these 'cyclical liquidity' debts."[24]

In other words, once "normalcy" has been attained, the yearly increase in United States foreign assets must, in order to be effective domestically, be equivalent to *the total non-American contributions to the World Fund and one-half the total lending powers of the World Bank,* subsequently increasing at compound interest with the increase of national income. To envisage these orders of magnitude is sufficient to accept them as a *reductio ad absurdum.* Nor must it be forgotten that the Fund is not meant to serve as a long-term source of finance, and that the Bank is only to lend on "sound projects." The accumulation, within a score or so years, of foreign assets running into hundreds of billion dollars, yielding some 2½ per cent to 3 per cent at least, is altogether out of the question. Nor would it be permitted by the borrowers themselves, who would pass under an absentee economic domination of the United States which would become quite intolerable politically and socially. The "liquidity approach" to multilateral full employment belongs to the realm not of utopias but nightmares.

This impracticability of large accumulations was accepted when the Clearing Union plan was dropped. The Bretton Woods Act provides a remedy for the exhaustion of the stock of any currency in the Fund resulting from a continued excess of exports of the country concerned, by rationing that currency, that is, introducing multilateral discrimination against that country's exports. But because of the distortion of the world economy already discussed, and the arithmetic of the Fund, unless the limits on borrowing are waived (and the voting power of creditors is cumulatively strengthened, that of the debtors weakened when borrowing takes place), the time which might

[24] *Ibid.*, p. 161.

elapse during a period of acute shortage of a currency before it is declared scarce might be up to four years. During that time, only devaluation and (or) deflation might be used by other members to maintain the balance between the supply and demand for the potentially scarce currency. Under these circumstances it might be impossible to avoid a deflationary pressure. If, however, the "surplus" area consents to lend or make direct investments, the scarcity of the currency might not arise at all. In that case the rest of the world could not maintain full employment except by domestic "anti-cyclical" measures which might well involve serious frictional unemployment—apart from the loss of financial independence.

The further discriminatory measure to be permitted (but which is outlawed so far as Britain is concerned by the Anglo-American Financial Agreement) is the discriminatory quantitative control of imports. But it is doubtful whether this would be sufficient to protect countries which have to rely on industrial exports for their existence. Each country must take these discriminatory measures *unilaterally*. There is no reason to suppose that third countries will discriminate in favor of "dear" countries, i.e., countries which are not depressed. The limited reciprocity implied in the permission of including bilateral deals under certain conditions cannot operate quickly and widely enough to provide for this case.

### C. APPROACH TO A SOLUTION OF THE STABILITY PROBLEM

We must certainly continue our attempts to achieve international stability within the framework of multilateralism (once the readjustment of Western Europe has been achieved).

The first can consist in pressing for a reinterpretation of the Final Act of the Bretton Woods Conference and more especially the extension of functions and the integration of the mechanism of the International Bank and the Fund. If these should be expanded into an International Investment Board[25] furnished with power to create international purchasing power, accepted by all members of the Fund and with authority to direct con-

[25] Cf. *New Plans for International Trade, Oxford Institute of Statistics Bulletin*, Supplement, 1943.

tracts arising out of international public works programs towards those mature industrial countries which suffer from "induced" balance-of-payments deficits, we should indeed be nearer to the solution of our troubles. And this development of the Bank would not even involve a "social" cost to countries which as a result of domestic depression developed surpluses in their balance of payments. Their excess of exports would mitigate their depression and maintain their national income.

Unfortunately, even this scheme has its drawbacks because it engenders counter-cyclical fluctuations in the poor countries. Whenever there is prosperity in rich countries, the investment program in poor countries will have to cease. While this may not be catastrophic, because in the meantime demand in the richer countries will have also increased, it might create considerable friction and unemployment.

The second, more negative, aim is a further amendment in the ITO Charter, giving the absolute possibility of maintaining imports through direct commercial agreements.

A clear distinction must be officially recognized between excesses or deficits in the international balance of payments caused by:

1. economic fluctuations (derived balances) and
2. divergent development unconnected with such fluctuations of efficiency earnings relative to those in other countries (spontaneous or classical balances).

If an excess is caused by *deepening* depression, that is, in the first instance by a fall in imports (the increase in exports is a secondary phenomenon: i.e. the cause of the depression in a country while others are not *equally* depressed), then I hold firmly that those countries which *maintain* their employment (and imports) are justified in safeguarding their position by at least not letting their *imports rise*. Hence, immediate discrimination against the depressed country's exports *at least* to that extent should be permitted. If in spite of this the reserves of other countries are exhausted by the *fall* of their *exports* to the depressed country (that is, after the first degree of discrimination is put into effect) because the depressed country is not putting its own house in order, then they should be permitted to put in further and stricter discrimination cutting down the pre-depression level of their imports from the depressed country (that is, the exports of the depressed country) to the new (depressed) level of the imports of the depressed country (that is, of their exports to the depressed country).

This procedure would: (a) give the depressed country some breathing space to put its own house in order (at the cost of the full employment countries losing reserves, but this loss would not be unbearable, and it would be limited to the *decline of the imports* of the depressed country which is usually manageable, while nothing is known about how much excess that country would accumulate if full employment is maintained elsewhere by an additional increase in exports); (b) show quite clearly that the degree of discrimination is entirely determined by the failure of the depressed country, and can be reduced by its own unilateral domestic action.

The proposals adopted by the London Preparatory Committee of the U. N. Conference on Trade and Employment aimed to ensure an increase in the relative international demand of a depressed country, such as appreciation of its currency, reduction of its tariffs, and so on, should be embodied in the Charter. This has not been done in the meetings either at Geneva or at Havana.

The grave danger in the present trend of official thought is that it almost exclusively concentrates on *negative safeguards.* However necessary these may be they are certainly not sufficient to maintain stability. It is easy to argue, for example, that discriminatory import restrictions imposed against a depressed country will minimize the net decrease in world income as a whole. Yet the prospect of periodically opening and closing trade routes and new sources of supply as the business cycles develop in leading countries is not a priori a very attractive one for the poorer areas. This is one of the most decisive arguments against the Bretton Woods scarce-currency clause.

Multilateral stability will depend on the extension, to a very much greater extent, of planned economies, if periodic breakdowns are not to occur. This is one of the arguments in favor of regionalism, which combines the advantages of multilateralism with some measure of direct control.

## *IV. The Problem of Equality of Opportunity*

Yet even if such a complicated system of multilateral discrimination were to be accepted by the United States, it still seems important to emphasize that, without obtaining permission for long-term reciprocal purchase agreements, or other preferential arrangements, Western Europe[26] will not be able to ensure real stability, nor will it be able to create really large-scale and secured markets. Even if American instability is guarded against, the principle of non-discrimination as applied by the Havana Charter will tend to perpetuate the present superiority of the United States in relation to other industrial exporters. The two wars have violently upset a world economic equilibrium which was the outcome of a slow development over a century and a half. The distribution of population had adapted itself to that equilibrium and it is impossible to readjust it even in scores of years. Moreover, a brusque alteration has taken place in the relative productive power of continents and a premature "opening" of economic frontiers (while maintaining the nineteenth-century political units for the purpose of a twentieth-century world economic organization) threatens to create a new class of proletarian industrial countries uneasily and meagerly living without reserves and without hope of relative betterment because they will be barred from the most productive industries monopolized by others. It is well known that classes which had such a fate have in many countries caused political instability. Is there reason to suppose that internationally the result will be happier?

The rupture of the world economic equilibrium has not only resulted in increasing the degree and area of economic instability but it also weighs heavily on the absolute level of Western Europe's standard of living. The problem can be put in different words: can the principle of "nondiscrimination" be accepted, in a world of such unequal national economic units, as equivalent to the principle of "equal opportunity," or would it lead to a domination of one country by economic (as opposed to military) force (or ideological affinity)? Can the principle of com-

[26] As against "developing" countries.

parative cost be applied—apart from the problem of underemployment—on the basis of current private money costs in countries at widely differing stages of social and economic development?

The theoretically simple case in which money demand expresses social needs and where optimum supply is determined by free competition is, in practice, rare in the extreme. In all other cases, however, long-run real social cost is not equal to current money cost and, what is more important, cannot be made equal by a simple policy of tariffs and subsidies. The classical analysis completely disregards the vitally important influence of risk, especially of the risk differential between home and foreign trade. The existence of a large home market, protected by taste and connections, if by no other more direct interference, which in addition enables the development of mass-production methods, secures advantages which cannot be challenged except by a country having complete state monopoly of its foreign trade and, even then, only if it concludes reciprocal purchase agreements. The scale of industrialization of a country as a whole is one of the most important determinants of costs. From this point of view the whole industrial structure of a smaller or poorer country can be regarded as "infant." This is not to say that really unalterable comparative differences between countries will not continue to exist. They certainly will. But any division of labor between countries founded on comparative social differences (including capital intensity) which are alterable by policy will tend to stabilize inequality and must therefore be rejected as a criterion of policy.

A liberal migration and lending policy would certainly render these inequalities between countries less intolerable than they are, but it would not solve the problem altogether. It would need to be supported by the creation of more equal trading partners—by permitting smaller and poorer areas to form regional units—in order to diminish inequality and the resultant tension. The general principle of nondiscrimination, to work fairly, requires a specific structure of the world economic system and the existence of equivalent economic units. Such structure does not now exist and the proposals now under discussion would render its establishment impossible. (Especially as there seem to be certain "legitimate exceptions" to nondiscrimination—tied loans, subsidies, and so on—which all tend to give "to him who hath"). Yet only the conviction that a visibly just order is being established will bind the nations together and will induce them to accept sacrifices whenever the "rules of the game" so decree. The differences in the living standard and economic power between the nations will, in any case, present awkward problems. But if the poorer countries begin to suspect that—under the guise of attractive slogans—their relative and absolute inferiority is to be stabilized and their social stability is to be sacrificed to renewed economic fluctuations, there remains little hope that they will keep their bonded word.

This has been recognized at the Havana Conference so far as *underdeveloped* countries are concerned. The gravity and basic causes of the *European* malaise have *not* received similar attention.

It is true that the United Kingdom and Western Europe are peculiarly dependent on a flourishing export trade. This, however, does not mean that a system of uncontrolled nondiscrimination in foreign commerce is the best means to achieving this aim. The new rules outlaw long-term reciprocal agreements and (except in conditions which are highly unlikely to be realized; compare Article 42 and Article 95 of the Charter) prohibit the establishment of new preferential arrangements which would generally restore the balance and thus tend to increase the volume of international trade and in particular help the United Kingdom in achieving such an increase in her exports as would be required to sustain a desirable living standard and full employment. Even after the fundamental disequilibrium in the world's balance of payments arising from the war and the slow recovery of the old world has been overcome the disequilibrium between the United States and the rest of the world is likely to persist. This disequilibrium is due to the discrepancy in order of magnitude of the economic power of the United States and any other single country, except perhaps the U.S.S.R. in the long run. The devastation of Europe and Asia has no doubt been responsible for the peculiar form in which our present dollar crisis developed, but it would be exceedingly rash to predict, as the British Board of Trade seems to do, that once the production crisis in Europe has been overcome the crisis in the economic relations between the continents will also have been solved, and more especially that Britain can stand to gain by our insistence that other countries should open up their frontiers to us in the same way as we are promising to do to the United States of America. If the experiment fails, Britain will be in a particularly vulnerable position as her dependence is in terms of food and raw materials and she cannot long continue to exist should her export trade come under pressure as a result of a breakdown in the United States, the dominant economy of the new bloc of multilateral trading partners which is being established by these instruments. To say that the West is in fact not establishing such a bloc but aims at "one world" is a misstatement of the true position. By ruling out special relations (except the reduced Empire Preferences and temporary bilateral agreements) these instruments, moreover, perpetuate the predominance of the United States—unless the United Kingdom immediately forms a complete customs and currency union with the Dominions and Western Europe, which attempt is doomed to failure for political reasons. Far from establishing "fair" rules of the game, the Agreement and the Charter, by their differentiation against partial currency and customs unions, freeze the unbalance in the world economy caused by the wars. Indeed, the United Kingdom and the United States are essentially competitive economies and because of the higher competitive power of the United States, due to a considerable extent to her greater size and greater riches as well as her initial advantage in the greater intensity of capital equipment, it must be feared that this agreement, together with the Bretton Woods instrument, is going to press heavily on Britain's effort at reconstruction and more especially on her efforts to achieve a measure of economic and financial independence from the United States.

It is this persistent discrimination against efforts to establish a large-scale economic territory in Europe and its complementary areas capable of development on the basis of long-term planning (and the permission to form full customs union is both impracticable and irrelevant) which is the real threat against our future contained in the postwar agreements. The Bretton Woods agreement, moreover, prohibits reciprocal-payments agreements which are the sole means of promoting trade between countries which suffer both from deficiencies in their balance of payments and, at the same time, do not produce staple standard products with recognized world markets (in respect of which bulk sales are possible). The new system of prohibitions, elaborated in these postwar economic agreements, tends to reduce Europe's capacity of restoring the disturbed balance between the Eastern and Western hemispheres, and also between agriculture and manufacture. Finally, the fact that neither the General Agreement nor the Charter outlaws tied loans—a most powerful and discriminating means to promote exports—shows that the United States, well aware of its war-promoted superiority, means to retain it.

It would be a profound mistake to regard the Western European malaise as a mere consequence of "inflation," "excess liquidity," and the overvaluation of currencies to be treated by monetary panaceas irrespective of the consequences internally and for the world economic system.[27] Only by creating mass-unemployment could we hope to balance Europe's international payments on a basis of returning to sound finance and free-market economies by devaluation—involving unnecessary hardship if not starvation. International trade would have to be even more severely cut than if the present more discriminating methods were continued. The maldistribution of scarce supplies through grossly unequal distribution of income would add to the unnecessary and intolerable loss through unemployment. Politically such an attempt would certainly lead to catastrophe.

Western Europe's crisis is not a temporary or short-lived departure from an "equilibrium position" to which it is easy to return. It is a historically unique, harsh break with all that has gone before, a fundamental structural crisis which, if it can be cured at all, can be cured only by a set of carefully planned and discriminating policies.

[27] For example, F. A. Lutz, *The Marshall Plan and European Economic Policy,* Princeton University Essays in International Finance No. 9 (Spring, 1948).

The first requisite is an increase in Europe's productive capacity. The war damage in Europe, including the enforced failure to maintain capital equipment and the dissipation of working capital (stocks) as well as foreign assets, is colossal. Its incidence on production is the more serious as the balance of the productive system has been destroyed. Marginal investment, however, just because of this lack of balance which paralyzes existing capital (for example, coal and steel) should yield exceptionally high returns. Reconstruction also implies a rationalization of European production by making use of modern techniques based on mass markets.

The second and hardly less important condition of success is the creation, by conscious and coördinated planning, of a large economic unit within which this productive capacity can be developed. Free-market economics cannot deal with this problem of large-scale change involving serious losses for part of the constituent national economic units. In conditions of extreme scarcity, moreover, free markets involve intolerable social injustice. The premature imposition of nondiscriminating multilateralism (burdened, moreover, with lopsided concessions to "underdeveloped" countries) on the relations of Western Europe with complementary overseas economic areas (for example, the British Commonwealth and colonies) will put an unnecessary strain on the delicate process of readjustment and might altogether jeopardize it. Once Europe, torn out of its former place in the world economy, has been successfully reintegrated by harmonizing a closer coördination in Europe with special ties to overseas—and other, for example, Eastern European—complementary areas the time will come when she can compete on equal terms with the more fortunate areas of the world, and the classical tenets on the international division of labor can once more be applied to the "real" world. Otherwise all efforts will end in creating dependent client states, unable to exist by themselves and a menace to social and political peace.

The more generous the treatment of the European nations by the United States in the coming years, the more enlightened the interpretation of the rules of the ITO as applied to the attempt to evolve a concerted program of rehabilitation in Western Europe, the sooner we may hope for a restoration of equilibrium in the world economy. It is more than welcome that after the rigid dogma of the first approach to postwar reconstruction, the practical solution of urgent political problems has resulted in the generosity of ERP combined with the flexibility of the treatment of the proposed Western Union. It is significant, however, that economists, as contrasted with practical statesmen and administrators, cannot claim much credit for this turn of events. It is much to be hoped that the price paid in renewed political conflict will not be too high, and that undue fiscal restrictions on the American administrators of the program will not result in humiliating and harmful dictates of policy leading to strife in Europe and worsened relations with America.

# *CONCLUDING REMARKS*

Seymour E. Harris

In concluding this book, which brings together the work of twenty-four experts, each with his own views, it may be helpful to make a few broad generalizations.

1. It is fashionable to minimize recent achievements in international economic coöperation. Yet the ITO, the Fund, the Bank and other international agencies are monuments to those who place their faith in international economic coöperation. Each of these agencies, and others, represent a bit of sovereignty sloughed off the sovereign states and grafted on to the international agencies operating on behalf of all countries. On paper at least, the major countries in the world, with the exception of the U.S.S.R., have agreed to fix exchange rates with some attention to international responsibilities, to limit the area of discrimination and quantitative restrictions on trade, and to take measures generally to expand trade. In practice, also, the achievements are substantial. Consider, for example, the reduction of tariffs effected since 1947, and the Canadian measures to protect her dollar position, which were pushed through with a sharp eye on the recently assumed obligations not to discriminate. The participating countries also acknowledge their responsibilities to maintain high levels of employment just because unemployment is an exportable commodity; and to renounce a sluggish adherence to fixed exchange rates which might be incompatible with economic well being. This marks a large advance over "respectable" policy in the prewar period.

2. A survey of economic conditions in six countries and Latin America of especial concern to the United States suggests the conclusion that disequilibrium in the balance of payments is a contagious disease; that once it affects large and important areas the patients are not easily quarantined; and that disequilibrium manifested in dollar shortage, becomes virtually a

world-wide phenomenon. The explanation in part is the improved relative economic position of the United States vis-à-vis the rest of the world; and in part the pressure put by countries confronted with adverse balance of payments upon countries supplying goods to them to finance them—the spread of dollar shortage to Latin America and especially Canada is explained in part by the financing of the United Kingdom by these countries. The U.S.S.R. and her satellites alone escape dollar shortage, an achievement made possible by deterioration of political relations and tight controls. Yet even these countries may be said to be short of dollars, the symptom being their virtual exclusion of United States goods badly needed by them.

3. Dollar shortage explains the origin of the ERP, which will provide additional dollars not only to Europe but indirectly to other countries whose exports to Europe will be financed by the United States Government. The success of this program in solving the production and the related dollar problem will depend largely upon the economic policies of the European countries being aided as well as on the political situation. Aid under the ERP is not likely to be much more than 5 per cent of the income of the countries involved; and the total income rise anticipated by the sixteen countries and Western Germany is many times the amount of that aid. Should these countries embark on a genuine program of economic coöperation, should they make effective use of the available resources, should they establish a proper proportion among consumption, investment, and exports, and should they introduce the minimum fiscal and monetary measures required of a well-functioning economy, and should the political situation improve, then the ERP may mark an important advance towards European recovery and the solution of the dollar problem. But courageous economic policies, which may annoy the average citizen, will not be forthcoming so long as important countries are ruled by governments constantly in danger of being thrown out.

Success of the ERP also depends upon economic policies of the United States. Here again political considerations may wreck the ERP. Tax reduction, excessive concern over so-called principles of free enterprise, a disposition to distribute resources according to the appraisal of economic policies of the European countries on our standards may well reduce the chances of a successful outcome. Unless this country can deal with the inflationary pressures which will be strengthened by the ERP, the program can greatly injure the American economy, with secondary adverse effects upon the rest of the world. This is the time for economic statesmanship.

4. Unfortunately, the theorist is able to give the practical man only limited help. There is disagreement concerning the symptom of disequilibrium, one view emphasizing the importance of large gold or exchange movements, the other drawing inferences from the state of employment and its relation to exchange rates. In the largely controlled and fully employed world of today, these barometers of disequilibrium will not be sufficiently revealing. Of course, when France loses three-quarters of her reserves in a few years, despite rigid controls of exchange, it is easy to conclude that disequilibrium prevails. Most economists will indeed then agree that the franc ought to be revalued; that prices are too high in France and should be brought down through fiscal and monetary measures, or at least that the rise of prices be stopped; and even that in the present situation, exchange control and quantitative restrictions are indispensable. But they will disagree on the correct value of the franc; nor will there be universal agreement on whether it should go up or down; on the extent to which reliance should be put upon measures within the authority of the French Government as against recourse to foreign aid. In fact, the relative contributions of orthodox measures, for example, higher taxes, reduction of monetary supplies; of semi-orthodox measures, illustrated by variations in exchange rates; and of unorthodox measures, for instance, exchange control and foreign aid, are still a matter of disagreement.

# INDEX

THE END